MEANING IN LIFE

MEANING IN LIFE

AN EVIDENCE-BASED HANDBOOK FOR PRACTITIONERS

JOEL VOS

First published 2018 by
PALGRAVE

Palgrave in the UK is an imprint of Macmillan Publishers Limited,
registered in England, company number 785998, of 4 Crinan Street,
London, N1 9XW.

Palgrave® and Macmillan® are registered trademarks in the United States,
the United Kingdom, Europe and other countries.

ISBN 978–1–137–57668–2 paperback

This book is printed on paper suitable for recycling and made from fully
managed and sustained forest sources. Logging, pulping and manufacturing
processes are expected to conform to the environmental regulations of the
country of origin.

A catalogue record for this book is available from the British Library.

A catalog record for this book is available from the Library of Congress.

I dedicate this book ...
... to my parents who showed me how to live a meaningful life.
... to my friends and relatives who make my life meaningful.
... to my colleagues with whom I share the passion of meaning.
... to my clients who show me the large diversity of meaning.
... to my students who teach me how to teach about meaning.
... to meaning as the energiser and compass in my life.

CONTENTS

List of Figures and Tables   x

List of Questionnaires and Handouts in the Treatment Manual   xi

Introduction   xiii
Aim of this book   xiii
Aims and method of meaning-centered practices   xv
Overview of chapters   xix
The best examples are personal   xxi
Exercises   xxiv
Key points   xxv

PART 1   **Scientific Foundations: Meaning in Life**
                 for Sceptics   1

1   Traditional Approaches to Meaning   3
   1.1   The four historical-cultural stages of meaning   3
   1.2   Teleology: the ladder from ancient Greece
         to the Middle Ages   3
   1.3   Scepticism: the flat earth of the philosophers
         and academics   12
   1.4   Functionalism: the skyscrapers of the McMeanings   17
   1.5   Meaning in non-western societies   25
   1.6   Implications for practitioners   30
   Exercises   33
   Key points   34

2   A Pragmatic-Phenomenological Approach to Meaning   36
   2.1   Early phenomenology: love for the sake of love   36
   2.2   Phenomenology in a nutshell   38
   2.3   An introduction to phenomenological methods   39
   2.4   Other phenomenological ingredients   44
   2.5   Scales of meaning   48
   2.6   Pragmatism   51
   Exercises   52
   Key points   53

3   Research on the Meaning of Meaning   55
   3.1   Definitions of meaning   55

3.2   Definitions of meaninglessness   61
3.3   Types of meaning: the meaning quintet   64
3.4   The development of meaning   69
3.5   Cold reflections on meaning in life   73
3.6   The hot flow of experiencing a meaningful life   76
3.7   Fundamental assumptions and life changes   82
Exercises   85
Key points   86

4 Working with Meaning   88
4.1   A brief history of meaning-centred practices   88
4.2   Meaning as a common therapeutic factor   91
4.3   Effectiveness of meaning-centred practices   93
4.4   The relevance of meaning   97
4.5   Implications for health care and insurance policies   100
Key points   101

PART 2   Practical Foundations: Practitioner Skills   103

5 Meaning-Centred Assessment Skills   105
5.1   General principles of assessment   105
5.2   Assessment skills   105
Key assessment skills   115

6 Meaning-Specific Skills   116
6.1   General meaning-centred principles   116
6.2   Specific meaning-centred skills   116
Key meaning-centred skills   133

7 Relational Skills   135
7.1   General relational principles   135
7.2   Specific relational skills   138
Key relational skills   144

8 Phenomenological, Experiential and Mindfulness Skills   145
8.1   General phenomenological, experiential and mindfulness skills 145
8.2   Specific phenomenological, experiential and mindfulness skills 146
Key phenomenological, experiential and mindfulness skills   173

9 Existential Skills   174
9.1   General existential principles   174
9.2   Specific existential skills   176
Key existential skills   185

PART 3   A Ten-Session Treatment Manual: Meaning-Centered
              Groups for Physically Ill Individuals   187

10 Overview of Treatment   189
Session overview   189
Evidence-based development   190

Practical recommendations   192
Preparation   193

11 Individual Assessment Session   194
   11.1 Overview   194
   11.2 Stages   195

12 Session 1: Introduction to Meaning in Life   201
   12.1 Overview   201
   12.2 Stages   202

13 Session 2: Changes in Meaning in Life   211
   13.1 Overview   211
   13.2 Stages   212

14 Session 3: Resilience as a Source of Meaning   222
   14.1 Overview   222
   14.2 Stages   223

15 Session 4: Materialistic-Hedonic Sources of Meaning   232
   15.1 Overview   232
   15.2 Stages   233

16 Session 5: Self-oriented Sources of Meaning   240
   16.1 Overview   240
   16.2 Stages   241

17 Session 6: Social Sources of Meaning   251
   17.1 Overview   251
   17.2 Stages   252

18 Session 7: Larger Sources of Meaning   262
   18.1 Overview   262
   18.2 Stages   263

19 Session 8: Being Here as Source of Meaning   269
   19.1 Overview   269
   19.2 Stages   270

20 Session 9: Doing Meaning in Daily Life   278
   20.1 Overview   278
   21.2 Stages   279

21 Session 10: Ending and a New Beginning   285
   21.1 Overview   285
   22.2 Stages   286

Questionnaires   288

Reading Suggestions   303

Index   305

LIST OF FIGURES AND TABLES

Figures

3.1   The Meaning Development Triangle   70

Tables

1.1   Characteristics of functional meanings in literature   24
3.1   The meaning quintet: evidence-based categorisation of
      different types of meaning in life   67
3.2   Examples of the development of meaning in a scoping
      literature review   71
3.3   Overview of possible changes after stressful life events   84
5.1   Selection of meaning-centred questionnaires   112
8.1   Overview of some unhelpful attitudes   152
8.2   Overview of some attitude-changing interventions   154
8.3   Examples of de-reflection interventions   156
8.4   Examples of self-transcendence   160
8.5   Hierarchy exercises   160
8.6   Possible Socratic questions   162
8.7   Examples of non-intellectualising exercises   169
9.1   Existential themes and moods identification skills   177
10.1 Overview of topics of each session, and typical steps
      within each session   189
10.2 Recommended inclusion criteria   192
21.1 Session overview   285

LIST OF QUESTIONNAIRES AND HANDOUTS IN THE TREATMENT MANUAL

Questionnaires to be sent and filled in by clients before assessment session

Meaning Quintet Questionnaire	288
Meaning-Centred Practitioner Skills Questionnaire	297
Meaning in Life Questionnaire	300
Goal Attainment Form	301

Assessment session

Handout 11.1	Session overview	199
Handout 11.2	Homework before Session 1	200

Session 1

Handout 12.1	Session overview	207
Handout 12.2	Group guidelines	208
Handout 12.3	Definition of meaning	209
Handout 12.4	Self-evaluation of today's session	210
Handout 12.5	Session 2 preview exercise: Identity before and after the illness	210

Session 2

Handout 13.1	Session overview	218
Handout 13.2	Changes in meaning	219
Handout 13.3	Evaluation of today's session	220
Handout 13.4	Homework (1) for Session 3: Preview exercise for Session 3	221
Handout 13.5	Homework (2) for Session 3: Meaningful moments exercise	221

Session 3

Handout 14.1	Session overview	227
Handout 14.2	Overview of theory on resilience	228
Handout 14.3	Homework for Session 4 (1): Preview exercise for Session 4	229
Handout 14.4	The meaningful objects exercise	230
Handout 14.5	Homework for Session 4 (3): Breathing exercise	231

Session 4
Handout 15.1   Session overview   236
Handout 15.2   Overview of theory   236
Handout 15.3   Homework for Session 5 (1): Preview exercise for Session 5   237
Handout 15.4   Homework for Session 5 (2): The meaningful pin-up board
                          (optional)   238
Handout 15.5   Homework for Session 5 (3): The safe place exercise   239

Session 5
Handout 16.1   Session overview   246
Handout 16.2   Overview of theory (1): Self-oriented meanings   247
Handout 16.3   Overview of theory (2): Self-acceptance   247
Handout 16.4   Homework (1) for Session 6: Preview exercise for Session 6   248
Handout 16.5   Homework (2) for Session 6: Body scan exercise   249

Session 6
Handout 17.1   Session overview   257
Handout 17.2   Overview of theory   258
Handout 17.3   Exercise: Whose meaning is it?   259
Handout 17.4   Homework for Session 7 (1): Preview exercise for Session 7   260

Session 7
Handout 18.1   Session overview   267
Handout 18.2   Overview of theory   268

Session 8
Handout 19.1   Session overview   273
Handout 19.2   Overview of theory   274
Handout 19.3   Lifeline exercise   275
Handout 19.4   Letter to a friend exercise   275
Handout 19.5   Homework for Session 9: Preview exercise for Session 9   276

Session 9
Handout 20.1   Session overview   283
Handout 20.2   Homework for Session 10   284

INTRODUCTION

Aim of this book

Human development is like walking on a thin rope: walking and balancing from ignorance to wisdom.

(Loosely based on: Nietzsche, 1879)

This book will not reveal the Ultimate Meaning of Life. It will not show you where you can find the divine ladder that will take you from daily mundanity to eternal bliss. You will also not find the secret to miraculously curing every individual of every problem in life. It will not tell you how you must live your life. It will not impose anything. It will merely invite you to keep your feet on the earth: explore what is meaningful to you and your clients, while maintaining a healthy dose of scepticism.

At the same time, you will not be invited to join the chorus of radical sceptics, for whom nothing else exists other than firing neurons and mechanistic social pressures. The rich subjective experiences of meaning and love can rise above these bleak materialistic and mechanistic perspectives. When we walk around in the landscape of our experiences, we are not doomed to wandering around like zombies on deserted planes, but we can climb into the mountains. We can experience love, excitement, passion, flow, satisfaction – and live life to the fullest. This book will invite you to explore the heights of what you and your clients experience as meaningful. It will not tell that 'anything goes' for any client and any therapist in any random direction. Instead, it will guide you. You will be directed by systematic research and clinical experience into the mountains, which will suggest how you can live a meaningful life, while using both your scepticism and your intuition as a compass.

This book is intended for practitioners and researchers who want to walk this thin rope, balancing between meaningful experiences and sceptical science. This balancing act is urgently needed. The traditional answers from clergymen and philosophers have lost their spell in our secularised era. Consequently, many individuals do not know how to live a meaningful life in the complex modern society. Many self-acclaimed experts have jumped in to fill this gap left by the fading answers to the quest for meaning. Every day, more than 10,000 new web pages are written, and the term 'meaning in life' yields millions of results in internet search engines. It seems as though everyone has become an expert on meaning – and possibly they are, as we are all experts about our own life. Many hits refer to New Age websites and abstract philosophical reflections, which can be inspiring but limiting in their actual usefulness in daily life. The tone of some authors is also black-and-white, leaving out individual freedom and scientific scepticism. A better balance between inspiration and a down-to-earth approach may be beneficial.

Several expert-practitioners have also jumped into this meaning-less gap and have written inspiring texts about their clinical experience, and theoretical and philosophical models on meaning. These works are extremely valuable as they reflect many years of experience. However, some texts are also biased towards the subjective opinion of the authors, as they are not grounded in systematic scientific research. To know what really works, it is crucial to test these ideas in unbiased studies. A litmus test is to ask for systematic evidence gathered by independent researchers in repeated studies and multiple samples. This evidence should not only support the overall effectiveness of the practices, such as testing whether the well-being scores of clients improve after receiving meaning-centred therapy, but the full underlying philosophy and all practitioners' skills need to be empirically validated – having a recipe for meaningful change is not good enough when the individual ingredients for that change are rotten. For example, we need to examine in detail how different individuals experience meaning differently. We need to understand why individuals ask questions about meaning: how does meaning matter, and how do possible problems develop? How does meaning change, and how can practitioners help clients? How do our activities as meaning-centred practitioners logically follow on from this (Kazdin, 2014; Vos, 2016)?

Therefore, to separate the wheat from the chaff, Part 1 of this book answers such questions. This will describe how different individuals in history have had different philosophies of meaning in life. This will be followed by scientific literature on meaning, and evidence-based skills that meaning-centred practitioners use. The term **evidence-base** refers to meaning-centred practices that have been studied systematically, with quantitative or qualitative research, or systematic philosophy and arguments.

However, scientific studies may not clearly tell us what to do in our daily practices. Research findings require a translation for practitioners. Therefore, this book also provides practical activities and exercises for practitioners to help their clients with meaning-centred questions, while these are explicitly rooted in the largest possible body of available systematic empirical research. Thus, the aim of this book is to use the body of scientific literature to provide practical guidance for meaning-centred practitioners such as therapists, counsellors, social workers, nurses and spiritual care workers who want to help their clients with meaning in life. This handbook does not offer a detailed introduction into each different type of meaning-centered practice, but it will offer an evidence-based overview of the common denominator across all meaning-centred practices. As Chapter 4 will describe, this common denominator is identified via comprehensive systematic literature reviews and meta-analyses of 'Meaning-Centered Practices'. This means that this book includes only these conceptual and practical components that are shared by most practitioners and that are supported by systematic empirical evidence. For example, Chapters 5 to 9 discuss specific practical skills and research evidence for each skill. The final part of the book consists of a common-denominator treatment manual based on the most effective meaning-centred practices.

Aims and method of meaning-centred practices

Background

In the past, working with 'meaning in life' was a task mainly reserved for priests and philosophers. Individuals turned to them when they wanted guidance on general directions in life. Meaning was often discussed in relatively abstract and philosophical terms, and those asking for help often received a dogmatic religious or philosophical prescription. This situation has radically changed: western society has become more secular and individualistic, and many individuals do not want to follow authorities but instead create their own meaning. For many, authenticity has replaced authority. But how can we experience meaning in life? In school, we learn how to read and how to do maths, but nobody teaches us precisely how to find meaning. Research even indicates that modern education gives less and less attention to life skills, although many students would benefit more from learning life skills than technical skills (Kronman, 2007; Appiah, 2008). Consequently, individuals try to find answers in spiritual retreats, mindfulness hypes and shelves full of self-discovery books. The benefits of such activities are not always scientifically explored, and thus it remains unclear whether they provide structural support in finding meaning or are mere bogus entertainment. In contrast, this book focuses on evidence-based ways of addressing meaning.

Without priests and philosophers telling us how to live our life, it seems inevitable that clients bring their meaning-related questions to the consultation room of psychotherapists, counsellors, coaches, pastoral care workers, nurses and other practitioners. Traditionally, most psychotherapeutic approaches have steered away from explicating meaning-centred topics. For instance, some psychodynamic psychotherapists have suggested that speaking about the abstract 'meaning in life' is an intellectual defence mechanism, shifting the attention from the real problems. Some behaviourists have argued that meaning should only be discussed outside the therapy room.

Such reductionist approaches deny the fact that often clients ask *themselves* about meaning. Research suggests that most clients want to discuss meaning, especially those facing life's limitations or at a crossroads in life, such as graduation, having a life-threatening disease or facing death (Section 4.4). The reason why certain clients ask for psychotherapeutic help can be explained by their underlying meaning-centred concerns. Therapists often experience this in their own practice when they ask clients what they want to achieve in therapy; the answer is seldom 'I want to get rid of my psychiatric diagnosis' (Vos, 2017). Rather, 70 studies reveal that therapeutic recovery for severe mental health problems 'is about building a meaningful and satisfying life, as defined by the person themselves, whether or not there are ongoing or recurring symptoms or problems' (Andresen, Oades & Caputi, 2011, 2003, p. 2). Meaning may even be regarded as a common factor in all effective practices (Vos, 2018). Thanks to these studies, the mental health field seems to be changing, and meaning is increasingly regarded as a clinically relevant theme that can be addressed effectively (Seligman et al., 2005; Seligman & Csikszentmihalyi, 2014).

This book describes an evidence-based way of working with meaning in any type of practices, regardless of whether you are a psychologist, psychotherapist, counsellor, coach, medical doctor, nurse, pastoral care worker or other professional practitioner. These practices are called **meaning-centred practices**. Although terms such as 'training' seem more client-centred, the term 'treatment' will be used throughout this book, to match the terminology of other psychological and medical treatments. Meaning-centred practices have proved effective for a wide range of clients (Chapter 3).

Aims of meaning-centred practices

The overall aim of meaning-centred practices is to help individuals to live a meaningful and satisfying life despite any limitations they may be experiencing; and by doing this, these practices help to improve clients' quality of life, mood and physical health.

The primary aim of meaning-centred practices is to help individuals to live a meaningful life despite their practical, physical, emotional, social and existential limitations. They do so by systematically and explicitly exploring a range of possible sources of meaning in life, and helping clients to experiment with and engage in meaningful activities and experiences. Meaning is the unique aim and method (Vos, 2016). Meaning-centred practices provide clients with a theoretical understanding about meaning, and offer a sense of normalisation and control in their life situation. Individuals also develop **meaning-centred skills**, which means they learn how to live a meaningful life even in challenging life situations. Individuals also try out and evaluate meaningful activities in their daily life.

The second aim is to increase the general quality of life, which includes stimulating **life satisfaction**, a sense of **hope** and optimism, **self-efficacy** and social well-being (Vos & Vitali, 2018). **Life satisfaction** is a general evaluation of how meaningful life is, and how this is experienced and realised in daily life (Section 3.6). **Hope** and optimism mean that individuals develop a long-term perspective and believe in the possibility of positive change. **Self-efficacy** means that individuals are able to set goals, plan, organise, evaluate and improve the way in which they live their lives, and regulate their emotions in a constructive way particularly in the face of challenging life situations. This also includes fostering greater acceptance: stimulating clients to accept the limitations of life and tolerate **paradoxical feelings**, and to think realistically and in a nuanced way about their situation, the world and themselves (Section 9.2). This also implies developing a coherent life story, and integrating their current life situation within this wider story. **Social well-being** means that individuals develop meaningful connections and a sense of belonging and contributing to the well-being of others.

The third aim is to improve clients' mood, which includes reducing psychological and existential stress, and increasing positive affects. **Psychological stress** includes, among other things, symptoms of depression and anxiety. **Existential moods** – of which **existential anxiety**, like I experienced, is an example – are moods which are not about a specific topic but about life in general (Section 9.2). Positive affects are experiences that people find pleasurable and preferable, such as happiness and joy (Section 3.6).

The fourth and final aim is to improve the physical health of individuals by improving health-related behaviour, physical activity and well-being. Health-related behaviour means that individuals engage in behaviour beneficial to their health such as physical exercises (Vos, 2016b). Individuals feel more motivated to live a healthier lifestyle and become more physically active. The result of this could be improvement in their physical well-being – such as improved self-reported physical well-being, for instance experiencing less intrusive and more bearable pain and physical limitations – immune system functioning, cortisol levels and other biomedical aspects (Vos, 2016b).

These secondary, tertiary and quaternary effects can be achieved by helping clients to explore and engage in meaningful activities, as research shows (Vos & Vitali 2018). That is, by helping individuals to live a meaningful life, their quality of life increases, their psychological stress decreases and their physical health improves.

General method

The method of 'Meaning-Centered Practices' can be generally described as systematically and explicitly exploring a range of possible sources of meanings in life, and helping individuals to experiment with and engage in meaningful activities and experiences. What precisely does this mean?

This book is based on a systematic literature review of all meaning-centred practices that have been systematically studied in empirical trials (Vos & Vitali, 2018). Over 60% of all effective meaning-centred practitioners discuss one particular type of meaning in one session (Vos & Vitali, 2018). For instance, there is one session on materialistic-hedonistic meanings, one on self-oriented meanings, one on social meanings, one on larger meanings and one on existential-philosophical meanings (Section 3.2). Typically, before the session in which the first **type of meaning** is discussed, some introductory sessions are given. These introductory sessions often consist of assessing how meaning is relevant for clients. This introduction also includes didactics about meaning. After the session in which the last type of meaning is discussed, one or more sessions are dedicated to creating priorities around what clients have learned and applying this in daily life.

Seventy per cent of the most effective meaning-centred practices use the following structure for an average session (Vos & Vitali, 2018). Most sessions consist of psycho-education, which involves didactic explanations about what meaning is and how this applies to clients. This psycho-education is often followed by a discussion, in which clients can ask their questions and share their thoughts and feelings about the topic. Some of the most effective practices use a guided **mindfulness** or meditation exercise, which helps clients to address their sense of meaning not only in a theoretical or cognitive way, but also in experiential, intuitive and embodied ways; these exercises seem to open clients up to broader explorations as to what they personally experience as truly meaningful, instead of focusing only on what their theories, the people around them or society tell them.

The heart of the sessions are reflective experiential exercises, in which clients are asked to reflect on how they relate in their daily lives to the theme that was described in the psycho-education exercise. For instance, clients are asked to describe a specific meaningful experience they have had, and how they could create the conditions in their lives in such a way that they can have more similar experiences. Clients share their experiences, which are followed by a **phenomenological** exploration of the different depths of their experience, for instance 'going to a soccer match' feels less meaningful than 'being a father'. Clients are encouraged to make a decision and a commitment for daily life, for instance to spend more time with one's daughter instead of going to all soccer matches. This decision is left entirely to the client, and the therapist only supports the decision-making process and not its content; this guidance is based on the depth of the **therapeutic relationship**, that is, having an understanding, positive and responsive relationship with the client. The session is usually concluded by explaining the homework for the next session, which usually consists of reading some texts, reflecting on some questions or trying out a meaningful change in their daily life.

Overview of chapters

Overview

The first part of the book answers the question of how it is possible to address meaning in life in an evidence-based way. Chapter 1 places 'Meaning-Centered Practices' within broader socio-historical contexts. This reveals how different clients may experience meaning in an entirely different light depending on their context. Experiencing meaning is inherently a socio-historical endeavour: meaning-centred practices are political. Therefore, practitioners need to be aware of the context in which they practice and of their own assumptions about meaning. This context also defines what we can consider as 'evidence', and this first chapter will therefore set the foundations for the rest of the book. There are many exercises in this chapter to help the reader examine their own context (**reflexivity**). The strong socio-historical embedding is a unique and innovative aspect of this book. Chapter 2 offers a modern pragmatic approach to meaning which posits the subjective experience of clients as central. These foundations are an essential part of the practitioner's **reflexivity**: we need to understand ourselves and the context in which we live and help our clients before we can actually help them. Chapter 3 gives an overview of empirical research on the experience of meaning, followed by Chapter 4 which summarises research on 'Meaning-Centered Practices'.

The second part of the book describes what practitioners actually 'do'; this will be called 'skills' and 'competences'. Some authors have criticised the use of these terms, as they appear to imply a **functional** approach: 'simply do this and all problems will be solved.' It will be argued that working in a meaning-centred way is about more than simply following a description of steps, as it may be described as a fundamental meaning-centred **attitude**. To describe the practical activities that practitioners may do when they have such an attitude, several competences and exercises will be described. The empirical evidence for each of the skills will be described. These skills seem to be the common denominator of these different approaches. To be able to tailor these general practices to the unique situation of the unique client, it seems important that meaning-centred practitioners understand this multiplicity of skills. Part 2 therefore includes chapters on assessment skills (Chapter 5), meaning-specific skills (Chapter 6), relational skills (Chapter 7), phenomenological, experiential and mindfulness skills (Chapter 8) and existential skills (Chapter 9). These chapters offer an introduction to the topics, brief instructions and some practical examples.

Part 3 concretises these preceding chapters with a specific meaning-centred treatment manual for working with individuals coping with limitations and change in life, such as a chronic or life-threatening disease. This treatment manual draws entirely from the evidence base described in Parts 1 and 2, and may be regarded as the common denominator of all effective meaning-centred treatments. This manual has been developed for and validated by clients who have experienced cardiovascular events or cancer, students with decision-making problems, and politically and socially disenfranchised individuals.

The following can be found in the Appendix: Meaning Quintet Questionnaire, Meaning Centred Practitioner's Skills Questionnaire, Meaning in Life Questionnaire and a Goals Assessment Form. A list of recommended further reading is also provided after the Appendix. The full list of references, as well as an online glossary briefly defining each term printed here in **bold**, can be found on the companion website: macmillanihe.com/companion/Vos-Meaning-In-Life

How to read this book

It is suggested that those new to 'meaning-centered practices' read all chapters. Readers who are particularly interested in 'how to deliver meaning-centered practices', may want to focus primarily on Parts 2 and 3. Part 2 includes many specific examples, which may not all be relevant for every reader – these examples can be used as a reference guide that can be consulted when working with specific clients who need a specific approach. The manual, in Part 3, can be used in full (as this is how it has been validated), but practitioners may decide to only use parts of it. Readers interested in the cultural, religious and philosophical background may want to focus on Chapters 1 and 2. Researchers and those wanting to know the empirical evidence for meaning-centred practices could focus on Chapters 3 and 4. As part of clinical training, it is recommended that students read Parts 1 and 2 in full, as the foundations of their practice; the focus of their training should be on Parts 2 and 3; and individual training sessions can be dedicated to the practising of specific skills as presented in Part 2 and to specific sessions as detailed in Part 3.

The best examples are personal

*What is meaningful? My shelves are full of books that offer many answers and raise even more questions. However, they do not cover what is meaningful for ME. Meaning is always about our own unique experiences (Chapter 2). Thus I can only answer this question by **phenomenologically** describing my own experiences; I cannot tell you what is meaningful for you.*

*For example, I have always been a writer. My first memories are of writing my first 'book' when I was four years old. As I did not actually know how to write, I invented my own letters. I filled a notebook with my scribbles and gave a public 'book reading' for the enthusiastic audience of my family – or rather, I invented a story and pretended this was what I had written. Fortunately, my scribbles have matured over the years, and my job activities mainly consist of producing articles and essays, and presenting at conferences. My priorities have apparently changed little since I was a toddler. Although writing academic texts feels meaningful, the ultimate goal in my life has always been to have a book published. Thus you are now sharing in one of the most meaningful experiences in my life: This fills me with an enormous sense of **fulfilment** and **satisfaction**.*

Why do people question meaning in life? Chapter 3 will give many possible examples, but a poignant example arose during the time I was writing this introduction. It was a dark rainy night and I was cycling home. I was reflecting on what to write. Shall I talk about my client Emma who felt life was meaningless after she was diagnosed with cancer? I could describe how I helped her to experience life as meaningful again? Or shall I talk about the man who booked a holiday after only four sessions, although he had not been out of his house for five years as he was suffering from generalised anxiety? Suddenly, the answer to my questions came from behind. A taxi overtook me and hit my front wheel. My tyre slipped, I lost my balance and the bicycle got stuck under the car. I fell on the tarmac. A sharp pain struck my back and radiated to my limbs, and I could no longer feel them. The ambulance arrived quickly. I was laid down onto a stretcher; the doctors carried out physical tests on me, and cables connected me to beeping machines. But I was not anxious; I did not need to be, as I deliberately focused on this book and what to write. Shall I tell about the man who decided to overcome his midlife crisis by fulfilling his childhood dream of climbing the Himalayas? Brainstorming what is so very meaningful to me helped me to cope with a frightening situation.

During the months after the accident and the spinal surgery that followed, I was bedbound and on strong pain killers. I tried to sit at my computer to write, but within minutes the pain would return. I could not work. One night, I woke up suddenly, with great anxiety and my heart pounding in my throat. I was not afraid of something specific, but it felt as if my life in its totality was pressing on me. I felt trapped by the limitations of my body. I felt determined by my situation, unable to control myself. I was afraid my body was falling apart; I may not be able to work again; I may have financial troubles, lose my house, be unable to socialise with friends…and there was nothing I could do. Thus not only did I think that I could not control the circumstances, I even thought I could not control my response to them: I felt unable to do anything meaningful in my life anymore, as my body defined me. I had lost my belief in my freedom.

I diagnosed and soothed myself with the thought that this was 'merely' an **existential anxiety** attack. I reminded myself of my research and therapy practice which had shown me in endless numbers of cases, that everyone – including potentially myself – can overcome such feelings of helplessness and regain a sense of control and meaning despite these experiences. Telling this to myself rid me of my most acute panic, but my low mood and worries remained. Subsequently, I started to worry about my symptoms and became almost obsessed with analysing my own mental state, as I had nothing else to do in bed. What is going on with me? Am I going crazy? Very quickly, I became stuck in a vicious cycle. My worries about my worries increased my worries.

My family doctor could only help me with a battery of anti-depressants. No, this was not a structural solution to my underlying problems. I knew I had to work on myself. I started to reflect on my vicious cycle and on what the psychiatrist Viktor Frankl has called **hyper-reflection**: my symptoms worsened as I was too focused on my problems. I needed **de-reflection**, that is, focusing on something more meaningful than lying in bed and my worries. What could I do that felt meaningful? I knew there was a hierarchy of activities that feels meaningful to me. Therefore, I started watching some of my favourite movies. Although it was great losing myself in engaging films, it was not enough to have nice experiences, as I felt I also had to reconnect with people. I phoned my friends, Skyped with family, and met my mates on better days. I also became involved in some political activities via Facebook and my phone; this helped me to not only be altruistic but also to contribute to some **larger goals in life** in trying to create a **just world**. These activities distracted me from the pain, but even more than this they gave me a sense of meaning and satisfaction in *life, despite my physical and emotional limitations: I transcended my situation (**self-transcendence**).*

However, I felt I was still missing something; my life did not feel as ful-filling as it had been before the accident. I needed to do something more meaningful: writing. I examined how I could work on this book despite my limitations. I was still physically unable to work behind a desk. However, I could start creating the conceptual structure of the book in my head, and begin collecting material I could include. On some good days, I could even write small parts. Step by step, I began working. Within days, I surprised myself when I heard myself whistling and humming. It felt as if seeing the mean-ingfulness of my life also reduced my pain experience; my back did not feel as limiting anymore. My physical recovery has made big leaps since then, and my back problems feel less limiting, although they are still there, even now that I am writing this sentence.

*What is it about writing this book that is so meaningful? No, it is not about becoming rich or famous; I have no illusions about that. There are far deeper experiences. I enjoy the process of writing (joyful experiences are meaningful for me); writing is a form of self-care that improves my mental and even physical well-being (the meaning of health); I feel proud that I have overcome my chal-lenges (overcoming challenges is meaningful), want to help other practitioners (altruistic meaning), get the best out of myself (**self-realisation**), contribute to a more just world (the meaning of justice); and writing almost feels like a call-ing or vocation in life (the meaning of spirituality). Via this node of multiple sources of meaning, I feel that I am **living a meaningful and satisfying life** again, despite everything.*

Many meaning-centred practitioners regard such **self-reflection** as a cornerstone of our practices. We can only empathise and understand our clients' quest for meaning when we understand our own struggles and how these may influence our relationship with our clients.

My personal example reveals many of the themes contained within this book: how can we help individuals, including ourselves, to live a meaningful and satisfying life despite our limitations? For instance, scientific research has shown that **de-reflection** works and that we can reduce our psychological stress by focusing on meaningful activities (Chapter 3). We can develop a sense of **self-efficacy**, **hope**, optimism and social well-being when we find ways to have meaningful experiences (Vos & Vitali, 2018). It seems as if we have a deep **will to meaning** which we need to fulfil if we want to achieve well-being. When we can regain a sense of meaningfulness during a period of disease, pain and physical limitation, our condition feels less intrusive and our immune system functions bet-ter, which can directly contribute to our recovery (Vos, 2016a).

These positive effects are achieved by connecting with activities and experiences that we intuit as meaningful. Most individuals experience many different types of activities as meaningful, and identify an **intuitive hierarchy** of meanings (Section 2.4), like I did: watching movies did not feel as meaningful as writing this book. One single activity – such as writing this book – can often have multiple meanings at the same time.

Losing the ability to engage in meaningful activities owing to a sudden life event such as an accident or physical disease can evoke an **existential crisis**, in which we are confronted with life's naked truths and limitations. However, we can always change our inner **attitude** and ultimately **transcend** our limitations, albeit in our mind, by conceptualising our projects. Although we may not be able to control everything that happens to us, we can control how we respond to our life situation. When we develop a **meaning-centred unconditional positive regard** about the possibility that our situation can and will improve, the actual improvement of our mental health has started. This is what I will share in this book, not only from my personal experience as a human being, but also from my professional expertise as associate professor in counselling psychology, clinical and health psychologist and philosopher.

Exercises

1. Explore initial meanings. Children often feel free from worries and setbacks. Therefore, their dreams are often more creative and ambitious. What dreams did you have as a child? Which dreams have you fulfilled? Which dreams are unrealised, and why did these remain unfulfilled? Imagine that you could do your life over again, what would you do the same and what would you do differently? Which unfulfilled dreams could you still realise?

2. Explore de-reflection. Think back to difficult moments in life. Have you ever felt that you were totally absorbed in your worries and could not escape from these? Were you worrying about your worries, and did these worries increase due to the worrying-about-the-worries (vicious cycle)? What helped you to get out of this cycle? Did it help to switch your focus to more meaningful activities (**de-reflection**) and, if so, how?

3. Explore **types of meaning**. What helped you to get through these difficult periods? For instance, did it help to engage in nice **materialistic and hedonic activities**, take care of yourself, and change your approach to how you were coping with the difficult situation, connecting with people or helping them, or focusing on **larger goals in life**, **justice** or **spirituality**?

4. **Goal-setting.** What made you pick up this book? Was this a rational decision or more intuitive? How do you know that this book will be meaningful for you? What are your personal questions that you will try to answer by reading this book? What are your questions as a professional? Can you set between one and three specific goals that you want to learn by reading this book?

Key points

> Meaning-centred practice explicitly address meaning in life as its primary focus with a systematic method. The aim of meaning-centred practice is to help clients live a meaningful and satisfying life, despite any challenges.

> Meaning-centred practices are always embedded in a socio-historical context, as will be elaborated in Chapter 1.

> Meaning in life is an evidence-based concept, and meaning-centred practices are effective according to rigorous clinical trials. This book is based on this research evidence, as summarised in Chapters 3 and 4.

> Working with meaning involves a wide range of therapeutic skills, which are inspired by many different psychological, philosophical and spiritual approaches. Parts 2 and 3 offer a common denominator of evidence-based meaning-centred practices.

PART 1

Scientific Foundations: Meaning in Life for Sceptics

1
Traditional Approaches to Meaning

1.1 The four historical-cultural stages of meaning

How can you speak about meaning in life? There is no meaning in life! There is only neurology and biology. Meaning is armchair philosophy, not reality.

I am often asked this question at public lectures. To me, this is an important question that needs to be discussed before we can continue our conversations. Some colleagues interpret this psychologically: 'What has happened to you to make you so sceptical?' Although the individual dimension should never be overlooked, I find it more helpful to address the historical-cultural context in which this question is asked. How we think and speak about meaning reflects not only our own experiences, but also our time and culture. We often assume that people in all times and cultures have asked questions about meaning in life in the same way we do, but – as I will argue in this chapter – this seems very unlikely. The ways in which we experience and speak about meaning – or are sceptical about meaning – are a product of our unique cultural history. Therefore meaning-centred practices are inherently **reflexive practices**: putting ourselves, our clients and our practices in the wider context. We can only be good meaning-centred practitioners if we can position ourselves, and understand where we and our clients come from, and how our individual and collective pasts influence the questions we have in the here and now. This chapter describes three historical-social perspectives: teleological, sceptical and functional meanings. Additionally, the next chapter will elaborate on the topic of phenomenological meanings.

1.2 Teleology: the ladder from ancient Greece to the Middle Ages

The individual quest for meaning is a modern western invention

Imagine the medieval peasant Godwin Rolfe. He was born in a wood-and-mud house in the manor of Lord Montagu. His parents cultivated a small piece of their own land for which they paid rent and worked on the land of the lord and the church. From early childhood, like all their family and friends, Godwin ploughed the fields, sowing and harvesting, day in and day out, season after season.

The only days that differed from this monotonous cycle were Sundays and saints' days, when Godwin went to church. Like other contemporaries, Godwin possibly did not follow the religion very intensely, but he did go to church because everyone he knew went and he had been going since early childhood. The church was also his only source of information and teaching, as he lacked access to education, television, newspapers, the internet or travelling. Often the Gospel was first dramatised in a play in the churchyard, and he depended on the subsequent sermon from the priest to understand this story from the Bible, as he was unable to read. Service after service he was told how he was expected to fulfil his role in society: receiving the holy sacraments, paying taxes to the church and not contesting the societal order, otherwise hell was waiting. As expected in his time, his eldest brother had become a priest; his second brother had inherited the farm, and Godwin was working on his brother's farm. His sisters had wedded local farmers and one married a shop owner; love was not involved – love for the sake of love did not exist, the partnership meant nothing other than a practical arrangement and if they were lucky they may have experienced some occasional moments of love. There was not one second when Godwin doubted this societal system, as he knew that any doubt implied excommunication and hell, and he also had no reason to doubt as this system was all he knew.

Imagine anachronistically, that Godwin met a meaning-centred practitioner who asked him the question: 'What is the meaning in your life?' Godwin would not know how to reply. Perhaps he would have answered: 'I simply live my life, do my duty, pay my rent and taxes, marry a wife to have children with, and that is it.' The medieval mystic Meister Eckhart wrote that individuals in his time usually understood the meaning of their life as being in service to the community, doing their duty and simply knowing their place (Eckhart, 1979, Sermon 9). It seems anachronistic to call this 'meaningful', as this was simply the way in which they lived their lives, and most people did not seem to have a sense of individuality or freedom of choice. The explicit quest for meaning is an invention of modern western society.

The societal-cosmic-divine order

The individual and societal order were apparently closely connected. The meaning for the individual was about fulfilling their place in the societal order, thus individual and social meaning were the same. As the societal order was decreed by God, this order was also a cosmic and divine one: 'human agents were embedded in society, society in the cosmos, and the cosmos incorporates the divine' (Taylor, 2007, p. 152). This societal-cosmic-divine order was communicated through a person's life and work.

This is also shown in the etymological origin of the word 'meaning', which is derived from the medieval German word 'Meinung' or 'meniti', which described something being communicated through oneself, such as being communicated to, being given an opinion, being signified, being given directions (Library of Babel; Oxford Dictionary of English Etymology). Meister Eckhart wrote that, in his time, the purpose of individuals was typically 'communicated' ('ge-meint') through their work, by being in service to the community. Thus Godwin's meaning was about the way in which his societal position and the divinity of God were communicated through his life and work, or in other words: his meaning was about successfully fulfilling the societal position he was born into.

Although the church reformer Martin Luther did not use this medieval word, 'Meinung', he kept with the metaphor of communication when he used the word 'vocation', which literally means being called (derived from 'vocare', to call). Luther used a visual metaphor to explain how individual meaning was about being called by God: God is milking the cows through the vocation of the milkmaid. We may initially see the individual milkmaid or peasant, but when we look closer we will see that it is God who is present and active in their service to society, and thus their individual face is merely a mask of God (Wingren, 1957; Billing, 1964). Thus living a meaningful life means recognising the place where you are living now, listening to the call that is communicated to you at your position and following this.

Meaning for individuals was about fulfilling their role in the societal-cosmic-divine order, and few would question this as there was no place outside this system. When individuals were unable to fulfil their role in society – for instance, owing to diseases such as leprosy – or when they deliberately decided to leave this order – such as in the case of vagabonds – their lives were literally considered meaningless. They did not fit into the system and the divine was not communicated through them. This narrow sense of meaning as fulfilling a successful position meant that such individuals were socially treated in – what we would call nowadays – an inhumane way; they were cast out from society to colonies, or even burnt at the stake, and this was regarded as normal as their lives, meaningless, relegated them to a position akin to that designated to animals and lower on the societal-cosmic ladder. Some human lives were also regarded as more meaningful than others if they were deemed higher on the societal ladder. Consequently those higher in status expected, for instance, to be served by peasants, women, slaves, and ethnic and religious minorities. These powerholders were in their rights to treat their servants poorly as they were considered less meaningful. (The unquestionable divinity of the social order and the meaningfulness of 'the Establishment' seem to partially continue in the present day; see Jones, 2013.)

In this societal-cosmic-divine order, there was no place for an individual quest for meaning. There was no 'quest', as meaning was dependent on the social position into which you were born. Individuals did not experience or verbalise the 'meaningfulness' of their position, as looking at yourself from a distance or doubting your position was sacrilege and there was no reason to do so: you simply did what you had to do.

The idealistic and conditional ladder of the ancient Greek philosophers

If we can anachronistically describe the meaning of the lives of individuals in the Middle Ages this was about a larger purpose that was lying behind their activities. In the way meaning for a seed is the end goal of becoming a full-grown plant, meaning for those in the Middle Ages was to successfully fulfil their role in society. For instance, love for the sake of love does not appear to have existed: the meaning behind having a partner was to start a family, share resources and have children who could help with the land. For instance, Godwin's purpose, or the meaning of his life, was to work the land of his brother's farm to produce food, sell the produce on the market, pay rent, start a family and serve the lord and the church. Thus the meaning of his work was not the work itself, but something higher and more purposeful: being of service in this hierarchical system. Servants worked for a lord, and believers went to church and practised their religious rituals to receive divine blessing and secure their place in heaven. The mystic Eckhart complained that many people went to church and received the holy sacraments only for the higher purpose of saving their soul; these individuals did not love God for the sake of God, but loved Him in an instrumental way for the higher purpose of their salvation (Eckhart, 1979, Sermon 9). People did not engage in activities for the mere sake of the activities themselves, but for a larger purpose. Meaning in life was defined as having an external purpose in life and all activities in life were directed towards this purpose.

Where did the idea of directing our lives towards a higher purpose come from? This could possibly be traced back to the ancient Greek philosopher Plato. He is well known for his metaphor of the cave. He describes how individuals are chained to the wall of a cave, facing a blank wall. During their lifetime, they can see only shadows projected on the wall from objects passing in front of a fire behind them, and these shadows are as close as they get to viewing reality. One day, a prisoner unchains himself, a philosopher, and he finds a ladder which leads him out of the cave. This philosopher understands that the shadows on the wall do not make up reality at all, as he has now seen the real objects near the fire, and even the objects in the sun outside the cave. Thus the Platonic ladder starts with the shadows on the walls, via the real objects near the fire, and ends with the true objects outside in the sun. The highest viewpoint, the sun, is what Plato calls 'the Good', which some individuals, such as philosophers, can see, but which most individuals cannot see as they are bound to the darkness of the cave and the shadows of the objects. However, there is an ultimate good beyond everyday life, and this goes beyond the functioning of ordinary people. The ancient Greek myths offer many examples of what these Good virtues and moral heroes look like. Only individuals who have developed their mind – as Aristotelean *animal rationale* – can see this abstract, eternal Idea. Therefore, the meaning of our life is to practise use our rational mind – in an attempt to become like these philosophers or mythical heroes – and connect with the 'Ideal Good' (whatever that may be).

Plato did not use the terms 'meaning' or 'purpose', but he did set the stage for other philosophers, by making a distinction between the meaning-less dark cave and the lighter meaning-ful Good outside. The ancient Greek philosopher Aristotle agreed with Plato that there is an idealistic world towards which our individual being develops. All beings are directed and moving towards a specific purpose or goal, 'telos'. When individuals reach their end goal, they participate in the Ideal Good, such as the telos of a seed to become a fully grown plant. Our human telos is also to flourish like this plant. However, to reach this end goal, individuals must fulfil several conditions. The material (*hule*) that a being is made of must be good – the seed for instance was not a poor type of grain or rotten. The seed also had the perfect form (*eidos*), like every being fulfilling their purpose. Everything purposeful is also the result of successful work (*energeia*), such as the seed growing perfectly in the sun, with the aid of water and air.

What happens when you fulfil your purpose? According to Aristotle you may experience well-being or flourishing (*eudaimonia*, which literally translates as *eu* meaning 'good' and *daimon* meaning 'spirit'). For Aristotle flourishing is the result of successfully actualising our moral virtues (*arete*) and our practical ethical wisdom (*phronesis*). For example, it is more likely that we will achieve *eudaimonia* when we properly develop and use our highest mental capabilities, particularly by leading a political-ethical life, serving the community and living a philosophical-contemplative life. This implied that individuals did not create their own purpose: each person's place was defined by the social-cosmic-divine order, and the harmony of the whole is the good to be pursued and our highest purpose. Although everyone can serve the community by doing what is expected of them in society, true *eudaimonia* seemed restricted to a small elite group, as many steps had to be fulfilled before we may experience *eudaimonia*. Women, slaves and many others would by definition be unable to attain these necessary attributes.

To summarise, for something or someone to fulfil their purpose, they first had to be successful in all the requisites of *eudaimonia* of having the perfect material, form, work and purpose. Eckhart compared the Aristotelean telos with the roof of a house, which first assumed that it has stable foundations and walls; but not everyone is so fortunate to have a stable ground on which to build their house or to have the materials necessary to build proper walls (Eckhart 1954, Saying 21). This narrow sense of meaning as a conditional purpose had profound societal consequences. Individuals did not seem to fulfil any purpose when their lives had not successfully ticked all of these Aristotelean boxes. This idea of a meaningful life as a conditional life was reflected in the inhumane treatment of slaves, women, ill individuals and social minorities in the Greek, Roman and medieval eras. A full meaningful life was conditional, and most conditions could only be fulfilled by a privileged few as this required a certain social standing, education, intellectual capacity and ascetic skills. Meaning was like a ladder, and most people could only reach the lowest rungs.

Self-discipline and self-denial

Thus, during the era of the ancient Greek philosophers until the Middle Ages, meaning was about a pregiven societal-cosmic-divine order which did not take into account individuals, their unique being and context. At birth, individuals were given a unique purpose which they had to fulfil in a linear way, similar to an acorn which is only allowed to grow in the direction of becoming a fully grown oak tree, and could not, for instance, become a pine tree. One must stick to their pregiven role. Like the hands and feet need to serve the head, humans beings needed to understand their place in the social order and fulfil their role at this position accordingly.

So how can we do this? How can we know our place and successfully fulfil our role? One answer can be found in the philosophy and training – which we may even call psychotherapy *avant la lettre* – of Stoicism, which began in the ancient Greek era but became particularly dominant in the Roman empire (Robertson, 2010). The Stoics taught the development of self-control and fortitude and stressed that these were a means of overcoming destructive emotions, so that individuals can become aligned with the larger order: '*Virtue* consists in a *will* that is in agreement with Nature' (Russell, 2013, p. 254). Thus a meaningful life was one that falls in line with the natural order, instead of fighting it. One Stoic described how a wicked man is 'like a dog tied to a cart, and compelled to go wherever it goes'; but, in contrast, a Stoic of virtue would amend their emotions to suit the world: individuals could die 'sick and yet happy, in peril and yet happy, dying and yet happy, in exile and happy, in disgrace and happy'. The core Stoic skill was to transform emotions to develop clear judgement and peace of mind, via ascesis, using their rational mind, self-discipline and the development of the virtues of wisdom, courage, justice and temperance. Consequently, unhappiness and evil – and possibly meaninglessness – were seen as the result of a lack of self-development and of not following one's social duty and the natural order. Therefore, Stoics would suggest that individuals who question the meaning of their life should analyse their thoughts and behaviour and try to align these with the natural and societal order. We need to learn to fit into the pregiven linear order (some Stoics had a more phenomenological perspective on meaning, which will be described in Chapter 2).

Adhering to this social ladder almost inevitably led to self-denial, particularly in Western Europe (see Verhaeghe, 2012). People were expected to deny their own desires and needs and fulfil their position on the ladder, be in line with nature or allow God to communicate through them. Self-denial was a crucial skill for some ancient Greeks. Philosophers taught that *hubris*, excessive self-confidence, is morally condemnable: individuals need to transcend their own interests and act according to their social nature as community animals, *zoon politikon*. Hedonism – which follows that pleasure and happiness are the purpose of life – was condemned and instead the stoic discipline of controlling one's emotions was hailed. This anti-hedonic teleology was taken over by church fathers such as Augustine: salvation depended on living a virtuous life, following the holy sacraments and accepting our place in the societal order. Ultimately, individuals must deny their self to serve God. This required that they do not trust their own experiences and embodied nature to tell them what is meaningful. For instance, the figures of the flagellant and the ascetic immured monk were highly praised. Modern forms of self-denial became particularly widespread across North-Western European countries, under the influence of the church reformer Calvin who focused on the innate sinfulness of humans: we need to work hard and deny our human urges (Weber, 2002). Consequently, self-denial seems to have become a fundamental characteristic of modern western societies, by which individuals mistrust their inner subjectivity and may consequently start to question meaning in life (Heidegger, 1927/2001).

Eschatological oppression

The ancient Greeks and Romans described the purpose of an individual as always pointing towards something higher on the societal-cosmic-divine ladder. At the bottom were minerals, metals and stones, which existed for the use of higher beings such as plants, trees and animals. These living beings were, in turn, there for the common people who served the free people and the leaders of the city, and even their being was directed to larger beings, such as demons, angels and gods. Thus humans held a unique position between the spiritual domain and physical creation, and their essence was ultimately directed towards spiritual service to God.

The early church fathers embraced this Aristotelean 'scala naturae', or ladder of nature, and merged it with the divine ladder (Solle, 2001). For instance, they focused on the biblical story about Jacob who 'dreamed, and behold a ladder set up on the earth, and the top of it reached to heaven: and behold the angels of God ascending and descending on it' (Genesis 28: 12). According to Thomas Aquinas, all things have an order or arrangement, and work for an end. The order of the universe cannot be explained by chance, but only by its purpose; this purposeful design of the universe is created and directed by God and all beings need to serve Him. As the Westminster Catechism instructed, 'Man's chief end is to glorify God, and enjoy Him forever.' In the Middle Ages, this order was translated into a societal order: all living beings were there for the common people who served nobles, who in turn were lower than princes, clergy and finally the king who was the closest to God and had divine rights, and the natural order expected all people to serve and obey him; the meaning of their lives was directed towards him. In the family, the father was head of the household; below him, his wife; below her, their children.

Judeo-Christian prophets, saints and church fathers added an eschatological vision to this ladder-thinking. This was a vision about the final judgement and destiny of the soul, the final reward or punishment for living a good or bad life respectively, like climbing a ladder from the mundane world to salvation and heaven. People were told that there is a 'ladder to paradise' (John Climacus), 'a pilgrimage of the soul to God'

(Giovanni Bonaventura) and 'a ladder to excellence' (Walter Hilton). This eschatology seemed to hold the societal order in its place. This belief was reinforced by continuous PR campaigns by the church, royals and nobles. During every mass, laymen were taught the natural order and their duties. Owing to this, most people would not even consider contesting this teleological order, as this was the only system they knew: there were few alternative perspectives, there was little education for commoners and even the mass was in Latin which few understood. Many people may also have internalised the teleological ideology and devotedly believed in it. As the risks of challenging the system were too great, the only option left was to change one's inner opinion and adhere to the social system (what we call **cognitive dissonance reduction**). Finally, if someone did question this order, they risked excommunication and even their salvation. Indeed, to rebel against the societal order would lead to prosecution by the king's army. Dissenters were labelled 'witches' and burnt alive at the stake, as their lives were considered meaningless. Those higher up on the societal ladder clearly benefited from this teleological perspective.

This sociological perspective seems to suggest that the individual quest for meaning is also inherently a political quest. In meaning-centred practices, individuals are empowered to explore their individual experiences of meaning. For instance, they choose to open themselves up to experiencing meaning in social relationships, family life, work and altruism, for the mere sake of love and altruism, and not because they are told by political and spiritual leaders what their place on the societal ladder is and what they should experience as meaningful.

Summary

Philosophers, priests and nobles created a meaningful context in which everything and everyone had a purpose within a coherent meaning-system. This system gave meaning to the individual. It was not up to the individual to create or seek meaning. It was simply to live one's destiny or purpose as part of the larger whole and social and natural order. These teleological meanings were held in place by the success of the privileged few and the political oppression of commoners.

The teleological perspective seems to be gaining popularity. Since the end of the twentieth century, many new books, lectures and training courses have been created about ancient Greek philosophers aimed at the general population. Philosophers passionately defend Plato and Aristotle as guides for daily life, while they do not always place these philosophers in the wider socio-historical context, as in this chapter. This uncritical revival could be a response to the meaning-less vacuum left by secularisation and postmodernism in the twentieth century (as will be described in Section 1.3); this seems to have created a desire for a clear understanding of the world order and our position in it. However, alternative perspectives are possible, as Chapter 2 will show.

Meaning-centred practitioners could meet clients who feel that they live in a teleological system. The problems that they may address could be about their difficulty in identifying a purpose, or that purposes may contradict each other, or that they may not be able to fully achieve their purpose, for instance as a consequence of their socio-economic limitations in society. Ladder thinking could therefore lead to the feeling that life can never be truly meaningful, as there is always a higher rung on the ladder, there is always another higher purpose which you could fulfil, you are never finished climbing. I have seen in many clients how this may lead to feelings of existential exhaustion, chronic failure and low self-worth. The internalisation of these feelings may lead to symptoms such as guilt, depression, burnout or midlife crisis. Clients in my practice have coped with such feelings via denial, substance misuse or outbursts of anger and violence. For these reasons, this book does not merely address meaning as fitting a pregiven position on a ladder or climbing the ladder toward the sky, but opens up other approaches to meaning (Chapter 2).

1.3 Scepticism: the flat earth of the philosophers and academics

Godwin Rolfe lived his life according to his position on the societal-cosmic-divine ladder. His life seemed less meaningful than the lives of those higher up the ladder. This hierarchy was an uncontested given. However, there have also always been individuals who questioned this hierarchy: sceptics. *How can we know what is more and what is less meaningful? The teleological knowledge claim is unfounded: there are no ladders, there is only flat earth and any ladders are manmade!* However, their scepticism most likely did not reach the largest part of society until the sixteenth century. Different types of scepticism can be distinguished: theological, philosophical, scientific, social, existential and reductionist scepticism.

Theological scepticism

Several medieval priests contested the idea that individuals need to fulfil a predetermined social role on a ladder, which seemed mainly based on God's decree and which the clergy had to make laymen believe in. Two famous individuals were particularly sceptical about this social order, and were excommunicated by Rome (posthumously revoked in the twentieth century). Meister Eckhart criticised the idea that meaning in life meant that everything we do needs to serve a higher purpose. As mentioned above the medieval German word for meaning, 'Meinung', means aligning oneself to a larger purpose to which our activities are directed, as part of a larger societal order. Instead, Eckhart told his audience to focus on meaning for the sake of the meaning which he called 'wise ane wise', which can be translated literally as 'a way without a way'. For instance, love for the sake of love, not for the sake of God or society expecting this from you. Several centuries later, the reformer Martin Luther added other examples. He wrote that he feared that people were merely trying to find penance and salvation: they go to church and follow the rules of the Bible simply to fulfil their duty and safeguard the future of their soul. People should not obey God out of selfish intentions or for the mere sake of following the teleological order and societal rules. Instead, people should choose in all freedom to serve God for the sake of God. God has given us the freedom to make the conscious decision to follow or reject Him.

Thus, according to Eckhart and Luther, meaning in life is not about a higher purpose in a societal-cosmic-divine order, but about our inner intentions. To differentiate this subjective meaning from teleological meaning, they started to use the word 'Sinn' instead of the teleological word 'Meinung'. This word is derived from the Latin word *sentire*, which means perceiving and is associated with using *all our senses*. During the Reformation, the word 'Sinn' was quickly popularised, and many languages now use this as the primary word for meaning (except for English, in which only the word 'meaning' is used, and 'making sense' does not mean the same as 'Sinn'). While the word 'Sinn' gained popularity in Continental European, Slavic and Russian languages ('Sinn', 'Zin', 'Sense', 'Sensida', 'Smesl'), these languages started to use the word 'meaning' in negative and mundane ways, with connotations such as subjective random opinion, vulgarity, childish desires and so on. This reveals a fundamental revolution, when the teleological order was refuted and the teleological word 'Meinung' was replaced by 'Sinn'. This was a revolution of the sceptics.

Philosophical and scientific scepticism

The word 'scepsis' is derived from the ancient Greek word for 'paying close attention' ('skeptesthai'). This implied a perceptive attitude and temporary putting aside of our own theories and biases ('epoche'; see Chapter 2). Over the years, this word became more generally used for a critical investigative perspective. Thus philosophical scepticism has been defined as the willingness 'to question any knowledge claim, asking for clarity in definition, consistency in logic and adequacy of evidence' (Kurtz, 1986, p. 20).

There is a long philosophical tradition of scepticism, which started possibly with the Skeptikoi, who were ancient Greek philosophers whose aim was to assert nothing in life. Pyrrho of Ellis told us that we should suspend our judgement. Protagoras suggested that our subjective perception and evaluation are the only existing measure or guidance which we can use in life (*homo mensura*). During the Muslim Enlightenment, the idea of measuring effects and conducting experiments emerged. Empiricism says that all information needs to be well supported by evidence. During the European Enlightenment, Rene Descartes used the method of systematic doubt about everything in life, until he realised he could not doubt the existence of his thinking ('I think, therefore I am'). Other philosophers followed his sceptical method, such as Michel de Montaigne in France and David Hume in Britain. The philosopher Immanuel Kant introduced the slogan *Sapere Aude*, or 'dare to know': discover what is meaningful for yourself, instead of assuming the truth of what others tell you or of uncritically fitting yourself into a teleological societal order (although Kant's philosophy did still include some teleological aspects such as the categorical imperative and synthetic a priori judgements). The twentieth century continued this sceptical tradition, particularly in response to the loss of trust in ideologies, as the two world wars had shown where uncritical acceptance of ideas could lead to. Many post-ideological philosophies developed, such as existentialism, nihilism, relativism and postmodernism.

This stereotypical overview sketches some sceptical trends which centre on the idea that we cannot believe in a teleological ladder falling from the sky. The philosopher Daniel Dennett (1995, p. 135) writes that sceptics realise that 'skyhooks do not exist': we invent our own ladders and try to climb these to reach heaven, but we have no evidence that there is a God by whose decree the teleological order can exist. The ladder has fallen to earth and cannot be put up again towards heaven. Consequently, we should give up on our hopes for larger meanings: 'I entreat you: remain true to earth and don't believe those who speak to you of super-terrestrial hopes: they are despisers of life' (Nietzsche, 1891/2017).

Social scepticism

The societal consequences of this scepticism have been significant. By literally bringing down the statues and the sculptures, the reformers in the Netherlands and Germany brought down the teleological ladder. The result is that nowadays these are among the most secular countries in the world, with a strong atheist objection to teleological heights (although modern forms of spirituality are very common). Since the Renaissance, more individuals began to be sceptical about the social order, and many social movements emerged to resist hierarchical societal structures, ranging from the French Revolution to the suffragettes, the civil rights movements and LGBTQ empowerment.

These societal changes were based on an increasingly widespread scepticism about the pregiven social order, which could for instance be found in texts from authors writing in the Enlightenment through to the communist and anarchist traditions. The Marxist sociologist Marshall Berman (2009) wrote how meaning and social empowerment evolved together, that is, in the sixteenth century, a new middle class emerged in the cities. They experienced more freedom and had time for reflection and the opportunity of wealth to choose between alternatives. Berman claims that the distribution of wealth and the emergence of a middle class in the cities gave people the opportunity to choose meanings that felt in line with their own identity: authenticity. If you are struggling for your survival and have no alternative options, you do not have the luxury to reflect and choose other options. And vice versa: the experience of individual authenticity helped individuals to liberate themselves from oppressing teleological societal orders. To some extent, Berman's explanation is teleological in nature and focuses on the privileged few, but it seems likely that the development of both social empowerment and sceptical meanings were symbiotic.

Existential scepticism

The evolution of widespread philosophical, theological, scientific and social scepticism fuelled the existential scepticism that individuals began to experience about their own meaning in life, that is, individuals became sceptical about the way in which they had been living their lives. This scepticism was fuelled by scientific advances, larger scale education and the invention of the printing press which allowed ideas to be distributed widely and quickly. The most significant 'invention' was possibly that of asking questions about one's own meaning in life. Up until the Renaissance and the Reformation, individuals most likely did not ask such questions as 'what is the meaning of *my* life?' Individuals' lives were simply part of the collectivist teleological order, and individuals merely fulfilled their role in that system, like the hand serves the head. This subjectivisation of meaning was fuelled further by Romanticism, which Georg Wilhelm Friedrich Hegel observed as individuals in his time starting to live their lives according to the uniqueness of their own experiences and taste ('Besonderheit der Empfindung'). This subjectivisation of our meaning has culminated in the functional meanings in the twentieth and twenty-first centuries, which will be explained in the next section. The stereotypical example is the anti-hero in Johan Wolfgang von Goethe's novel *Die Leiden des Jungen Werthers* (The Sorrows of Young Werther), who doubts everything while focusing on his feelings as a source of meaning.

Reductionist scepticism

Scepticism can be either **reductionist** or non-reductionist. **Reductionism** is an approach whereby a phenomenon is reduced to nothing other than ... For instance, meaning is nothing other than physical, biological and evolutionary processes (materialistic reductionism), social expectations and pressures (social reductionism) or a denial of life's primary meaninglessness and absurdity (**existential reductionism**).

For example, existential reductionism suggests that meaning is our human response to the overwhelming human condition (Vos et al., 2015): life primarily lacks structure, meaning and morality. We are not born with an instruction manual to tell us 'this is what the meaning of your life is going to be'. Life is primarily about potentiality – having possibilities from which we can choose (see Heidegger, 1927). However, without teleological guidance to tell us how to deal with this potentiality, we experience this as a choice overload. In confrontation with this absurd potentiality, we often feel overwhelmed and experience **existential moods**, such as existential anxiety, death anxiety, disgust and boredom. To cope with this, we try to deny or distort reality as it is (**existential defence mechanisms**). For instance, we create the illusion that life does have absolute meaning, while it actually does not. Thus some existential philosophers argue that meaning is a way to cope with existential threats, and meaning is *nothing more than* an existential defence mechanism.

Extreme forms of reductionism have been criticised for being based on erroneous reasoning. The main phenomenological argument against reductionism could be metaphorically described as the **map/landscape fallacy**: it is illogical to say that 'there are no differences in height in reality, because my map is flat'. Having a two-dimensional map of a landscape doesn't refute the existence of a three-dimensional landscape. Thus the ability to explain how individuals experience meaning in life does not imply that meaning does not exist. Love still exists, although we can identify its neurological correlates. Sceptical reductionism has been described as self-undermining, as it doubts everything but not itself. For instance, how can Darwinists be convinced about the truth when their own perspective is the product of social evolution? Reductionists describe meaning as a physical reaction to a physical world, and base their interpretations on the assumption that there is a world of physical meanings; however, the **phenomenologist** Husserl questioned why first setting out this physical world is more true than starting from the world of our lived experiences ('Lebenswelt'). Most reductionist studies are also based on correlations, which do not show any causal relationships: the fact that meaning and certain biological processes happen simultaneously, does not mean that biology causes meaning. Reductionism could also be ethically rejected, as scepticism could lead people away from meaning, although meaning is an important buffer against stress and helps people to altruistically contribute to each other's lives and build society (Chapter 3). Society seems to benefit more from a meaningful vision than from self-acclaimed realism (Lerner, 1997, 2006). Thus rigid reductionism seems difficult to defend logically and ethically.

It seems impossible to ignore the legacy of scepticism in our postmodern era, and it would be equally controversial to return to the reductionist teleology from the Middle Ages. Therefore, Chapter 2 suggests the alternative position of non-reductionist scepticism. The phenomenological approach in that chapter creates a space for meaning in life for sceptics.

1.4 Functionalism: the skyscrapers of the McMeanings

'MAXimise your life!' (Pepsi Max commercial)

Characteristics of McMeanings

The sceptical revolution has fundamentally changed the way in which individuals live their lives in western countries. It is not just scientists and philosophers who have embraced a sceptical attitude. The student revolution, the human empowerment movement and the flower power movement in the 1960s broke with societal conformism and teleological meanings on a large scale. We can all define our own meaning and there is no ultimate meaning in life; 'anything goes'.

However, scepticism did not entirely replace teleology: there are modern versions of Godwin Rolfes. Many individuals seem to experience a hybrid of teleological and sceptical meanings, which may be called 'functional meanings'. To a wider audience, I usually call these 'McMeanings', as we see these meanings as though they were something we could buy at a McDonald's: they provide instant happiness, can be demanded from life, but we quickly feel hungry again and want more which may lead to addiction. These meanings seem to be characterised by modern forms of teleology, a culture obsessed with feelings and particularly with happiness and our public face, assuming the randomness, mechanical functionality, *replace*-ability and unsatisfiability of our McMeanings, creating the illusion of control, and feeding a culture of competition and guilt in a capitalist system (Vos, 2014). These meanings seem to give many a sense of meaninglessness (Frankl, 2010; see Section 3.2). These components will now be elaborated.

Feeling culture. In sharp contrast with the collectivist teleology, in modern society meaning is a matter of subjective taste. In 1807, the philosopher Hegel wrote that individuals were beginning to design their lives according to the uniqueness of their individual experience and taste. At that time, the sceptical revolution had started to defeat traditional teleology. The French Revolution had created the political freedom for individuals to design their own lives. The emergence of a middle class living in relative wealth in cities had also created the materialistic possibility for individuals to define their own meanings (Berman, 2009). Yet if there are no longer rigid societal conventions and institutions to instruct us on the meaning of our lives, then where can we find meaning? The answer is from within ourselves. This was the counter-Copernican revolution of the subject, whereby individuals no longer revolved around universal meanings, but rather the universe began to revolve around their subjectivity. Our meanings are no longer merely determined by our societal duties but instead by our subjective rights, as reflected in modern law and human rights. We live in an 'Experience Society': many people make decisions and build their identities according to their subjective experience and taste. External purposes – others' expectations, the way in which individuals fit within the larger system, and divine-cosmic meanings – have become less important than an individual's inner purpose (Schultze, 1992).

Hedonic culture. What is the subjective taste on which individuals base their meanings? Often, our taste is narrowed down to McMeanings: demanding ready-made meanings that provide instant gratification (Vos, 2014). For example, this may be in the form of focusing on material wealth, possessions, financial safety, holidays, entertainment, social status, quick visible success and so on. McMeanings focus mainly on hedonic pleasure. Many empirical studies confirm that material and hedonic meanings correlate with lower general well-being than other types of meaning (Section 3.3).

Technical meaning-making. It has been suggested that the ways in which we organise our lives are related to how we organise our work, and particularly how we use technology (Sennett, 2004). For instance, instead of being aware of where we are and using our experience, we trust the GPS in our phone; similarly, we are often disoriented in life and trust the guidance from others and from books (Dreyfus & Kelly, 2011, p. 208). Every western bookstore has a self-help section with book titles such as 'think and grow rich', 'the success principles' or 'seven habits of highly effective people'. These books not only suggest that we focus on discrete purposes such as being rich, successful or effective, but they also promise that we can demand these meanings through a small number of steps. Thus meaning in life is described technically as a means to reaching a goal (Visser, 1998, 2008). This reveals a new teleology, which is not based on a collectivist order but rather on our subjective experience.

Where did this transition come from? By the end of the nineteenth century, the craftsman was being replaced by the factory worker. Whereas craftsmen had been responsible for the quality of the entire product, from A to Z, based on the training and experience they had acquired over many years, factory workers became responsible for only a small specific part of the production chain which did not require lengthy training or experience. Not only did their working lives became more specific, but they no longer demanded much expertise or character formation, like in the Ford automobile factories (Sennett, 2008, 2011). Their entire life seemed to become Fordified, and based on the idea that meaning can be manufactured like a product, with short small bursts of effort like the specific activities of the factory worker. The focus moved from living a meaningful life – like living as a craftsman – to doing specific activities like the factory worker. Job activities no longer required an understanding of the whole process and the complete final product, nor of how all the specific steps connected; in a similar way, individuals seemed less interested in developing a broad philosophy, overview or coherence of life.

Having a general sense of meaningfulness was broken down into specific meanings. Jobs started to require specific outputs in terms of discrete 'goals', and similarly, during the 1990s, it became popular – particularly for commercial trainers – to break the experience of meaning down into what they called specific 'life goals' or 'life aims'. The culmination of this are self-help books with titles such as 'seven steps to a happy life'. Similar to a commercial product, the idea developed that if a meaning could not be realised, it could be randomly replaced by another meaning. For instance, several psychological therapies were developed in which clients were advised to randomly pick another value or meaning from a checklist if another had become unattainable. The lifelong process of acquiring expertise and intuitively connecting with multiple meanings in life was reduced to a tick-box exercise. One mainstream idea is to make a list of priorities that you want to achieve before you die, a 'bucket list', and you only need to fulfil these steps to have lived a meaningful life. Thus, like a manager at work, individuals became managers of their own life, demanding specific activities to create the end product.

Viktor Frankl warned psychotherapists not to envision meaning like discrete objects from which we could randomly pick a meaning (Frankl, 1986), as if from the shelves in a shop. If we were to envision and select meanings in such a manner, we deny the totality of our socially, historically and embodied lived experience. This technical approach only shows meaning as a goal/result and not as a process (Fromm, 1941/2002), and may not necessarily resonate with who we truly are in our total experience. As the next chapter explains, what it means to live a meaningful life entails much more than being a functional machine, setting goals and creating means to an end. Furthermore, Chapter 3 includes a literature review of empirical studies which reveal that goals are only one specific type of meaning, and many individuals also experience non-goal-oriented meanings, such as love for the sake of love. However, meaning is often seen as a thing we 'make', and some psychotherapists even call their approach 'meaning-MAKING therapy'.

Mechanical functionality. The clearest example of a reductionistic and functionalist approach can be found in Gary Becker (1976), who wrote that all economic behaviour can be explained by the individual's ability to increase their economic utility or efficiency. This includes love, which means, according to him, that individuals derive utility from each other's utility: 'It can be said that Mi [Man i] loves Fj [Female j] if her welfare enters his utility function, and perhaps also if Mi values emotional and physical contact with Fj.' In other words, Becker writes that meaning is about a relationship that increases each other's well-being. This is not love for the sake of lovek, but for the sake of the functionality of the relationship. This utilitarian approach has made love vulnerable to manipulation and commercial exploitation. Whereas love seemed to be a romantic mystery half a century ago, it has now become the domain of goal-oriented behaviour on internet dating sites and in Hollywood movies and reality TV shows. This marketisation of love may give the idea that true love can be easily demanded and achieved – like ordering a 'Burger McLove'. If you want love, you simply go online, send Valentine cards and roses, and you will have the perfect partner. However, despite this trend, for many individuals love is not merely a calculation about 'from whom will I benefit most' but it is about meaning that transcends the functionality of the relationship. Romantic love is irrational and blind, guided by passion and not reason (Bruckner, 2012). Similar to the irreducibility of love, for many individuals meaning in life is more than setting functionalistic goals or fulfilling social expectations.

Aiming and reaching the max. After the sceptical revolution, teleology was no longer about climbing collective theological-political ladders but about building our own subjective ladders and climbing these as high as we can. The German philosopher Peter Sloterdijk (2014) published a book with the title *You Must Change Your Life*, to describe how individuals in the twentieth and twenty-first centuries have a deep wish to optimise their individual lives and can do so through what he calls 'antropotechniques'. This is what the human potential movement in the 1960s and 1970s preached: whatever you do, optimise it. The Pepsi commercial later followed their lead with their slogan: 'live life to the max!' The twenty-first century continued with similar slogans on social media such as YOLO – You Only Live Once – and FOMO – Fear Of Missing Out. The sociologist Max Weber (2002) argued that the Calvinist teleology created a culture of maximisation in North-Western Europe. Despite secularisation, the biblical metaphor of optimising our individual talents is stronger than ever. Several modern western philosophers, such as Alisdair McIntyre and Charles Taylor, motivate individuals to direct their life towards actualising a telos or ideal of life that is yet to be. You MUST live life to its max: you are free in the content, but unfree in the goal-directedness. Choose whatever you want, as long as you do it optimally. Lifestyle magazines seem to shout to their readers: you MUST enjoy life, and not moderately or undeliberated, but you must actively decide to enjoy it completely. You MUST attain the highest education possible; you MUST have as many friends as possible; you MUST know all the news about what is going on in the world; you MUST go on retreats to become mindful (how mindful is that?).

Aiming for the max does not suffice; we also need to reach the max. For instance, some enterprises use a rank-and-yank system. At the end of every year, employees are ranked in accordance with their individual productivity, and those with the lowest productivity will be fired. There is no place for suboptimal results, vulnerability or lessons to be learnt. This is a meritocratic system: societies run by people selected according to meri, who are educated and able individuals (Sennett, 2011; Verhaeghe, 2014). The meritocratic culture starts from a young age, and even children in nursery schools undergo tests before they can progress to a higher class. Throughout all their years of education, pupils and students are expected to achieve the highest grades, and aim for the highest, although only a few privileged individuals can reach the highest educational distinction of professorship (Verhaeghe, 2014). This meritocratic culture significantly impacts on how we live our lives.

Our life goal becomes maximising our human potential, however we may personally define this potential. The philosopher Oswald Spengler (1921/1991) wrote that the skyscraper is the symbol of our obsession with infinitely reaching higher and higher towards the sky. Consequently, the sky is the limit and we fantasise continuously about the sky. Underlying this meritocracy is our belief in the ultimate malleability of society and of our own lives, ideas that emerged in the Enlightenment. Nothing is determined, everything can change, and WE can change everything (see Verhaeghe, 2014). Meaning and identity become things we MAKE instead of discover. Consequently, individuals who fail to reach the highest potential in life have only themselves to blame.

Becoming our public image. This meritocratic system reveals a social paradox. On the one hand, individuals define meaning according to their own subjective taste. On the other hand, individuals orient their taste towards others, and are very sensitive about their social image. That is, without a teleological measure of what is meaningful, people seem to turn to others to tell them what their taste should be. For instance, lifestyle magazines, fashion shows, television series and blogs thrive on our uncertainty about what is meaningful. The reality show *Big Brother* highlighted the importance of public opinion by giving voters the option to decide via text message which show members and what activities are the most meaningful. If there is no objective criterion to instruct us on what is meaningful, the number of 'likes' on Facebook end up defining what we regard as 'meaningful'. Individuals may start to believe that they need more adventure trips and funny pictures: this attracts many 'likes', thus this must be meaningful for me? This makes our subjective experiences vulnerable to manipulation by businesses who are looking to sell their products and services. We focus on meanings that give us a positive social image: we present ourselves as able and successful, show off our productivity, and embark on education to improve ourselves as much as we can. Our self-image is based on our social image and the measurable effects of our work, instead of what feels truly meaningful to us personally (Verhaeghe, 2014). Our technology seems to alienate us from ourselves and from our phenomenological meanings (see Visser, 2013).

Capitalism. Several authors have associated functional meanings with capitalism, an economic system that focuses on private companies selling their products on the free market. Capitalism is inherently embedded in a wider functional context, and this functional meaning culture has enabled capitalism to grow exponentially. Capitalism is economic teleology: the meaning of individuals is to serve the market; our illusion of self-determination disguises our obedience to a continuously judging societal tribunal (Foucault, 2008; Verhaeghe, 2014). The liquidity of our identity and the subjectivity of our meanings make us vulnerable to the influence of commercial industry.

The meaning industry has become a new economic sector, alongside agriculture, industry and services (Schulze, 1992). The most obvious example of meaning products are self-help books, training courses and retreats catered towards helping people to find their own meaning. In the current market of overproduction, producers need to sell their product not by the quality of the product but by the meaning they can give. Individuals buy products mainly for the associated meanings (Bernays, 1928/2005). For example, although Nike, Adidas and Puma provide similar material quality, customers identify themselves as 'I am a Nike person who would never wear another brand'. Books instruct companies on how they can sell more by suggesting that they do not sell products and services but that they sell meaning – for example, *Marketing PRopaganda: From Attention to the Meaning Economy*. Commercials tell us that life is not meaningful if we do not buy such and such. Furthermore, business gurus recommend increasing employees' productivity by creating meaningful organisational structures – for example, in books such as *Meaning Inc.: The Blueprint for Business Success in the 21st Century, Doing God's Business: Meaning and Motivation for the Marketplace* and *Make It Better: How Managers Can Motivate by Creating Meaning*. Thus, the meaning of customers and employees is manipulated to increase profit. Commercials continuously reinforce the idea that products have meaning, and that they are even necessary for living a meaningful life. This creates a self-reinforcing cycle between the commercial industry and the hedonic culture of functional meanings.

Mental health crisis? Thus, capitalism seems to reinforce the functionalist focus on materialistic, hedonic and self-oriented meanings. Consequently, capitalism shifts the focus away from social and larger meanings in life (Section 3.3). As these types of meaning are associated with lower well-being compared to social and higher types of meaning (Section 3.3), capitalism seems to be contributing to the large-scale mental health crisis in modern society. Research seems to indicate that many individuals in modern western countries suffer from the Capitalist Life Syndrome, which is based on six criteria: living in a capitalist society, superficial types of meanings (materialistic, hedonistic, self-oriented meanings), functionalistic approach to meaning, capitalistic fatalism, identification with capitalist life, existential concerns and psychological, social and professional concerns (Vos, 2018). Thus the functionalistic focus on superficial meanings in western countries has been associated with a sense of meaninglessness and mental health problems. For example, worldwide Gallup surveys reveal that individuals in non-capitalist countries such as Togo and Niger experience more happiness and life satisfaction than in capitalist countries like France and Scandinavia (Oishi & Diener, 2014). Sociologists have described similar trends towards functional meanings, and how these may be causing structural psychological stress in clients. Table 1.1 details symptoms that they have observed. Some have argued that these meaning-centred problems are so widespread that they have created a mental health crisis in western countries.

However, at the same time, sociologists have revealed another trend in western countries, whereby individuals are starting to reject the functionalist perspective and to focus instead on social and larger meanings. For example, the sociologist Ronald Inglehart (1990) has showed through his World Values Survey, which has been running since 1981, that people's values have been increasingly shifting away from materialistic values – such as economic and physical certainties – towards post-materialist values – such as self-expression and making a meaningful contribution to the world. Economists and sociologists identify a similar trend in consumption of moving away from the aspirations of money and consumption towards meaning, knowledge and community. The next chapter will elaborate on this trend.

Table 1.1 Characteristics of functional meanings in literature

Characteristic	Description	Reference
Chronic lack of fulfilment	Functional meanings only provide temporary satisfaction and momentary happiness.	Verhaeghe (2014)
Addiction (literal or symbolic)	To compensate for their chronic lack of fulfilment, individuals try out many functional meanings ('going from kick to kick'), and need more and more extreme meanings. Full diary, chronic exhaustion.	Kunneman (2009)
Fat ego	Individuals become self-obsessed as a consequence of focusing on materialistic-hedonic and self-oriented meanings.	Kunneman (2003)
Uncertainty	There is no absolute guidance from church or parents. The world and the self have become uncertain. Social roles and identities have become liquid. Consequently, there is an obsession with risk aversion.	Beck (1992); Bauman (2013)
Guilt	We set and optimise our own goals. If we fail, we have only ourselves to blame. We overgeneralise the extent to which we can determine our lives, and are unrealistic about the influence from for instance socio-economic status or government.	Verhaeghe (2014)

Flexible relationships	As there is no prescribed social order, social and professional relationships are flexible and often change. Friends and relationships are measured according to personal taste, instead of the social context determining our social context.	Sennett (2011)
Commitment	Resilience, perseverance and commitment to long-term meanings are replaced by short-term gratification.	Sennett (2007), Benn (2003)
Choice overload	As there is no teleological guidance, and people do not use their intuition, which creates an overload of choices, and therefore difficulties in making decisions.	Schwartz (2004), Swenson (2014), Kahneman (2012)
Double standard	False tolerance; lack of honesty; political correctness; 'Yes, but' culture.	Pfaller (2002), Zizek (1996)
Little happiness	Individuals in western countries are less happy. Happiness paradox: we are healthier than ever, but our happiness has not increased.	World Happiness Report (2016), Skidelski & Skidelski (2012)
Neo-conservatism and extremism	In response to chronic emptiness and dissatisfaction, individuals become more conservative, extreme and teleological.	Gray (2004)

1.5 Meaning in non-western societies

This chapter has focused on the experience of meaning in life during the last millennia in western countries. The historical trend, as described, was that the initial teleological approach was replaced by scepticism and functionalism. Chapter 2 will follow on from this to describe a modern trend in western countries towards **phenomenology.**

Historical and anthropological research suggests that this western perspective on meaning cannot be applied directly to non-western cultures. For example, psychological researchers have been trying to translate English questionnaires about meaning in life into other languages, but they often get stuck in translation, as different languages and cultures conceptualise meaning differently. For example, individuals in western countries often approach meaning as one specific static 'thing' that they only need to discover once in their lifetime, and that they can know cognitively, manipulate and replace with any random meaning (see the section above on functionalism). However, non-western cultures and other eras show more dynamic, social, intuitive, behavioural and less monolithic concepts of meaning. The following is a brief sketch of trends in other cultures and eras (see also Hoffman, Kang, Kaklauskas, & Chan, 2009).

As far as we know, the Bronze Age was dominated by relatively fixed social positions, with aristocratic families at the societal top, and this hierarchy was often justified by religious stories and rituals. Individuals most likely did not explicitly ask questions about their individual meaning, but lived according to their allocated spot on the societal-cosmic-divine ladder, like medieval Europe. In the Axial Age (c. 800 BC to 300 BC), the status quo of pregiven societal, cosmic and divine structures came to be questioned by philosophers and spiritual leaders across the globe from Confucius to the ancient Greek philosophers, and the founders of the three major religions in the Middle East (Voegelin, 1985/2000; Armstrong, 2006; Jaspers, 1949/2011). Possibly for the first time in history, explicit attention was given to individual questions about meaning in life instead of embedding oneself in a pregiven social-divine-cosmic order (Neville, 2002). This development seemed to go hand in hand with the development of new technologies (Lent, 2017) and neurological evolution (Peterson, 1999).

Many texts from the Axial Age reveal a sceptical attitude towards following rules for the sake of rules and living life according to pregiven goals. Instead, many prophets and philosophers suggested personal meditation practices, behavioural training or mystic devotion, to help individuals **phenomenologically unpeel** their experiences, to get rid of societal and selfish hindrances to finding true spiritual meaning. For example, early Indian authors of Vedic books such as the *Upanishads*, the *Brahma Sutras* and the *Bhagavad Gita* do not speak about end goals but about the fourfold system of *dharma* (a moral way of living, following duties and laws), *artha* (finding meaning in means of life such as food, shelter and wealth), *kama* (finding meaning in experiences such as pleasure, desire, sex and love) and *moksha* (spiritual meaning, liberation from the life–rebirth cycle, or self-realisation in this life). It is only the dynamic totality of this fourfold system that can be called meaningful (Agarwal, 2015). These meanings can be realised via a complex system of *yoga*, which are physical, mental and spiritual practices. These philosophical ideas about meaning have influenced many religious developments in Hinduism, Buddhism and Jainism. In most Asian languages the terminology for 'meaning' still refers to this historical complexity, although different individuals interpret this philosophy differently.

Many Asian traditions seemed to focus on **phenomenological unpeeling** (see Chapter 2). For example, several Hindu philosophers focus explicitly on unpeeling daily life experiences to realise that there is no world or self. According to this tradition, the *mayan* (mundane) world and individuality (*atman*) that we perceive in our daily life are actually already one with *Brahman*, the One Ultimate Reality. The purpose of life is to realise this. In latter Buddhist traditions, individuals search for meaning by **phenomenologically bracketing** their mundane experiences and focusing on the true Reality. Similarly, in Daoism, individuals phenomenologically bracket their daily life meanings – that is, they set these meanings temporarily aside – to let what is meaningful reveal itself. The masters Laozi and Zhuangzi talked about *wu wei*, which can be literally translated as not-acting; they seemed to refer to a way of living that does not focus on materialistic or self-oriented purposes. A similar attitude to *wu wei* can be seen in medieval mysticism; Meister Eckhart described a similar attitude which he called *Gelassenheit,* which can be translated as a process of letting go of, for instance, mundane and self-oriented purposes and allowing what is meaningful to reveal itself. *Gelassenheit* later returns in the work of existential and phenomenological philosophers such as Arthur Schopenhauer, Friedrich Nietzsche and Martin Heidegger (Caputo, 1978; Chong, 2006; Visser, 2008). Seen from the daily life perspective of the individual, the phenomenological unpeeling implied in several Asian traditions that social, larger and existential-philosophical meanings were prioritised over materialistic, hedonistic or self-oriented types of meanings, and that meaning was experienced in phenomenological and non-technical ways (see Chapters 2 and 3).

Many Asian philosophies and religions have also paid attention to the sensorial and embodied experience of meaning, for instance via physical meditative techniques, rituals or moral behaviour. For example, in Confucian philosophy, individuals pursue the unity of the self and the divine order via contemplation and the building of a harmonious community by doing the right actions. Thus, in these Asian traditions, meaning is not merely something we theorise as a goal towards which we strive, it includes all our feelings and behaviour. A similar behaviour-oriented approach to meaning can be found in Roman philosophers and Stoics. This behavioural focus has led to specific forms of behavioural therapies. In Morita's therapy (1998), clients learn from their actions and not merely from cognitive reflection. Clients get out of their daily life routines and engage in new occupational activities such as gardening and it is assumed that individuals will intuitively develop more meaningful activities. Thus Morita therapists focus on helping clients to be in the **hot inside flow of experiencing** instead of **cold outside theoretical reflection** (see Chapter 3). They assume that behavioural change can develop a renewed sense of meaningfulness.

In Japanese, the term *Ikigai* is used (Garcia & Miralles, 2017). Similar to the **meaning triangle** which will be described in Chapter 3, *Ikigai* assumes that meaning can be found at the intersection between what we can or cannot, must or must not and want or do not want to do. To be more precise, *Ikigai* is the combination of what you love, what you are good at, what the world needs and what you can be paid for. Thus, the concept of meaning incorporates behaviour and embodied experiences, in contrast with the theoretical approaches to meaning in many western religions and psychological therapies.

This brief world history of meaning shows the complexity and multi-dimensionality of meaning in life. Martin Heidegger has also argued that many ancient Greek philosophers had more complex and multifaceted philosophies about meaning than how we often interpret them nowadays (Visser, 1998; Brogan, 2005). For example, Aristotle discussed four different causes of behaviour of nature and all beings (form, materialistic, agent and purpose), but in our modern western era we seem to ignore most causes. Instead, in the sixteenth century, the scientific revolution brought the idea that everything is functional: everything we do is a means to a larger goal. Consequently, many individuals in modern western countries see meaning as one specific purpose that they need to strive towards.

However, it is too simplistic to describe all non-western philosophies as phenomenological and as rejecting all mundane experiences. For example, many Vedic philosophers are positive about materialistic and hedonistic meanings, as long as *Artha* and *Kama* are not standing in the way of *Dharma* and *Moksha*. Some Hindus have also interpreted Vedic philosophies as a societal-cosmic-divine hierarchy which can be found in the caste system and ideas about reincarnation. This means that at birth individuals are born into a caste, and this prescribes their meaning, often including their occupation, ritual status and customary social interaction and exclusion (Smith, 2000).

Religions in other parts of the world also seemed to experience hier-archical meanings, often with the sky as the highest position in the hierarchy. They often intertwine an individual's sense of meaning with cosmology and astrology. For example, ancient Egyptian religion saw the purpose of an individual's life in the context of a larger cosmological order, of which the pyramids are a clear symbolisation. Similar pyramids can be found with the the Aztecs in Southern America, who adhered to the concept of destiny. The Aztecs had an annual calendar, guiding individuals according to their date of birth, which was intertwined with their personality, psyche and fate. Individuals did not contest the book of destiny, as the Creator God and Goddess had made both time and the calendar (Boone, 2007). Some tribes and nomadic groups in African and Middle Eastern countries also had strong social hierarchies, which were assumed to be given at birth and which were experienced not only as a social order but also as a divine order, ordained by God. These tribal structures seemed to prescribe how individual tribe members should live their lives and what they should experience as meaningful (Harvey, 2015). In some animistic cultures, this societal-cosmic-divine order was also intertwined with nature. Individuals in animistic traditions believe that gods can be found everywhere in nature and in inanimate objects, and meaningful rituals should help to appease the gods. In Native American and Amerindian religions, nature also plays an important role, particularly through the all-encompassing Spirit which is assumed to guide and direct individuals in their lives.

Chapters 1 and 2 describe how the history of meaning in the modern west contrasts with many of the traditions described in this section. The Judaic, early Christian and Islamic religions have seen some strong hierarchic interpretations of meaning in life. The complexity and sceptic traditions in the ancient Greek philosophies of meaning seemed to disappear in the interpretations from early church fathers such as Augustine and Aquinas. This led to the medieval societal-cosmic-divine ladder that determined an individuals' meaning at birth, as this chapter has described. The old German term for this reductionist experience was *Meinung* which later came to refer to mundane and random opinions and which became differentiated from the term *Sinn* which reflects a larger complexity and embodied sense of meaning like in other traditions. The medieval mystics and the protestant reformers criticised the idea that individuals had to follow a cosmic-divine law like Judaism and early Christian church fathers had described; instead, they described how Jesus' concept of love replaced the Judaic behaviour-oriented focus on the Law, *Halakhah*. They described how these orthodox Judaic concepts could be unpeeled phenomenologically to uncover a wider understanding of meaning. This transition from hierarchic meanings towards phenomenological meanings will be elaborated in Chapter 2.

This brief world history of meaning is reflected in the different terms – and their underlying different worldviews – in modern languages. In most English-speaking, African and Middle Eastern countries, people use terms that are etymologically derived from the reductionist term *Meinung*. In Continental Europe, Slavic countries and Russia, terms are derived from the fully embodied term *sintere*, as described earlier in this chapter. In Asian languages, many terms have been derived from *artha*, although this is usually embedded in a more complex understanding of meaning, such as *Ikigai* in Japan. In Old Chinese, the term *Qi* is often used in this context, which refers to the life force or energy flow in life (the practice of cultivating and balancing *qi* is called *qigong*), and which has been associated with how someone ought to behave and justice.

Despite clear linguistic and conceptual differences, there are also remarkable overlaps between the different terminology. In totally different eras and continents, philosophers used the same metaphor of the way of life to describe meaning: the term *Dao* emerged on the Chinese planes around 600 BC which can be literally translated as 'way', and the term *Sinn* became popular in medieval Continental Europe which has also been etymologically associated with a way or travelling. In the Middle Ages, Meister Eckhart introduced the term *Sinn* which he associated with a way in life – in contrast with the static term *Meinung* (see Smith, 1987/2004). In line with Eckhart, the nineteenth-century philosopher Wilhelm Hegel used the metaphor of the way with an explicit reference to the *Dao* (Magee, 2001). Martin Heidegger took this metaphor when he described Being as moving and meaning as the the *Woraufhin*, the point of direction, towards which individuals are thrown in life (Ma, 2007). Several years later, Viktor Frankl (1948/1986) seemed to refer to this metaphorical history when he spoke of a certain number of 'main ways' ('Hauptstrasse') to meaning (see Section 3.3). This association of meaning with a journey on different ways of life though time and space seems in contrast with the more static term 'Meinung', that can be found in Anglo-Saxon, African and Middle-Eastern languages. However, in our era of globalisation, it may be expected that linguistic and conceptual differences on the topic of meaning between different cultures may disappear.

1.6 Implications for practitioners

World-scale trends often translate directly into the consultation room with individual clients. Regardless of the practitioner's opinion, clients may have different experiences of what is meaningful, and these experiences are always embedded in a wider historical-social context. The individual's quest for meaning cannot be removed from its social embedding, which in modern western countries is dominated by a self-reinforcing focus on functional meanings.

Practitioners may be able to support clients by helping them to identify what is meaningful for them, but also to investigate the historical-social context of their meanings, and to assess whether their perspective on meaning is what they really want it to be or whether they feel forced into this. Does a client focus on teleological, sceptic or functional meanings? Is their focus beneficial? Are they aware of their focus? Did they choose this focus or is it due to social pressure and lack of self-insight? Which type of meanings do they ignore through a narrow focus? This awareness often develops over multiple sessions and during discussions about what the client experiences as meaningful and not meaningful. When clients have developed a basic understanding of how their meaning has evolved, an explicit discussion about their historical-social context could stimulate insights, for instance into why their meanings may intuitively feel unsatisfactory, or how they respond to pressure from people and media around them.

For practitioners, it is important to set their own assumptions about meaning temporarily aside (phenomenological bracketing), and use strong **relational skills** to connect with the client's understanding of meaning instead of imposing their own concept. For example, the practitioner could ask clients which term they would like to use. For instance, previous clients preferred the terms mojo, doing your thing, importance, values, virtues, Sinn and Ikigai. The use of different terms seems to be associated with different historical and cultural backgrounds, and may imply different subjective experiences and different therapeutic practices.

This exploration can only progress in a neutral context, in which practitioners try not to impose their values. That is, since the topic of meaning in life is fundamental to our being, meaning-centred treatments not only touch on the experiences of the client but also those of the practitioner. As a large body of literature shows, the practitioner's personal perspective and experiences can influence the client and the meaning-centred treatment (Vos, 2017). Therefore, it is recommended that practitioners be aware not only of their own values, meanings and meaning-centred struggles, but also how these could influence the treatment process (**self-reflection**). It is equally important that practitioners can place any meaning-centred encounter in the wider cultural-historical context of which both the client and the practitioner are part (**reflexivity**). Practitioners should be aware of how they have created a meaningful life within their socio-historical context, their limitations, their alternative perspectives, and how they may explicitly or implicitly impose their perspective onto clients. However, it may be impossible for practitioners to be entirely value-neutral – as we all have preferences and blind spots. In these situations, it may be advisable that practitioners initiate an open conversation with clients about their own perspective. It is important that the practitioner recognises that there may not be a right or wrong perspective, but looks at multiple options and makes a deliberate decision about which meaning perspective intuitively fits with the client. To become aware of the socio-historical context of their own meanings, practitioners may benefit from personal therapy, supervision and individual exercises such as keeping a diary in which the practitioner writes about their own experience, doubts and wishes for the sessions with specific clients (Hedges, 2010).

Example

A random day in my psychology practice. The first teleologic client talks about his orthodox Christian background, and how he believes that there is only one big God-given purpose in his life, which he is yet to find. We explore where this expectation comes from, and how realistic it is that he can directly know his 'Big Purpose'. He concludes that this expectation puts him under a lot of stress, and that it is more helpful to trust that this purpose may be intuitively revealed over time, for instance through praying. The second sceptic client is a high-functioning autistic maths student. When reflecting on our last sessions, he states: 'I still believe meaning in life does not exist. But I do experience it and need it. I do not want to live a meaning-less life anymore. It is better to be ignorant and happy, than scientifically correct and depressed.' Later in the day, a hedonistic teenager told me that he lives day by day, partying and drinking a lot, but he feels that life is not truly fulfilling and that he must get more and more out of life. We explored a range of other, longer last-ing and authentic meanings in addition to his hedonistic meanings. This day reveals how different (sub)cultural perspectives directly influence our practices. I identified each client's (sub)cultural perspective, examined to what extent they can and want to see other perspectives, and helped them within their personal perspective, while not imposing my own.

Metaphorical overview of the four perspectives

Up until the Middle Ages, many people seemed to live their lives as though they were standing on a ladder. At birth, every individual, animal and even object was allocated its position on the ladder, with the inanimate objects on the lowest rung, the average citizen on the middle rung, and the landowners, kings, clergy and God on the high-est. This societal-cosmic order was justified and stabilised by a skyhook, something higher, a God, the Greater Good and so on. In contrast with the sky-ladder, sceptical meanings are like the flat earth. Although there were individual sceptics in ancient times, scepticism has become widespread only since the sixteenth century, with the rise of urban life, the printing press and empirical research. Sceptics define meaning as a phenomenon not coming from gods or the Greater Good in the sky, but rather that can be explained by earthly mechanisms, such as biophysical mechanisms and survival of the fittest. Scepticism seems to have led to new types of meaning, which are manmade and where 'anything goes'. In the nineteenth and twentieth centuries, functional meanings leave the flatness of the earth, not via ladders, but via large shiny skyscrapers: individuals can ascend quickly into the sky by manmade eleva-tors. This is down to the influence of commercials, the entertainment industry and PR campaigns telling us to 'live life to the max', albeit that we create this max ourselves

▶

◀

via materialistic, hedonic and self-oriented meanings. Functional and teleological meanings have created artificial hierarchies in life, although scepticism remained on the flat earth. In the twentieth century, many philosophers have recommended that we stay down to earth, while acknowledging that the earth is not flat. There are natural mountains and valleys in life. That is, when we stay faithful to our experiences, we experience differences in height, between the less and the more meaningful. But these heights do not miraculously fall from the sky, they are not flat, and they are also not merely manmade: they are the heights within our actual psychological experience. This is the subject of the chapter that follows: meaning not as a ladder attached to a skyhook, flat earth or artificial skyscraper, but as mountains. This book intends to offer a map into these mountains, and help people to trust their inner compass.

Exercises

1. Rank meanings. Write ten activities or experiences – small or big – from last week that felt meaningful to you. Try to rank these in order of importance for you. For instance, does watching movies feel more or less meaningful than your work or being with friends? Ask yourself, how do you know what is more important and what is less important?

2. Switch between scepticism and meaningfulness. Play the devil's sceptical advocate by explaining why you call the meanings in the first exercise meaningful (e.g. 'social pressure', 'genetics'). Subsequently, play your own advocate and argue why this is actually meaningful. What is more important for you: believing in scientific truth or living a meaningful life?

3. Distinguish meaning from success. Have you experienced moments when life felt meaningful even though you were not successful in your activities? Did you experience meaningful moments when you did not feel happy? And vice versa? Find several examples, and use your experiences to answer the question of whether you need success and happiness for a meaningful life.

4. Reflect on the political nature of meaning-centred practices. Do you agree with the medieval idea that life is less meaningful when you are born with a physical handicap, are an orphan, grow up in poor socio-economic circumstances, or become chronically ill? Is life less purposeful when you are a slave or a woman? Why (not)? Based on these arguments, reflect on the hypothesis that our modern perspective on meaning is inherently political. How does our perception of

meaning influence how we organise our society? How are meaning-centred practices inherently an act of empowerment and social justice? The philosopher Richard Rorty described the position of liberal-irony as tolerating different meanings in the public domain and having our own meanings and scepticism in the private domain. Meaning-centred practices seem to exist between the public and private spaces, as clients meet with a practitioner to speak about meaning. How might a meaning-centred practitioner work in a liberal-ironic way with clients who rigidly believe in their meaning, such as religious extremists? How might a practitioner be a liberal-ironic in working with rigid sceptics? How might practitioners develop liberal-irony?

5. Experience that meanings are not random. Divide a paper into two columns. In the left-hand column, write down ten activities or experiences that feel meaningful. These can be small or big. In the right-hand column, write down a random alternative meaning for every meaning given in the left-hand column; for instance, I might put down 'writing this book' on the left and 'reading a book' on the right. Compare the left and right columns. Do both columns feel equally meaningful? Can you imagine a moment in your life when the meaning in the right-hand column feels equally or more meaningful than that in the left-hand column? Can the meaningful activities (left column) be replaced with any other random activities (right column)?

6. Identify McMeanings. Look at examples of meaning in the previous exercises. Do you recognise characteristics from Table 1.1, and if so, for which examples? Viktor Frankl wrote that every era requires a different type of therapy; can you identify arguments for why meaning-centred therapy would be the best therapy for our era?

Key points

> All experiences of meaning are embedded within a socio-historical context. This chapter discussed three dominant contexts: teleological, sceptical and functional meanings.

> Teleological meanings are presented through the metaphor of a ladder, ranging from the least to the most meaningful, and hypothesised as being attached to hooks in the sky such as a belief in God or the Greater Good. Life focuses on external goals (telos), popularised by the ancient Greek philosopher Aristotle. Teleology may involve a linear approach and a denial of individuality and individual context, as well

as idealism, self-discipline or self-denial. If prescribed to other individuals, teleology leads to social oppression.

➤ Sceptical meanings are compared with the flat earth. Scepticism involves questioning any knowledge claim, asking for clarity in definitions, consistency in logic and adequacy of evidence. Examples are philosophical, theological, scientific, social and existential scepticism. Scepticism can be either **reductionist** or **non-reductionist**.

➤ Functional meanings (also called 'McMeanings' in this book) are likened to manmade skyscrapers, whereby individuals use elevators to reach artificial heights as quickly and as high as possible. This is experienced by individuals in western countries in the twentieth and twenty-first centuries, and characterised by modern forms of **teleology**, a culture obsessed with feelings/emotions (particularly happiness and our public image), assuming the randomness, replaceability and unsatisfiability of meanings, creating the illusion of control, and feeding a culture of competition and guilt within a capitalist system.

➤ Practitioners are recommended to practise reflexivity and self-reflection: being aware of their socio-historical context in which they live their meaningful life and meet their clients.

➤ The next chapter describes a pragmatic-phenomenological approach, which is compared to mountains. Phenomenology transcends the opposition between teleology/functionalism and scepticism, as it includes both a sceptical attitude (no ladders on skyhooks or artificial skyscrapers, but staying on earth) and a focus on intuitive heights in the individual's experience (the earth of our experiences is not only flat). This involves continuous **reflexivity** and **self-reflection**.

➤ This chapter has focused mainly on western history of meaning in life. Other cultures and religions, which predate modern western cultures, seemed to have a more all-encompassing understanding of meaning, which also included behaviour, an embodied sense of meaning and **phenomenological unpeeling** as will be elaborated in the next chapter.

2

A Pragmatic-Phenomenological Approach to Meaning

2.1 Early phenomenology: love for the sake of love

The brief world history of meaning in Chapter 1 started with the **teleological** order. This implied that individuals lived their lives according to their position in a pregiven uncontested societal-cosmic-divine hierarchy. For instance, being born a peasant's son meant fulfilling your role as a peasant and serving the landowners, clergy and king. This teleological structure was reflected in the original use of the word 'meaning' ('Meinung'), which referred to the external purpose of someone's activities in a collectivist context.

However, since the sixteenth century, more and more individuals began to question this teleological order, due to developments such as increased wealth, widespread education and the Protestant Reformation. The rational purpose of Aristotelean teleology, becoming an **animal rationale**, disappeared and instead individuals started to give meaning to their lives according to their own subjective taste. These non-teleological types of meaning assumed that individuals can control, randomly choose and replace meanings and maximise meanings that give instant satisfaction and follow public and commercial influences. Some sceptics totally rejected the concept of living a meaningful life, as they entirely explained away all meanings as nothing other than physical, social or existential processes. This **reductionist scepticism** sometimes led to existential indifference, anything goes and a lack of responsibility. This was also reflected in the later etymological development of the word 'meaning' in Continental European languages, which started to refer to mundane-negative experiences: meaning is about random, changeable and subjective experiences.

However, at the same time another term for meaning became more popular. Medieval mystics such as Meister Eckhart started to use the German word 'Sinn' in contrast with the teleological or mundane-negative word 'Meinung'. This term 'Sinn' was derived from the Latin word 'sentire', which may be translated as 'perceiving' and which can be found in most Continental European and Slavic languages ('Sinn', 'Zin', 'Sense', 'Sensida', 'Smesl'). This word comes from philosophers such as Cicero who spoke about the importance of perceiving ourselves and our situation. They rejected the teleological primate of higher purposes, rationality and fitting ourselves into a pregiven teleological societal order. For instance, we do not need to strive towards higher goals on the societal ladder of life, but instead listen to nature, the phenomena themselves. To understand what is meaningful, we should not impose our rationalised teleological order on nature. We will start to see nature when we perceive nature as it shows itself instead of foisting our ideas onto it.

For example, instead of saying 'I do this activity for this higher purpose that I think is important', the medieval priest Eckhart suggested to focus on activities for the mere sake of these activities. For instance, I love God not for my own purposes, but for my love for God. If I want to truly serve God, I need to let go of God, or more specifically formulated, I need to get rid of all images and rituals about God from which only I benefit, such as trying to safeguard my place in heaven. I merely need to perceive God in the way in which He reveals Himself. Similarly, my social connections are meaningful for me not to achieve another purpose, but for the sake of connecting and loving others. There is something irreducible in my love for my friends. This was a revolutionary concept, as marriages and friendships were until then often not formed for the sake of love but for practical reasons. Thus meaning is revealed in my relationship to a phenomenon itself, and not in a pregiven rational or functional purpose. I need to listen to nature and myself as it reveals itself. Eckhart wrote that when I have emptied myself of all the expectations that are imposed by society and myself onto myself, I will be filled with a deeper meaning. Protestant Reformers further popularised this shift from external teleology to subjective perception. For example, Luther wrote in his famous pamphlet *Freedom of the Christian* that individuals should serve God, not for their own salvation or for doing what everyone else does, but for the love of God. The inner intention matters. Many early authors stand in this tradition of perceptive meanings, such as Soren Kierkegaard, Friedrich Nietzsche, Martin Heidegger and many Taoists, Buddhists and Hindus. Also, nowadays many positive psychologists follow this approach, such as Mihaly Csikszentmihalyi (2002, p. 67):

> The key element of optimal experience is that it is an end in itself ..., a self-contained activity, one that is not done with the expectation of some future benefits, but simply because the doing itself is the reward.

2.2 Phenomenology in a nutshell

At the beginning of the twentieth century, Husserl (1901/1973) used the
term 'phenomenology' to describe this perceptive method of focusing on
the things, phenomena, for themselves, instead of imposing our rational
explanations and expectations on the phenomena. Phenomenology
offers a third option to naïve teleology/functionalism and reductionist
scepticism.

On the one hand, phenomenologists focus on hierarchical meanings.
They assume that there can be a difference between low and high, meaningless and meaningful. These hierarchies are not based on naïve assumptions, such as an artificial teleological ladder falling from the sky, or
finding a quick fix with McMeanings such as alcohol and drugs. I examine sceptically what I experience as meaningful: I identify possible explanations and I subsequently evaluate these intuitively. Do I authentically
find this activity meaningful or is that I merely follow the expectations of
others? For example, I experience writing this book as meaningful, but I
am also aware that this desire may be explained by my upbringing, with
my parents stimulating my writing. This explanation helps me to distinguish more authentic meanings from less authentic ones. Yes, my parents
stimulated my writing, but this explanation does not tell me that I should
not do this. If my parents had forced me, against my will or nature, to
become a writer and I had internalised their expectations, I could conclude that writing this book is not authentic. Thus intuitively perceiving
what is meaningful is different from blindly climbing pregiven external
ladders: I intuitively evaluate what is meaningful and what is not. Thus
the phenomenological method starts with non-reductionist scepticism,
such as analysing the biological, social or existential conditions under
which our meanings are formed. As our meanings are always contextualised and embodied.

Being sceptical towards myself and explaining my meanings does
not necessarily change my experience of this activity as meaningful. Writing this book is still meaningful, although I can explain
why I started to write this. Having a sceptical explanation is like a
two-dimensional map of my surroundings, which does not remove
the third dimension from my three-dimensional experience of the
landscape (**map/landscape fallacy**): 'Yeah, of course I have a map of
the mountain. So what? That does not change the fact the mountain
is still a three-dimensional mountain and that I want to hike here!'
Thus phenomenologists use **non-reductionist scepticism**: scepticism
destroys false hierarchies and helps us to focus on true hierarchies in
my experience. This is not a metaphysical difference between earth and
sky (like a ladder), but an experiential difference between valleys and

mountaintops on the earth. We cannot rationally explain or demand this (like functional meanings) but need to perceive this meaning with all our senses, like the etymology of the word 'Sinn' indicates. The philosopher Wilhelm Dilthey suggested that we should phenomenologically *understand* meaning, and not try to *explain* it in a teleological or functional way. After initial scepticism, we simply need to intuitively look around in our life and we will see what is meaningful, authentic, true – like the mountains only need to be perceived and are not created by us.

Thus phenomenological meanings include both the subjective experience of mountains ('transcendence') and down-to-earth scepticism ('immanent'). This combination has been called 'immanent transcendence' (Hayes, 2012), and can be compared with mountaineering. When I focus on my subjective experiences, I experience the world around me and my experiences are influenced by the world, but the way in which I experience this is not merely a flat earth. I experience heights and depths in life, and these heights are not artificially created but begin with earth and nature: biological, social and existential soil. Phenomenological meanings are a third position next to teleological/functional and sceptical meanings, combining hierarchical meanings and scepticism. Many individuals seem to experience this combination as difficult, as they argue that you believe either in teleological/functional hierarchies or in scepticism, but not both. Phenomenologists have a **dual awareness**: being simultaneously aware of two perspectives, tolerating feelings of paradoxes, ambiguities and uncertainties (Vos, 2014). Examples of modern philosophers climbing the mountains of our experience are Martin Heidegger, Emmanuel Levinas, Otto Duintjer, Gianni Vattimo, Giles Deleuze, Michel Henry, Theodor Adorno and Peter Sloterdijk.

2.3 An introduction to phenomenological methods

The unpeeling process

How can phenomenologists help individuals to discover their phenomenological meanings? Which steps could they use?

The teleological approach suggested that we have a direct understanding of what is truly meaningful. We have a direct access to 'reality' and directly know what our absolutely God-given meaning in life is. Phenomenologists doubt whether we have direct access, as we often conceal our experiences and make them inaccessible to ourselves. For instance, we veil reality by being too theoretical, following others, ignoring our embodied intuition or having an unhelpful attitude (see Heidegger, 1927). We may also mask our meaningful experiences by focusing too much on teleological or functional meanings, or by being too sceptical. Therefore, phenomenologists suggest a process of removing the veils from our experiences, to uncover more authentic and true meanings.

Thus the core phenomenological process is unpeeling our experiences like an onion or a mango. Of course, we cannot be entirely certain that when we start unpeeling our experiences we will arrive at a core, as with a mango. That is, we cannot be sure that 'authenticity' and 'true self' exist, like Buddhists claim; it is possible that our self-experiences are nothing other than layers, and there is no core, like an onion. Thus the unpeeling process could lead to an 'essence' or 'reality', but it could also be the case that we continue unpeeling until nothing is left: we may not know what the end point will be. This philosophical question of where our unpeeling will lead is pragmatically irrelevant, as the unpeeling process itself has proved beneficial to individuals. Whatever the result of unpeeling is, clients seem to benefit from this process: they experience their lives as more meaningful and experience a better quality of life, lower psychological stress and better physical well-being (Chapter 4). The pragmatic-phenomenological approach in this book focuses on the process instead of on the metaphysical result of unpeeling. The following briefly outlines how unpeeling could work in practice.

Exercise

What do you see in this picture? What do you see first in this picture before you interpret this?

Possibly you see no pattern among the dots at all, but when you look long enough you will see a dog drinking water. However, when we focus on our primary experience, there is no dog; there are only dots on paper which our brain seems to connect secondarily. William James (1842–1910) wrote that reality does not exist of separate phenomena, but it is our mind that separates phenomena from each other. Therefore, he advised us to focus on the primary 'stream of consciousness', before this separation occurs. In this raw experience there is no dichotomy between subjective and objective, because reality emerges from the interaction between 'raw material' (things in themselves which we cannot directly know) and 'our mental faculties' (Spinelli, 2002). The philosopher Jean-Paul Sartre wrote more specifically that before we can experience any meanings in life ('essences'), we are already experiencing ourselves and are embedded in a world and social context ('existence': 'existence precedes essence'). We need to return to the dots and the chaos in our immediate self-experience, so that we can become aware of the process of how we often create secondary meanings.

However, the picture of the dog shows how difficult it is to temporarily put aside our interpretations. Human beings seem to be chronic meaning-makers, starting even with such a simple exercise as seeing dots on a piece of paper. Developmental neurological studies show for instance how babies initially have the primary experience of dots, unstructured chaos and few meanings, but relatively quickly they identify meanings in this chaos (e.g. Spreen, Risser & Edgell, 1995; Temple, 2014). Complete sensory deprivation experiments (Zubeck, 1965) have also shown that when all our senses are blocked, individuals will soon start hallucinating as a way to make sense of the lack of sensory input; apparently, our brains function in such a way that they always need to experience meaning. Existential laboratory experiments also show that when individuals are confronted with stories about a meaningless, chaotic or threatening world, such as terrorist attacks, they will use cognitive avoidance and start thinking about meanings in own life (e.g. love, children, work) (Greenberg, Pysczinski & Koole, 2014).

What interpretative steps do we make in our experience of, for instance, this picture of the dotted dog? Primarily, we experience raw experiences of the world, such as the immediate straightforward experience of black dots on white paper. Secondly, we interpret the world, such as reflecting on our primary experience of the dots. Thirdly, we are embedded in a wider world, as we use our previous experiences of what dogs look like to interpret this picture. Fourthly, we can develop a sense of a 'self' in these three steps. That is, in the first step we were not aware of ourselves as the subject experiencing the object of this picture: we did not experience a subject–object difference. However, finally, we could become self-aware of a conscious 'self' that is experiencing and interpreting; the phenomenological experience of this self-aware self is different from the self-unaware 'I' in the first step.

This process of phenomenological unpeeling could make us aware of these interpretative steps, and could help us to trace back how we have distorted our primary experiences in the second, third and fourth steps. We may possibly not be able to return entirely to the primary experience, and look with the new eyes of a newborn baby to our primary experiences. For instance, now that you have seen the dog, it is difficult to see the picture as a mere collection of dots again. However, we may become aware of how we have transformed the dots into our interpretation of a dog, and this awareness could help us to see the dots again, or to imagine what it was like when we saw the dots instead of the dog. In a similar way, meaning-centred practitioners help clients to become aware of how they have interpreted and covered their primary experiences of their authentic or true meanings. This awareness could subsequently help clients to experience their authentic meanings and imagine what it would be like to experience authentic meanings.

Three phenomenological steps

Many phenomenologists follow three steps to uncover our original experiences of meaning. These three steps follow mystic traditions and will be explained briefly (Spinelli, 2005).

First, we need to get rid of approaches that do not bring authentic meaning. For instance, we sceptically examine our life and the roots of our activities and set aside those experiences that hold teleological, reductionist-sceptical or functional meanings. Husserl called this **bracketing**: we need to temporarily bracket our own assumptions. We set aside our individual hopes, expectations and social pressure. We suspend our judgement and stay open-minded. We are sceptical even about our own scepticism. Applied to the dotted dog, this means that I open myself up to the idea that there is possibly no dog in this picture; when I do not want to let go of this interpretation of a dog, I will not be able to understand how I came to see this dog. We need to 'destruct' the inauthentic meanings which block our intuitive understanding. Applied to working with clients, like all practitioners, before I meet a client, I often have preconceived ideas about them, albeit on the basis of their name, or the brief phone conversation, or referral letter; I try to set all this information aside and listen openly to the client.

Since the perspective from which we look at our experiences determines what we perceive, phenomenologists suggest to vary aspects of the example, what we can do with it and how we relate to it. We can look at our experiences from many different perspectives. For instance, when I turn the paper with the picture of the dotted dog upside down, I stop see-ing the dog, and become aware of the dots instead of my interpretation of the dog. Van Deurzen (2002) suggests individuals explore different ways in which they relate to themselves, their physical, social and spiritual world. In line with Van Deurzen, it will be suggested in Section 3.3 to ask clients to describe how they may experience materialistic-hedonic, self-oriented, social and larger meanings in their past, current or imagined future. Therefore, the treatment manual in Part 3 of this book is built around the **meaning quintet**, which helps clients to vary the different perspectives on their lives to discover what they intuit as most meaningful in life.

Second, phenomenologists try to describe and not explain their experiences (Dilthey, 1897). This means trying to perceive the situation neutrally with all our senses, and not only in a theoretical-intellectual way. What do you feel? What do you see? What is there? Stay with your initial experience of the dots, and do not focus on the dog.

Third, phenomenologists try to avoid placing any *initial* hierarchies of significance or importance upon the items of description. That is, we initially treat all experiences as having equal value or significance. For instance, often when I ask clients what they experience as meaningful in life, they start to speak about Big Ultimate Meaning and peak experiences. From a phenomenological perspective, such experiences may not neces-sarily be more important than the more modest meanings in our daily life.

Applied to the metaphor in Chapter 1, this means that I simply perceive where I walk in life, instead of trying to build ladders or skyscrapers. What may happen in this experiential process of walking is that individuals start to experience absolute differences between heights and lows in their life, even though they are bracketing their assumptions, and stay descriptive as much as they can. That is, they do not experience initial hierarchies they have imposed *onto* their experiences before they started experienc-ing, but rather when they are perceiving the flow of experiences they may start intuiting authentic hierarchies *in* their experiences. Martin Heidegger described this last step as having removed all covers, and then allowing what is meaningful to reveal itself. Instead of imposing my ideas onto the mountain, I experience the mountain as it is. Martin Heidegger called this 'truth' in line with the Greek word *aletheia* which means uncovered (see Vos, 2014). The destruction stage removes the covers from the truth, so that we will be able to perceive truth. We can perceive this truth not by explaining it with rational-sceptical explanations but merely by describing our experiences. Meister Eckhart and later Friedrich Nietzsche and Martin Heidegger called this 'Gelassenheit', which literally means 'letting-be'. Metaphorically speaking, when we walk in the mountains we do not need to do anything other than letting the mountain show itself as mountain. In life, we need to let what is meaningful show its meaningfulness.

Example

Robert is an Oscar-winning actor. Before I met him, I had many expectations about him, his stereotypical glitter and glamour, and his life being fulfilling due to his multiple-award winning career. When I met him, I quickly realised that I had to set these expectations aside (**bracketing**). My questions were focusing so much on his acting, that I could not hear what was authentically meaningful for him. He talked about how he had developed severe depression, because everyone was pigeonholing him: 'But I am much more than an actor!' He described how Hollywood creates a merely **functional** social context with red carpets, champagne and big parties, where VIPs use alcohol and drugs to sedate their gnawing lack of deeper meaning. His fame made it difficult to imagine himself engaging in other meaningful activities. He felt that 'This is all there is to life. Everyone looks up to my life, so I must be satisfied, but I am not.' He felt he had lost touch with what is truly meaningful to him. As a first step, we decided together to temporarily set aside this lifestyle in his mind, as this does not seem to be authentically satisfying. Second, I taught him to listen more to his inner experiences via mindfulness exercises. Subsequently, we systematically explored many possible meanings in the **meaning quintet**, such as **hedonistic-materialistic, self-oriented, social, larger** and **existential-philosophical meanings**. I asked questions such as 'Find an example of when you felt deeply connected with others; how does this connection feel?' I asked him to 'simply feel' and describe his experiences and not theorise and explain these. Third, I asked him not to put any initial preferences to his experiences, but stay with this **flow** of experiencing. He started to see that he had been missing authentic relationships, playing music, and achieving a larger goal such as working for a charity. In the next sessions, he explored what he could practically do to engage more in these activities. Over time, when he had been engaging in new meaningful activities, he started to realise that the most important things for him were social relationships and charity work, and music and acting came second.

2.4 Other phenomenological ingredients

The phenomenological approach includes many ingredients, some of which will be described below.

Intuition. How do we 'know' or 'feel' the difference between authentic and inauthentic interpretations? We could use our **phenomenological intuition**. Intuiting what is authentically meaningful is like a sculptor who can 'see' the sculpture being there in the stone even before he has started to cut and shape; his art involves revealing what is already there (Heidegger, 1962; Wrathall, 2011). Although the term 'intuition' may also have some spiritual connotations, in everyday English we often use the term intuition for a generic psychological sense. To define this, our **phenomenological intuition** is our embodied, full-sensory receptivity towards our true being and an unconscious understanding of what is meaningful and valuable, and what is not. Clients have described this as 'just knowing', 'just so', 'click' or 'mojo'. Speaking along the metaphorical lines introduced in Chapter 1, intuition is the compass that directs individuals in the mountains of their lives (Vos, 2014). It directs me away from inauthentic or teleological/functional meanings towards more authentic phenomenological meanings. We seem to be able to use this intuitive compass by becoming permeable, 'opening ourselves up', 'trusting the guidance', 'letting it be', and allowing intuition to show us how to navigate in life (Heidegger, 2000; Visser, 2008; Vos, 2014). An exponentially growing body of evidence-based research is validating intuition as a well-defined empirical experience, and is suggesting many ways in which intuition can be used beneficially (Gladwell, 2002; Duggan, 2007; Pretz & Sentman Totz, 2007). Chapter 8 describes therapeutic examples.

Embodiment. The experience of meaning is primarily embodied according to phenomenologists, and only secondarily do we put this into rational explanations. Maurice Merleau-Ponty (1945) writes that the full body is involved in the process of perceiving our phenomenological meaning, and not only our conscious theorising self. Being an embodied being as we are means that we are:

> open to moods that can direct us and reveal the world as meaningful, just is to be a being who extends beyond what we can know about ourselves. The project, then, is not to decide what to care about, but to discover what it is about which one already cares.
>
> (Dreyfus & Kelly, p. 230)

Case study

John studied Business & Finance because his 'life aim is to work at the stock exchange'. However, he experienced that he felt an unfocused sense of unhappiness in his life; he was procrastinating and 'doing many things except studying'. It was remarkable that when he spoke about what he cognitively regarded to be his life aim, his body looked tense. When we explored other meaningful experiences in his life, such as his love for art, his body became relaxed. He also told me that he had recently started having headaches and nausea when he tried to force himself to study. It seemed that non-verbally his body showed his disgust for the meaning that he tried to enforce on himself. We did mindfulness exercises to help him reconnect with his body and he started keeping a diary of how his body was feeling in different life situations. After several sessions, he told me that his body had shown him that he should study art, as his body was the most energised and he felt most alive when he was painting. He brought along a painting of an image that had come to him in a dream: he was sitting in a dark cage, with his arms stretching through the bars to reach for food that was lying beyond his reach outside of the cage. He said that he realised that art was the food he needed, and that his current course was a cage which he had been put in because of his parents' expectations.

Our behaviour reveals our intuitive hierarchy. Intuitively, we experience a hierarchy in our meanings which we may automatically act on in daily life. That is, certain meanings are more important than others, such as writing this book is more important than cleaning my house. In my daily life, I do not first consciously create a hierarchy of what is meaningful and subsequently decide how to fill my time. For instance, a client told me he was convinced that there is no hierarchy in his life. I asked him to describe which decisions he had made this morning, from the moment he woke up until now. He told that when he woke up he decided to snooze a bit, after which he had a shower and then went for breakfast. Subsequently I asked him what activities he had not chosen but which seem to have simply happened; he told me how his body simply told him to lie in a bit longer, that he had forgotten to do the dishes after breakfast, and that without consciously meaning to he had taken a different route to work. 'Precisely! Your actions reveal that you have a hierarchy, albeit unconscious: going to work via a longer different route felt more mean-ingful than doing the dishes. You may become angry that you did not do the dishes – possibly because you want to please others or tick the box of being "a good husband" – but this morning, intuitively, you accepted the hierarchy: you did not want to waste your limited time doing some-thing so mundane as dishwashing when you could have a nice detour.' As this example shows, unconscious processes often drive our meaningful actions, without the intervention of our conscious decision-making mind. Psychoanalysts such as Carl Jung and Jacques Lacan have analysed how our lives are often determined by unconscious meanings (Chapter 8).

Social. Many people construct meaning socially in the context of their wider group, such as the traditional context of a tribe or religion (see Chao & Kesebir, 2013; Mikulincer & Shaver, 2013; Neimeijer, 2001; Stillman & Lambert, 2013). Therefore, meaning-centred practitioners examine what the expectations from someone's social context are, and explore to what extent an individual feels free to develop their own meaning independently. Cultural values may be explored, as, in collec-tivistic cultures, individuals may want to develop their meanings in a social way instead of individualistically. With young people, the quest for meaning can be influenced by their process of individuation-separation, in which they start to make decisions in their life independent from those who raised them (Section 4.4).

Double hermeneutics. Practitioners undoubtedly attribute their own meaning to the events and experiences being recounted by the client. It could be that the practitioner's own meanings in life influence how the client's narrative is interpreted and the communication is directed; Freud called this 'countertransference'. From a phenomenological perspec-tive, the practitioner would try to become self-aware of the subjective biases and countertransference. This involves strong **self-reflection** and **reflexivity**: practitioners interpret the meanings that are revealed in the client's narrative, and they subsequently interpret how they interpret the client's narrative and how this could have been influenced by their own life narrative; this has been called 'double hermeneutics'. This book holds a pragmatic-phenomenological stance: we may never be able to develop perfect self-insight and to phenomenologically bracket all unhelpful intrusions of our own destructive meanings into the therapy process. The aim is to become aware of how the practitioner's own meanings influence the relational-therapeutic process with the client. We create some **self-distance**, and gain some freedom to either set our meanings aside ('phenomenological bracketing') or use our own meanings in conversation with the client, as some of the practitioner's meanings may get in the way, or they may be a gift to the client. The question is not how to prevent all personal meanings transferring from the practitioner, but how to use them in a constructive way for the client. Of course, practitioners should never impose their own thoughts, feelings and images on the client, but rather sensitively share these as a hypothesis with nuanced formulations such as: 'When I hear your story, this reminds me of ...'; 'I may be totally wrong, but I wonder whether ...; 'If I were in your shoes, I may ... but this may probably tell me more about myself than about you'; 'How do you feel when I share this?' The practitioner can become a role model of authenticity by revealing how they experience and critically use meanings themselves. This can help to foster relational depth, where the client can feel safe to explore their own meanings. This is possibly one of the most difficult practitioner skills to master, to find the right sensitive balance between being authentic and imposing their interpretations onto the client. Many practitioners when they are starting out seem to be either too self-absorbed or too personally neutral and client-obsessed. Personal therapy can help to further self-insight, and supervision and intervision could be important sources of learning to work with the double hermeneutic process:

> Because values cannot be taught, they must be lived; nor can meanings be given by a teacher. What a teacher may give is not a meaning but an example: the example of his personal dedication and devotion to the great cause.
>
> (Fabry, 1968, p. 113)

Multiple worlds. Meaning is revealed in many parts of our lives. Martin Heidegger speaks of different types of 'care'. On the basis of Heidegger's work, therapist Binswanger described the different meanings individuals can experience in their physical environmental world ('Umwelt'), inner world ('Eigenwelt') and social world ('Mitwelt'). Van Deurzen (2012) has added a spiritual world

('Uberwelt'). Section 3.3 will add an existential-philosophical world, and shows how the phenomenological differentiation between these worlds or dimensions in our experiences are validated by empirical research.

Becoming who you are. The philosopher Friedrich Nietzsche wrote we should 'become who we are', instead of focusing on external (functional) goals. Meaning is about perceiving our self; if we do decide to have goals, these goals come from who we are (or who we perceive we are).

Friedrich Nietzsche and other philosophers have described how our sense of self, others and meaning always develop in a social context, and how there is a subtle or sometimes explicit indoctrination from our upbringing (socialisation), our culture or religion. Social Darwinists have suggested that what we see as meaningful or meaningless may be a random 'struggle of the most functional meaning': we will see activities that may improve our survival as meaningful; in their opinion, there is no absolute hierarchy between lower or higher meanings except functional survival value. For example, we may see religion as meaningful because social values and the sense of community could benefit our survival. Other authors have argued that this evolution of functional meanings may start from birth onwards, when we start to internalise the meanings from the people that we depend on: as we do not want to be rejected by those who raise us as our physical survival depends on them, we copy their ideas and values (Greenberg et al, 2014). However, according to Nietzsche we have the ability to become aware – at least to some extent – that we have developed our meanings merely for functional or existential reasons. Instead, we may start affirming our widest potential – which may reach beyond the range of meanings that we had internalised before – and within this regained freedom become ourselves. This is what Nietzsche called 'Superman' ('Ubermensch'), which is the **duality** of being both human – which includes all our possibilities and impossibilities in life – while simultaneously having the ability to reach beyond our current situation. For example, in our childhood we may have wanted to become a fireman, a doctor, or a parent. However, during our lifetime we may have learned that we are more than a role that we could play; our potential reaches far beyond professional roles, and far beyond the expectations and images that we grew up with. We can un-cover our wider potential in life and listen intuitively to who we want to be, here and now, and thus become ourselves. Thus, we do not strive to be bankers, policemen or doctors but we strive to be ourselves (Thompson, 1928).

2.5 Scales of meaning

Stereotypically, when people use the term meaning they refer to The Meaning of Life. However, this book also focuses on smaller meanings. There are different scales of meaning. There are meanings that are more defined and integrated than others, and small meanings may synthesise into larger meanings and vice versa. For instance, the meaning of writing this sentence is to efficiently convey the essence of this chapter, which contributes to this book, and publishing this book helps to me to fulfil my meaning of being published as an author. Thus everything refers to each other, from micro-level, via meso-level, to macro-level (Heidegger, 1927). For didactic purposes, I differentiate these three levels, although in our phenomenological experience levels cannot be easily separated (Vos, 2017b).

Micro-meanings are about the subjectively lived experience of specific situations at specific moments by specific individuals. How do I make sense of my specific life situation? For instance, what does drinking this cup of coffee at this moment mean to me? What is the meaning of writing this section in this book? How do I cope with an illness? How do I interpret the loss of a loved one? Micro-meanings are always embedded within the context of meso- and macro-meanings; for instance, this sentence can only be understood as part of the larger context of this section and the entire book.

Meso-meanings are groups, categories or patterns of micro-meanings. These groups may have emerged over time and/or between individuals, and they could, for instance, be identified via **thematic analyses**. Section 3.3 will describe five categories of meaning in life: the **meaning quintet**; these categories are created on the basis of thousands of participants' answers in empirical studies to the question, 'What do you experience as meaningful, valuable, important or purposeful in life?' Their answers revealed materialistic-hedonic, self-oriented, social, higher and meta types of meanings. These categories are nothing more than groups of meaningful micro-experiences. For instance, the meso-group of social meanings consists of many small moments in my life that I found meaningful in connecting with my friends – Peter, Emma and so on. My awareness of this meso-group could subsequently lead me to invest more time in micro-meanings that fall into this meso-group; for instance, I see that in general social meanings are important to me, therefore I can decide to search for more friends and spend more time with them.

Thus experiencing meaning includes both bottom-up and top-down processes.

Macro-meanings are the largest group or category, and describe a general sense of meaningfulness of life. I feel my life is meaningful in general. Many questionnaires measure this macro-meaningfulness, but few measure the specific types of meso-meanings (Chapter 11). It has been argued that the repeated experience of meaningful moments (micro-/ meso-meanings) could become generalised and create a general sense of meaningfulness in life. This general sense of meaningfulness in life may be nothing more than the perception of what happens at the micro-level (Dennett, 2002).

Scaling-up exercise

Some clients find that they are so strongly focused on large meanings and peak experiences in their life that they find it difficult to perceive how meaningful their daily life already is. It has helped with some to do a step-wise scaling-up exercise.

1. Describe ten activities you have done today, preferably those that you do frequently or that you feel are important. For example, I have been drinking coffee.

2. Describe how you felt when you were drinking coffee? For example, I was enjoying my coffee.

3. What micro-meaning did drinking this coffee have for you at the moment you were drinking? To answer this question, it may be helpful to look at what was your motivation, value and commitment, how you dealt which possible challenges in the situation, and what this tells you about how you feel about yourself and how you understand the world around you (Section 3.1). For example, I was motivated to drink this because coffee helps me to wake up, and I also value enjoying its taste. Although it was challenging to drink the coffee as I was in a hurry, I was committed to drinking it, thus I quickly made and drank it. I felt it was worth listening to my coffee-drinking habit and arriving slightly later at work. This means that my self-worth is relatively important compared to my work.

4. Does this micro-meaning actually show a more frequently experienced meso-meaning in your life, and if so what does this meso-meaning look like? To answer this question, it may help to answer the following questions. Do you do similar activities more often? Find some other examples, and try to find what it is that unites these experiences? It could be the case that you cannot find a meso-meaning; in this case, you could look at other examples of activities you did today. If you would generalise this experience – that is, make it applicable to other situations as well – what would this look like? What meaning do you need to be able to experience this micro-meaning? For instance, I not only value drinking coffee, but also other drinks and food; the common factor is that I enjoy food and drink. Enjoying myself is apparently an important meso-meaning. To be able to enjoy myself, I believe I am worthy of enjoying myself; thus self-care and autonomy are also important meso-meanings for me.

5. When you have identified multiple meso-meanings, what do these meso-meanings tell you about the general meaningfulness of your life? To answer this question, it may help to answer the following questions. Which meso-meanings feel more important and which are less important? Try to find more micro-examples for each of the meso-meanings; close your eyes and imagine each example one after the other, so that you are now in the situation of experiencing each micro-meaning; how does this feel? For example, self-care feels more important than the physical enjoyment. When I imagine other examples of self-care, such as taking a long bath or buying clothes, I start to feel a sense of meaningfulness.

▶

◀

6. Scaling-down exercise. Where could you find more examples of when you could experience the meaningfulness in your daily life? What could you actually do? For example, I could decide to go to good restaurants with friends or take long baths more often, as these are examples of self-care which feel meaningful to me.

2.6 Pragmatism

Does meaning start at the top of the mountain which allows the mountaineer to engage in his meaningful journey at its base? Or does meaning start with the mountaineer in the valley who makes the decision to go up the mountain? That is, do we work top-down or bottom-up? And is meaning discovered or constructed? Is there an absolute difference between authentic and inauthentic meanings? These questions have engaged many theologians and philosophers throughout history. This debate is also reflected in discussions between meaning-centred practitioners. This book will follow the idea that these questions may be metaphysically unanswerable (metaphysics is about the philosophical-abstract foundations and truth in life). However, when we focus pragmatically on the phenomenological flow of experiences of clients, they seem to experience both top-down and bottom-up processes at the same time, discover and construct meanings at the same or different moment in their lives. Despite their scepticism, individuals have meaningful experiences such as love. Therefore, this book proposes a phenomenological-pragmatic approach which will focus on creating a **dual awareness** of how multiple perspectives could be occurring at the same time.

This book is pragmatic by assuming that different clients have different needs: some have a teleological perspective on meaning, and others are more sceptical or functional. For instance, some want to identify specific purposes in life via specific steps, and others want a more intuitive process which may not result in specific purposes but a general sense of direction in life. The phenomenological approach offers a meta-perspective which gives practitioners and clients the option to work within a teleological, sceptical or functional framework if this is how the clients experience meaning and this is what they want. It is important to acknowledge these four different approaches, both as part of the **reflexivity** and supervision of the practitioner and as part of the **meta-communication** with clients. This also depends on the **practitioners' mandate** that the client has provided: if a client asks the practitioner to help within a teleological framework, it seems unethical for the practitioner to enforce a sceptical perspective. However, clients may benefit an explanation of what their options are before they decide to work within a certain perspective; that is, **psycho-education** about these different teleological, sceptical, functional and phenomenological perspectives may help clients to make a well-informed decision. This assumes that any work between a practitioner and a client starts with an assessment and psycho-education regarding the experiences, needs and preferences of clients (Chapter 11). This also assumes a client-centred approach (Chapter 7).

Metaphor

Together with African friends, I developed a metaphor about stereotypical differences between western (teleological/functional) and non-western (phenomenological) approaches to meaning. There is a fire, and a westerner and a non-westerner are standing at a river which they need to cross to escape the fire and reach safety. There are two boats on the shore, one nearby and one upstream. The westerner takes the nearest boat and paddles in a straight line to the other side. However, the current is strong and it is hard work to paddle against the stream, to keep his straight line. The westerner arrives at the other side totally stressed, exhausted and with muscle pain. The non-westerner looks at the river, looks at how the current flows, walks a bit upstream to jump at the right location into the boat, and with a minimum of paddling he lets the currents direct him to the other shore. The journey takes longer for the non-westerner, and he may not arrive precisely at the same destination as the westerner, but his trust and wisdom about the water helped him to cross the river in a less stressful and exhausting way.

Exercises

1. Explore meanings-in-themselves. Think about your friends. How did each friendship start, and how has it evolved? Are these friendships for-the-sake-of-friendship, or are these functional relationships? Why do you continue these relationships? Ask similar questions about your daily life activities, such as your work, living together, leisure activities and so on. Do you engage in these activities because they are meaningful in themselves, or do they serve another purpose?

2. Experience phenomenological freedom. Throughout history, many philosophers have spoken about our experience of 'free will'. Immanuel Kant concluded that we cannot prove the existence of the free will, but

we have to assume that it exists, as our daily life experiences 'phenom-enologically' tell us there is free will, and it is important for our per-sonal and societal well-being to believe in its existence. Do you feel we have free will? Or is free will an illusion, something we could rationally explain? What is more important for your psychological well-being, being scientifically correct by saying that you do not know whether you have free will, or submerging yourself in the daily life experience of making free decisions (although you may be scientifically incorrect)? What is ethically most important for society, being scientifically correct or believing in free will? What is best for your clients?

3. Go with the flow. Are you more like the westerner or the non-westerner in the metaphor, or are you both in different situations? Why or why not? Give examples. Who would you like to be, and how could you become this person? Who do your friends, family and soci-ety want you to be? Do you trust the currents in your life or are you afraid of them?

4. Sceptical destruction. Look at your previous examples of meanings in this and the previous chapter. Which experiences of meaning are merely teleological, sceptical or functional? Play devil's advocate with yourself. Which meanings are not really meaningful for you? Carry out a peeling exercise: which activities in your life are the least mean-ingful to you (e.g. cleaning or paying taxes); and after you have peeled these meanings away which activities are the least meaningful and so on. Continue this peeling away until you feel there is as little as pos-sible left to uncover as you have arrived at a core, or there is nothing meaningful left.

5. Phenomenological construction. What does your intuition tell you after doing these two exercises? Is there any ground left after your sceptical destruction? If you were allowed to keep only three meanings in your life, which would they be? What are the hierarchies of mean-ing in your life. What is more meaningful and what is less meaning-ful? Do you trust your intuition in revealing what is meaningful and what is not. Why or why not?

Key points

➤ History has revealed several approaches to meaning which combine scepticism with personal meaning. Traditionally, this was found in mystic spirituality, which was further stimulated by Protestantism and

Romanticism, and then elaborated by phenomenologists and existentialists in the twentieth century.

> **Phenomenological meanings** are self-contained experiences, which are meaningful in themselves and do not depend on an external reward in the future, such as accomplishing a higher purpose (teleological meanings) or functioning as instant gratification or happiness-making manipulation (functional meanings).

> Phenomenological meanings focus on what individuals intuitively perceive as meaningful for themselves. This intuitive perception implies both a sceptical analysis of what they initially assumed to be meaningful and an openness to their subjective flow of experiences which may reveal what they may experience as 'authentically meaningful'. This **phenomenological intuition** is embodied, embedded in someone's historical-social context, often unconscious and experienced at many scales in many parts of their life (also called 'worlds'). Phenomenologists have developed several methods to develop such an intuition, and psychologists have shown intuition to be an evidence-based construct which can be effectively used in treatments.

> This book follows a pragmatic-phenomenological approach, which helps clients in a systematic way to critically explore what they phenomenologically intuit as meaningful. This approach does not reject teleological, sceptical and functional meanings, but creates a context in which clients and practitioners can explore the perspectives of clients in an open way. The next chapters elaborate the phenomenological method and describe specific practitioner skills and exercises.

3

Research on the Meaning of Meaning

3.1 Definitions of meaning

This chapter describes what researchers have discovered about what meaning means for people in daily life. Of course, this starts with the question: what is meaning in life? Ask individuals in the street, and you will get a plethora of answers. Philosophers and theologians are no different, as their answers diverge widely. However, if we turn to empirical research, we seem to find more consensus. Seven aspects are frequently mentioned and are validated by a large body of empirical studies (Vos, 2016a): meaning seems to be about the combination of motivation, values, understanding, situational commitment, worthiness of the self and self-regulation (Wong, 2013; George & Park, 2014; MacKenzie & Baumeister, 2014). Some authors also argue that meaning is inherently about how we cope with life's existential givens, such as freedom and responsibility (Vos, 2014; Wong, 2015).

Motivation

Motivation describes how individuals move in a forward direction in life. That is, individuals usually do not stand still in life, but move. Their movements are also not random, but rather they move towards specific directions. That is, most individuals do not chaotically live their lives, but show patterns: they have selected certain directions and deselected others, albeit that they do not always consciously decide which way they go. All our behaviour is about consciously or unconsciously selecting and deselecting options, revealing specific directions in life.

What makes people move and not stand still? Motivation. This word 'motivation' is etymologically derived from the Latin 'movere', which means 'to move'. Chapter 1 showed how different individuals in different times and cultures have different motivations (**teleology, scepticism,**

functionalism). This book focuses on **phenomenological** motivations: moving in the direction of something that is important and valuable in itself, and not because individuals try to fit into a societal-cosmic-divine order or impose their theoretical ideas. Meaningful movement is directed towards realising something important and valuable that is not there yet at this moment in life. We try to achieve something better than the here and now (Sloterdijk, 2014). Thus people are moving and future-oriented (see Heidegger, 1927/2001). Thriving describes how individuals move in a forward direction in life.

Individuals do not need to be aware of their motivation or consciously decide for it. Although much research focuses on cognitive aspects of motivations, from a phenomenological perspective, meaningful motivation can be thought and felt emotionally and physically. Meaning involves cognitions, affects and embodied actions (Chapter 2).

Furthermore, individuals do not need to reach the future situation they had hoped for, as in their movement towards future directions, they could face challenges, change direction or strategy in response to the challenges, or re-evaluate the here and now. The amount of success is irrelevant for the definition of thriving: individuals can thrive despite their circumstances. For example, Frankl (1948/1985) described how inmates found the motivation to stay alive in concentration camps. Therefore, thriving is broader than having a specific life purpose or goal, as it describes the forward orientation without the need of realising a specific destination (Wong, 2012; Martela & Steger, 2016). Although motivation often has the form of a specific purpose or goal in life, this is not always the case (Chapters 1 and 2). Practitioners should address motivation in a broad way, as they could limit their clients when they focus only on purposes and goals.

Other authors, such as Frankl, speak in this context about a **will to meaning**, psychodynamic analysts about drives, existential-humanist authors about the human need for **self-transcendence** and self-growth, others about 'personal strivings' (Emmons, 1986) or 'wants' (Cooper, 2012), and some spiritual authors about a 'spiritual pull'. Frankl hypothesised that the **will to meaning** implies that all humans strive and crave for meaning, and this contains an internal contribution, that is the individual who is striving and craving, and an external contribution, that is the meaning potential of the situation (Lukas, 1986/2014). Although Frankl's hypothesis is empirically unverifiable, all authors have in common that they describe the forward movement of individuals in life. There is abundant empirical evidence showing that most people search for and/or experience meaningful motivation, although the precise percentages differ per measurement instrument, population and study (Brandstätter et al., 2012; Steger, 2012; Shin & Steger, 2014).

> **Case example**
>
> John came to see me as He said 'he felt not motivated in life'. I asked him to describe
> an average day. He told he wakes up next to his wife, goes to his work as a carpen-
> ter and so forth. I asked him what other options he may have chosen: sleeping with
> another partner, working in a factory and so on. He realised that his actual behaviour
> shows that he is already moving towards specific directions. However, in his daily life
> he usually does not reflect and label this as meaningful: 'I simply do what I do; how
> can that be meaningful?' He started to see that his current directions were based on
> motivations from the past which felt less valuable to him now. Consequently, he had
> lost the passion for these directions (Section 3.4). In the next sessions, we explored
> old and new values, and how these could motivate him again.

Values

Motivations are usually based on **values**. Values are about what individuals experience phenomenologically as important or worthy, or
functionally as useful. Motivation per se is not enough for meaning, as
individuals need to be aware and experience this as valuable and significant (Emmons, 1986; Little et al., 2007). These values can be reflected,
explicit and consciously developed before any action, but they can
also be revealed implicitly in someone's decisions and direction in life
(Section 2.4). For example, individuals can have materialistic, hedonic,
self-oriented, social or larger meanings in life (Section 3.3).

Understanding

Meaning also describes how individuals understand themselves, what
happens in their life, how they relate to the world around them and
how they experience a spiritual world (also called 'cosmic meaning').
This offers a sense of coherence (Martela & Steger, 2016). These four
materialistic, self-oriented, social and spiritual worlds have been described
by Binswanger (1956) and Van Deurzen (2002), and are validated by a
review of the types of meaning which are discussed in Section 3.3. This
understanding may not need to be explicit and reflected, but is often
implicit, embodied and evident in the actions of individuals (Section 2.4).
An example is a priest who understands her own self as being a pious person, relating to others as a pastoral carer and theologian, living a responsible life in the way in which God would expect from a priest and feeling
connected with a spiritual world.

Worthiness

Meaning implies that individuals experience their life as worthy, significant and relevant (this has also been called 'existential meaning'). This describes the experience that their life is worth living (Pfarrer, 2013). They feel they are worthy to move in certain directions in life in line with their values, instead of staying passive or living a random chaotic life without direction, or following others. Self-worth may also involve self-esteem, which means having confidence in one's own skills. An example is the message about self-worth and positive reinforcement that parents and teachers in western countries seem to be trying to give to children, telling them that they should decide their own direction in life.

Situational commitment

Meaning also implies that individuals *actually* commit to a specific direction in life in a specific situation (this has also been called 'situational meaning'). That is, they give attention to their motivation and values, adhere to these, translate them into concrete actions and dedicate their time and energy to this, rather than other directions. Thus meaning involves a commitment which implies attention, adherence, action and dedication. A stereotypical example of commitment is the total commitment by a politician to a political cause.

Regulation

Experiencing meaning also implies that individuals know how to regulate their meaning in real life. That is, they translate meaning into real actions and stick to their commitment, but are also able to flexibly adjust to changing circumstances. Research shows that the awareness of motivation alone may not be sufficient for mental health, but that individuals need to feel that they are progressing, in control, know how to work towards attaining meaning in daily life, able to overcome challenges, and engaging in meaningful activities in daily life (Emmons, 1986; Austin & Vancouver, 1996; Koestner et al., 2002; Wiese, 2007). According to self-regulation theory, self-regulation implies that individuals know how to select meaningful situations, modify situations when necessary, pay attention towards the situation, appraise the situation (that is, cognitively evaluate the possible threat and resources to cope with the situation) and respond in an appropriate way (Gross, 1998). This also includes being able to cope in meaningful ways with challenges in life, such us our limitations and finitude (Chapter 9; Vos, 2014). A historical example of meaningful self-regulation is that of yogis and Zen masters who train individuals to regulate their lives, starting with the physical.

Existential meaning

Some existential philosophers have argued that the experience of meaning cannot be separated from how we cope with life's givens, such as our free-dom of choice, responsibility, physical limitations and mortality (Yalom, 1980). Other authors seem to reduce meaning to a defence mechanism to fend off our awareness and anxiety about existential facts of life (Becker, 1973). For example, when New Yorkers were subliminally confronted with memories of the attack on the Twin Towers on 9/11, they suddenly shifted their attention to their family or work, or became more nationalistic and so on (Pyszczynski, Solomon & Greenberg, 2003). The experience of 9/11 seemed to evoke so much existential stress, that these individuals needed meanings to ward off their awareness. Research shows that such denial of reality may relieve stress in the short term, but results in a lower sense of meaning and fulfilment longer term (Jim et al., 2006; Vos & De Haes, 2007). We can attempt to hide behind a façade of meanings, but reality will ultimately creep through its cracks, crumbling these inauthentic walls.

Thus meaning is often related to how we cope with existential threats. However, this does not imply that all experiences of meaning are nothing other than defences or are inauthentic. We are free either to use mean-ing to deny the existential facts, or to experience authentic meanings while facing the facts of life (Vos, 2014). Some clients may temporarily need to deny reality, for example when they are in a crisis situation or risk mental breakdown. Meaning-centred practitioners help clients to be flexible and ultimately experience authentic meanings while accept-ing reality. For example, I accept the reality of my physical limitations, while simultaneously using my freedom within these limitations to live as meaningfully as possible. Chapter 9 describes this **dual attitude**. Existential topics may not be relevant for each client in every life situa-tion; therefore, existential meaning will be described in Section 3.3 as a specific existential-philosophical type of meaning.

Package deal

These seven characteristics are like a package deal: when you focus on one aspect, you will also get other aspects due to their intertwining. Many empirical studies show that these aspects are strongly correlated, and both from a clinical and statistical perspective these experiences are difficult to differentiate. The meaningfulness of life is about the total experience of all these aspects together, and not only one specific aspect (as shown in many correlational studies). This package has also been described as unique: each person has their own interpretation of each aspect. The individual is responsible for experiencing their own unique meaning: no one else can define what your meaning is. It is superfluous to mention that from a phenomenological perspective **meaning in life** is also not a fixed permanent experience, but a **unique** experience which may differ per individual per life period:

> Few things irritate Frankl as much as the question 'What is the meaning of life?' ... But Frankl's important point is that each man can answer it only for himself, and never for more than the moment. For the man and the situation are constantly changing, and with them the meaning that he is required to fulfil.

(Fabry, 1968, p. 33)

Metaphor

Many clients find it helpful if the definition of meaning is explained in metaphors. I often speak about sailing. When we sail, we often head in a specific direction instead of randomly floating – for instance, I direct my sailboat towards a specific point on the horizon, such as a lighthouse (motivation). When I am a sailor, I also have specific values. For instance, I feel I should never use a motor, but rather only use my sails (values). When I sail, I often feel strongly connected with nature and really alive; meaning is about the moments that you feel most alive and connected with the world around you (understanding). I also feel worthy by making the effort of getting my sailing boat out of storage, preparing the boat for sailing and charting my own direction on the water, without needing others to tell me where I should go in life (self-worth). I could only reach the lighthouse when I perform specific actions that will lead my boat in that direction, such as raising the sail, using the wheel and so on; I am committed to carrying out these actions (commitment). When I am sailing, I evaluate frequently whether I am still sailing in the right direction or whether I need to change tack, possibly because there was a sudden gust of wind that made my boat drift off course a bit. I could also change the direction in general; I could for instance decide not to sail in the direction of that lighthouse anymore, but head in the direction of that church on the horizon (self-regulation). I could see sailing as a battle against nature's elements and feel defeated by the wind; alternatively, I could see the wind as giving me the possibility to sail quicker and have a more intense sailing experience (meaning as coping with existential facts of life). Experiencing meaning is about the dynamic totality of this experience of sailing; a sailor needs all aspects to be able to sail, and cannot sail when he has, for instance, only a sail or a goal.

3.2 Definitions of meaninglessness

As far as we can discern, the sole purpose of human existence is to kindle a
light of meaning in the darkness of mere being.

(Jung, 1989, p. 230)

When clients discuss meaning in life, some raise the topic of meaninglessness. They often seem to assume that meaninglessness is the opposite
of meaningfulness. However, this is not necessarily so: individuals can
experience meaninglessness and meaningfulness at the same time. It has
been argued that meaning-centred therapy is about helping clients to live
a meaningful life despite life's meaninglessness (Vos, 2014). Therefore,
an important aspect of meaning-centred assessment is identifying the
type and possible cause of the meaninglessness that clients experience
(Chapter 5). Based on my clinical experience and philosophical knowledge, I often differentiate the following types of meaninglessness.

Primary meaninglessness or 'absurdity' is our existential awareness that
we are born without any pregiven meaning in life, and that all meanings are constructed by human beings to make sense of the chaotic world
around us ('constructivism'; e.g. Neimeyer, 2001). At birth, we were not
given a guideline telling us what the meaning of our life was going to be.
Individuals can become aware of this primary meaninglessness when they
are confronted with life changes (Chapter 9). Primary meaninglessness
and meaning are two different dimensions which could go hand in hand
with each other (Vos, 2014); this non-reductionist scepticism is called
dual awareness. For instance, I could believe that being an author is
authentically meaningful for me, although I do not think that this meaning is given by a teleological decree from God and I see how this meaning
has been influenced by my social circumstances and some in-born skills.

Secondary meaninglessness or 'existential guilt' is the experience that
in life we have an endless number of possibilities, and that any meaning
we experience implies that we do not commit to other meanings at that
moment. Doing one thing often implies we cannot do something else.
Martin Heidegger (1927/2001) writes that being is being-in-possibilities,
and that therefore there is inherently a nothingness in the process of
experiencing meaning as it closes possibilities for other meanings. For
instance, I could feel guilty that I have spent all my time on writing and
had no time to meet my friends. In some of my clients, the experience of
secondary meaninglessness has been related with their perfectionism or
decision-making problems. On social media people call this FOMO: Fear
Of Missing Out.

Tertiary meaninglessness, or the lack of meaning, is the experience that
at this moment in life there is no meaning. However, these individuals

believe that it is theoretically possible to find meaning, but they are not experiencing this now. This has been called a liminal situation, a state in between the current meaningless situation and the meaningful future. For instance, shortly after their emigration many refugees seem to struggle with the fact that old meanings have fallen away, while they have also not yet built a new meaningful life in the new country (Vos, 2014, 2006).

Reductionist scepticism tells us that all meanings are nothing other than illusions and self-deception (Section 1.3). Scepticism and meaning are mutually exclusive (one-dimensional view), and **dual awareness** (two-dimensional view) is impossible (Vos, 2014). This is sometimes called nihilism. In my experience as a practitioner and public speaker, reductionist existential scepticism is often associated with a high educational level, existential indifference, and sometimes autistic traits and disconnection from emotions. In my experience, this is a difficult group to treat due to high levels of intellectualisation (Section 3.5).

Existential indifference is the inability to experience differences and hierarchies in life: everything feels grey (see Schnell, 2010). For instance, the loss of a loved one or one's own wedding feels like ordinary daily life. Existential indifference may be associated with psychological dissociation and derealisation, autistic or schizoid traits, which are characterised by a lack of connection of affects with their cognition and behaviour. Some psychodynamic authors suggest that this may be due to traumatic life experiences, neglect, insecure attachment or narcissistic damage, usually in early childhood (Section 4.4). Assessment of the cause may be important, and treatment of these underlying problems by a mental health professional may be necessary before the client is able to benefit from meaning-centred practice. If existential indifference is related to a recent loss, meaning-centred bereavement therapy may be considered, which may include a systematic phenomenological exploration of the loss experience and the stimulation of continued bonds with the lost person or lost experience (Neimeyer, 2013).

Structural existential emptiness is the experience that life is empty, regardless of the quantity and quality of meanings that an individual may experience in life. In line with psychoanalyst Lacan, this may be explained as the difference between wanting something and desire: an individual can receive what was wanted, but the larger desire is still unfulfilled. Structural existential emptiness could be developed in multiple ways. For example, individuals could focus merely on **functional meanings** ('McMeanings') which may not provide long-term fulfilment; meaning-centred practices can be very effective with these clients. Frankl suggested that when individuals have often been frustrated in realising their meaning in the past, they could experience an **existential vacuum** (Section 3.5). Structural personality difficulties could also lead to existential emptiness, such as with Borderline Personality Disorder. Meaning-centred practitioners often attract individuals with structural borderline traits, as these clients hope that the practitioner will be able to fulfil their deeper desire. In this case, the practitioner may after a while fail in the eye of this client, and the client may project their own frustration about the structural emptiness on the practitioner. In response, the practitioner may feel a sense of failing themselves (psychoanalysts call this 'projective identification'). If a client shows strong Borderline Personality traits, it may be recommended to have a mental health professional help the client to develop basic structural psychological functions. One of the most effective treatments for Borderline Personality Disorder is Dialectical Behaviour Therapy (Linehan, 2002) which integrates cognitive-behavioural, psychodynamic, mindfulness and some meaning-centred techniques, although it may be considered to include more meaning-centred skills.

Hopelessness and helplessness. Individuals could start feeling hopeless or helpless in confrontation with the overwhelming experience of meaninglessness. They feel they cannot cope, because repeated attempts of finding meaning have failed ('learned helplessness') or because they believe that it is principally impossible to experience meaning despite meaninglessness. They feel that they do not have the possibility or capability to cope with the meaninglessness. Meaning-centred treatments can significantly lower this feeling of hopelessness and existential anxiety, and will give the experience that it is possible to live a meaningful and satisfying life despite meaninglessness (Chapter 9).

Example

'I am afraid of death and therefore I do not dare to live life to the fullest.' These were Emma's first words when she entered my therapy room. I had been told by colleagues that I had to use a cognitive-behavioural treatment manual for general anxiety disorder, but I decided to put this temporarily aside. Instead, we **phenomenologically** explored what her death anxiety meant for her, with empathic and specification questions such as 'What do you mean by this?', 'Could you give examples?' and 'How does this make you feel?' I saw that it was not death per se that she was afraid of, but the temporality and changeability of life. She had become aware of this **primary meaninglessness** when she had emigrated from another country, as this had taught her that everything in life can change. She asked me 'How can something be meaningful when it is about to disappear?' It seemed that she was expecting meaning to be permanent – like her life before the emigration which felt stable – but

▶

◀

after the move she can no longer find a sense of permanence. I gave some **psycho-education** on the *dual attitude*: meanings do not necessarily need to be permanent; we are able to live a meaningful life despite realising the fundamental temporality and changeability of life. Instead of creating the illusion that meaning must be permanent and pushing away her anxiety, I helped her to embrace feelings of anxiety and temporality. Simultaneously I asked her to write in a diary mini-moments of meaningfulness in daily life, such as enjoying a bird in the park; although the bird had stopped singing – it was temporary – she had enjoyed it and felt connected with nature. She also used the six characteristics of meaning (Section 3.1) to identify what is meaning and what is not. Initially she did not identify the bird moment as meaningful, but when she examined this, she realised that she felt motivated to go to the park; she knew where the park is, how to get there and to commit her time to listen to the birds; this followed from her values and understanding about nature, and she had felt it worthwhile going to the park instead of making dinner for her family precisely on time that day. Over the sessions, her hopelessness disappeared and she said 'Although I have lost my naivety about life after emigration, I have learned how my daily life can feel meaningful despite understanding that nothing in life is permanent'.

3.3 Types of meaning: the meaning quintet

Multiple interpretability of meanings

To understand what individuals phenomenologically experience as meaningful in life, researchers have asked them what they experience as meaningful, valuable or important in life. A systematic literature review of 108 empirical studies on this topic which included 45,710 individuals revealed five groups of meanings (Vos, 2018). This **meaning quintet** is in line with other categorisations from, for instance, Langle's 'Fundamental Motivations' (2014) and Binswanger as elaborated in Van Deurzen's framework of 'worlds' (2015). The meaning quintet can be interpreted as the most comprehensive and validated typology of meanings from individuals worldwide.

Every experience of meaning could be placed in one or more of these five categories. This is called **equifinality** and **multifinality**. Equifinality means that every type of meaning can by attained by different means (Austin & Vancouver, 1996). For instance, I can achieve the meaning of intimacy in many different ways, with different partners, in different situations. Multifinality means that any one means can serve for a range of meanings. For instance, being close with friends can offer intimacy, but can also be functional, for instance in finding a job via professional networking. Thus one activity may have many meanings, and one meaning may be realised in many activities. Research suggests that individuals often strive for multifinality, that is, synergy between different meanings (Chun et al., 2011).

The meaning quintet

Materialistic-hedonic types of meaning describe the value of material and physical well-being and hedonic experiences. This includes experiencing meaning in material conditions (e.g. finances, housing, possessions, practical activities, physical survival), professional-educational success (e.g. general success, professional success, educational success, social status, power), hedonic-experiential activities (e.g. hedonism; fun, leisure and joyful activities; aesthetic enjoyments, such as music, art, food and drink and so on; sex; nature and animals; peak experiences; pain avoidance) and health (being healthy, a healthy lifestyle, sports).

Self-oriented types of meaning describe the value of the self. This includes experiencing meaning in resilience (i.e. coping successfully with difficult life situations – for example, demonstrating flexibility, perseverance and hardiness, accepting challenges, effective coping skills, positive and hopeful perspective), self-efficacy (i.e. effective actions in daily life – for example, setting specific activities or goals, planning, organising, being disciplined, evaluating and adjusting daily life activities or goals, being in control), self-acceptance (e.g. self-insight, self-acceptance, self-worth, self-esteem, self-compassion), autonomy (e.g. self-reliance, non-selfish balance with social context), creative self-expression and self-care.

Social types of meaning describe the value of being connected with others, belonging to a specific community and improving the well-being of others and children in particular. This includes experiencing meaning in feeling socially connected (e.g. sociability, friends, family, intimate relationships/partner), belonging to a specific community (e.g. family, community, history and society), following social expectations (i.e. doing what is socially expected, following social virtues, conformism, tradition), altruism, and giving birth and taking care of children.

Larger types of meaning describe values of something bigger than their materialistic-hedonic experiences, themselves and other human beings, primarily for the sake of that larger value. This includes experiencing meaning in larger specific purposes in life (e.g. specific larger goals, purposes, aims or dreams in life), personal growth (e.g. authenticity, true self, self-development, self-transcendence, self-realisation, fulfilling one's potential, authenticity, wisdom), temporality (e.g. sense of coherence, future-oriented, reflection on the past, legacy and afterlife), justice and ethics (e.g. following ethical standards, being treated in a just way, contributing to a just world), spirituality and religion (e.g. beliefs, worship and religious practices; insight in cosmic meaning; spiritual union; peace, harmony and balance; Platonic Idea or Highest Good).

Existential-philosophical types of meaning describe the value of life as such. This type does not have a specific content like the other types of meaning but is more abstract: the mere fact that someone is breathing and is able to make unique decisions with freedom is a gift for which one may feel grateful, and may wish to respond with responsible decisions. Most of these meanings are mentioned in conceptual texts by existential philosophers and therapists. This type of meaning can be implicitly present and underlie the other types of meaning. It includes experiencing meaning in being alive (e.g. being born, feeling alive, being until death), uniqueness (e.g. the unique individuality of one's own experiences, own life, own world and own self), connectedness with the world and others (e.g. being in the world, being in context, being in relationships), individual freedom (e.g. freedom of choice, freedom to decide one's attitude towards a limiting situation in life, the possibility to leave a legacy), gratitude to life as a gift (e.g. experiencing the mere fact of being born as a gift or miracle that one did not ask for but that one regards as highly precious and special, and to which one responds with gratitude) and responsibility (e.g. individual responsibility for oneself to live a meaningful life according to one's highest values).

Implications for practitioners

Many meaning-centred practices have been built around the **Franklian triad**. That is, Frankl (1949) hypothesised that individuals may find meaning on the basis of three 'main routes' ('Hauptstrasse') or values: **phenomenological experiences** and describe **phenomenological** modes, productivity-creativity and **attitude**. This triad seems to describe modes of being which can apply to each type of meaning. For example, you can experience materialistic meanings, be creatively producing materialistic meanings, and you can have a specific attitude towards this, for instance by rejecting materialistic values. However, some therapists seem to have interpreted the Franklian triad as three specific types of meaning. They have built their full treatment around the meanings: in each session, they ask about another Franklian type (e.g. Breitbart & Poppito, 2015). For example, they ask when individuals had positive experiences, were productive or creative, and had a helpful attitude towards life. Interpreted in this narrow sense, the **Franklian triad** has not been validated by this review: the **meaning quintet** shows that there are more types of meaning (Vos, 2017). This implies that more types of meaning could be discussed in treatments. It also seems more effective to discuss a larger number of possible meanings and not only these three categories, as on average, meaning-centred treatments cover 41% of all possible types and subtypes of meanings; and the more meanings are addressed the greater the psychological improvements, the higher the participation rates and the lower the attrition rates in clients (Vos, 2017). This is understandable, as discussing a wider range of possible meanings makes it more likely that clients recognise and identify within themselves some meaning types/subtypes.

Therefore, it is recommended to explore an exhaustive list of meanings with clients, and not simply focus on a small selection on meanings. The **meaning quintet** is the most comprehensive and validated list of meanings. In each session, each type and subtype can be briefly introduced theoretically. Subsequently clients can explore to what extent they experience each type/subtype as important, are already trying to realise this or want to try to realise this. Formulated in the Franklian ways, clients can **phenomenologically** explore for each type of meaning, how they **phenomenologically experience** this, decide their **attitude** towards this and

Table 3.1 The meaning quintet: evidence-based categorisation of different types of meaning in life

I. MATERIALISTIC-HEDONIC DOMAIN OF MEANINGS

Underlying value: the value of having material goods, objective success, nice physical experiences

- A. Material conditions
  Finances, housing, possessions, practical activities, physical survival
- B. Professional-educational success
  General success, professional success, educational success, social status, power
- C. Hedonic-experiential activities
  Hedonism; fun, leisure and joyful activities; aesthetic enjoyments, such as music, art, food and drink and so on; sex; nature and animals; peak experiences; pain avoidance
- D. Health
  Being healthy, a healthy lifestyle, sports

II. SELF-ORIENTED TYPES OF MEANING

Underlying value: the value of the self

- A. Resilience (coping successfully with difficult life situations)
  Flexibility, perseverance and hardiness, accepting challenges, effective coping skills, positive and hopeful perspective
- B. Self-efficacy
  Effective in daily life (setting specific activities or goals, planning, organising, being disciplined, evaluating and adjusting daily life activities or goals), being in control
- C. Self-acceptance
  Self-insight, self-acceptance, self-worth, self-esteem
- D. Autonomy
  Self-reliance, non-selfish balance with social context
- E. Creative self-expression
- F. Self-care
- G. Authenticity
  Following the perceived true self

(Continued)

III. SOCIAL TYPES OF MEANING

Underlying value: the value of being connected with others, belonging to a specific community and improving the well-being of others and children in particular

    A. Feeling socially connected

        Sociability, friends, family, intimate relationships/partner

    B. Belonging to a specific community

        Family, community, history and society

    C. Following social expectations

        Doing what is socially expected, following social virtues, conformism, tradition

    D. Altruism

    E. Giving birth and taking care of children

IV. LARGER TYPES OF MEANING

Underlying value: values of something bigger than their materialistic-hedonic experiences, themselves and other human beings.

    A. Purposes

        Specific larger goals, purposes, aims or dreams in life

    B. Personal growth

        Self-development, self-transcendence, self-realisation, fulfilling one's potential, authenticity, wisdom

    C. Temporality

        Sense of coherence, future-oriented, reflection on the past, legacy, afterlife, position in life span, little time or few resources left

    D. Justice and ethics

        Following ethical standards, being treated in a just way, contributing to a just world

    E. Spirituality and religion

        Spirituality and religion; beliefs, worship and religious practices; insight in cosmic meaning; spiritual union; peace, harmony and balance; Platonic Idea or Highest Good

V. EXISTENTIAL-PHILOSOPHICAL MEANINGS

Underlying value: the value of life as such. This type of meaning does not have a specific content like the other types of meaning but is more abstract: the mere fact that someone is breathing and is able to make unique decisions with freedom is a gift for which one may feel grateful and may wish to respond to with responsible decisions. Most of these meanings are mentioned by existential philosophers and therapists in conceptual texts. This type of meaning can be implicitly present and underlying the other types of meaning.

    A. Being alive

        Being born, feeling alive, being until death

    B. Uniqueness

        The unique individuality of one's own experiences, own life, own world and own self

    C. Connectedness with the world and others

        Being in the world, being in context, being in relationships

    D. Individual freedom

        Freedom of decision, freedom to decide one's attitude towards a limiting situation in life, the possibility to leave a legacy

    E. Gratitude to life as a gift

        Experiencing the mere fact of being born as a gift or miracle that one did not ask for but that one regards as highly precious and special, and to which one responds with gratitude

    F. Responsibility

        Individual responsibility for oneself to live a meaningful life according to one's highest values flexibly commit to productive and creative actions in daily life. Part III provides an example treatment manual built around the **meaning quintet**.

3.4 The development of meaning

> There are three transformations in the development of humans: the camel who carries all burdens, the lion who destroys everything with his growling, and the baby who plays innocently.
>
> (Loosely based on Nietzsche, 1891/2017)

Many academic texts describe how individuals develop meaning during their lifetime. A scoping review of academic literature revealed over 50,000 search results. There are particularly many texts about how their upbringing leads individuals to internalise the **values** from their social context, and how they develop their individual meaning during their adolescence. Most studies are theoretical texts or show correlational research (e.g. 'What type of childhood did most individuals with strong social meanings have?'). Unfortunately, these studies do not provide definitive evidence about how individuals precisely develop meaning, as there is little information about what caused what (causality). As a comprehensive literature review exceeds the aims of this book, this section only summarises main trends and describes a simplified structure which resulted from **thematic analyses** in line with previous reviews (Kruithof, 1967). This is called the **Meaning Development Triangle**: every meaning seems to develop from the tensions between what an individual must (not), can(not) and (does not) want to do in life (Figure 3.1; Table 3.2).

Must. Many people, such as parents and teachers, tell us what our meaning must or must not be about. They communicate their expectations verbally and non-verbally, for example: 'You should become a decent citizen', 'You must have a good career, partner and children', 'It does not matter which direction you go in life as long as you are happy,' and so on. Individuals can internalise these expectations and experience these 'musts' as coming from themselves, although they have forgotten the origin of these meanings (Nietzsche, 1887). **Teleological** societies are often dominated by many musts, and individuals try to fit in with the societal-cosmic-divine order that they are expected to follow (Section 1.3). In **functional** societies, individuals may experience the pressure to maximise their life and live up to the expectations from their public life and commercials (Section 1.4).

Can. During the life course, individuals can develop an understanding of what they can and cannot attain. Up to the age of 30, many individuals seem to focus on their possibilities, learn many new skills and are full of hope and expectations about their potential. However, failures also teach them their limitations. For example, although some individuals may have initially tried to become president or a millionaire, their failures taught them that these aims may be too high.

Want. During the early years of life, children often focus on what they are expected to do (must/must not) instead of on what they want for themselves, although this differs according to culture, as children in modern western societies may be encouraged to go after what they want. Adolescence is often characterised by a testing of boundaries: what must I do, what do I want, and what can I do? Individuals develop a stronger sense of what they want, independent from their upbringing. This is called **separation-individuation**: individuals learn to separate their individual wishes and expectations from those of others around them.

Overlap. There is often a strong overlap between what individuals can do, must do and want to do. For instance, because they **internalise** what other people tell them, the musts from others around them become their own wants. Often, what individuals must do, want to do and can do is influenced by their social-historical context: collectivist and religious societies seem to focus less on what individuals must do than what they want to do, and individualist societies focus more on wants than musts. Individuals can reflect on this process, evaluate whether their wants originate from within themselves or are internalised meanings, and decide whether they want to continue with this meaning. Practitioners could use this Meaning Development Triangle to explore with clients how their sense of meaning has evolved. Clients often interpret cans, musts and wants as mutually exclusive: 'How can I make totally free decisions when I am born here, in this context, with this IQ, etc.?'

Practitioners may want to explore ways to support clients to develop a more realistic sense of **dual awareness**, for instance by using metaphors. As an example, in life we may be given a bandwidth that tells us what we must (not) and can(not) do; and within this bandwidth we can make free decisions, and over time we may even widen it.

Figure 3.1   The Meaning Development Triangle

Table 3.2 Examples of the development of meaning in a scoping literature review

	Examples
Can(not)	Social-historical context
	Biology
	Personality
	Structural physical and mental disorders
	Attachment
	Life stage
	Life experiences
Must (not)	Social-historical context
	Family/social context of upbringing
	Education
	Social institutions
	Peers
	Culture
	Media
	Socio-economic situation
	Reinforcements (rewards and punishments)
	Lifestyle and subculture
(Do not) Want	Social-historical context
	Freedom of choice
	Influences on what one can(not) or must (not) do

Example

In a decision-making training group for students, trainees reflected on how they made difficult decisions in the past. For each decision, they filled in three columns entitled 'I can(not)', 'I must (not)' and 'I (do not) want', respectively, and they identified patterns between decisions. For instance, Jenny made most decisions based on what she thought she must do according to parents and peers. Adam focused on his immediate wants and ignored expectations from other people. Peter felt overwhelmed by his limitations due to a spinal injury. Subsequently, we analysed where the patterns came from. Jenny realised she had developed her social conformism in response to meeting her mother's needs, who was a psychiatric patient. Adam was angry at his parents who had often put him down. Peter's illness had led to low self-esteem. Everyone decided how they would like to make decisions in the future, and we practised this each week by completing the column-exercise for current decisions, while particularly focusing on the column(s) they had been ignoring in the past. Jenny focused on what she wanted, Adam on social expectations and Peter on what he could do within his limitations. At a follow-up session three months later all participants had made big life decisions. Jenny described her decision to take a year's break to travel the world as 'very meaningful'. Adam said he 'finally had'

▶

◄

a girlfriend. Peter's procrastination in his study had stopped, and he was finishing his master's thesis, as his self-esteem had improved. This four-session training had brought about large effects in making 'more meaningful life decisions' and 'better psychological well-being' in 157 participants, which was significantly more than in the 200 participants who were following spiritual training in a quasi-experimental trial (Vos, 2009).

Developmental insight exercises

1. Create columns entitled 'situation details (date/location/situation)', 'I can(not)', 'I must (not)', 'I (do not) want', 'The decision I actually made' and 'Blind spot'. In the rows, write different decision situations in the past. Complete the columns with several decisions. Do you see a pattern? For instance, do you make many decisions based mainly on what you can do, must do or want to do? Where does this pattern come from? How has this decision-making pattern influenced what you experience as meaningful? Is this pattern what you want? How could you make decisions that are more in line with what you want to achieve? Fill in the columns for current decisions with a specific focus on the column that you usually ignore. How does this feel?

2. Make a list of meanings that your parents, relatives, closest friends, teachers and other important individuals have/had. Which meanings did/do they explicitly or implicitly expect you to have? To what extent does your experience of meaning in life derive from them? Do you feel free to deviate from their examples and expectations? How can you focus on your own meanings while being loyal to them? How can you explain to others that you would like to follow more of your own meanings?

3. How would you describe your personality? Do you know other individuals with your personality type, and what do they experience as meaningful? How does your personality influence what you experience as meaningful? How can you deal with the limitations of your personality?

4. This question follows Erik Erikson's developmental model (Erikson & Erikson, 1997) and the existential questions that are associated with each developmental stage (given in brackets) (Macnow, 2014, p. 220). What do you know about the developmental stages of your life? That is, how did you develop physically? Infancy (0–18 months): how did you develop a sense of trust or mistrust of other people (virtue of hope; can I trust the world?)? Early childhood (2–4 years): how did you develop a sense of autonomy or shame/doubt (virtue of will; is it OK to be me?)? Preschool age (4–5 years): how did you develop a sense of initiative or guilt (virtue of purpose; is it OK for me to move and act?)? School age (5–12 years): how did you develop productivity or a sense of inferiority, which is not only about attaining visible results, but also about developing self-esteem and experiencing self-growth and education as meaningful (virtue of competence: can I make it in the world of people and things)? Adolescence (13–19 years): how did you develop your social identity or feel socially confused in your adolescence (virtue of fidelity: who am I? who can I be?)? Early adulthood (20–39 years): how did you develop intimate

►

◀

relationships or feel isolated (virtue of love: can I love)? Adulthood (40–64 years): if relevant, how did you become generative via work, family or otherwise, or feel a sense of stagnation (virtue of care: can I make my life count)? Maturity (virtue of wisdom: 65 years+): if relevant, to what extent do you look back at a meaningful life or experience despair (is it OK to have been me)? When you look at how you developed yourself in each of these periods in your life, how did every stage influence what you experience now as meaningful? Finally, how have these developmental stages influenced what you experience now as meaningful in life? There is some empirical evidence for this model (e.g. Marcia, 1966), but research suggests that these stages may not be sequential and may not be rigidly fixed to certain ages.

5. When have you felt that you are free in making decisions? How did it feel to be free? What do you need to feel free?

3.5 Cold reflections on meaning in life

People say I should find the meaning of life, but meaning means nothing to me. What does matter to me is feeling alive. Possibly that is lived meaning. It is like you do not theorise about love. You simply live it.

(Mary, a client)

The previous sections described meaning in a theoretical way. However, in daily life we often do not reflect on the directions in our life, as we simply live it. We often live in the moment, committed to actions, following implicit motivations and values, and immediately understand ourselves, the world and people around us. This inner experience is associated with hot feelings, such as flow and happiness (Section 3.6). In contrast, the outer experience from theorising about meaning is emotionally devoid, characterised by cognitive distance from our emotions.

This difference can be heard in the terms people use. Clients describe their inner experience often with verbs or the present participle (-ing), for example: 'I feel I am living a meaningful life, when I am hiking or mountaineering.' In contrast, when clients speak about 'meaning in life' as a noun, they often seem to have a reflective distance from their emotions: 'I do not know what the meaning of my life is.' To underline that meaning is more than a reflective state but also an experiential process, I prefer the verb 'living a meaningful life' instead of the noun 'meaning in life'. Other psychologists use other verbs such as flourishing or thriving (Peterson, 2012). A simple exercise to help reflective clients return to experiencing meaning is to ask them to express themselves with present participles.

This section describes this cold outer experience, and the next section (3.6) elaborates on the hot inner experience of a meaningful life. Chapter 8 discusses specific techniques which practitioners can use to help clients shift from the cold outer perspective to the hot inner perspective.

Theorising. We are not experiencing a meaningful life from within when we merely reflect on ourselves in a philosophical-abstract way (Heidegger, 1927/2001). For example, when we only look at life in a **reductionist sceptical** way, we explain life from an outer perspective, instead of understanding it from the inner. Rigid reductionist sceptics seem to lack the motivation to go within their lived experience of a meaningful life, because they think they already know what that is. Metaphorically formulated, they seem to have no urge to go into the mountains, because they think they already know what it is like to be there, as they know the map (**map/landscape fallacy**).

Lack of awareness. Meaning is like the walls of our house within which our daily life activities take place. We are usually unaware of the walls, as we simply live between them. We do not need to be aware of the walls to be able to live a meaningful life. On reflection, we may see that everything within the house is positioned in such a way that it always refers to the possibilities and limitations of the walls (Vos, 2014).

Automatic pilot. Often we live our daily lives on automatic pilot and our actions are about functionally taking care of things instead of meaningful care (Heidegger, 1927/2001). We are not in the present with our full attention, for instance because we are too hurried or overwhelmed by daily life. We can rationalise for ourselves why we are doing things, but we are not really connecting this meaning from within: 'I know cognitively that my children make my life meaningful, but I cannot really feel that right now because I am busy taking care of them, as I need to make their food, take them to school and drive them to football lessons.' It often seems realistic to live on automatic pilot, because this saves energy and time as we do not need to make time-consuming conscious decisions all the time (Kahneman, 2012).

Following others. We can follow others' expectations instead of making authentic decisions every moment in our lives: we follow commercials, our Facebook friends and so on (Section 1.4). The next section shows how it is also possible to be authentic.

Hyper-reflection. A common example of **hyper-reflection** is clients telling themselves: 'I must sleep; if I do not sleep, I will not be able to function well tomorrow.' Subsequently they focus more on their not-sleeping and their anxiety increases, which creates more hyper-reflection. Frankl described how individuals can increasingly focus on how they are performing and become obsessed with themselves and their problems. This circling around oneself could lead to overreacting to minor failures, being hypervigilant to mistakes, and having an overly negative image and unrealistic demands of oneself, which could lead to anxiety and emotional crises. In addition, individuals may excessively try to force something (**hyper-intention**), which aggravates the hyper-reflection. **Hyper-reflection** and **hyper-intention** exacerbate the problems of clients, as they are standing outside their lived experience and their subsequent focus on feeling like an outsider makes them feel even more of an outsider, which makes it less likely that they can focus on inner experiencing. According to Frankl, this could, in the long term, lead to an **existential vacuum**: the experience that life structurally lacks meaning, is empty or boring. An existential vacuum can also be caused by long-term frustrations about their **will to meaning**: the more often you have failed in trying to achieve your goals, the more likely it is that you feel like an outsider to a meaningful life. To help these clients, Frankl suggested going against their inclination to increasingly focus on what is going on within themselves and instead focus on their meaningful experiences in the real world around them (Chapter 9).

Crisis. Frankl used the term 'noogenic neurosis' (derived from *nous*, etymologically implying meaning) to describe how a frustrated will to meaning could make an individual ill (Raskob, 2007). Nowadays, a more frequently used term is crisis. A **crisis** is a situation of extreme difficulty in which the individual explicitly experiences questions about life and may need to make critical decisions. Four different types of crises can be identified in the therapeutic literature: crises regarding meaning (what makes life worth living?), spirituality/religion (where are we called to go in life?), identity (who am I?) and existence (what does life demand from me?) (Vos, 2011). Individuals may try to suppress or deny these questions about life, which may be called a latent crisis. Thus although clients may not directly experience and mention such questions, they may experience a general discontent or dissatisfaction about life. At one point, individuals may not be able to contain the crisis anymore, possibly due to a depletion of resources, changed perception or life events. This could lead to a manifest crisis in which they explicitly ask questions about life, or experience pathological levels of stress, anxiety or depression. When the questions about life become explicit and/or stressful, this may mean that clients have already been through many stages of latent crisis and failing coping skills.

Example

Many clients seem to have lost hope that their life is meaningful because they are too engaged in the **functional** activities of daily life. Some clients mainly connect theoretically with the sessions and do not engage emotionally; consequently, they feel even less meaningfulness – Lukas (2004) calls this 'iatrogenic damage'. For example, when my colleagues referred George to me, they told me they had given up on him as he had received all possible cognitive and psychodynamic treatments that my mental health service could offer. When I met him, I saw that George's mental health deteriorated when session after session he was speaking about philosophers and theories about life: 'Nietzsche wrote that God is dead; anything goes! Why should I even try to live a meaningful life? There is nothing meaningful.' As a hypothesis, I asked him whether his **hyper-reflection** may prevent him from experiencing **flow** in life (**psycho-education**). Therefore, I invited him to do some **mindfulness** exercises, to focus on his feelings instead of his thoughts. Mindfulness made him feel worse; as he became more focused on himself, he felt a greater distance from his feelings, and felt he was a failure as he was often distracted by his thoughts during the exercises. I understood that mindfulness increased the 'cold' focus on his inner world, and instead he needed 'hot' engagements with the outside world. We started to explore where 'hot' meanings could already exist in his daily life activities that he may not have been aware of, like the unseen walls of his house (Vos, 2014). He searched for examples when he had (briefly) felt a meaningful **flow**. He remembered he had felt truly alive when he was engaged in physical activities in nature such as rock-climbing and running. He understood that these activities felt meaningful, as they literally forced him to ignore his thoughts. He decided to try out a regular running group and a climbing group, which made him into another person. Two sessions later, he told me he had a girlfriend, which he had not had for seven years. After a total of ten sessions, his depression had disappeared and for the first time in ten years he did not need further therapy.

3.6 The hot flow of experiencing a meaningful life

What is it like to be inside the **phenomenological** experience of living a meaningful life? Answers can be found in the field of **positive psychology**, which often focuses on the positive inner experiences of living a meaningful life (e.g. Seligman et al., 2005; Ivtzan et al. 2015). This section outlines some trends from empirical positive-psychological research, which suggest that when individuals are living a meaningful life, they may experience flow, mindfulness, peak experiences, happiness, life satisfaction and authenticity.

Flow

Flow describes the mental state of absorption, where the abilities of an individual meet the challenge of the situation. Examples are achieving goals or improving skills, for instance in work, education or sports, regardless of how good they are at the task. Csikszentmihalyi (2002) describes how flow can be found in doing an activity that is meaningful in itself, which implies a balance between how challenging a situation is and what someone's abilities are: intense concentration, lack of fear of failure, a merging of action and awareness, and an absence of distractions, self-consciousness and sense of time. Csikszentmihalyi (2002, p. 67) suggests that flow can only be experienced when there are phenomenological meanings, or what he calls 'autotelic experiences', which refer to a self-contained activity, one that is not done with the expectation of some future benefits, but simply because the doing itself is the reward. This seems to imply that teleological, sceptical and functional meanings are less likely to lead to flow than phenomenological meanings (Chapters 1 and 2).

Mindfulness

When we are living a meaningful life, we often feel in the here and now. This is called **mindfulness**, which can be defined as an individual being completely grounded in the present moment, by having an intentionally focused awareness of their immediate experience. Focused awareness means that someone has a conscious moment-by-moment attention to situational elements of an experience, such as thoughts, emotions, physical sensations and surroundings. They observe the arising and passing of the experiences, do not judge experiences and thoughts and do not try to explain or change anything. In particular, Southeast Asian religions, such as Buddhism, focus on the importance of mindfulness for a meaningful life.

Since the 1990s, western psychologists have also used mindfulness. However, mindfulness-based treatments have been criticised for being too distant from warm experiences, as mindfulness exercises explicitly instruct clients to observe their experiences instead of identifying with them (e.g. one instruction tells us to visualise our thoughts and feelings as clouds in the sky, and allow them to pass by rather than focusing on one specific thought or feeling). On the one hand, it may be argued that mindfulness-based therapy makes it more difficult for clients to immerse themselves inside a meaningful flow. Consequently, in hyper-reflective clients, mindfulness exercises can exacerbate symptoms. On the other hand, mindfulness can help clients on automatic pilot to become aware of their stream of experiencing, and could help rigid/obsessive clients to look at their experiences from a greater distance. Mindfulness can also be used as an **unpeeling technique** (Section 2.3), to turn the focus towards a more authentic and meaningful stream of experiences. Several therapists have suggested using other forms of meditation such as Transcendental Meditation to combine the internal flow of experiencing the here and now with emotional heat (Baer, 2003; Cahn & Polich, 2006; Goyall et al., 2014). An alternative option can be found in the treatment manual in Part 3, where mindfulness exercises are immediately followed by experiential exercises which focus on the client's warm inner experiences of meaning. Meaning-centred therapies that include mindfulness or meditation exercises have proved to be more effective in improving meaning-centred skills and psychological well-being (Chapter 4).

Peak experiences

Individuals in a meaningful situation may also report **peak experiences**. Flow and mindfulness do not necessarily assume personal accomplishments or euphoria, but peak experiences describe meaningful achievement. **Peak experiences** are specific moments of euphoric mental state where an individual actualises oneself, such as scientific discoveries, extreme sports activities or musical experience: 'Think of the most wonderful experience of your life: the happiest moments, ecstatic moments, moments of rapture, perhaps from being in love, or from listening to music or suddenly "being hit" by a book or painting, or from some creative moment' (Maslow, 1962). An individual in a peak experience will lose the sense of time and space, feels part of a larger whole or harmony, is fully in the moment and fully functioning by using all capacities and capabilities, does not experience struggle or fear, but feels spontaneous, creative and free.

Example

When clients are asked in the first session about meaningful moments in life, they usually refer to peak experiences, such as their wedding, exceptional concerts, extreme holidays or drug trips. Such memories are like anchors of hope, which they cling to in their daily life. Often, peak experiences are like *teleological* goals for them, towards which they design their life. Consequently, individuals feel that they are lacking a sense of immediate meaning in their daily life, as they expect to continuously experience exceptional moments. Several clients came to see me after having a peak experience, such as a wedding or promotion. A famous rock star told me he felt disappointed: 'Is this all there is to life?'; and he did not know what could ever be meaningful after this peak: 'I will never be able to reach such a peak again.' It helped to discuss how meaning can also be experienced in non-teleological ways. Meaning is not merely about peak moments: in any mountain range, although there are not many peaks there are many heights. A mountaineer can be hiking at height without being at the peak. People can be living a meaningful life without achieving the highest. The rock star benefited from identifying how he could experience meaning not only on the stage, but also in more mundane situations in daily life, starting with holding his child in his arms, looking her in the eyes and feeling a warm connection.

Happiness

Meaning does not necessarily offer **quick happiness**, but it can foster a sense of **slow happiness**. That is, many studies found only a small relationship between meaningfulness and happiness measured as a state of positive emotions or hedonic pleasure. This is possibly most obvious in the repeated study finding that raising children does not make people happier, although they often experience taking care of children as meaningful (Baumeister et al., 2012). This lack of happiness has been explained by the fact that taking care of children often involves a busier life, a child-centred focus which shifts the attention from other meaningful aspects in life, and worries about the development of the child. However, raising children is also experienced as providing a different type of happiness in the long term, which results from a long-term commitment to the value of raising children, which raises someone's self-worth as a parent, educator or caregiver.

This type of happiness is like the deep currents in the ocean, while quick happiness or busyness are superficial waves. Such deep currents are experienced as slower, like a state of tranquility or harmony below the surface. The slowness of this type of happiness has been given different names by different traditions, for example *ataraxia* in ancient Greece, *sukkha* in Buddhism and *oikeion* in Roman Stoa. I call this kind of happiness based on phenomenological meanings **slow happiness**. As research suggests, I distinguish it from other types of happiness (see Diener, 2000; Ryan & Deci, 2001; Huta, 2013; Huta & Waterman, 2014). **Quick happiness**, in contrast, is often about functional meanings and temporary states, which do not require a commitment to values, but can even be artificially created by drugs or alcohol. Quick happiness is about fulfilling one's own needs and desires that one demands from reality; slow happiness is about being immersed in reality. That is, slow happiness is about connecting with the real world and being inside the flow of experiencing the here and now, but quick happiness can even be artificially manipulated in a state detached from the world (Layard, 2012).

Is quick happiness not meaningful? According to the definition in Section 3.1, slow happiness can be meaningful, as this is a way in which individuals commit themselves to actions motivated by the value that happiness has for them, for instance going to parties or using mind-enhancing substances. Surveys confirm that when individuals worldwide are asked what meaning is for them, one of their answers is about hedonism and happiness (Section 3.3). However, many studies show that striving for happiness is self-defeating, as it makes people unhappier and lonelier (e.g. Mauss et al., 2011; Maus et al., 2012; Schooler, Ariely & Loewenstein, 2013). The quest for happiness can even lead to depression

(Ford et al., 2014). Research also indicates that materialistic-hedonic and self-oriented types of meaning are experienced as less meaningful and satisfying, and are correlated with lower long-term well-being, while social and larger values are associated with better well-being (Baumeister et al., 2013; Nielsen, Gantt & Thayne, 2014; Vos, 2017). This is also called the happiness paradox: constant pleasure-seeking does not yield the most happiness in the long run (see Sidgwick, 1874/1984). Thus focusing on quick happiness may not necessarily provide a long-term sense of meaningfulness and slow happiness. Although researchers know these facts, the '(quick) happiness industry' is flourishing (Davies, 2016).

Authenticity

> The highest form of excellence can only be achieved by living in accord with one's true self.
>
> (Loose translation of Aristotle, 1998)

Section 3.3 described how individuals can experience materialist-hedonic, self-oriented, social, larger or existential-philosophical types of meaning. Can we randomly select any meanings or copy from others? Is any type of meaning sufficient to feel meaningful? The phenomenological experience of individuals rejects this idea: meaning needs to be authentic (Schlegel et al., 2009; Schlegel, Smith & Hirsch, 2013). That is, research differentiates the experience of more authentic meanings from less authentic meanings, and suggests that the more authentic we are the more we experience life as meaningful.

Authenticity has been defined as the perceived congruence between someone's primary experiences, their self-awareness and their behaviour and communication (Barrett-Lennard, 1998). In simpler terms, this means that authenticity is on the one hand about being open and aware of our experiences, and on the other hand being open and transparent about our own experiences in our behaviour and communication with others (Lietaer, 1993; Schmid, 2001; Wood et al., 2008). Thus authenticity means that we experience and behave in line with being ourself and our actions follow accordingly. This is etymologically derived from 'authos' – meaning self – and 'hentes' – being or doing. Authenticity means being the author of our own meanings (Nietzsche, 1887).

Research indicates that meanings that feel more strongly connected to our true self lead to a stronger sense of meaningfulness (Bellah et al., 1995; Debats, Drost & Hansen, 1995; McGregor & Little, 1998; Krause, 2007). Thus the more we feel we are doing activities that are meaningful – and not because others told us to, or because they are internalised values from others, but because they feel more authentic – the more we will experience our life as meaningful. Furthermore, how we see ourselves influences what we experience as meaningful, and we value decisions more when we have made these in line with our self-concept (Schlegel, Smith & Hirsch, 2013). Focusing on our true self is also good for our well-being, mindfulness, vitality, self-esteem and active coping skills (Andersen & Williams, 1985; Schimel et al., 2001; Kernis & Goldman, 2006; Lakey et al., 2008).

However, who is the true self or authos whom we are listening to? The concept of a true self may be tenuous at best (Schlegel, Smith & Hirsch, 2013). Possibly the self is nothing more than the meanings we give to our world (Neimeyer, 2012), and focusing too much on the self may even distract us from actually living a meaningful life (Epstein, 2006). However, from a pragmatic-phenomenological perspective, it can be beneficial to focus on the experience that clients have of different **degrees of authenticity**: clients experience that there are different degrees to which they are true to their person, spirit or character. For example, many people experience that they are fulfilling different roles, and there are different sides to their experiences or personality; they describe some of these roles or sides as more authentic than others, even though the concept of authenticity may be metaphysically untenable (Ryan, LaGuardia & Rawsthorne, 2001). Meanings which we experience as more authentic are covered by many layers of socialisation, expectations, examples and reinforcements from our society, and by our own fears and desires. Phenomenological practitioners can help clients to **unpeel** the inauthentic layers. However, we cannot know metaphysically whether an ultimate authenticity hides under these layers of inauthenticity. Therefore, clients may only aim at being authentic enough.

Several authors, such as Carl Rogers, have developed theories around why individuals may become incongruent and how clients can learn to become more authentic (Wyatt, 2001). For example, to become authentic, individuals may need to learn to listen to themselves, and trust that it is okay to listen to themselves behind all layers of inauthenticity. This depends on their self-worth. This can be defined as 'I am worthy of listening to (myself)'. Research shows that individuals who have not developed a strong sense of self-worth are more likely to experience life as less meaningful. They feel more alienated from their flow of meaningful experiences and instead follow others (Zika & Chamberlain, 1992). Research suggests, for example, that individuals with insecure attachments feel that they are less authentic and live less meaningful lives. These clients may benefit from focusing the treatment towards self-discovery: it is OK to listen to what I am experiencing, and I am worthy of being listened to (Langle, 2014).

Case example

An art expert asked me how he could become more authentic. I returned the question, How does he know whether a painting is authentic?, He answered that this is often not a black-or-white answer, but a likelihood: at its best, it is 'likely authentic'. You can make some estimations about the likelihood that a piece of art is authentic. For example, you look at the use of colours, how the brush is used, the type of canvas, the discolouring over the years, anachronisms in the scenery, altered frames, etc. The best we can get is a painting which is 'likely authentic', based on a number of indicators. However, even the highest likelihood could actually be inauthentic. For instance, many had difficulties revealing Tom Keating as an art forger. Sometimes, the difference between authentic and inauthentic becomes blurred, particularly when a forged painting becomes a beautiful piece of art: although this started with pretending as if, this became an authentic piece of art. At the end of our conversation, the expert decided to create a list of indicators for himself of when he is authentic.

Life satisfaction

Another aspect of experiencing a meaningful life is **life satisfaction**. That is, individuals can evaluate their life in general and feel to a greater or lesser extent satisfied by it. **Life satisfaction** can be measured according to different standards, ranging from being able to successfully fulfil your role in the teleological order and being successful in achieving functional goals to phenomenologically living a meaningful life (Chapters 1 and 2). For instance, individuals may be satisfied about the meanings that they have been actualising or that they could potentially actualise in future. They may also have a general lack of satisfaction, for example because they have been living their life according to what those around them find meaningful, and have been ignoring what they intuitively feel as more meaningful than their current life. To acknowledge that the mere presence of meaning does not necessarily imply life satisfaction, I usually define the aim of meaning-centred practices as 'living a meaningful *and satisfying* life'. Research suggests that experiencing life satisfaction is associated with positive well-being (Diener, Inglehardt & Tay, 2013).

3.7 Fundamental assumptions and life changes

In daily life, we can stay within the hot flow of meaning, because the context of our lives feels stable and we have no need to step outside our routine and reflect (Vos, 2016b). We believe life is predictable, we are in control of what happens, we are invulnerable, life is benevolent, and good things happen to good people and bad things to bad people (Janoff-Bulman, 1992). We stay in the flow as long as we believe such positive assumptions. For instance, we commit ourselves to our job or raising children, because we assume our life will not suddenly radically change and we will not suddenly lose control, for instance due to illness. If we were to believe that we may fall ill soon, we would possibly make different decisions and not commit to long-term goals that we may not achieve. Of course, when we reflect on it, we know that life is not totally predictable, and we are not completely in control and invulnerable. However, to be in a meaningful flow, we need to not pay too much attention to this reality, or pretend that we are oblivious to it. If we are too aware of everything bad that could hypothetically happen, we would not take risks or even dare to cross the street out of fear of being hit by a vehicle.

However, life events can make us suddenly aware of the reality that we were hiding behind our positive assumptions in daily life. These events challenge the status quo, such as the diagnosis of a life-threatening disease, the loss of a loved one or sudden unemployment. In the era of global mass media, collective events also often confront people with this reality. For example, 9/11 busted the myth that western countries are safe from terrorist attacks (Vos, 2006). The traumatic aspects of these events may not be the events themselves, but the shattering of our fundamental assumptions. We are confronted in an undeniable way with reality. The more directly physical the events are felt, the more individuals are unable to deny reality: it is impossible to believe in full control or invulnerability when we lose our job or our spine is crushed in a traffic accident. Individuals in such situations often express frustration, anger and ask reflective 'why' questions: 'Why did this happen to me?'

Individuals may try to deny the reality: I am not really ill; I have not been fired; this is only temporary; it will change. For example, a client focused obsessively on her work after she was diagnosed with cancer, which created a latent crisis; in the long term, this exhausted her and she developed a severe existential and meaning-centred crisis (Vos, 2016b). Research shows that denial can reduce psychological stress in the short term, but in the long term it depletes our psychological reserves and leads to low well-being (Chapter 9).

The central question that people ask after a life-changing event is: 'How can I get in the flow again of living a meaningful and satisfying life, despite these physical, psychological and existential limitations?' (Vos, 2016b). Individuals can answer in many ways, depending on how threatening they feel the challenges are and the resources they have to cope with these. Generally, people realistically change their assumptions about life, they adjust the meanings they were hoping to realise, or do both

(Park & Folkman, 1998). For example, a cancer diagnosis could lead an individual to conclude that she is not as invulnerable as she had thought, and she may lower her goals by replacing the aim of 'having the most successful career' with 'simply doing my job'. Thus individuals develop more realistic positive assumptions, such as 'I may not be totally in control of everything in life, but I can control how I respond to it', 'Although I may be vulnerable, I can still achieve small goals' and so on. This enables them to experience meaning and flow again.

The change process is often characterised by a period of frequently alternating between being inside the meaningful flow at some moments and being aware of the positive assumptions at other moments, and shifting their attention from the reality of life's limitations to meaningful activities. At one moment they may be crying and feel overwhelmed by their lack of control and vulnerability, and at other moments they seem happy and act as if they were in complete control and invulnerable. Over time, people seem to learn to switch flexibly between having life's limitations in the background to having them in the foreground of their attention (Vos, 2016b).

In conclusion, life-changing moments can lead to changes in specific meanings and people's general perspective on life (Table 3.3). Embracing such change seems to be psychologically beneficial; a study showed that individuals experience their life as more meaningful when they are asked to identify important decisions and events in life, and subsequently imagine how their life would have been without these events (Kray et al., 2012). However, some individuals may continue to feel overwhelmed by life's limitations, and may benefit from existential counselling (Chapter 9).

Table 3.3 Overview of possible changes after stressful life events (Vos, 2016b)

Changes in specific meanings ('micro-meanings', Section 2.5)
• A specific pre-event meaning becomes more valuable • A specific pre-event meaning feels less valuable • A specific pre-event goal is adjusted • A specific pre-event meaning become unattainable • A specific new meaning develops
Changes in general perspectives ('macro-meanings', Section 2.5)
• General priorities in life change • Experiencing life more intensively • Focusing more on authentic meanings (Section 2.6) • Such a narrow focus on life's limitations that other meanings are forgotten or denied • Hyper-reflection or hyper-intention (Section 3.6) • Experiencing meaninglessness (Section 3.2) • More realistic about life's limitations (Section 3.7) Existential moods, e.g. existential anxiety (Chapter 9)

Exercises

1. Identify meaning. Write down moments in your life that have felt meaningful to you (for example, use answers from previous chapters). Use the definition of 'meaning' in Section 3.1: to what extent are experiences about meaning or about other experiences? Which types of meaning can you identify (see Section 3.3)?

2. Identify meaninglessness. Find examples of meaninglessness in your clients, friends, family or yourself. Which type of meaninglessness is this? How would it be possible to combine this meaninglessness with meaningfulness?

3. Differentiate cold outer and hot inner experiences. Set your alarm clock for every hour. When it goes off, close your eyes and feel what you are experiencing in the moment. Rate on a scale from one, 'completely not', to seven, 'completely', how meaningful this moment feels. Rate how strong ('hot') your feelings are. Rate to what extent you are theorising. Rate to what extent you are in the here and now. After several days, examine whether there are relationships between these scores.

4. Differentiate inner and outer experiences. Nozick (1989) asks what it would be like if we were able to attach ourselves to a machine that would give us a feeling of happiness; this would not be true happiness, as we would miss the freedom and true meaning. Watch the movie The Matrix or read Brains in a Vat (Putnam, 1992). What do these tell you about the positive assumptions we have in daily life? How do we know which reality is true (being inside or outside the Matrix/Vat)? Would you take the red pill or the blue pill, and which character would you be in the movie? How does it feel to be inside the Matrix/Vat? How does it feel to be outside? Can we flexibly step outside and inside the Matrix/Vat; if so, how?

5. Identify crises. Have you ever experienced a crisis in life or know someone who has? What were the symptoms and which type of crisis was it? Was there a latent phase, and if so, what were the latent signs? Why did the crisis become manifest? If there were multiple crises at the same time, how did these different crises relate to each other?

6. Differentiate happiness and meaning. What is more important to you: living a happy life or a meaningful life? Why? Find examples of when you felt meaningful but not happy, and moments when you felt happy but not meaningful. Can happiness be manipulated, for instance with drugs or alcohol? Can meaning be manipulated?

7. Identify resilience. Think about moments of small or large change in your life. How did this disrupt the way how you were living daily life? How did you feel initially? How did you respond? Did you ask meaning-related questions? How threatening did the situation feel? What resources helped you through this period? What changes in specific meanings or general perspectives did you experience? What have you learned about life?

8. **World-assumptions** exercise. Try this three-chairs, as if exercise which often works well with clients who have difficulty coping with life changes due to black-or-white thinking. For example, sit on the chair to the left, close your eyes, and imagine you are completely in control, invulnerable, life is good, etc. How do you feel, what activities do you do in daily life, what do you achieve, etc.? Now sit on the chair to the right, and repeat the exercise while imagining you lack all control, are completely vulnerable, etc. Finally, sit on the middle chair, and feel what it is like to sit between both extremes. How does life feel here? What activities do you do and achieve here, etc.? Which chair do you prefer? Have you had moments in life where you felt you can stand up from a chair and move to another one? What do you need to move more freely between chairs or sit more often on the middle one?

Key points

➤ Meaning has been defined as the combination ('package deal') of motivation, situational commitment, values, understanding, worthiness and self-regulation.

➤ Different types of meaninglessness have been defined: absurdity, guilt, lack of meaning, reductionist meaning, existential indifference, existential emptiness/vacuum, hopelessness and helplessness.

➤ Five types of meaning have been described (**meaning quintet**): materialistic-hedonic, self-oriented, social, larger and existential-philosophical meanings.

➤ The development of meaning has been sketched as negotiating between what individuals must (not), can (not) and (do not) want in life. Individuals may experience free will within the bandwidth of social expectations and the possibilities and limitations in life; over time, they could try to stretch this bandwidth slightly.

➤ Individuals can examine meaning in their life from a cold outer perspective, for instance by theorising, lack of awareness, living on automatic pilot, following others, hyper-reflection or experiencing crisis.

➤ When individuals are inside their experience of living a meaningful life, they may experience flow, mindfulness, peak experience, happiness, satisfaction with life and authenticity.

➤ Individuals can stay in their flow thanks to assuming they are in control, invulnerable and so on. Negative life events could shatter these positive assumptions, and consequently individuals may need to change their specific meanings or general perspective on life.

4

Working with Meaning

4.1 A brief history of meaning-centred practices

Early history

Asking for individual support with our personal questions about meaning is a modern western invention (Chapters 1 and 2). Until the Middle Ages, most individuals seemed to fit into a pregiven societal-cosmic-divine order which determined both their position in society and their personal meaning. If they did receive advice, it was from philosophers, the clergy and spiritual leaders, who referred them to this order. This changed during the sixteenth century, with the spread of scepticism and individualisation. Individuals started to define their own meaning, and with this a market emerged for meaning-centred practitioners. Around the beginning of the twentieth century, the meaning-centred revolution accelerated, as individuals began to ask more often for individual support from professionals. The discipline of psychology was born. Simultaneously, the role of priests was transforming from offering penance and general guidelines for life to listening and advising as pastoral care workers (Evans, 2000). Meanwhile, the academic discipline of philosophy developed an identity crisis as it became popularised and many individuals became homegrown philosophers (see Sloterdijk, 2014).

At the start of psychology as a profession, typically meaning was not explicitly addressed in the consultation room, as meaning was considered irrelevant, a psychopathological symptom, defence mechanism or cognitive bias (Vos, 2016a). However, these **reductionist** practitioners were opposed by psychologists and psychiatrists such as William James, Karl Jaspers and Alfred Adler who revealed how meaning-centred experiences are essential to the psychological realm. Adler showed how the experience of meaning is engrained in our personality and fulfils crucial functions in our psychological development. Karl Jaspers (1919) wrote that meaning is particularly important in situations of suffering, pain or death, which he called 'boundary situations in life'. At such inevitable crossroads, we can choose to sink into despair and resignation or take a leap of faith towards 'transcendence', that is, reaching beyond the reality of the here and now to 'what can be' and 'what ought to be' (Lukas, 2004), and thus transcending the situation in space and time, accepting our freedom to decide and developing a larger, more authentic and meaningful perspective on life (Vos, 2016a).

Viktor Frankl

Self-transcendence was also at the heart of the work of the psychiatrist Frankl. He wrote a paradigm-shifting book about his experiences as an inmate and psychiatrist in a Nazi concentration camp, originally entitled *Saying Yes to Life in Spite of Everything,* which later became known as *Man's Search for Meaning* (1948/1985). He wrote that inmates' ability to identify meaning and imagine the future affected their longevity. Meaning can be found in every moment of living, and life never ceases to have meaning, even in suffering and death. Frankl developed the idea from his experiences that prisoners' psychological reactions are not solely the result of his or her life situation, but also from their freedom of choice, which they always have, even in severe suffering. He believed that every individual has the freedom in every situation to modulate their inner attitude, similar to what Jaspers described as the inner leap of faith from despair and resignation towards experiencing a meaning that transcends the situation. Ultimately, life means a responsibility to take the initiative in finding the right answer to its problems and fulfilling the tasks which it constantly sets for each individual. Everyone is driven primarily by a striving to experience meaning and this sense of meaning enables us to overcome painful experiences. Thus, life always offers potential meaning that transcends the here and now, even in the most dehumanising and painful moments (Vos, 2016a).

Frankl's work was based on three central pillars: the assumption that all individuals have an inner striving towards meaning ('will to meaning'); that everyone is always free to take a stance on how they respond to any condition in life ('freedom of will'); and that every situation has the potential of being meaningful, even in times of the tragic triad of suffering, guilt and death (Lukas, 2014). Frankl's practices have often focused on three main techniques: **de-reflection, modulation of attitudes** and **paradoxical intention** (Chapters 6–9). Frankl called his new non-reductionist therapeutic approach 'logotherapy' (derived from the ancient Greek word 'logos', which may be translated as word, meaning or wisdom) and 'existential analysis'.

Frankl's legacy

Many practitioners have further developed Frankl's work, which evolved in different directions (Correia et al., 2014). Chapters 5–9 will describe the wide range of the most frequently mentioned techniques. Thus Frankl's legacy has been broad, although logotherapy has not developed into one unified therapeutic school (Raskob, 2005). This may be explained by Frankl's belief that logotherapy is a 'supplement rather than a substitute for psychotherapy' (1948/1986, p. xii), and that therapies should not be led by 'gurus' (Frankl, 1969/2002).

Frankl's anthropology also centres around the uniqueness of individual clients, which means that treatments are tailored to individual clients and therefore it has been argued that 'a standardised guide would be more hindrance than help' (Lukas, 1986/2014, p. 129). Consequently, meaning-centred therapies have seen little standardisation and systematic research until recently. This has created the scientifically unsatisfactory situation that, despite the existence of hundreds of training institutions and tens of thousands of meaning-centred practitioners worldwide, practices are used that have not been validated in accordance with current academic standards (Vos, 2016a). This lack of validation may explain the marginal role that meaning-centred practices usually play in public health care. Therefore, despite ideological arguments against standardisation and trials, pragmatic reasons may justify rigorous outcome studies (Vos et al., 2015).

Since the turn of the millennium, there has been an exponential growth in the number of meaning-centred trials (Vos & Vitali, 2018). The way to this research has been opened up by an impressive body of studies validating the core clinical, aetiological and therapeutic assumptions of meaning-centred practices: meaning is no longer a disputed phenomenon, but a well-established measurable psychological experience (Chapter 3).

The surge in meaning research may also be a response to the dominant focus on functional meanings ('McMeanings') in modern western countries, which may lead to a structural lack of meaning and deep happiness in some clients, which some authors have dubbed a chronic mental health crisis in the west (Section 1.4). There seems to be a growing dissatisfaction with standard mental health care, as mainstream approaches do not systematically address these underlying meaning-centred causes. Popular treatments such as cognitive behavioural therapy seem to focus more on coping with negative symptoms, such as anxiety and depression, and are often based on a medical model that does not appear to take into account the totality of the client's lived experience. In response to this medical approach, the movement of positive psychology has been booming in the last few decades, and aims at transforming mental health care from merely treating mental illness to including positive psychological experiences such as meaning (Seligman et al., 2005). Meaning is promoted as essential to clients' personal recovery: 'recovery is about building a meaningful and satisfying life, as defined by the person themselves, whether or not there are ongoing or recurring symptoms or problems' (Andresen, Oades & Caputi, 2011, p. 2). Thus, although Frankl's initial formulation of logotherapy and existential analysis may not be practised very widely, many researchers and practitioners follow in his footsteps with their focus on meaning.

4.2 Meaning as a common therapeutic factor

Franklian meaning-centred practitioners do not have a monopoly on helping clients to live a meaningful life. Rather, a systematic literature (Vos, 2018a) reveals a meaning-centred continuum, ranging from treatments which explicitly and systematically address meaning as the primary aim and method, to therapies which implicitly address meaning as one of multiple aims and methods. Explicit systematic primary meaning-centred practices explicitly address meaning within a systematic method as the primary focus of the practice, and include, for example, classical logotherapy, general meaning-centred therapies and logo-analysis, and key authors such as Viktor Frankl, Elisabeth Lukas, Joseph Fabry and Alfried Langle. Explicit systematic secondary meaning-centred practices explicitly and systematically address meaning as one core aspect of the intervention, alongside other aims and processes, such as Acceptance and Commitment Therapy, dignity therapy and narrative therapies. Implicit non-systematic secondary meaning-centred practices address meaning implicitly as one of its multiple outcomes or processes, and not always with a systematic method such as in the case of transactional analysis, schema therapy, hope therapy and motivational interviewing. Explicit systematic meaning-centred non-therapeutic practices address meaning not via a therapeutic approach, but in an explicit and often systematic way, such as pastoral care, life coaching, philosophical counselling and meaning in life education.

Thus many treatments directly address meaning in life. It may even be argued that all treatments are attempts to reconstruct meaning (see Neimeyer, 2010) and help clients to live a meaningful life despite their problems (Vos, 2018a). For example, at face value, behavioural therapy may appear to reject meaning-centred themes, but it may also be interpreted as a systematic way of understanding the meanings reflected in the client's behaviour, leading authors in the field of behaviourism to confirm that existential themes need to be addressed (Van Bruggen & Vos, 2014).

There are strong arguments supporting the hypothesis that addressing meaning in life is a common factor in all effective treatments (Vos, 2017b). For example, it has been argued that individuals benefit from any type of treatment, because asking for professional help is in itself meaningful: clients engage in the meaningful ritual of frequent sessions and interaction with a professional; the expectation of meaningful change is created; and practitioners offer meaningful explanations for their problems. Many clients also seem to ask for help because of underlying meaning-related problems, particularly in transition moments in life (Chapter 3). It seems a tautology that clients who request psychological support have difficulties in living a meaningful life: either the psychological problems make it more difficult to fulfil their usual meanings in life, or the lack of meaning could lead to hyper-reflection and worry. Many clients do not seem to expect a cure for their mental health problems, but want to be able to live a meaningful and satisfying life despite their problems (Andresen, Oades & Caputi, 2003, 2011). Research also indicates that not all long-term psychological problems can be structurally solved, but clients can learn to live with these limitations (Park & Folkman, 1997; Folkman, 2008; Park, 2010; Vos, 2016b). They do not change simply because they follow the practitioner's instructions, but because they are motivated to change: change is meaningful (Prochaska & Vlicer, 2009; Lundahl et al., 2013). Their motivation for change can be influenced by their contact with the professional. As will be elaborated in Chapter 7, the relationship between client and practitioner has a social meaning to the client, and is particularly meaningful when both agree about the goals and method of treatment. The deeper their relationship, the deeper the topics that may be discussed, and vice versa.

Thus all effective treatments include meaningful processes for clients. Consequently, treatments become more effective when they explicitly and systematically address meaning in life. A review of 392 clinical trials in 38,808 clients revealed that those treatments which explicitly and systematically address meaning have greater effects on psychological well-being and quality of life than treatments that do not. Clients improve more with these explicit systematic meaning-centred treatments thanks to the improvement in their meaning-making skills (Vos, 2018a,b).

Although all treatments may provide some meaning to clients, the more explicit and systematic practitioners help clients to find meaning, the more effective the treatments become. The meaning-centred practices in this book differ from other practices which may to some extent address meaning. (For the remainder of this book the term 'meaning-centred practices' refers to these explicit systematic meaning-centred treatments.)

First, their primary (or sole) aim is to improve the client's ability to live a meaningful and satisfying life despite problems. Second, these meaning-centred practices explicitly address meaning; other approaches may address this only implicitly. Third, meaning is addressed in a systematic way, and the practitioner does not simply address meaning once or only certain aspects that feel relevant to the individual practitioner. Meaning-centred practitioners try to explore the widest range possible of what clients may experience as meaningful, and not only a brief checklist or a practitioner-imposed selection of meanings. The system described in this book is comprehensive and evidence-based. Fourth, the meaning-centred practices are non-reductionist (Chapter 2), as opposed to several psychological approaches that seem to have a reductionist sceptical approach towards meaning. Clients are not forced to randomly find any meaning, like McMeanings, for instance by ticking boxes in a list with values. In contrast, meaning-centred therapists explore what feels meaningful for clients. Fifth, in contrast to some religious-spiritual and teleological approaches, meaning is addressed in a relatively neutral and sceptical way (Chapter 2). Sixth, although there is a phenomenological approach when clients explore what they experience as meaningful, this does not imply that the practices are unstructured: structured meaning-centred practices are the most effective (Section 4.3). Finally, meaning-centred practitioners integrate a wide range of evidence-based skills, so that they can help different client populations (Part 2). It is the combination of these components that seems to make meaning-centred practices effective; as restaurant chefs say, it is not single ingredients by themselves but their combination that creates a tasty meal.

4.3 Effectiveness of meaning-centred practices

What effects do meaning-centred practices have on clients? A systematic literature review and meta-analysis examined 60 clinical trials published in 11 languages, with a total of 3,713 participants (Vos & Vitali, 2018). Different types of meaning-centred treatments were included across different populations, including those with chronic physical illness, transition moments in life and clients with primary psychological problems. The effects of the treatment were compared with control groups considered gold standard in the field, such as cognitive behavioural therapy.

Overall effects. Immediately after the last session and at follow-up, meaning-centred treatments create significantly large improvements in the client's quality of life and psychological well-being. Compared to other treatments in the control groups, meaning-centred therapies also have a greater effect on the client's quality of life and psychological well-being, both immediately and at follow-up. The improvements in quality of life included general quality of life, meaning in life, hope and optimism, self-efficacy and social well-being. The psychological improvements included a reduction in anxiety, depression and existential anxiety. Ten trials also included physical outcomes in physically ill populations, showing moderate to large improvements in the client's self-reported and biological well-being (Vos, 2016b). These results confirm that explicitly addressing meaning in a systematic way improves the client's quality of life, psychological stress and physical well-being.

Variation. The effects of meaning-centred practices are not influenced by study characteristics. For example, all types of meaning-centred practice are equally effective. Therefore, this book focuses on the common techniques and skills of all treatments and does not promote one specific type of treatment over another. The practices were also equally effective across all populations; thus meaning-centred therapy can be recommended for any type of client, regardless of country, religion, socio-demographic background, educational level or gender.

Practitioners' skills. Although overall all types of meaning-centred treatments had relatively similar outcomes, using specific practitioners' skills made the treatments slightly more effective. That is, **thematic analyses** showed that the 60 clinical trials in this meta-analysis used 39 common **practitioners' skills** (Vos, 2016). Although all 39 skills contributed to the overall effectiveness, some resulted in significantly greater improvements in clients' well-being. Meaning-centred practices had greater effects when these did not include religious-spiritual formulations, were structured, explicitly stimulated clients to set and experiment with achievable goals in daily life, used mindfulness exercises, explicitly discussed one type of meaning per session, addressed self-worth, discussed existential limitations, mentioned the coherence of time, and focused on creating a positive therapeutic relationship. These findings suggest that practitioners should use these 39 skills, and particularly these significant skills. Part 2 of this book explains each of these 39 skills, and provides additional empirical evidence for the effectiveness of each one. Part 3 offers a treatment manual based on these skills.

Number of meanings. Within each of the 60 trials, the number of meanings that was systematically addressed in the treatment was calculated. This showed that the more types of meaning were discussed, the greater the effects of the meaning-centred practice were on both quality of life and psychological stress (Vos, 2017). This suggests that meaning-centred practices should include the largest number of types of meaning as possible, as identified in the **meaning quintet** (Section 3.3), rather than the

Franklian meaning triad. Therefore, the treatment manual in Part 3 is developed around this quintet.

Session structure. The mean number of sessions was 8.65 (Standard Deviation = 3.3). The average structure of the included trials was identified via **thematic analyses** (Vos, 2016a). The session structure of most treatments was so similar that it was impossible to test which structure was the most effective. This average session structure is the basis of Part 3.

Most practices started with an assessment and introduction phase. This focuses on understanding the facts of the client's life situation, problems and strengths, exploring hopes and expectations, exploring the relevance and history of meaning for the client, and building a constructive therapeutic working alliance. Often, acute suffering and recent life events are explored, such as the experience of having a life-threatening physical disease and how life has changed because of this. This exploration of the recent history frequently focuses on grieving over lost meanings or a lost meaning potential, and clients are invited to explore how they could experience meaning despite the loss and thus transcend their suffering in the current life situation. Several manuals position the client's current experience of suffering and loss within the broader context of their life history, for instance via an autobiographic life review, and clients may be asked to describe what they experienced as meaningful in the past and how they overcame previous hardships.

The meaning-exploration phase is the backbone of many manuals and consists of systematically exploring clients' values and meaning potential. In this phase, meaning-specific and existential therapeutic skills are used. Typically, one session is spent on each group of values from the Franklian **meaning triad** (one session on the value of experiencing, one on productivity-creativity and one on attitude modulation and clients phenomenologically explore their experiences, their attitudes and opportunities for creativity and productivity for each type of meaning), although it may be advisable to replace this with the **meaning quintet**. Clients are guided in their explorations of what they experience as valuable and meaningful via practical exercises and direct questions or structured techniques.

The evaluation and application phase aims to evaluate the values and potential meanings that were explored in previous sessions and apply these to everyday life. Clients are, for instance, invited to create an intuitive hierarchy of values and meanings – for example, by drawing a mountain and putting different meanings/values at different heights, reflecting differences in value and authenticity. This evaluation is followed by assessing to what extent the client already lives their life according to this hierarchy and what may need to change in their lives to recreate the mountain range exercise in their daily lives. Subsequently, clients are encouraged to translate this into concrete goals and plans and experiment with this. The following sessions evaluate these experiments and, if necessary, adjust aims and methods and create long-term commitments. In this phase, clients are often confronted, with limitations in life, such as meanings that are difficult or impossible to actualise; in response to this, practitioners use their existential skills to help the client explore and tolerate imperfections, tensions and paradoxes in life, while stimulating pragmatic problem-solving. The final session often explores existential feelings of termination, autonomy and being responsible for their own life (see Lukas, 1984/2014).

Average session. It was impossible to examine which structure of an average treatment session was the most effective, as either this was not explicitly discussed in the publications or the structure was too similar. An average session starts with an emotional check-in, and a discussion about the previous session and homework. The aim of this is to understand any developments in life since the last session, and to connect with the emotional process and progress of the client. This is often followed by explicit psycho-education on the theory and practice of a central topic of the session. Often, a guided exercise is performed to help clients apply the theory to their own lives, for instance by searching for examples of how the theory manifests in their lives. Some practitioners introduce these exercises with a guided mindfulness exercise to help clients connect with the topic not only on an intellectual level, but also on an experiential-embodied level. The guided exercise is sometimes followed by identifying which examples in their daily life feel most valuable and authentic. This sometimes leads to an evaluation and a decision regarding questions such as 'What do I want to change in my life?', 'What can I realistically change?', 'What do I need to accept that cannot be changed?', and 'How can I cope with this situation in a positive way?' These questions sometimes lead to the decision to change something in one's life, to set goals and to make an action plan. Most sessions end with homework and an evaluation. A similar structure is used in Part 3.

Professional background. All meaning-centred practitioners seemed equally effective. No significant effects were found for different professional backgrounds, possibly because all practitioners had the relevant educational background, such as psychological counselling, psychotherapy, psychiatry or nursing, and had multiple years of clinical experience. Everyone also received meaning-centred training and supervision/intervision, and engaged in **self-reflection/reflexive** practices. Therefore, based on these evidence-based trials, it may be advisable to determine the eligibility of future practitioners on an individual basis, following the formula: relevant educational background + years of experience + skills + knowledge + training + supervision + self-reflection/reflexivity.

4.4 The relevance of meaning

The meta-analysis shows that the effects are greater than those of alternative psychological treatments in the control groups. The extent of the overall effect seems similar to or better than that of other widespread treatments such as cognitive behavioural therapy (Roth & Fonagy, 2013). Meaning-centred therapy also works effectively across different populations. However, the way in which clinical trials have been designed may have created selective samples. As in other research studies, there must have been a self-selection by clients who were motivated to participate in this trial. That is, the assessment procedure was part of the research procedure and not of the therapy process, so that it remains unclear how many clients enrolled on the treatment because meaning-centred therapy was relevant for them. However, the assessment may be regarded as part of the treatment (see Chapter 5). It may be argued that meaning-centred therapy must be relevant to clients, as some individuals have different needs at different stages in their life: one size may not fit all (see Section 3.4). Therefore it is crucial to carry out a good meaning-centred assessment to assess the needs and the therapeutic tasks for a specific individual.

With which clients should practitioners explicitly and systematically address meaning? From the statistical perspective, the answer would be, always – as meaning-centred practices are equally effective across different populations. From a clinical perspective, more specific recommendations could be provided. Over the years, practitioners have offered many suggestions about who needs professional meaning-centred help. These suggestions are mainly based on personal clinical experience and have relatively little empirical validation (Raskob, 2007; Lukas, 2009). Thus there is little systematic evidence to answer this question. However, Chapter 3 provided an overview of clinical-aetiological assumptions of meaning-centred practices. Several recommendations may be deduced from this.

First, individuals may explicitly ask questions about their motivation, values, situational commitment, understanding, self-worth and regulation of meaning (Section 3.1). For example, clients may lack a sense of competence and **self-efficacy**, which is the extent to which they believe in their own ability to do what is needed in the current situation to achieve meaning (Steger et al., 2008).

Second, individuals may have difficulties living a meaningful life in the face of life's meaninglessness (Section 3.2).

Third, individuals may have difficulties in experiencing certain **types of meaning**. For example, they may not be reaching important life goals – for instance, they may be failing in their career (Kosine, Steger & Duncan, 2008; Steger & Dik, 2009). That is, they may feel they are not attaining what they find important in life (**frustrated will to meaning**; **existential vacuum**; see Dyck, 1987; Reker, Peacock & Wong, 1987; Krause, 2004; Raskob, 2007). Individuals may have problems balancing the various types of meaning, or have conflicting goals, such as balancing their work and private life (Bonebright, Clay & Ankemann, 2015). Individuals may also be focusing on only a small number of important meanings in life (**pyramidal meaning system**); for instance, in modern western societies many individuals mainly focus on their career and neglect other possible meanings in life (see Verhaeghe, 2014). It may also be that individuals have too many equally important meanings (**broad meaning system**), and consequently do not know which option to choose. Practitioners may help clients to develop a parallel value system in which there a few important values – for example, four or five – which provides a focus and offers clients flexibility when one value becomes lost or unattainable (Lukas, 2014). Clients may also be focusing too much on materialistic-hedonic and self-oriented meanings, which are known to be less satisfying and psychologically beneficial in the long-term (Section 3.3). In particular, social meanings have proved important for long-term well-being, and individuals may feel dissatisfied about life due to social problems (Steger et al., 2008; Chao & Kesebir, 2013; Lambert et al., 2013). Sloterdijk (2014) also argued that individuals may ask meaning-centred questions because all humans strive to improve themselves, even if they are already experiencing a basic level of meaningfulness. Individuals may also be struggling with existential-philosophical questions, which will be addressed in Chapter 9.

Fourth, clients may have developed meanings which are too one-sidedly focused on what they must (not), can(not) or (do not) want in life: they have blind spots or do not know how to negotiate between these (Section 3.4).

Fifth, individuals could be outside their stream of meaningful experiences, for instance because they are reflecting too much. This is most explicit when they ask questions about life or experience a crisis (Section 3.5).

Sixth, they may have difficulty immersing themselves inside the hot stream of meaningful experiences and lack flow, mindfulness, peak experience, happiness, life satisfaction and authenticity (Section 3.6).

Finally, individuals may have difficulty accepting and coping with life changes, as they may need to change specific meanings or their general life perspective (Section 3.7). Meaning functions as an important source of resilience in times of stress (Vos, 2016b). For example, traditional psychotherapies only have small effects in individuals with a chronic or life-threatening physical disease, most likely because these treatments do not systematically address the meaning-centred concerns; in contrast, meaning-centred therapies have substantial effects in physically ill patients (Vos, 2016b).

Furthermore, it may be argued that everyone can benefit from improving their skills in living a meaningful life, as numerous studies show that perceiving life as meaningful is moderately to strongly correlated with higher quality of life, lower levels of psychological stress and better physical well-being (e.g. Ryff et al., 2004, 2006; Brandstätter et al., 2012; Steger, 2012; Roepke et al., 2014). Formulated the other way round, a lower sense of meaning is correlated with higher stress levels and psychopathology, such as depression and anxiety. Thus all clients may psychologically benefit from meaning-centred practices. Clinical trials also confirm that meaning-centred practices are effective across many populations (Chapter 4). Practitioners need to assess the relevance of meaning for clients (Chapter 6).

A specific example is suicidal ideation. Research suggests a relationship between a low sense of meaning on the one hand and thoughts, intentions, plans and attempts to commit suicide on the other hand (Edwards & Holden, 2001). This relationship seems to be a tautology, as suicide is about losing 'a reason to live', that is, a lack of meaning and having lost hope in the possibility of change (**demoralisation**). Cross-sectional studies show that when individuals are frustrated in their meanings, such as in the case of chronic or life-threatening illness, they are more likely to consider suicide (Vos, 2016b). Thus suicidal ideation is associated with low meaning, but does this also mean that suicidal clients should receive treatment about meaning? Is the lack of meaning an underlying cause of suicidality? Or is a lack of meaning the result or symptom of suicidality? International suicide guidelines suggest not to primarily treat meaning-centred questions, but focus instead on cognitive behavioural problems such as worrying and biased thought patterns. They suggest that questions about meaning should be seen as the consequence of such cognitive behavioural issues, and meaning should only be addressed when these issues have first been treated (Jacobs et al., 2010). However, cognitive behavioural treatments are not always successful, and seem to create an artificial distinction between cognitive behavioural functioning and meaning (**form/content fallacy**). A danger of such treatments is increased **hyper-reflection** and **hyper-intention**, as cognitive behavioural treatments stimulate clients to focus even more on themselves and their problems. In contrast, meaning-centred treatments stimulate **de-reflection** and **self-transcendence**. This also takes their subjective request for help – questions about meaning – seriously, which may increase their motivation and adherence to treatment. Several trials show that focusing on meaning reduces suicidal ideation, demoralisation and the wish for hastened death (Vos & Vitali, 2018). Thus suicidal clients may benefit from addressing

meaning and not increasing **hyper-reflection** and **hyper-intention**, particularly when other treatments have failed.

4.5 Implications for health care and insurance policies

Meaning-centred practices are not structurally included in national
health care guidelines or health insurance policies. The only exception
is the governmental funding of Meaning in Life Education in Taiwan,
and agreements between individual practitioners and health insurance
providers. This book is the first publication that systematically reviews
the evidence base of meaning-centred treatments, and proposes a treatment manual, which may be regarded as the common denominator of
all effective trials. The empirical support may be compared with the most
frequently funded treatments, such as cognitive behavioural therapy (Vos,
2016a–c; Vos & Vitali, 2018). Therefore, health care policy makers and
insurers are advised to include meaning-centred practices. This section
summarises the main arguments discussed in this book.

➢ Meaning-centred practices significantly improve the quality of life,
  psychological and physical well-being of clients in any population and
  country (Section 4.3).

➢ Meaning is relevant for many clients (Section 4.4), and many clients explicitly ask for support with meaning-centred questions
  (Section 4.2). One example is individuals with a chronic or life-
  threatening physical disease, most of whom ask meaning-centred
  questions. Possibly owing to ignoring meaning-centred questions,
  usual care practices often have relatively few effects in this population,
  while meaning-centred therapies show substantial effects (Vos, 2016b).

➢ Meaning-centred practices offer what the conceptual treatment model
  promises: greatly improving the sense of meaning and psychological
  stress levels thanks to improving the client's meaning-centred skills
  (Section 4.3).

➢ Health care policies and insurance providers may include any type of
  meaning-centred practices, as all are equally effective (Section 4.3).
  It is recommended to mainly include practices which include the session structure, a wide range of meanings and the **practitioners' skills**
  discussed in Section 4.3.

➢ Empirical research confirms the clinical-aetiological model underlying
  meaning-centred practices (Chapter 3). Meaning is a valid and reliable

psychological phenomenon, which has been shown to correlate to but be distinct from other psychological experiences. Research shows that most humans strive and crave for meaning. A perceived sense of meaning is related to greater psychological well-being, less psychopathology and better physical well-being, both in the short and long term. Individuals with meaning-centred coping skills cope better with changes and threats in life, such as a diagnosis of a chronic or life-threatening disease, psychotrauma or bereavement. Phenomenological studies indicate that individuals experience a hierarchy in their meanings: they find experiences more meaningful than others. There is some evidence that authentic, social and higher oriented meanings are more beneficial for an individual's well-being than materialistic and hedonic meanings.

➤ Meaning can be addressed in a pragmatic and down-to-earth way, and not only in philosophical or spiritual-religious ways (Chapters 1 and 2). A phenomenological approach can be used to tailor the therapy to the individual and avoid imposing the practitioner's opinion.

➤ Working with meaning is a common factor to many effective treatments (Section 4.2; Vos, 2018b).

➤ Meaning-centred practices are likely to be cost-effective, as shown in one study (Spek et al., 2016). The average number of sessions is eight, which is relatively few (Section 4.3).

➤ Meaning-centred practices can be easily taught, for instance through this book.

Key points

➤ Meaning-centred practitioners help clients in explicit and systematic ways to live a meaningful and satisfying life despite life's challenges. Viktor Frankl was one of the founders of this approach, which has been further developed by many others.

➤ All effective treatments (also non-meaning-centred) implicitly or explicitly address meaning, and help clients to live a more meaningful life despite their problems. Clients improve thanks to their improvement in meaning-centred skills.

➤ A meaning-centred continuum of treatments can be formulated, ranging from treatments explicitly and systematically addressing meaning as primary aim and method, to treatments implicitly addressing meaning as one of multiple aims and methods. Explicit systematic meaning-centred treatments are the most effective.

➤ Meaning-centred practices largely improve quality of life, psychological stress and the physical well-being of clients.

➤ All types of meaning-centred practices are equally effective across different populations. Treatments have significantly greater effects when these exclude religious-spiritual formulations, are structured, explicitly stimulate clients to set and experiment with achievable goals in daily life, use mindfulness exercises, explicitly discuss one type of meaning per session, address self-worth, discuss existential limitations, mention the coherence of time, and focus on creating a positive therapeutic relationship. The more types of meaning are addressed, the greater the effects.

➤ Practitioners may consider addressing meaning when clients report meaning-centred questions, meaninglessness, difficulties in experiencing different types of meaning, developmental problems, difficulties in immersing themselves in the flow of meaningful experiences, or problems coping with life changes. In general, individuals may benefit from improving meaning-centred skills, particularly when they report suicidal ideation.

➤ On the basis of the research literature, this book provides an overview of: the scientific foundations on which effective meaning-centred practices are based (Part 1); the skills that meaning-centred practices have in common and that are further supported by empirical evidence for their empirical effectiveness (Part 2); and a treatment manual that uses the common skills and structure of these previous meaning-centred practices and which has shown effective in several trials (Part 3). Thus this book offers the common denominator of evidence-based meaning-centred practices. Introductions and handbooks about each individual type of meaning-centred practice can be found elsewhere (see overview on the companion website).

PART 2
Practical Foundations: Practitioner Skills

5

Meaning-Centred Assessment Skills

5.1 General principles of assessment

Assessment skills are about evaluating the life situation, needs, preferences and capacities of clients. On this basis, the client and practitioner develop a meaning-centred treatment plan. Several research studies show that psychological treatments are more effective when starting with such assessments and tailoring treatment to the client (Schulte, 1996; Eifert et al., 1997). For instance, treatment is more effective when the client and practitioner have assessed and agreed on the treatment goals and the methods to achieve these goals (Tryon & Winograd, 2011).

Despite these general benefits, few meaning-centred practitioners have explicated the assessment process. Often, assessment is only described as part of scientific research and not of the treatment; thus there is an assessment, but this is not expanded upon. Therefore, the next section describes – and somewhat extends – the small number of assessment skills (Lukas, 2004). In contrast with treatments such as cognitive behavioural therapy, meaning-centred practitioners usually do not test a specific diagnostic or clinical-aetiological model, but explore the general relevance of meaning from the client's subjective lived experience. Chapter 11 provides an example assessment session.

5.2 Assessment skills

1. *Assessing the request for support*

Phenomenological. The assessment process is usually non-reductionist and phenomenological in nature (Chapter 2). This means that the totality of the client's lived experience is not entirely reduced to a diagnostic label. Any collected information is regarded as one possible way in which the client tries to make sense of the current life situation, and not as a fixed label. The practitioner tries to empathically understand the client's perspective. This starts, for example, by asking clients to describe in their own words why they asked for support, what made them ask for it specifically at this moment, how their concerns have developed over time, and what limits and helps them in life. Chapter 8 will elaborate how a phenomenological examination of the client's request for support could reveal the direction of the treatment. For example, a general sense of discontent or dissatisfaction in life may suggest an implicit understanding that something needs to change.

Holistic. Essential to all meaning-centred practices is the focus on the totality of the client's lived experiences, which embraces the somatic, psychological and spiritual (Lukas, 1994), and the widest range of meanings possible (Section 3.4). For example, clients may be asked to describe how they experience materialistic-hedonic meanings in their life and which problems they experience regarding this, and similar questions could be asked about self-oriented, social, broader and existential-philosophical meanings. Of course, clients have not received any psycho-education on the types of meaning yet, but an initial assessment may reveal relevant information.

Pathoplastics (coping with problems). Frankl suggested that 'beyond the pathogenesis, there is a pathoplastic factor consisting on how the person responds to the illness' (Marshall & Marshall, 2012, p. 17). That is, what plasticity or flexibility hides behind their problems? Practitioners should not only assess what clients experience as problematic in their life and what their therapy goals would be; they should also examine what the client has done to cope with this problem, what has helped and what did not. Ultimately, this is about exploring what helped clients get through a bad day despite their problems. What keeps an individual going in life? What meanings are implicitly present in the fact that a client has not committed suicide? When clients suggest suicidal ideation, why have they not killed themselves yet: what keeps them alive?

Meaning of the request for help. It may also be beneficial to examine what meaning the treatment could have for the client. To establish this, the client could be explicitly asked what the goals for therapy are, and write these down, for instance on a Goal Assessment Form (Cooper & Mearns, 2014; see page 295). Simultaneously, it is recommended that practitioners are aware of any implicit meanings. What does the client unconsciously try to get from the practitioner? Ultimate answers to their quest for meaning? Developing skills to cope with challenging life situations? A meaningful relationship to break their loneliness?

2. *Immediate needs*

Specific life situation. All meaning-centred concerns are embedded in the wider context of the individual's social, professional, physical and individual life. Therefore, clients are asked to briefly describe their general life situation. What made them specifically ask for support now? Are there any specific events or situations in life which triggered the concerns? What can clients do (not do) and what must they do (not do) in their current life situation? (Section 3.4).

Immediate needs and other support. Meaning-centred practices do not have a monopoly on solving client's problems. Therefore, practitioners should explore other kinds of practical, social and psychological resources which clients can use to cope with problems. What would meaning-centred practices add to these? Practitioners should also assess whether there are other more urgent concerns that need to be addressed before the client can work with meaning. For example, clients could be referred to a medical doctor in the case of an untreated somatic disease, or to a social worker to address concerns in their practical life situation. In some cases, clients may want to ask in the first place for support from their friends and family before the meaning-centred treatment commences.

3. *Meaning-centred case formulation*

Definition. Many health services expect practitioners to develop a case formulation, as research suggests that treatments are more effective when these are based on such a formulation (Page & Stritzke, 2006; Kendjelic & Eells, 2007). Case formulations are used to examine which treatment would be suited to the client, and what effects can be expected. When any problems arise in the treatment process, the initial case formulation may be used as a guide to resolving them (Teachman & Clerkin, 201). Meaning-centred therapists often develop a non-systematic case formulation, which risks missing out important aspects. Our meta-analyses showed that the clearer the inclusion criteria or case formulation are, the more effective the meaning-centred practices (Vos & Vitali, 2018). A good case formulation has been defined as clear and as brief as possible, holistic, precise and empirically testable, and the hypothesised mechanisms of the aetiology and the treatment should be evidence-based (Dawson et al., 2016). Therefore, the following format for meaning-centred case formulations is developed, following evidence-based case formulations in other therapies (Eells, Kendjelic & Lucas, 1998), and as suggested by meaning-centred practitioners (Lukas, 2014).

  I. *Field-specific case formulation.* Depending on the field that the meaning-centred practitioner is working in, common case formulation components should be described, such as the medical situation or psychiatric diagnosis.

  II. *Phenomenological description of concerns.* This provides a comprehensive overview of the problem in the words of the client, with as little interpretation and theorising from the practitioner as possible.

III. *Evidence-based description of meaning-centred concerns.* The symptoms
are described in terms of meaning in line with the evidence-based
literature summarised in the previous chapters, and justified with
specific examples from the client. This could be based on check-
ing the following possible components of relevance (based on
Section 4.4):

A. *Social-historical context* (Chapters 1 and 2): teleological, sceptical,
functional or phenomenological meanings.
B. *Meaningfulness*: What does the client experience as meaningful
and/or experiences problems with? What commitments does the
client have in life, motivation, action, values, self-worth and self-
regulation? Explore this by asking for specific examples when life
felt meaningful, and examine to what extent these six aspects of
the definition of meaning are covered. To what extent do they
feel competent and self-efficacious to achieve goals in life? This
could for instance reveal a lack of commitment, unclear values,
low self-worth or difficulties in specific motivated actions or
regulation of oneself (Section 3.1).
C. *Meaninglessness*: Does the client report meaninglessness and, if
so, what kind of meaninglessness? Is the client able to experience
meaning despite meaninglessness? (Sections 3.2)
D. *Types of meaning*: To what extent does the client have self-insight
into what is meaningful in life? Further, what types of meaning
does the client report (Section 3.3)? Which types of meaning are
problematic (Section 4.4)?
E. *External perspective on meaning*: To what extent does the client feel
they are standing outside the stream of meaningful experiences?
Does the client experience any latent or manifest crisis in life?
(Section 3.5) What are the possible causes of this (Section 3.5)?
F. *Internal perspective on meaning*: To what extent does the client
feel immersed within the stream of meaningful experiences, and
experience flow, mindfulness, peak experience, happiness, life
satisfaction and authenticity? Are there any problems experiencing this?
G. *Impact*: What is the general impact of the meaning-centred
concerns on the client's psychological, physical and social
well-being?

IV. *Aetiology.* How has the client developed a sense of meaningfulness or meaninglessness in life? This includes a description of any
life events which may have triggered the concerns, the duration
of the concerns, and specific situations in which the concerns are
experienced as more present or less present, and whether anything

has helped the client to deal with these concerns in the past. The practitioner explores the general development of meaning in the client's life, in line with Section 3.5. This includes hypotheses about the triad of what the clients can (not) do, must (not) do and (do not) want to do in life, and whether the client feels specifically drawn to a particular corner of the triad, has any blind spots or has difficulties negotiating between the three. This could be uncovered by analysing specific recent or current life decisions, as described in the exercise in Section 3.4. It is particularly important with young individuals to examine concerns with life stage and separation-individuation.

V. *Meaning-centred mechanisms.* Based on the previous components of the case formulation, the practitioner creates hypotheses about the meaning-centred mechanisms that led the client to experiencing the concerns and asking for help. This can be regarded as a meaning-centred summary of the case, which could provide an indication for the focus of the treatment.

VI. *Treatment indicators.* The practitioner examines arguments pro and contra offering meaning-centred practices to the client. For example, is this a meaning-centred problem, are there other more urgent concerns that need to be addressed first, or does the client have other social and inner resources that could be more beneficial in solving the concerns? Any inclusion criteria could be checked. Although meaning-centred practices have proved equally effective across many different populations (Section 4.3), it is recommended that alternative treatments are suggested first to clients with cognitive impairment, psychoses or severe personality disorders. Other treatment indicators include the client's motivation, self-awareness and self-insight, adaptive coping styles, social support, and existing strengths and skills (Eells, 2007).

VII. *Treatment aim.* Clients are asked to formulate specific goals that they want to achieve in treatment. These goals could be written down and assessed according with a Goal Assessment Form (Cooper & Mearns, 2014; see page 295). Working with goals may help to focus the treatment, motivate clients and provide a means to assess progress (Chapter 6).

VIII. *Treatment process.* Based on the therapeutic aims and the meaning-centred mechanisms, the practitioner formulates how the client could benefit from a meaning-centred therapeutic process. Any specific benefits and concerns for the therapeutic alliance and dangers of ruptures in the relationship are described.

IX. *Self-reflection/reflexivity.* The practitioners reflect on their own position and possible biases in the assessment process (Section 1.5).

4. *Start of treatment process*

Assessment is the first step to change. The assessment can help clients to identify meaning-centred concerns and alternatives, which can be the first step to meaning-centred change.

Prevent iatrogenic damage. Meaning-centred practitioners have warned of the potential iatrogenic damage of the assessment process (Lukas, 1986/2014). This is the damage that assessment may do to individuals. The assessment may cause clients to intellectualise or **hyper-reflect** on their meaning-centred concerns, which could alienate them even more from having a sense of meaningfulness. This can be avoided by not only focusing on the clients' weaknesses but also on their strengths and positive meanings (e.g. Lukas, 1986/2014). Therefore, Lukas (1986/2014) suggests developing a 'dual diagnosis' based on questions about both weaknesses and strengths of the client. For instance, a client could be asked to describe not only their problems, but also what aspects in their lives they experience as meaningful. This is reflected in the case formulation.

Relational. The assessment is based on relational principles, as will be described in Chapter 7. These include genuine listening, empathy and using one's own intuition as a practitioner. Chapter 7 will introduce how clients and practitioner can make a shared decision about the aims and method of treatment.

5. *Using meaning-centred assessment tools*

Many questionnaires have been developed to assess a client's experience of meaning. Most questionnaires lack norm groups, so that scores cannot be interpreted as higher or lower than average. However, questionnaires may reveal some general patterns, and provide the means to compare scores on different (sub)scales, such as 'on average this client scores very low on general meaningfulness in life', or 'The scores On the scale of social meaning are lower than on self-oriented meanings, which shows that this client experiences social meanings as less important than self-oriented meanings'.

Aims. Using questionnaires could help to: (1) assess possible meaning-centred strengths and weaknesses; (2) provide suggestions for possible treatment aims and processes, and tailor the treatment to better suit the client; (3) minimise possible subjective biases from the practitioner; (4) allow a more systematic exploration of the client's preferences, needs and strengths, instead of being ignored due to the blind spots of the practitioner and/or client; and (5) in evaluating improvements, for instance by allowing the client to fill in the questionnaires every five sessions.

Phenomenological interpretations. Phenomenologists have criticised the use of questionnaires as reducing the totality of the client's subjectively lived experience to mere numbers. However, questionnaires can be used in a pragmatic, non-reductionist way. The client's experience may be described as a diamond, casting light from different angles which will reveal different facets of the totality (Vos, 2014). Using only that revealed from a phenomenological angle or only a questionnaire angle would leave other – possibly relevant – facets in the dark; therefore, it may be advisable to combine different perspectives. This does imply that the outcomes of questionnaires are regarded as hypotheses, which need to be further discussed and validated by conversation with the client. Any differences between the questionnaires and the conversations are particularly worthwhile exploring. It is recommended that the practitioner does not separately report the scores of individual sub-scales of each questionnaire, but uses a holistic profiling approach in which all individual scores are related to each other. For example, a high score on the sub-scale search for meaning from the Meaning in Life Questionnaire (Steger, 2012; see page 295) needs to be interpreted entirely differently if this is combined with either low or scores on the sub-scale for presence of meaning. Individuals seem to be in a crisis when they both experience no meaning and search for it, but when individuals search for meaning while they also experience meaning this may indicate a **dual attitude** and an open an flexible sense of meaning (see Chapter 9).

Types of tools. Table 5.1 provides an incomplete selection of questionnaires frequently used in studies on meaning-centred practices (Vos & Vitali, 2018). It is recommended that multiple questionnaires be combined, to develop a broad understanding of the client's experiences. Four questionnaires are used in the treatment manual in Part 3. The Meaning in Life Questionnaire (MLQ) assesses the presence and search for meaning (Steger, 2012). The **Goal Assessment Form** (Cooper, 2015) can be used in the assessment and/or the first treatment session, to ask clients to formulate treatment goals. After every session or multiple sessions, clients can evaluate whether the treatment is helping them with these goals and/or whether they would like to adjust them, which helps to better tailor the treatment to the client (Cooper, 2015). Two questionnaires are directly derived from this book, and are still in the developmental stage. The Meaning Quintet Questionnaire (MQQ) assesses the five types and 25 subtypes of meaning in the **Meaning Quintet** (Section 3.4). This questionnaire helps clients to assess how important each type/subtype of meaning is, to what extent they are already experiencing this or would like to do so more in life. The **Meaning Centred Practitioner's Skill Questionnaire** (MCPS Q) assesses to what extent practitioners use the 39 evidence-based skills described in Part 2. It is recommended that this is filled in for

Table 5.1   Selection of meaning-centred questionnaires

	Selection of questionnaires
General sense of meaningfulness: relatively strong focus on self-reflection (Sections 3.1 or 3.5)	**Meaning in Life Questionnaire** Purpose in Life Seeking of Noetic Goals Post-Traumatic Growth Inventory Logo-Test
General sense of meaningfulness: relatively strong focus on positive affects (Section 3.6)	Life Satisfaction Test Life Fulfillment Scale Authenticity Scale Self-Congruence Scale Life Orientation Scale Flourishing Scale Ryff's Conceptual Well-Being Scale
General meaninglessness (Section 3.2)	Existential Anxiety Questionnaire Death Attitudes Profiles Tragic Optimism Scale No Meaning Scale
Types of meaning (Section 3.4)	*Scales measuring multiple types of meaning:* **Meaning Quintet Questionnaire-V0.1.** Personal Meaning Profile Quest for Meaning Scale Basic Psychological Needs Assessment Scale Sources of Meaning Profile Meaningful Life Measure Schedule for Meaning in Life Evaluation Major Life Goals Measure *Scales measuring specific types of meaning:* Hedonism Scale Hedonic Experience Scale Financial Worries and Illness Perception Questionnaire Rosenberg Self-Esteem Scale Altruism Scale Social Connection Scale World Assumptions Scale Sense of Coherence Scale Self-Realisation Scale Spirituality Questionnaire Freedom Questionnaire Responsibility Scale Gratitude Scale
Meaning-centred coping (Section 3.7)	Meaning Reconstruction Scale Grief and Meaning Reconstruction Scale Finding Positive Meaning Scale Flexibility Scale (AAQ) Psychological Resilience Scale Hardiness Scale Stress Appraisal Measure Coping Schema Inventory – Revised Trent Attribution Profile

Specific moments of meaning in specific situations (Section 2.5)	Phenomenological methods Cognitive subliminal experiments
Projective tests	Thematic Apperception Test Rorschach Test Sentence Completion Test
Therapeutic relationship (Chapter 8)	**Meaning Centred Practitioner's Skill Questionnaire (MCPS Q)** **Goal Attainment Form** Working Alliance Scale Relational Depth Inventory
Observation	Non-systematic: e.g. behaviour, care and style of clothing, speech

Questionnaires in **bold** can be found at the end of this book. References and more examples: Van Bruggen et al. (2015); Pyszcynski, Greenberg & Koole, 2010; Brandstatter et al. (2012); Wong (2012).

every session, particularly for the first meaning-centred treatments that the practitioner gives. This may help to examine which skills can be improved. This skills questionnaire could also be discussed in supervision and intervision.

Meaning-centred profile. It has been recommended to focus on the relationships between different questionnaires and scales and create an overall profile of the client, instead of discussing each scale separately from other scales (see Eurelings-Bontekoe & Sneller, 2003). For example, an individual may be searching for meaning, but this quest could be interpreted in multiple ways, particularly when individuals simultaneously experience the presence of meaning (Steger, 2012). This profiling approach helps to formulate hypotheses about the meaning-centred mechanisms, which could be verified through conversation with the client and which could guide the treatment process. For example, a client should be treated in a different way if the meaning-centred concerns are associated with a personality disorder instead of with a current life situation.

For example, a practitioner could use a theory-driven profile based on Frankl. This would first describe to what extent a client experiences a will to meaning (e.g. self-insight in meaning, balance of different types of meaning, life satisfaction) and to which extent this will to meaning is frustrated. Second, this would examine whether this frustration is structural (e.g. symptoms related to the social-historical context discussed in Chapters 1 and 2, social pressure, practical concerns, self-worth, existential moods) or situational (e.g. life situation, life stage, coping skills, hyper-reflection, self-realisation, suicidal ideation).

Case study

Questionnaires. I met John when he was 19 years old. Before the assessment session, I asked him to fill in some questionnaires which he returned to me, so that I could develop a preliminary questionnaire-based profile which I subsequently used as hypotheses in our face-to-face conservation. The scores on the questionnaires showed a combination of limited meaning-centred self-insight and self-worth, strong teleological meanings, high social pressure and life stage-specific concerns. A recent life change was that John had moved out of his parental home into a student flat. These interpretations were shared during the assessment session, and John confirmed these conclusions.

Description of meaning-centred concerns. When I met John, I initially bracketed these preliminary findings and created a relatively unbiased space in which we phenomenologically explored his experiences. I observed that he was relatively shy and uncertain in our conversation, and his clothes looked neutral. He described phenomenologically that he felt unhappy and dissatisfied in life: 'Everything feels grey, not black, but just not really interesting.' The explorations during our conversation suggested that he focused strongly on the teleological meanings from his strict Christian upbringing, combined with his lack of self-worth and not trusting his own experiences as a source of meaning in life. He described feelings of tertiary meaninglessness, as he identified that 'It is possible to experience meaning in life; I simply do not know how to do this.' His biggest concern seemed to be his lack of being in the experience of flow, mindfulness, peak experiences and slow happiness. He could describe different meaningful experiences in life, but none of these felt particularly satisfying. This seemed to lead to a low mood, which he had been experiencing for several years and which I diagnosed as dysthymia. There was no crisis. This description of his meaning-related concerns during our conversation was in line with the scores from the questionnaires.

Aetiology. During the conversation, it became clear that John had grown up in a cohesive family with a strict religion, in which he was expected to follow what his parents and his church described as meaningful. He had learned to mistrust his own experiences and intuitions as sources of meaning. Moving out of his parental home had made him aware of the social pressure of his parents and cultural group, and how this had made him feel unsatisfied about life.

Meaning-centred mechanisms. The main reason for John's dissatisfaction seemed to be his inability to stay loyal to his parents while living his life according to his own values. This seemed indicative of an uncompleted separation-individuation process.

Treatment indicators. John was very motivated to receive treatment, and showed a quick understanding of meaning-centred topics when we discussed these. There were no negative treatment indications.

Therapeutic aims. John wrote the following aims: learning to listen to what I feel is meaningful; trying out new activities that I feel are meaningful; staying in touch with my parents.

Therapeutic process. It seemed likely that John's mood and life satisfaction could improve by focusing the treatment on meaning. The treatment would be structured

▶

◄

around an experiential exploration of the meaning quintet; in every session we would discuss another type of meaning, with a specific focus on mindfulness exercises and exploring what he experiences as meaningful and what other people experience as meaningful. There seemed to be a positive practitioner–client relationship and no specific indications for relational ruptures.

Self-reflection/reflexivity. I wondered whether my extensive experience as a practitioner working with clients from conformist Christian backgrounds could have created a bias in me. Therefore, I checked the questionnaires which confirmed high levels of conformism and rigidity, which I had initially overlooked. In the conversation, I had explicitly played devil's advocate, saying my thoughts out loud that his conformist religious background has nothing to do with his current issues. John responded strongly to this, confirming that it is this background that has led him to the current meaning-centred concerns.

Shared informed decision-making. I explicitly shared these analyses and the interpretation from the questionnaires, and asked John to share his thoughts. He suggested some minor adjustments, and agreed with most of it. I explained what meaning-centred treatment could offer, and what it could not offer. I offered him the possibility to receive individual meaning-centred treatment. He initially agreed, but I suggested that he take a few days to think about the decision; however, he said he was eager to start and did not need this time.

Start of treatment. This assessment helped John to explore possible reasons why he felt unsatisfied about his life, and he developed a sense of hope when he saw how this situation could be improved. During the assessment, we had discussed both strengths and weaknesses, meaningful and less meaningful aspects in his life. I had shown empathy and was transparent in the assessment process, and I felt we developed the foundations of a positive practitioner–client relationship.

Key assessment skills

1. Exploring the client's request for support in a non-reductionist and multidimensional way.

2. Assessing the immediate needs and life situation of the client.

3. Developing a meaning-oriented case formulation.

4. Using assessment at the start of the meaning-centred change process.

5. Using meaning-centred assessment tools.

6

Meaning-Specific Skills

6.1 General meaning-centred principles

Meaning-specific skills help to explicate, systematically explore and improve meaningful aspects of the client's experiences. This includes skills shown to be effective in other therapies such as didactics and guided exercises but specifically applied to meaning.

6.2 Specific meaning-centred skills

6. *Providing meaning-centred didactics*

Meaning-centred didactics are about theoretically explaining how individuals can live a meaningful life, how a sense of meaningfulness can be developed, how to deal with challenges in life, and what specific actions can be undertaken to improve the sense of meaningfulness. Typically, the first session starts with explaining what meaning is, the second session talks about how life experiences – such as negative life events – can challenge the sense of meaningfulness, and each of the next sessions explore one specific type of meaning, often finishing with sessions on making meaningful changes in life. Different didactic tools can be used. Usually some core concepts are explained, often in interactive ways, and tailored to the specific clients, for instance by asking them for examples about the theory. The theory is explained as simply as possible, with many examples. Subsequently, clients are encouraged to discuss the theory, by asking questions and sharing their thoughts; sometimes, the practitioner asks questions to start a debate. To facilitate the understanding and integration of the theory, the practitioner asks whether the clients can give some personal examples. Part 3 shows specific didactics for every session. Research indicates that didactics and psycho-education have some positive effects on clients (Lincoln, Wilhem & Nestoriuc, 2007; Donker et al., 2009).

7. *Focusing on long-term meaning instead of short-term gratification and pleasure, and revealing the potential benefits of this focus*

Previous chapters described how clients may focus on short-term gratification and materialistic, hedonic and self-oriented meanings (Sections 1.4 and 3.3). However, social and higher meanings lead to better well-being in the long term (Vos, 2017). Delaying gratification and setting long-term goals can help individuals to build resilience and self-efficacy, from which they may benefit in the long term as they are confronted with challenges in life. Meaning-centred practitioners recommend exploring with clients how they may benefit from this long-term meaning perspective (Wong, 2014; Batthanya, 2014).

Clients may not be used to focusing on long-term meanings, as their personal habits and socio-cultural context may be focused more on instant gratification (Section 1.4). Consequently, they may be resistant – or even drop out – when pushed to commit to long-term meaning (Section 3.1). The meaning-centred approach to personal change suggests that clients should never be forced to make certain life changes, unless these feel meaningful for them. Therefore, practitioners can explain the general benefits of long-term meaning, but they cannot impose them. They could invite clients to explore and evaluate how they have benefited in the past from long-term meanings, and compare these with short-term meanings. In this way, clients may phenomenologically discover the benefits of a long-term perspective.

A possible challenge is that clients often confuse meaning with pleasure and expect continuous peak experiences (Section 3.6). The practitioner can help them to understand this difference via meaning-centred didactics (see point 6 above) and reframing their stories (see point 8 below). For instance, the practitioner could ask: 'Is this an experience you just like or is it something more than that? Is this more important than ordinary daily life experiences? Does this offer a direction or set an example in your life?' A useful exercise is to ask clients to rank a series of experiences from 'just liking' to 'very meaningful'. For instance, a pop concert can be enjoyed, but it is not as meaningful as the birth of someone's child. The difference between pleasure and meaning may not always be clear-cut, but on an experiential-phenomenological basis clients can usually identify the most important and valuable experiences.

8. *Identifying and explicating meaning-centred topics in clients' experiences*

Practitioners can help clients by identifying and explicating meaning-centred topics in their stories. That is, the stories of the clients are rephrased in terms of meaning, and connected with the theory about meaning, such as: 'I feel that you are now telling me that you feel you can no longer do some of the activities that gave you a sense of meaning in the past. This is precisely what today's session (Session 2) is about: becoming physically ill can limit the doing of certain activities that felt meaningful in the past, but at the same time it is always possible – in any life situation – to find other ways to attain a sense of meaning, fulfilment and satisfaction in life.'

Practitioners may use different ways to draw attention to the meaning-centred components in the client's narrative. They could simply restate or repeat the words of a client. They could explicitly refer to the feelings or emotions of the clients, or address non-verbal behaviour. Or they could summarise and paraphrase the client in meaning-centred terms. It is important, though, to keep the formulations close to the client's experience, and not over-interpret these. For example, research suggests that interpretations should be formulated in a tentative and not an absolute way: 'Could it possibly be the case that ...' The interpretations should not be too far away from the client's level of self-insight, and thus just slightly at the back of their awareness. They often need to be repeated several times. Interpretations usually happen later in the treatment, when a positive relationship has developed between the practitioner and client. This could also include explicit feedback about the client's behaviour and the effects of the behaviour, such as: 'I feel that you are often speaking in an abstract way about meaning. I wonder whether thinking so much may possibly increase your feeling of meaninglessness?' The effectiveness of rephrasing, reframing and interpreting is supported by some empirical evidence (Hill et al., 1988; Allan et al., 1996; Williams, 2002).

Example

Being unexpectedly admitted to hospital is possibly one of the most frightening and disorientating experiences for many individuals. The routine and flow of daily life are broken, and people feel disconnected from experiences that give them a sense of meaning and satisfaction in daily life. Therefore, I often help hospitalised patients to see meanings in the present and the past, and meanings which could be waiting for them when they return home. When I do my rounds, I closely observe anything that could reveal some meaning for the client, and I invite them to talk about this: flowers at the bedside, a family picture, a book, a card, a ring, a watch, clothes, a TV show they are watching and so on. These questions break their social isolation and connect them with a larger meaningful and social world. I also recommend patients bring meaningful objects to the hospital or when on holiday, when they feel socially isolated or meaningless. For example, I met Ms Jansen in an English hospital, where she was treated for cancer. She was suffering from extreme anxiety, and was even too afraid to take anxiety medication. Other psychotherapists had unsuccessfully

▶

◀

tried cognitive behavioural techniques such as challenging, her fatalistic thoughts and cognitively reinterpreting her situation as less threatening. When I saw her, her hands were trembling severely. Her bedside looked sterile: nothing meaningful I could address. I asked whether her name is Dutch, and whether she is Dutch. She told me that her grandparents had emigrated from the Netherlands. I said I recognised her name, as I am originally Dutch as my surname shows. Her eyes lit up, and I felt she strongly connected with me. I asked whether she had ever been to the Netherlands. She started to talk passionately about how she went there with her parents when she was a child, during the celebration of Sinterklaas. While she was speaking, her hands stopped trembling and she began to smile. When she had finished, I asked her to look at her hands and feel her smile. She surprised herself. I told her: 'This shows that although your situation can feel overwhelming and lonely, you can simultaneously feel meaningful and connected. Your anxiety is not the only answer to this situation.' Subsequently, Ms Jansen accepted anxiety medication, which helped her to relax and made it possible for her to undergo life-saving surgery. This shows that anyone can carry out meaning-centred interventions, even with limited time and skills. Nurses, medical doctors, friends and family can help hospitalised patients by empathic meaning-centred observing, listening and questioning.

9. *Offering clients a guided discovery of their meaning potential*

Many meaning-centred practitioners use guided exercises to help clients examine what they experience as meaningful, deepen their experiences and facilitate greater emotional arousal and expression. This discovery is guided, as the practitioner uses specific instructions or a questioning approach (Chapter 8). For example, clients are explicitly asked to generate three examples from the previous week when life felt meaningful. Clients are then asked to make a drawing of a mountain where they position the names of meanings in order of importance. These exercises help to make the meaning-centred didactics more specific and directly applicable to the client's unique situation. Guided exercises usually follow meaning-centred didactics, are tailored to the unique situation of the client and activate all the senses and not just theoretical reflection. Exercises do not impose meaning on clients, but create a neutral space in which clients can explore their experiences. Each discovery is explained before the exercise is started, and clients are asked whether they would like to participate in this (relational skills in Chapter 6). Many examples can be found in Part 3. Research suggests that guided exercises are to some extent effective (e.g. Greenberg et al., 2002; Orlinsky et al., 2004). Research also suggests that doing emotional processing exercises per se may not produce positive change, as they need to be followed by cognitive processing, such as expressing and reflecting on the exercise (Bohart, 1980).

10. *Showing an unconditional positive regard about the possibility of finding meaning*

Frankl was strongly convinced that clients are always able to find ways to live a meaningful life. This is possibly one of the most contested aspects of his work. However, Frankl did not say which specific type of meaning individuals would find; he did not say finding meaning (again) is an easy process; and he did not say that meaning solves all suffering. We may not be able to achieve the specific goals we want, but we can find meaning in attempting or coping with the challenges: a physically ill patient may, for instance, find meaning in making it through the day, although no higher meanings may be achieved. Although we may need to change our goals and expectations, we can experience meaning. We always have potential options and can experience some meaning in any life situation. This seems to be a tautology about human experience, as the phenomenology of meaning has shown: all individuals continually experience at least some micro-meanings, such as the enjoyment of a cup of coffee (Chapter 2). Frankl argued that even in limiting circumstances, individuals can change their inner attitude towards that situation. He exemplified this with his concentration camp experiences when he refused to despair, but instead fostered hope and helped his fellow inmates.

Thus Frankl underlined the potential within everyone, while accepting the realistic limitations. It seems important to be realistic. For example, some practitioners encourage the unrealistic belief that individuals can reach any goal they want: 'You can do this, as long as you believe in it!' Such strong statements lack empirical evidence and may evoke scepticism from clients. Research indicates that when practitioners offer a realistic sense of optimism, unconditional positive regard and hope, clients strongly improve (Farber & Doolin, 2011).

Practitioners can address the meaning potential in many ways. For example, clients may be asked to reflect on similar difficult life periods, identify what helped them to get through this period, how they created a sense of hope and meaning, and what they could learn from this to apply to their current situation. A practitioner could also explicitly tell us that: 'Not being able to achieve what you hoped for is always frustrating. But don't let this make you lose hope. I am convinced that your feelings will change, like they always change in life. You will be able to have some meaningful experiences again, although I cannot tell you which specific meanings, where you will find these and how they will feel. But I know from research and having treated many clients that you will. Even if you cannot change the factual situation, you can change how you feel in that situation, like Frankl in the concentration camp.'

Unfortunately, this unconditional positive regard could unintentionally give the implicit message that if clients do not feel meaningful or hopeful, they are to blame for this: 'You can always find meaning. Why did you not find it yet? You are not doing your best!' On the one hand, this guilt may motivate clients to change. On the other hand, it could lead to perfectionism or undermine their treatment: 'I am worthless, as I am not a hero like Frankl.' This may create an additional burden: 'Not only do I have my psychological problem, but I even have a problem in the way in which I cope with it.' Therefore, practitioners need to offer realistic hope, be sensitive to the client's situation and empathise with their struggles.

11. *Addressing the totality of possible meanings in the client's life*

Rationale: Meaning-centred practitioners try to address meaning as broadly as possible. The importance of this broad-based approach may be metaphorically compared with a dietician who tells an obese person to add at least two spoons of vegetables to their diet every day. Although the additional vegetables may make a small improvement in the client's well-being, nothing radically will change if the client does not make further changes, such as to their sedentary lifestyle and or consumption fast food. Similarly, it seems of limited use to discuss only a small number of meanings with clients, while they continue to focus predominantly on McMeanings in daily life (Section 1.4). The more different types of meaning are discussed, the more effective the treatment is (Vos, 2018a). Furthermore, the more potentially relevant meanings are discussed, the more likely that the treatment will feel relevant for the client, and thus will increase their motivation and adherence, and reduce dropout.

Phenomenological and pragmatic: How broadly should meanings be addressed in the sessions? Following the phenomenological-pragmatic approach in this book, this depends on the unique situation of the client (Chapter 2). It also depends on practical aspects, such as the number of sessions that are funded. Thus there is often a balance between being complete and pragmatic. For example, the treatment manual in Part 3 is intended as a time-efficient group treatment, built around the **meaning quintet**. In each session, another type of meaning is systematically explored. It is very likely that clients do not experience every type as meaningful, and they may use these five as examples to reflect on and will only phenomenologically connect with some aspects. Metaphorically speaking, a treatment manual uses a wide fishing net to be time-efficient, instead of waiting for the fish to jump out of the river themselves.

Structure: Using the structure of, for instance, this treatment manual means that practitioners follow a plan and agenda for the sessions, and address some predetermined topics. This helps to systematically address a wide range of experiences and avoid blind spots. In contrast, some practitioners prefer an individual-phenomenological approach, where they follow the client in an unstructured way, and let this reveal what is meaningful for them, instead of starting with a wide structure. However, research shows that meaning-centred practices are much more effective when they are systematic and structured (Roth & Fonagy, 2013; Vos & Vitali, 2018). Thus the fishing net approach is more effective in research, although some practitioners argue that some smaller nuances of the individual's experience may be lost in the wide holes of the net structure.

Multi-sensory: Empirical research indicates that meaning is something that we can speak about not only theoretically, but also experientially. For instance, asking clients 'What do you think is meaningful for you?' or 'What does your intuition say is meaningful?' may elicit an entirely different answer from 'What do you feel is meaningful for you?' (Vos, 2011). Both answers may differ from each other, and often individuals are not able to directly intuit what feels meaningful for them, and prefer to speak about meaning initially on a theoretical level, possibly also because theorising feels less threatening and intimidating than directly exploring and expressing their deepest feelings. Therefore, meaning-centred practices are more effective when addressing both theoretical and experiential experiences via a multiplicity of techniques, such as didactics, reflection, experiential and mindfulness exercises (Vos & Vitali, 2018).

For example, the **meaning quintet** includes many dimensions, such as professional and personal life, internal meanings (e.g. inner attitude) and external meanings (e.g. behaviour), hedonic and self-transcending. It also includes a discussion of meaning as striving towards specific goals (linear, goal-directed, future-oriented) and non-goal-directed (non-linear, such as one's inner attitude and experiencing in the here and now). This also includes balancing stress-causing meaning (e.g. positive aspects of stress and striving towards goals) and leisure time (e.g. relaxing after striving and working hard towards goals). An overview of experiential and mindfulness techniques can be found in Chapter 8.

Spiral structure: Educational research shows that individuals learn better when the content is addressed in multiple ways, for instance because different individuals have different learning styles (Rider & Sadler-Smith, 1997; Schmeck, 2013). This implies that the same topic crops up several times, but each time with a different method. Meaning-centred treatments often have a similar spiral-like structure. That is, for each type of meaning there are multiple rounds of exploring this meaning. For instance, clients are asked in homework before a session to find examples of a certain type of meaning – e.g. examples of social meanings; in the session the practitioner explains what social meanings are (didactics), which is followed by a group discussion that focuses on further explaining and theoretically understanding the theory. This could be followed by a mindfulness/relaxation exercise to help clients focus their attention on their inner experiences and move away from a mere cognitive perspective. While the clients are in this meditative-experiential state, the practitioner offers a guided exercise, for example by asking questions about this type of meaning. Subsequently, the clients share their examples, and at the end of the session they identify the most meaningful examples discussed in this session. In the final sessions, clients can look back and rank the meanings addressed in all earlier sessions in order of importance. Some clients explain that the repetition of the same topic 'Feels like a vicious circle: I am always finding the same answers.' The practitioner can explain the rationale behind this, and compare it to a spiral instead of a vicious circle: in each new round, the client explores the topic at a deeper and more meaningful level.

12. *Concretising and specifying meaning in daily life*

Clients are often inclined to speak in generalised, abstract or philosophical terms, particularly about meaning in life, and **hyper-reflection** may worsen their problems (Section 3.5). Therefore, it is not unexpected that research shows that clients benefit from specifying the topics they are speaking about (Roth & Fonagy, 2013). Practitioners can encourage clients to concretise and specify in many ways: 'Could you specify this? What do you mean precisely? Could you give an example? What does this look like in your daily life? What actions would a video camera record?'

Meaning-centred coaches in corporate contexts often use the STAR technique: Situation, Task, Action, Results. The client is asked to present a recent Situation. Subsequently, the client identifies the specific Task or meaning to be achieved. Then the client is asked about the Action, what the client did, why this was done and what alternatives there were. Finally, the Results of the actions are examined; what did the person achieve through the actions, and to what extent was this a meaningful experience, and what did this situation teach?

13. *Stimulating effective goal-management*

Meaning-centred practitioners often stimulate effective goal-management. This involves stimulating clients to set concrete aims for daily life; planning, experimenting, evaluating and adjusting the aims and methods; and making long-term commitments. Its effectiveness is strongly supported (e.g. Lapierre et al., 2007; Arends et al., 2013). There are many ways to set goals (Little, 1983; Heckhausen & Gollwitzer, 1987; Austin & Vancouver, 1996), some of which are included in the following approach. This is included in treatment Session 9 in Part 3 (Chapter 20).

Steps. First, clients explore what they experience as meaningful in life in general (e.g. via the **meaning quintet**). Without first knowing what their general motivation and values are, clients may not be able to commit to action (Section 3.1). *Second*, they decide which meaning is the most important at this moment in life, for instance by using a **mountain range exercise** in which they rank meanings in order of priority. *Third*, clients analyse why they have not realised this yet, and try to find ways to overcome this. For example, they imagine a desired future (e.g. 'I would like to have a partner'), followed by the current negative problems that are in the way of realising this (e.g. poor social skills, which may be improved with social skills training). This process of mentally contrasting the idealised future with realistic hindrances is different from both merely indulging in positive dreams about the future and simply dwelling in ruminations about the negative reality (Fantasy Realisation Theory; Oettinger, 2009). This leads to an intention: 'I want to do X to achieve Y, and to be able to achieve this I may need to do/overcome Z.' *Fourth*, they translate this into specific goals and subgoals, with the help of the criteria of helpful goals (below). *Fifth*, they make a realistic plan, which includes detailed steps and contingency plans in case some challenges arise. The practitioner could help with specification questions: 'What does your plan of action look like? What will you do first, second, etc.? Is this realistic? What problems could you face, and how might you cope with these?' *Sixth*, the client acts. *Seventh*, along the way, and/or at the end of the action, the client evaluates both the end result and the process. The client may decide to adjust the goals or action plan, and decide whether and how to attempt these again. The latter is important: individuals need to receive feedback about their progress – either feedback they give themselves or feedback received from others (Locke & Latham, 2002). *Eighth*, clients formulate what they have learned about themselves during this process. For example, they may take pride in their attempt, even though the desired end goal is not completely achieved. The client may have learned that having tried is more important than not having attempted at all. Or the client may have learned that goals that are too large do not work.

Criteria of helpful goals. To be able to experience flow (Section 3.6), goals should be set within the optimal range of being both realistic and challenging (Csikszentmihalyi, 1997). If goals are too simple for someone's abilities, they may not lead to a full sense of meaning and flow. When a goal is set too high, the individual may struggle too much and therefore not be able to experience flow (Section 5.3). Furthermore, research indicates that individuals perform better and experience better mental health when individuals aim for goals which are:

➤ important (Austin, 1996; Moskowitz, 2012),

➤ specific and simple (Locke, 2002; Sheeran & Webb, 2012),

➤ not too far in the future (Locke & Latham, 2002),

> challenging (Locke & Latham, 2002; Wiese, 2007),

> attainable (Emmons & Diener, 1986; Sheldon & Elliott, 1999; Wiese, 2007),

> mutually conducive (in the case of multiple goals) (Chun et al., 2011),

> focused towards something positive rather than negative – approach instead of avoidance; for example, instead of saying, 'I want to be less socially anxious', individuals could say, 'I would like to make more friends' (Klein & Elliott, 2006; Elliott & Friedman, 2007); this approach also seems helpful because trying to avoid something also assumes that one has to think about the thing that is being avoided, which actually makes it more salient (Kahneman, 2011).

Small playful projects. One challenge that clients often face in my clinical experience is the threshold from inaction to action. One individual told me: 'I know what I want to do, and am motivated. But it is such a big step to move into action, to show myself in the world and risk failing. It sounds so serious. Therefore, I have made the action smaller for myself by calling these "small projects", trying out and playing with them.' The term 'life project' describes a specific well-defined action with a clear deadline in a not too distant future, and to which individuals want to commit themselves for a short period, for which they are motivated as this follows on from their higher values, they know which specific steps to do, they try this out and they develop a sense of self-efficacy and self-worth (Little, Salmela & Phillips, 2007). A life project is an experiment, creative and playful, and the client a 'joyful scientist' (Nietzsche, 1882/2010). The aim is experiencing meaning in the attempt, and not necessary reaching the end goal. By experiencing the joy of small projects, individuals may experience flow, and develop a sense of hope and self-efficacy, which could motivate them to engage in larger projects in the future.

Clients often expect a project to be perfectly meaningful. However, they may be advised not to look for perfection, but to lower the bar to prevent disappointment, frustration and depression. For example, individuals could expect that 70% of their working time will be meaningful – instead of 100%; the other 30% of the time they may have other duties to fulfil (see Lees, 2017).

A project can also be presented as an addition or temporary try-out, and not as a replacement of old meanings: 'Try to work fewer hours, and evaluate after a month; you can always return to working as many as you are now.' If a practitioner saidy, 'Replace your old workaholic behaviour with a more relaxed lifestyle', clients may respond defensively or feel destabilised. Clients may experience such practitioners as a ringmaster asking trapeze workers in a circus to let go of the bar they are holding onto, and jump into the darkness where they cannot see a new bar, nor a safety net, even though the ringmaster tries to convince them there is another bar. Motivation research suggests that individuals feel better prepared for attempting change, and experience less fear, when they perceive the safety net of being able to return to the old situation (Vos, 2014, 2016b). Clients can experiment with incrementally more challenging and complex projects.

Treatment goals. Meaning-centred practices can be interpreted as a project with specific goals. Research has shown that goals can help the treatment to be more focused and client-centred. The overall aim of meaning-centred practices is to learn to live a meaningful and satisfying life, despite life's challenges. This overall aim can be broken down into specific goals and subgoals. For example, some clients aim to develop more meaningful relationships, others want to develop better self-care and so on. They can learn to set, adjust and achieve goals in treatment, and generalise this skill for use in their daily life. Treatment goals should not be conceptualised as rigid and unvarying targets that clients should be pressurised to construct and pursue, but the emphasis is on helping clients clarify and explore the goals that are already there, in terms of being implicit in the structure of the person's engagement with his or her life (Cooper & McCleod, 2009). It has been recommended that goals are set relatively early in the treatment process, preferably at the end of the assessment session, based on the meaning-centred case formulation, and adjusted after several sessions. For instance, clients fill these in on the Goal Assessment Form (see p. 295). The treatment goals should be formulated in such a way that they can be realised and generalised to other situations in daily life. This could help clients to learn how to set and work towards achievable goals. It has been suggested that at the start of the treatment clients are asked to rate the extent to which they have already achieved the goal, to evaluate and assess this halfway through treatment and at the end of the final session (Cooper, 2018). It is advised to focus not only on the accomplishment, but also on the way in which the client has attained it, and to reframe this as a meaningful learning experience.

14. *Stimulating the client to connect with the larger temporal experience of past–present–future legacy*

Obsession with the present. In ancient Greek, Roman and early Christian times, the meaning of individuals seemed to depend on their societal position, on where they fitted on the societal-universal-cosmic ladder (Section 1.2). They connected their individual being with the larger social and temporal perspective: 'I am Godwin, Rolfe's son, who was the son of … Born a farmer, I will serve the landlord and church, and hopefully rent my own farm which I can pass on to my children, which they can hand over to their children…' Since the sceptic revolution in the sixteenth century (Section 1.2), people increasing turned to their individual experiences. In our era, meaning is primarily regarded as an individual process (Section 1.4), and many types of meaning are self-oriented, materialistic or hedonic (Section 3.3). Thus individuals seem to connect their individual meaning less with the bigger temporal and societal-universal-cosmic perspective. Their primary focus is often on meaning in the here and now, signified by the popularity of books such as Eckhart Tolle's *The Power of Now*. However, many meaning-centred practitioners underline the importance of transcending the individual here and now (Frankl, 1986).

Obsession with the past. Frankl criticised psychodynamic and Adlerian therapies for focusing too much on the past and on what is no longer meaningful or possible. For example, he doubts whether it is beneficial to spend many sessions on examining the roots of problems, when clients could use these sessions instead to learn how to commit to meaningful activities in the present. Thus he criticised these approaches for being too deterministic, and forgetting the freedom and potentiality of clients.

Obsession with the future. In contrast, Frankl had a future focus, giving attention to how individuals can use the potential of the future to create a more meaningful life. How can individuals create a more meaningful future despite limitations in the past and present? This future-focus may include not only the client's future but also beyond the client's death. For example, many studies show that clients benefit psychologically from thinking about the legacy they would like to leave after their death. This could range from leaving material possessions to one's offspring to contributing to transforming the world into a better place. What do you want to leave behind for your children, relatives, friends and the world? Thus this is about focusing on social and higher types of meaning (Section 3.4). Understanding what clients want to leave behind can help them to know what to do in the present to ensure they will be able to leave this legacy. Breitbart and Poppito (2014) state that it is particularly important to address legacy with clients in palliative care. This can also help clients to cope with death anxiety (Chapter 9). Frankl's approach has been criticised for ignoring problems from the past which may still influence clients, and for disconnecting clients from being in the flow of the present by focusing too much on the theoretical future (Section 3.6).

Coherence of time. Several meaning-centred practitioners have developed treatments that address the totality of time, and create a sense of coherence between the past, present, future and post-mortem legacy. For example, Breitbart and Poppito formulate this as: 'the legacy you were given, the legacy you live, your future legacy, and the legacy you will give.' Meaning-centred treatments that focus on the coherence of time improve clients' psychological well-being more than treatments which are too one-sided and focus on either the past, the present or the future (Vos & Vitali, 2018). This is in line with research showing the importance of a sense of coherence for meaningfulness and psychological well-being (Antonovsky, 1987; Martela & Steger, 2016). The sense of belonging to a socio-historical totality and attachment helps individuals transcend their individual problems in the present or past, and connect them with generations before and after them (Chao & Kesebir, 2013; Mikulincer & Shaver, 2013; Lambert et al., 2013). These meaning-centred practitioners address the past, present, future and post-mortem legacy over the course of multiple sessions. This creates a sense of coherence of time, by which individuals not only focus on the present, but feel they are part of a larger stream of life which started before them and flows through the person who they have become, that they have somewhat directed the flow of this stream through their individual impact in the past, present and future, and that the stream will continue to flow after their death in a slightly adjusted direction. Thus individuals experience their self as part of the larger enfolding and ever dynamically changing process of social history (see Part 3, Chapter 19 – Session 8).

The focus on the coherence of time has been called the spiritual aspect of meaning-centred practices. Many philosophers have described how history reveals itself through us; as individuals, we are taking part in Being (e.g. Soren Kierkegaard, Arthur Schopenhauer, Friedrich Nietzsche, Martin Heidegger). They were directly and indirectly inspired by mystic traditions and religions. Hinduism describes, for example, how the individual life (*atman*) is part of larger ultimate reality (*Brahman*). Judaism tells of how we walk in the footsteps of God, which were there before us and will still be there after individuals' lives (Levinas, 1986). The coherence of time also assumes that time is cyclical, like in nature religions. Several phenomenologists criticise the modern western concept of time, which they describe as reductionist, linear and teleological (Visser, 2011).

Exercises

1. Writing. Clients are asked to write their life story, with a beginning, a middle and an end. For example, in every session another aspect of their life story is explored and written about. They could be explicitly asked to focus on the continuity of the story, how the past led to the present and so on. They could read their stories aloud, and the practitioner and clients could bear witness and validate the story.

▶

> ◀
>
> The **meaning quintet** could be used to identify the different types of meanings in their story.
>
> 2. Post-its. Individuals are asked to fill out 10–15 Post-its, describing the highlights and depths in their life. The first Post-it describes the context in which they were born, other Post-its note other meaningful events in their lives, and one Post-it is left empty to represent their future and another about their possible legacy. If this exercise is done in a large room, clients could stick the Post-its on symbolic places in the room, such as putting a Post-it on the floor when this felt like a low point in their life, and putting one on a lamp when this was perceived as an enlightening experience. The client explains their life story via the Post-its, and particularly focuses on how they developed from one Post-it to the next. A variation on this exercise is to add a piece of rope between all the different Post-its, to literally connect all life events.

15. *Exploring meanings in the client's past, as a potential source for improving self-esteem, hope and inspiration for future meaning.*

What have you done with the legacy that you were given in your childhood? Many meaning-centred practitioners re-interpret the past as a source of meaning for the present and the future, for instance via life reviews (Westerhof et al., 2010; Chochinov, 2012). Reviewing your life has proved beneficial for someone's quality of life and psychological well-being (Westerhof, Bohlmeijer & Webster, 2010). Breitbart and Poppito (2014) describe history as an important source of meaning, particularly for palliative care clients, as their future prospects may be short, but by reinterpreting their past they can develop a sense of **life satisfaction**. They focus their exercises on how individuals have been able to transcend limitations in their past and find meaning.

For example, practitioners may first explore the legacy that clients received from their upbringing (e.g. Where did you come from? How did your parents, teachers or socio-economic circumstances influence your life? What expectations did they have? Which were significant life events?). Second, practitioners may examine how clients transformed this legacy that was given to them in the past into something more meaningful, to follow Frankl's example of 'transforming tragedy into triumph' (e.g. How did you overcome problems from your upbringing? What did you achieve? How did you overcome stressful life events?). By re-interpreting the past, for instance realising that they were not merely a victim of the situation, clients can see to what extent they are free to change situations, and develop a sense of hope and **self-efficacy** (Yes, I can change my situation). Third, practitioners can examine how the tragedies and triumphs from the past influence clients' here and now (What did your life experiences teach you? Do your current values come from your past? How free do you feel to define your own life? How responsible do you feel?). Fourth, practitioners can help clients to re-interpret the past (What can you still change from the legacy that was given to you? What do you want to change?). This seems to follow the Serenity Prayer: *'God, grant me the serenity to accept the things I cannot change, the courage to change the things I can, and the wisdom to know the difference.'*

Clients often have difficulties in finding examples of positive meaning in the past and/or only explore positive experiences superficially, depending on their mood. Research shows that memory-retrieval processes are often mood-congruent: when someone feels depressed or meaningless this individual will usually retrieve mainly negative memories (Barry et al., 2004; Matt et al., 2012). It has been suggested that finding mood-incongruent examples of meaningful moments in the past may help to improve one's mood; it has also been suggested to ask specific questions about the past and not just globally explore their general memory of an event, with specific questions such as: 'Where were you? Who were there with you? What did you see? What did you hear? What did you smell? What did you taste?' Thus clients should not focus on a general period in their life, but on specific exemplary moments within that period. Evidence from a randomised controlled trial in which cancer patients were asked to review their life with such specific questions indicates positive findings (Kleijn et al., 2015), which seems in line with the effectiveness of other reminiscence trials (Bohlmeijer et al., 2003).

16. *Stimulating clients to give an independent but connected answer to the social context*

  'People need roots and wings' (Chinese saying)

In modern individualistic societies, individuals often seem to focus on their own individual meaning (see Section 1.4). However, individuals' decisions are strongly influenced by others and they may construct their experiences within their social context (Neimeijer, 2003; Chao & Kesebir, 2013; Mikulincer & Shaver , 2013; Stillman & Lambert, 2013). Social relationships, family and the sense of belonging are meaningful and psychologically beneficial (Lambert et al., 2013). By definition, every individual meaning is embedded in social meanings; for example, deciding to read a book alone implies not socialising at that moment. How do individuals balance the focus on making autonomous decisions and being socially embedded?

The answer to this question may depend on the cultural context, as for example in Asian cultures individuals seem to have a stronger focus on how they can align their meanings with others. Meanings may also not be experienced as individual but as inherently social (Section 1.2). Several practitioners mention the importance of balancing autonomy and social connections, and the effectiveness of this balance seems indicated by multiple studies (Mikulincer et al., 2013). For example, the **Meaning Development Triangle** could help to explain this (Section 3.4).

Based on family therapy, it has been argued that it is particularly important to be aware of the influence of family dynamics on what individuals develop as their sense of meaning. Families could be running a script which could create a life script for children (Lantz, 2010). For example, a child could implicitly or explicitly help parents with their relationship conflicts, or be used as weapon in parental conflicts. Families may also function on the assumption that 'If you really loved me, I wouldn't have to ask', family secrets, avoidance of disagreements or communicating indirectly, labelling or blaming each other or oneself, not allowing individuals to differ, and saying that others are 'trying to do what I want, but that is not what I really want'. Exploring family dynamics and the role of individuals can help to examine where an individual's meanings come from, and may help them to develop a sense of freedom and responsibility. This could support **individuation-separation**, which may be particularly helpful in work with children and young people (Section 3.7).

It has been argued that individuals are often very loyal to their social context, even if the life script is detrimental to the individual. Therefore, family therapist Boszormenyi-Nagy has suggested that to help clients develop a sense of freedom within, they draw on connections and a balancing between give and take between people, instead of totally cutting ties with the context and only taking and not giving anything anymore. Severing ties goes against our loyalties and could be detrimental to our mental health. It could be that clients do not physically meet with their parents anymore – for example, when the relationship is too detrimental – but they can still be aware of how they are both connected and free. To foster this sense of individual freedom within the limitations of relationships, Boszormenyi-Nagy and Krasner (1986) suggested a self-transcending procedure, in which individuals recognise the intergenerational patterns and meanings. For example, a client may recognise how their parents behaved the way they did – including the ways in which they hurt the client – because they were also partially the result of their upbringing. Thus every individual is explicitly acknowledged as being both victim and active agent. This **dual awareness** could help clients to develop a sense of individual meaning, while acknowledging the limitations from their context. Lantz (2000) has integrated family therapy with meaning-centred practices, which he bases on some empirical evidence for its effective-ness; he discusses many specific exercises in his book *Meaning-Centered Marital and Family Therapy*.

17. *Focusing on meanings that are based on and that stimulate self-worth and self-compassion*

Clients feel more meaningful and have a better sense of well-being when they focus on authentic meanings in line with their true self (Section 3.7). Meaning-centred practitioners will therefore help clients to avoid self-destructive behaviour. Some practitioners have also used self-suggestion exercises called 'appealing technique', in which clients tell themselves they are meaningful and worthy beings.

This has also been associated with 'self-compassion', the experience of compassion towards one's self, particularly in times when an individual feels inadequate, like a failure or is suffering (Neff, 2003). It includes self-kindness, common humanity and mindfulness. Self-kindness is about being warm towards oneself, when encountering pain and per-sonal shortcomings, rather than ignoring them or hurting oneself with self-criticism. Common humanity involves recognising that suffering and personal failure are part of the shared human experience. Research shows that self-compassion is not only associated with greater psycho-logical health, but also with a stronger sense of meaning, greater life satisfaction, wisdom, goals, personal responsibility and resilience (Neff, 2003; MacBeth & Gumley, 2012). Practising self-compassion exercises has proved psychologically beneficial (Neff & Germer, 2013). Such exercises generally consist of either a writing exercise, role-playing or introspective contemplation. For example, clients can imagine how they would advise a friend in a similar situation; give themselves a self-compassion break; write a letter to themselves from the perspective of a loving friend; reflect on themselves by occupying different 'chairs' as criticiser, criticised, and compassionate observer; reframe critical self-talk; journal from the per-spective of self-kindness, mindfulness and common humanity; identify what they really want; practise self-forgiveness; and engage in self-care.

Example

Logotherapists sometimes use the Appealing Technique, which directly appeals to change for the better, regardless of circumstances. This often includes making indi-viduals aware of their freedom and responsibility ('I am not a victim, I can make a decision'), and autosuggestive techniques. Dezelic (2014) offers the exercise called

▶

◄

'Accessing the defiant power of the spirit' to strengthen self-compassion. She first begins with some auto-suggestive or hypnotic techniques: she suggests the client bring their attention to their body, and feels any tension leaving the body as it becomes more and more relaxed. Subsequently, when the client is in a relaxed state, she suggests:

[Now that] your body is resting gently and quietly, and the feeling of complete calm and safety is ever present, your spirit states: I have willpower, I am strong, I am able, I am well (repeat suggestion). A colour of your choice comes to mind, for which when you this particular colour of yours, you become empowered, resilient, full of strength, wellbeing and joy. Picture this colour all around you like flowing scarves in the wind of your soft and soothing breath. See this colour vividly, which awakens your spirit, and your spirit states: I have willpower, I am strong, I am able, I am well. Now allow your attention to drift back to your resting and calm body. Your colour has gradually permeated the air around you and you are now able to breathe this colour in and out, which washes over your body in gentle waves as you exhale. As you breathe your colour in and out, you are feeling empowered, resilient, full of strength, wellbeing and joy. See and feel that your resilient spirit allows your body to feel calm, at peace, and full of joy. Your mind and your body alike state: I have willpower, I am strong, I am able, I am well.

Key meaning-centred skills

6. Providing meaning-centred didactics.

7. Focusing on long-term meaning instead of short-term gratification and pleasure, and revealing the potential benefits of this focus.

8. Identifying and explicating meaning-centred topics in clients' experiences.

9. Offering clients a guided discovery of their meaning potential via specific exercises.

10. Showing an unconditional positive regard about the possibility of finding meaning.

11. Addressing the totality of possible meanings in the client's life.

12. Concretising and specifying meaning in daily life.

13. Stimulating effective goal-management.

14. Stimulating the client to connect with the larger temporal experience of past–present–future legacy.

15. Exploring meanings in the client's past, as a potential source for improving self-esteem, hope and inspiration for future meaning.

16. Stimulating the client to give an independent but connected answer to the social context.

17. Focusing on meanings that are based on and that stimulate self-worth and self-compassion.

7

Relational Skills

7.1 General relational principles

I do not know what helped me the most: your explanations and exercises, or your trust and support. Possibly both; without our deep connection, I would not have dared to look behind my daily life. I trust you; I knew that if you said I could do this, I could actually do this. We did this together. Above all, you showed me the possibility, no the importance, of having meaningful relationships; you inspired me to connect deeper with friends and family.

(Jan, Client)

The relationship between the client and the practitioner is possibly one of the least explicated aspects of meaning-centred practices. Many textbooks and treatment manuals focus on the content of meaning. However, research shows that the more meaning-centred practices explicitly focus on the practitioner–client relationship, the more effective these are (Vos & Vitali, 2018). In general, empirical research findings emphasise the quality of the practitioner–client relationship: between 17% and 30% of improvements in clients may be attributed to the positive relationship (Lambert, 1992). This is the case not only in relationship-centred psychotherapies such as humanistic therapies, but also in cognitive behavioural therapies, as shown in numerous empirical studies (Vos, 2017b). This chapter analyses some relational skills in meaning-centred practices. Guidance on working at the relational depth can be found elsewhere (Mearns & Cooper, 2005; Cooper & McLeod, 2014). This chapter is based on the assumption that relational depth and meaning-centred depth go hand in hand, and that using a clear structure goes together with a strong relationship.

Relational depth and meaning-centred depth go hand in hand

Both theoretical arguments and empirical research support the hypothesis that the deeper the practitioner–client relationship is, the more likely that meaningful topics will be addressed (Vos, 2018b).

Openness. Practitioners create a positive context in which clients feel safe and able to be open to express what is truly meaningful for them. Clients feel safe to **unpeel** the layers in their experiences and show their vulnerability. When practitioners are perceived as uninviting and unsafe, clients may focus more on superficial, inauthentic experiences. Empathy helps the practitioner to understand the client's lived experiences, and offer better tailored questions and suggestions. Thus meaning is more likely to be explored in its depth and totality when there is a positive relationship.

Modelling. Carl Rogers has suggested that congruence in the relationship between practitioners and clients helps clients to become more congruent with themselves (Wyatt, 2001). When you learn to be authentic in the sessions, you may also become authentic in daily life. Thus clients experience the relationship with the practitioner as a model for how relationships could be outside the consultation room.

A positive relationship is meaningful. Research suggests that clients change in particular when clients and practitioners meet each other at a deep level (Vos, 2018b). This has been called 'working at relational depth', which can be defined as:

> a feeling of profound contact and engagement with a client, in which one simultaneously experiences high and consistent levels of empathy and acceptance towards that other, and relates to them in a highly transparent way. In this relationship, the client is experienced as acknowledging one's empathy, acceptance and congruence – either implicitly or explicitly – and is experienced as fully congruent in that moment.
>
> (Mearns & Cooper, 2009, p. 25)

Many descriptions of relational depth are reminiscent of those describing meaningful experiences (Chapter 3), such as aliveness, profound connectedness, exhilaration, heightened awareness, a sense of being in the moment, open and co-creating (Vos, 2018b). The relationship could function as an example to the client of what meaningfulness in life can be about – although there may be a danger that clients become dependent on this relationship and no longer see a need to search for meaning outside of the consultation room.

Structure and relationship

There has been much debate about what structured meaning-centred practices should look like. Proponents argue that using a clear and systematic structure helps to focus the treatment and avoid blind spots, and thus make meaning-centred practices more effective (Vos & Vitali, 2018).

Opponents say that using a structure goes against phenomenological and relational principles. That is, clients' individuality may not be recognised enough when they receive a one-size-fits-all treatment: 'a standardised guide would be more hindrance than help' (Lukas, 1986/2014, p. 129).

However, this debate stems from a false dichotomy. Using a structure and a tailored approach can go hand in hand. In clinical practice, structured practitioners also have deep relationships. To understand this, the relationship between the practitioner and the client needs to be differentiated into macro-, meso- and micro-levels. These three levels may be compared with future students choosing a place of education to study at. At the macro-level, they speak with a student advisor and receive brochures in which all possible modules are listed, each with their own aims and methods. At the meso-level, the individual follows the structure of the chosen study. At the micro-level, they have their own learning style, and give their own unique answers to exercises and examination questions.

Macro-level. At the macro-level, meaning-centred practitioners aim to work collaboratively with clients to help them identify what they want from therapy and how they might achieve it, similar to the approach of pluralistic therapists (Cooper & Mearns, 2011, p. 27), and develop a unique therapy for every unique client in every unique situation (Jung, 1979). Meaning-centred practices are often characterised by explicit dialogues and negotiations about the goals, tasks and method of the treatment. Therefore, meaning-centred practitioners have a broad toolkit, being prepared to create something meaningful in different situations with different clients. Practitioners inform clients what meaning-centred practices can offer and what they cannot, and explore whether this is what clients can, must and want to do in their current situation (Chapter 5). At the macro-level, the practitioner tries to establish a deep working relationship, and uses a relatively **non-directive** approach in their ongoing meta-therapeutic dialogue.

Meso-level. The communication at the macro-level leads to the decision to follow certain aims and practices; one possible way of working is to use a semi-structured treatment manual as described in Part 3. The practitioner can be relatively **directive** in following the direction, didactics, questions and exercises from such a manual, but the practitioner will continuously check with the client at the macro-level whether this still fits the client's situation, preferences, needs and skills, for instance by using macro-communication and questionnaires (Section 5.2). Thus this meso-level consists of the specific actions that the practitioner brings in, as agreed upon and as continuously evaluated at the macro-level.

Micro-level. The micro-level describes the specific experiences and examples of clients. At this level, the practitioner is entirely phenomenological, sensitively following the lived experience of the client in a non-directive way, and neither imposing nor suggesting what the client must do, say, think or feel (Chapters 2 and 8).

7.2 Specific relational skills

18. *Tailoring the practice to the needs, skills and wishes of the client*

The treatment needs to be tailored to the needs, skills and wishes of the client, as initially evaluated in the assessment session (Chapter 4). Although there is some evidence for the effectiveness of using structures and treatment manuals (Chapter 6), it is also important to remain relatively flexible and tailor therapy to the unique situation (Schulte et al., 1992). Thus it seems important to tailor the general approach to the client, albeit by having regular macro-communication about the general aims and method of the treatment, and being phenomenologically sensitive to the specific micro-experiences of the client, by asking questions such as: 'How does this treatment manual feel to you? What is helpful? What could we change? Or would you prefer a different approach?' Treatment manuals such as in Part 3 should always be used in a flexible client-centred way.

19. *Shared decision-making*

Macro-level communication. The meaning-centred assessment should be a joint process between practitioner and client (Chapter 5). This implies that the practitioner is transparent about the reason why certain questions are asked ('I would like to ask you this question, because ...'), and any ideas should be tested as hypotheses and not as truths ('I wonder whether it might be the case that ... How do you see this?'). The practitioner discusses the hypothesised case formulation, and asks the client for feedback as clients are the best expert on their own life.

Rationale. Being transparent about the methods – especially in the first sessions – can be helpful for clients to 'own' the therapy process and take responsibility for their own therapeutic development. Transparency can also stimulate members in a treatment group to contribute more actively to each other's development, as they understand what the aim of the sessions is. Some disadvantages of being transparent are that it is time-consuming, could lead to intellectualising and may be difficult for individuals with little self-insight.

Informed decision. The client should not experience any hidden agendas. Practitioners must explain what meaning-centred practices can and cannot offer. Details about the treatment are discussed, such as the frequency of the sessions, where thy will take place, the number and content of sessions, whether they are group or individual, and aspects of the treatment (e.g. theory, reflective questions, mindfulness, homework). The client and practitioner decide together whether to start meaning-centred treatment, or whether another solution is more appropriate.

Reflection on process. During treatment, where appropriate, the practitioner could start a macro-dialogue with the client, to explore whether the goals, method, structure and relationship are still what the client wants and needs. Such explorations can be particularly beneficial when there are disruptions in the relationship, a client is stuck in the developmental process, or the client shows implicit or explicit resistance (Cooper & Mearns, 2013). A practitioner may express their own relational experiences (e.g. by saying 'I feel that ...; I may be wrong ... how do you feel about this?') and connect this with the general goals and methods (e.g. 'I wonder whether this [issue] has to do with the general goals, the way in which we work, or our relationship? At the start, we agreed that ... do you feel this still applies, or would you like to change this?'). Subsequently, they explore whether and how to continue.

20. *Exploring and macro-communication about which meanings the client expresses in the relationship with the practitioner*

Every relationship has a meaning. What meaning does the relationship between a client and a practitioner have? Many theories have been developed about the therapeutic relationship, with psychodynamic terms such as transference and countertransference describing this meaning. It is usually not an explicit aim and part of meaning-centred practices to explicate the relational dynamics. However, particularly when there are relational ruptures, practitioners should examine what meaning the sessions have for the client, and possibly address this in macro-conversations with the client.

Examples

Clients come to me for different reasons, in line with the **meaning quintet**. **Materialistic-hedonistic meaning**: for some clients, our sessions have become a familiar habit and enjoyable experience, with no further implications in daily life. **Self-oriented meaning**: other clients own the treatment and use the sessions to set goals, plan and organise their lives. Some merely seek recognition of who they are, or express themselves. **Social meaning**: many clients find a sense of social connection or belonging in the therapy groups, and those who participate in research trials feel they are altruistically contributing to the development of better practices. **Higher meaning**: clients also use our conversations for self-growth or coping with crisis. **Existential-philosophical meaning**: some clients report that our sessions remind them of feeling alive, free, responsible and connected with the world and history.

For many clients, the relationship with the meaning-centred practitioner becomes a unique experience, offering a glimpse into what is possible in life. By explicitly exploring the meanings of the relationship, the practitioner could help clients to set goals and experiment with these meanings outside the consultation room. For example, when I explored with a client what she was looking for in our sessions, the client realised that she was using me to get recognition for her achievements, and subsequently she decided it was more effective to ask her manager for feedback. Thus whatever is going on in the relationship between the client and the practitioner could be used to open new meanings in daily life. **Self-reflection** and supervision may help practitioners to reflect and experience the meanings that clients could be looking for in the relationship. Research suggests that practitioners who are aware of transference and countertransference, and deal effectively with this, are slightly more effective (Goldfried et al., 1997; Gelso & Hayes, 2002). Practitioners who are interested in further developing this skill may study psychodynamic or pluralistic therapies.

21. *Improving and deepening the practitioner–client relationship*

Meaning-centred practitioners use many skills to strengthen and deepen the practitioner–client relationship. Research shows that the strength of the working alliance strongly predicts the general effectiveness (Martin et al., 2000; Norcross, 2002). Practitioners who are experienced as more authentic, genuine, open or trustworthy seem to be slightly more effective (Orlinsky et al., 2004; Burckell & Goldfried, 2006). Self-disclosure about relevant meaning-centred topics may be slightly effective, as therapists who reveal something personal may be associated with lower symptom distress in the clients and a more positive relationship (Van de Creek & Angstadt, 1985; Hanson, 2005). This implies for example that practitioners share their own meaning-centred experiences, where relevant and within the reasonable boundaries of the client–practitioner relationship. Another important skill is the ability to repair alliance ruptures, that is, a tension or break down in the collaborative relationship between client and practitioner (Safran et al., 2002). This includes a wide range of skills, such as acknowledging the problem, exploring the cause of it, finding solutions and apologising where needed. Other effective relational aspects can be found elsewhere (Norcross, 2002).

22. *Following the client's tempo*

It may be frustrating for practitioners when clients do not improve quickly. From their personal and professional experience, practitioners may be quicker to understand and change than clients. It is important for practitioners to see how fundamental meaning is for the client: it is not merely about some random behaviour, but about the most important experiences, which have often been formed over many years. Research indicates that treatments are more effective when these are tailored to the specific stage of change for the client (Prochaska et al., 2009). Or formulated in meaning-centred terms: clients will only change to the extent that change is meaningful for them. Clients improve quicker when practitioners follow their tempo, although there is no one generic formula on how all clients develop. This also implies that practitioners adjust treatment manuals when these go too quick or too slow for an individual. The practitioner can check how accurate the tempo is via empathy, intuition and macro-communication.

23. *Empathising with the client's struggles in life, and stressing that existential struggles are common to all human beings*

Empathy is an important aspect of effective treatments (Bohart et al., 2002). This means that practitioners enter the private perceptual world of another and have an accurate, felt understanding of their experiencing (Cooper, 2008). This implies that practitioners empathise with the client's struggles in life, and stress that all humans struggle (Yalom, 1980; Yalom & Lesz, 2005).

This may help to normalise the – often frightening – situation: 'It is normal to ask questions about meaning when you are in such abnormal life situations; it would be abnormal if you did not ask such questions.' Practitioners explicitly help clients to mourn the loss of meanings: 'How does it feel that you cannot do this anymore? What has this meaning given you in the past?'

The existential therapist Van Deurzen seems to focus much on this core skill. She describes how life appears to perpetually oscillate between suffering and joy. She writes that 'life is an endless struggle where moments of ease and blissful happiness are the exception rather than the rule', and reaching heaven-on-earth is unlikely (Van Deurzen, 2015, p. 181). Individuals' positive intentions are inevitably confronted with injustices, paradoxes and failures in endless numbers of boundary situations, such as suffering illness and death, as Jaspers reports (1925). Individuals often find it difficult to accept the reality that life is an endless struggle, for instance by fantasising about a perfect and problem-free life. Such unrealistic expectations may lead to frustration and more suffering, as these expectations will inevitably fail in daily life (Van Deurzen & Adams, 2011). By empthasising with clients in the role of a non-directive mentor and fellow human-being, Van Deurzen helps clients to embrace the totality of their being, and possibly wake up from self-deception, and in this process realise that they may be stronger than they think. This process of empathising with life's existential boundaries may help clients to move beyond a fear of life, discover life's potentiality and experience life as worth living (Vos, 2018b).

Empathy is often associated with a positive regard, which may be described as a warm acceptance of the other and their experiences without conditions, and which is moderately effective in most therapies (Cooper, 2008 p. 67). For example, practitioners are sensitive and non-judgemental about any experiences the client may have had. The client feels accepted and not judged by the therapist, and free to express their feelings. Empathy also implies that, although practitioners may give some feedback, they focus on soft confrontations and nuanced hypotheses (with formulations such as 'could it be that …') rather than direct or confrontational statements (e.g. 'you should …'; 'you must …'; 'it is true that …').

24. *Recognising the importance of existing meanings, and religious and cultural context*

Why would an individual change a behaviour or belief which feels meaningful? When it feels meaningful, the client will not be motivated to change. Motivation research suggests that it is ineffective to directly undermine behaviour or thoughts that are perceived as meaningful, such as addictions and obsessions. Therefore, meaning-centred practitioners often suggest 'trying out something new', instead of 'giving up something old for something new'. This is underlined by cognitive research showing that individuals are more aversive towards losing something than gaining something (Kahneman, 2012). Therefore, meaning-centred practitioners often explore a broad range of possible meanings, both existing and new meanings. Where there is a conflict between meanings, clients could try out a 'temporary small project', which they may abandon and return to the old situation if this does not feel satisfying. Practitioners also recognise the importance of the religious and cultural context of the individual, and how this shapes the meanings of clients, what this offers them and how they are loyal to their convictions. Research also shows that sensitivity to religious and culturally unique meanings increase the effectiveness of psychological treatments (Roth & Fonagy, 2013).

25. *Helping the client to develop ethical and authentic relationships; having an ethical stance towards the client and their situation*

Exercise

How would you treat Hitler who found meaning in killing Jews? How would you treat a terrorist who finds meaning by blowing himself up and interpreting this as an altruistic act? Who are we to say that this is not meaningful?

Meaning-centred practitioners have had heated debates about this question. At one end of the debate, practitioners argue that they should always remain neutral and provide space for clients to define what is meaningful. At the other end, practitioners such as Frankl strongly believe that every individual has an ethical conscience. For example, if a practitioner would have helped Hitler to **phenomenologically unpeel** his experiences, he would have discovered that his conscience was conditioned along the lines of the myth of a super-race, and that he mistook the dictates of the state for the voice of conscience (Fabry, 1968). Of course, the assumption that everyone can discover their ethical conscience seems difficult to verify empirically, although there is some evidence (Hauser, 2006).

The phenomenological method may offer some guidance (Chapter 2). All individual meanings are embedded in a social context. Practitioners can use self-reflection and **reflexivity** to identify how they could be imposing their values on clients. They could also recognise that helping clients with their individual meaning-centred questions is inherently a political act, seen from a social-historical perspective (Chapter 1). Clients are invited to transcend their own perspective, their materialistic-hedonist and self-oriented meanings and to connect with the larger social-historical perspective, and focus on meanings about the people around them. Practitioners could for example explore how clients have developed values in their social context, and recognise how these values may have emerged out of suffering; by blowing himself up, the terrorist takes away the meanings and freedom of other people, like other people have limited him. The practitioner may be able to humanise the client and connect with an underlying value, such as the terrorist wants to create a more just world. Subsequently, they could analyse whether terrorism is the most effective method and whether it is in line with the client's other values. For example, they could help the client to find ways to create a more just world without a cost to human life. Thus practitioners will not directly enforce their perspectives on clients, but invite them to explore other perspectives. In this way, the practitioner explores empathically what it is like to be ethical.

Perhaps the most important way to support clients in developing ethical relationships with others is by being a positive ethical role model. This implies empathic relational skills, **self-reflective and reflexive practices**, and having trained and prepared oneself optimally. If it is safe enough, practitioners may also consider explicitly discussing their ethical dilemmas. However, further research and debate is needed, and practitioners must always work within the ethical and legal framework of their discipline and country.

In my early professional years I was asking the question: how can I treat, or cure or change this person? Now I would phrase the question in this way: how can I provide a relationship which this person may use for his own personal growth?

(Rogers, 1995)

Key relational skills

18. Tailoring the practice to the needs, skills and wishes of the client.

19. Shared decision-making (macro-level).

20. Exploring and macro-communication about which meanings the client expresses in the relationship with the practitioner.

21. Improving and deepening the practitioner–client relationship.

22. Following the client's tempo.

23. Empathising with the client's struggles in life, and stressing that existential struggles are common to all human beings.

24. Recognising the importance of existing meanings, and religious and cultural context.

25. Helping the client to develop ethical and authentic relationships, and having an ethical stance towards the client and their situation.

8

Phenomenological, Experiential and Mindfulness Skills

8.1 General phenomenological, experiential and mindfulness skills

There are roughly two ways to address meaning: either we reflect on it from a cold distance, or we submerge ourselves in the warm flow of actually living a meaningful life (Sections 3.5 and 3.6). Clients often report that they have difficulties feeling this flow. How can meaning-centred practitioners help them to change from the reflective, cold distance to the warm flow of living? Some answers can be found in phenomenological, experiential and mindfulness skills. Although, strictly speaking, these are three different sets of skills, all help clients to develop a **phenomenological intuition** for what they experience as meaningful in their life. **Phenomenology** centres around exploring how clients experience meaning (Chapter 2). Experiential skills help clients to focus on their stream of experiences, including their emotions and behaviour, instead of mere reflections. Mindfulness and meditation skills are specific exercises to help clients submerge themselves in the flow of experiences in the here and now, in a non-judgemental way. A review of empirical and conceptual research (Vos, 2018c) indicates that phenomenological therapeutic skills can be effective in improving the well-being of clients, and particularly in addressing fundamental themes such as meaning in life and existential limitations (see Chapter 9).

Example

Bob told he knew perfectly how to live a meaningful life, as he had read shelf-fulls of books and followed countless self-discovery retreats. He told me that his long-term aim in life was to become a writer. However, he had not taken any of the

▶

◀

necessary steps to make this happen, as he was 'waiting for the right moment' to start. Consequently, he felt he lacked flow and happiness. During the assessment, I noted how much Bob was theorising about life instead of experiencing and acting. He had high demands of himself and was continuously monitoring himself, as a result of which he lacked the distance from himself to be immersed in the flow of activities in the world around him. I discussed my impression, and he agreed. We started with attention exercises to challenge his experiential avoidance. Via a questioning approach, he realised how his self-obsessive attitude blocked him from being in a meaningful flow, and therefore he decided to focus more on doing. We made a list of activities which he could do when he had the tendency to go inside himself. As he wanted to become a writer, he started a diary about his experiences, in which he would start writing without putting the pen down to get any experiential association with flowing. He also started some 'pilot projects', to try out new behaviour, instead of expecting immediate perfect results. Soon, he started dating and met a woman whom he fell in love; although he had difficulties trusting these loving feelings – he tried to rationalise them and had difficulty committing himself in the relationship – the relationship helped him to distance himself from his problems, trust his feelings more and transcend his own situation. This seemed to give him a greater sense of meaning and fulfilment in life.

8.2 Specific phenomenological, experiential and mindfulness skills

26. *Phenomenological unpeeling of experiences*

Some meaning-centred practitioners seem to work more in a phenomenological way (e.g. Langle, 2012) than others (e.g. Breitbart, 2015). At the core of phenomenology appears to be the process of **unpeeling** layers of our experiences (Section 2.3). There are many ways to do this, as phenomenology is not a unified school.

For example, existential-analysts follow four phenomenological steps (Langle, 2014): after description of the external facts of the situation, phenomenological analysis explores the client's experiences in more depth, followed by inner positioning in which clients evaluate their inner attitude and values, and finally clients reflect on acting on what they want to do.

As exemplified in Chapter 2, Ernesto Spinelli (2015) identifies three phenomenological steps (Section 2.3). Practitioners begin by temporarily setting aside their own assumptions and biases about the client ('bracketing'), ask open questions, and do non-leading exercises. Self-reflection, reflexivity, supervision and personal therapy can help practitioners to increase their self-awareness and bracket their assumptions. Subsequently, practitioners help clients to describe their experiences, for instance by empathising and taking a questioning approach (see Skill 30). Different aspects of the experiences are explored, such as asking: *When did you start to feel this? When do you experience this? What is the most meaningful aspect?* And so on. This implies that the client's experiences are specified and concretised, focused on daily life, embodied, contextualised in the totality of the individual's history and so on. The practitioner avoids placing any initial hierarchies of significance or importance in these conversations with the client. Anything the client tells them is initially regarded as equally meaningful. With this distant perspective, meaningful themes can emerge. For example, it may become clear that for a client materialistic-hedonic meanings are less meaningful than social or higher meanings. This experiential hierarchy arises from the client's story, and are not imposed onto the client by the practitioner.

The research evidence for phenomenological skills is built mainly on phenomenological studies, both philosophical explorations and empirical interview studies (e.g. Smith, 2010; Vos, 2014; Spinelli, 2015). Several trials suggest that clients may benefit from phenomenological practices (Koebbel, 2016; Rayner & Vitali, 2016). However, research seems to suggest that phenomenological skills alone may not be very effective, but combined with meaning-centred skills they may be (Vos, Craig & Cooper, 2015; Vos & Vitali, 2018; Vos, 2018c). Several specific phenomenological techniques are supported by strong empirical evidence, such as the Socratic dialogue (see Skill 30 below) and systematically addressing different types of meaning (Vos & Vitali, 2018).

This book follows a pragmatic phenomenological approach (see Chapter 2). This means that the phenomenological process aims to support the client in exploring their meaningful experiences, without the need for unverifiable metaphysical ideas, such as the ability to discover authentic true meanings. For example, Ernesto Spinelli (2006, 2015) seems critical about the idea that therapists should explicitly explore or develop the worldviews of clients – such as systematically exploring how clients live in different worlds (Van Deurzen & Arnold-Baker, 2005) or experience types of meaning (see Chapter 2). Instead, Spinelli aims to stay with the worlding process of clients, which is the process of immediate unrepeatable embodied flow of experiencing. According to Ernesto Spinelli, therapy aims to de-sediment fixed stances and re-own dissociated experiences, although this aim should not be enforced and clients may decide not to consider alternative ways of seeing themselves and their world. Thus Spinelli suggests staying with the client's existence as it is currently being lived. In a similar vein, this book focuses on the phenomenological and experiential process instead of on the identification of universal truth or absolute meaning like fundamental phenomenologists such as Husserl

(1901/1975). This is supported by research, as studies show that the **unpeeling** process is beneficial, regardless of whether the result is finding an absolute meaning or not (Section 2.6; Vos, 2018c).

27. *Stimulating an attitude of experiential acceptance*

Example

The treatment manual I was using with my client Berend suggested to ask him questions about specific moments when life had felt meaningful, such as 'Could you give some examples when relationships felt meaningful in your life?' or 'When did you enjoy something beautiful?' Berend was staring into space when he tried to answer these questions and gave few examples. He seemed unable to do these exercises because he did not know how to focus on and trust his experiences. When I shared this impression, Berend felt relieved that I had recognised he was struggling with my questions. We decided to do some basic experiential exercises. For example, he closed his eyes and described what he was feeling: where did his body make contact with the chair, how did his body feel, what was his breathing like and so on. Subsequently, as homework, he set his alarm clock every hour to briefly write down how he felt in that moment. He then went on to begin writing a diary of how he had been feeling during the day. Only when Berend had started to be able to accept his flow of experiences and develop the ability to focus without fear of his experiences, could he begin to differentiate between meaningful and less meaningful experiences.

Definitions

Phenomenological practitioners tell us that meaning is found in the subjective flow of experiencing. When we phenomenologically examine our experiences, we can differentiate between what we experience as meaningful and as less meaningful. From a pragmatic-phenomenological approach, it is irrelevant whether this difference is a metaphysical truth or constructed in our experiential process. What meaning-centred practitioners seem to agree on is that clients can use experiential introspection as a main path towards a more meaningful life. For clients to be able to use their experiences as a compass towards meaning, they first need to accept their experiences. *I accept that I experience what I experience; I will not try to deny or distort my experiences; I pay attention to the totality of my subjectively lived experiences, and take these seriously as signposts to future directions in life.*

Most meaning-centred practitioners appear to assume that clients have direct access to their flow of experiencing, accept these experiences and use them for self-discovery. However, this may not be the case. When practitioners do not first help clients with experiential acceptance, clients can feel manipulated, engage only superficially with the treatment or drop out. This may be referred to as 'a basic attitude of experiential acceptance': accepting we experience what we experience, being able to focus on experiences and trusting these experiences to show possible directions in life. Several meaning-centred practitioners have differentiated helpful from unhelpful experiential attitudes, which either help or block individuals from experiencing meaningful experiences, as will be explained in the next section.

Although phenomenological-existential and meaning-centred therapists have focused on experiential avoidance since the beginning of the twentieth century, its importance has only recently been popularised from a functionalistic perspective by Acceptance and Commitment Therapy, and its benefits have been validated in empirical studies (Hayes et al., 1996). The Acceptance and Action Questionnaire has often been used in this functional context (Bond et al., 2011). However, meaning-centred therapists seem to describe experiential avoidance in less functionalistic ways (Chapters 1 and 2). Etymologically speaking, meaning that is discovered via experiential acceptance has been called 'Sinn' in Old Germanic and Continental European languages ('Sinn'). This word is etymologically derived from the Latin 'sentire', meaning receptivity: individuals receive meaning by accepting their experiences. This receptive attitude contrasted with the demanding tone of the Old Germanic word 'Meinung' – from which the English word 'meaning' is derived – which means that a teleological or functional order was imposed onto the experiences (Chapter 2). Fostering experiential acceptance has been included in many meaning-centred trials, although it is not always explicated by other practitioners (Vos & Vitali, 2018). In general, experiential treatments seem to improve clients' well-being (Elliott, Greenberg & Lietaer, 2004; Elliott & Freire, 2010).

Basic attitude of acceptance

For many clients, going to a meaning-centred practitioner is a big step. This can be the first time in their life that they are paying attention to their experiences, which can be overwhelming. Therefore, practitioners must be non-judgemental and empathic, and invite clients to share anything they like. The basic attitude of practitioners could be described as one of acceptance, which may help clients accept their own experiences. Existential analysts, such as Langle (2014), have most explicitly elaborated the role of acceptance for meaning-centred practitioners.

Examples of acceptance that were found in meaning-centred treatments include, for example, acceptance that specific life events have
occurred (emotional acceptance and integrative acceptance which
incorporate a negative event with positive aspects of life); acceptance
that absolute certainty about what is meaningful for ourselves (absolute
existential meaning), about the meaning of the universe (absolute cosmic meaning) and about how my life fits into this cosmic 'Big Plan' (e.g.
'why did this happen to me?') may not be achievable; acceptance of the
world (e.g. acceptance of physical limitations such as an illness); acceptance of life (e.g. acceptance of one's own experiences); acceptance of self
(e.g. acceptance of and revealing who they are); acceptance of what they
experience as meaningful; acceptance that our perspectives and attitudes
are inherently limited; and acceptance of what is in our power to change
and what is not.

Use discontent as compass

The decision to ask for help shows that clients already have an initial
understanding of what is meaningful, and particularly that their current
life situation is not meaningful. It is the task of the practitioner to make
clients aware of the differences they intuitively make between meaningful and not-meaningful, for example during assessment (Chapter 5), via
identifying and concretising skills (Chapter 6) or through questioning
(see Skill 30 below). For instance, clients often report that they have a
general sense of discontent, 'something is wrong' and 'something needs
to change'. Clients often see such feelings as negative, but phenomenologists have reframed these feelings as a compass indicating initial
direction: the clients already know they should not be doing what they
are currently doing, and they are motivated for change. These feelings
are like a positive '[wake-up] call from the self to the self' (Heidegger,
1927/2001). Therefore, clients are asked to identify what their experiences 'are trying to tell them', to put their attention in a helpful direction
('reduction'; Heidegger, 1927/2001).

Develop self-distance

Some clients avoid their experiences because they are too overwhelming. For example, after traumatic life events such as the loss of a loved
one or the diagnosis of an incurable disease, clients may not immerse
them within their experiences, as these may be too painful. As a first
step towards experiential acceptance, these clients could be prompted to

look at their feelings, but not go within them. Logotherapists call this self-distancing (Marshall & Marshall, 2012): stepping out of our usual stream of experiencing and observing ourselves. We create the distance of observation between us and our circumstances. Distancing means that clients detect their thoughts and experiences, and see these as hypotheses rather than objective facts about the world. Logotherapists use a broad range of exercises to foster self-distancing, as will be explained in Skill 30 below: questioning, evaluating the helpfulness of their attitude, creative exercises and cognitive behavioural therapy exercises (Beck, 2000).

Identify unhelpful attitudes

If experiences are like a compass showing us the general direction in life, then our attitude is like a magnet that can distort the needle from our experiential compass. The phenomenological explorations of the client's lived experiences may help identify which attitudes clients experience as helpful and which as unhelpful in living a meaningful life. As a reference point, meaning-centred therapists have developed possible unhelpful attitudes and ways to change these (Ungar, 1997, 1998; Lukas, 2000; Frankl, 2004; Marshall & Marshall, 2012). Tables 8.1 and 8.2 are neither complete nor entirely based on systematic research, and should only be read for didactic purposes. These unhelpful attitudes may block clients from accepting their meaningful experiences.

Stimulate a dual attitude

Empirical research indicates that a helpful attitude towards living a meaningful life is a **dual attitude** (Vos, 2014). This means that two different options are not seen as each other's opposites, but as two independent phenomena which could be combined. For example, clients could say, 'I am frustrated because I cannot be successful in my work and at the same time be a good parent', but they may explore options where they are both successful in their work and a good parent. Thus clients examine whether their conclusion is based on a false dichotomy, on the fallacy that there can only be one ultimate solution, and on their inability to bear paradoxical feelings. They could try to see new meanings not as permanent replacements of old meanings, but as a small temporary project next to other meanings (see the discussion on 'life projects' in Chapter 6). The next chapter will explain how clients can learn to live with risks, tensions and ambiguities in life.

Example

Eve felt dissatisfied about her life because she was not doing the job that she had been dreaming of since early childhood. In our conversations, she started to realise that she had an either/or approach to her jobs: either she can only do the job of a legal officer but then she cannot follow her dream of being a hairdresser, or she totally gives up the legal job to become a full-time hairdresser. Subsequently, we explored whether it would be possible to be a hairdresser in the evenings and weekends, while she kept her legal position. Resulting from this exploration, she started a hairdressing course in the evenings and started hairdressing at home in the weekends. After a year, her hairdressing work was so successful and satisfying that she reduced her number of hours that she was working as legal officer. When she started her part-time job as hairdresser, the depression that she had been suffering from for many years disappeared, and she felt life as fulfilling.

Table 8.1   Overview of some unhelpful attitudes

Attitude	Description	Exercises
Provisionary attitude	Lack of aims and plans in life; not trying to reach goals; primarily directed by impulses and wishes; indecisiveness; lack of commitment; self-indulgence; bitterness; hopelessness	Explore meaningful experiences; experiment with small attainable goals
Fatalistic attitude	Belief that everything is determined and can be explained; sceptical about meaning; focused on materialism and hedonism; pessimism; inactivity; seeking control; superstitious Unhelpful because no belief in meaning at all	'Accept the things I cannot change, the courage to change the things I can, and the wisdom to know the difference' (Niebuhr)
Collectivistic attitude	Following majority opinion, trends; denying individuality and responsibility	Explore individual's flow of experiencing, connect with the experiences that feel the most important; tolerate feelings of uniqueness
Fanatical attitude	Elevate one meaning to absolute idealised level; risk of emotional crisis if meaning is lost or unattainable	Focus on more meanings

Passive attitude due to anticipatory anxiety	Excessive fearful reactions, panic attacks, or avoidance behaviours due to negative imaginings; quick reactivity to environment such as blushing or dizziness; vicious cycle of fear triggering by the feared scenario	Confront what is feared; learn to tolerate feelings of anxiety
Obsessive attitude	Obsessive ruminations; obsessive-compulsive behaviours; perfectionism; emotional response to stressful situations; fear of doing something unacceptable, leading to a continuous fight with themselves, and being stuck in the mind; vicious cycle due to being over-alert and exaggerating imperfections	Develop right passivity; comfortably ignore negative thoughts by not attributing special significance to them
Hyper-intention	Excessive forcing of something; excessive defensiveness; narrow focused on self; unable to let go; often materialistic-hedonic or self-oriented meanings; dichotomous world view (good/bad); focus on luck or fortune; boredom and emptiness if a desire gets satisfied; vicious cycle emerges: the more control is aimed for, the more control seems lost; dissatisfaction; addictions to fill boredom	Let go of intention; appreciate flow of experiences; develop a sense of wonder and awe for what experiences bring; self-transcendence
Hyper-reflection	Increasingly monitoring one's performance; fear of failure or diminished performance; hypervigilance and hyper-reaction to mistakes; negative self-image; unrealistic demands on oneself; anxious and vulnerable to emotional crises. Examples: insomnia, hypochondria, body image disorders, sexual dysfunctions	Develop a positive and realistic sense of self; identify hyper-reflection as a core problem; realise that our self-image may not necessary be true; develop a sense of humour; create a dialogue with oneself
Attitude towards a pyramidal meaning system	Small number of idealised meanings at the top and few other minor meanings at the base of the pyramid. Example: the fanatic	Parallel meaning system in which there are a few (four/five) important meanings
Attitude towards a horizontal meaning system	If an individual has a horizontal value system, the individual has many equally important values; not a specific focus or direction; indecisiveness	Parallel meaning system in which there are a few (four/five) important meanings

Table 8.2 Overview of some attitude-changing interventions

Attitude changing interventions	Example
Assessment	Focus on their discontent or lack of fulfilment; identify alternative positive directions
Didactics	Didactics about experiential acceptance and dual attitude
Questioning approach	Examine experiences and inconsistencies via questions and Socratic dialogue
Identifying & specifying meaning-centred skill	Highlight and explicate experiential and dual aspects in the experiences and stories of clients
Practitioner–client relationship	Lower anxiety; clients feel safe to explore alternative experiences
Confrontational experiential exercises	Confront experiences and paradoxes; experiential and creative exercises; experiential flooding by confronting the feared scenario; learn to tolerate feelings
Mindfulness	Learn to accept experiences and create distance
De-reflection exercises	Leave rational mode and immerse clients in flow of experiencing
Attitude change	1. Explore the client's current situation, and understand the cause of the suffering they experience 2. Look for the roots of the suffering and see where there are realistically limitations 3. Notice also the strengths and possibilities 4. Notice the unhealthy attitude which increases the suffering, and try to change this 5. Bring the findings to the awareness of the patient and discuss them openly 6. Help to affirm the belief in life's meaningfulness and one's unlimited personal worth (Marshall & Marshall, 2012)
Act as if	Pretend as if the alternative is already there
Gratitude	Be grateful about what was and what still can be (Schulenberg, 2001)
Faith, hope and love	Stimulate faith and hope about change, and focus on love (Frankl, 1987)

28. *Stimulating clients to immerse themselves in the flow of meaningful experiences*

> ## Example
>
> Bob was anxious about stepping into action. He could not distance himself from his fears, put these aside and take the first needed step. He was reflecting a lot, desperately wanting to have meaningful life experiences, but the more he wanted this
>
> ▶

◀

the further he seemed from realising it; he was worrying about his worries, and trying to explain why he was not successful, which even further increased his **hyper-reflection**. We hypothesised together that he may need to create more distance from his emotions and thoughts (**'self-distance'**), and transcend his own inner world by acting in the world around him (**'self-transcendence'**).

As described in the previous section, individuals may 'feel trapped in their own worry about a problem .... There is no situation that cannot be made worse by excessive worrying. A certain amount of worrying is healthy: it will get you medical or other help. But if you brood on a problem, eventually you will feel as if you are the helpless victim of a problem you cannot solve' (Fabry, 1986, p. 32). This is called **hyper-reflection**, which means that individuals are obsessed with themselves and their problems, and are stuck in a process of cognitive reflection on their problem, which exacerbates their symptoms. Hyper-reflection often implies a self-reinforcing cycle, by which individuals are reflecting and reflecting about their reflections and so on.

Additionally, **hyper-intention** means that individuals have a strong intention which aggravates the hyper-reflection: 'I must sleep; if I do not sleep, I will not be able to function well tomorrow'; and subsequently they begin to focus more on their not-sleeping and so their anxiety increases, which creates more hyper-reflection. Examples of hyper-reflection and hyper-intention are typically found in experiences which require letting go of thinking, such as insomnia, hypochondria and some sexual disorders (Marshall & Marshall, 2012). The self-observation and worry cast them out of their flow of experiences, and make them stuck in their mind. Sudden negative life events, such as a tragic loss or development of a life-threatening illness, could lead to hyper-reflection.

These individuals often believe that their thoughts are true or meaningful, and that there are no alternative options. Their habits of hyper-reflection and hyper-intention may have become so pervasive that it is ineffective to ask them to 'reflect less' or 'try less'. Requesting this could even strengthen their hyper-reflection and hyper-intention. Therefore, Frankl encouraged such clients to distance themselves from themselves and their problems, by paying attention to what the world around them could mean to them. If a problem is caused by too much reflection the help comes from *de*-reflection (Fabry, 1986). **De-reflection** means that clients leave their rational mode and immerse themselves in the process of experiencing. Thus, individuals look away from themselves and their performance, and look towards something more meaningful. Many exercises could help clients to 'get out there in the real world instead of philosophising from their armchair'. Several exercises are discussed below, some of which are supported by empirical evidence (Table 8.3).

Table 8.3   Examples of de-reflection interventions

Exercise	Example
Alternative list making	Develop a list of alternative activities that clients could engage in, instead of hyper-reflection – e.g. someone who cannot sleep could engage in mindfulness or fantasy exercises, or read, to create a distraction from oneself. Alternative activities should not be about self-concern, but about commitment to something external, such as love for a life's task or love. Effective in insomnia, sexual dysfunctions, addictions, psychosomatic disorders, alcohol misuse, chronic pain, burnout, families of schizophrenic individuals (Marshall & Marshall, 2012)
Mindfulness	Accept thoughts for what they are – mere thoughts – and do not attach too much attention; instead empty the mind of obsessive self-focus
Just do	Put clients in situations in which it is impossible to be hyper-reflective; 'just do' activities in the world commit to random actions and allow evaluation of the experience of not being hyper-reflective
Paradoxical intention	Clients are to deliberately practise or exaggerate a neurotic habit or thought, so that they stop fighting, identifying and undermining their problems. Effective in anxiety and obsessive-compulsive disorders (e.g. Hill, 1987). Breaking the pattern of anticipatory anxiety, which often presents itself as anxiety about anxiety, anxious self-observation (hyper-intention), fear of the physical consequences of fear (hyper-reflection), leading to a sensation of 'impending doom' and avoidance, and reinforcing the same symptoms that are feared (Marshall & Marshall, 2012). Possible steps: '1. Rule out any underlying medical concern that can cause the anxiety 2. Detailed explanation of paradoxical intention and the sharing of case studies 3. Collaborative exaggeration of symptoms in ways that appeal to the client's unique sense of humour' (Fabry, 1982, p. 35)
Sense of humour	Laugh, ridicule and relativise their own behaviour
Cognitive defusion	Regard feelings and thoughts as mere experiences and hypotheses, not as absolute truths. Examples could be found in Acceptance and Commitment Therapy (Hayes et al., 2012), supported by empirical evidence (Masuda et al, 2004; Hayes et al., 2006; Powers, et al., 2009)
Self-transcendence	Having a greater perspective on oneself and the situation (discussed in the next section)

29. *Phenomenologically exploring whether there are any hierarchies in the client's experiences of meaning*

In meaning-centred practices clients learn to identify differences between what is meaningful and what is less meaningful. Phenomenologically speaking, they learn to identify hierarchies in their experiences. For example, when I look at my experiences, I see that watching movies is less meaningful than having relationships, which at the time of writing felt less meaningful than fulfilling the larger purpose of writing this book (see Introduction). These are not hierarchies which clients or people around them impose, but clients identify with these hierarchies in their stream of experiencing (Chapter 2). Clients may be able to identify a hierarchy of meanings, like a mountain, starting with unimportant meanings at the foot of the mountain, progressing to more and more important meanings, until finally there is the most important meaning at the top of the mountain. The development of such an intuitive hierarchy of meanings could direct clients in life and help them make decisions. For example, if the family is more important than work, this could imply spending fewer hours in the office and more with the family. The creation of such a hierarchy is never final, but only reflective of the current experiences of the client, which may change in the future. To create such an experiential hierarchy, practitioners can follow several steps:

Step 1. Preparation

The previous sections describe how some clients need to do some preparatory work before they can identify what is meaningful. For example, practitioners can work with them on experiential acceptance, developing a helpful attitude and self-distancing. Take for instance John (p. 114), who practised mindfulness exercises as he was often theoretical-cognitive and not in touch with his inner feelings.

Step 2. Identify what is meaning and what is not meaning

Practitioners can theoretically explain what meaning is: making a commitment, being motivated, acting, having values, experiencing self-worth, understanding and self-regulating (Section 4.1). Clients may learn to use this definition by applying this to some examples. They could, for instance, every day write in their diary at least five experiences which they experience as 'meaningful', and, in line with the next session, for each of these experiences, clients could check the definition: 'Is this about meaning or about another psychological experience, such as quick happiness, social expectations or mundane daily life?' Subsequently, clients may identify whether and when they were within a meaningful flow and when they were not (Section 4.4). John wrote every day for ten minutes what had felt meaningful; during our sessions we examined which experiences were about meaning and which were not. He learned to identify those experiences that were meaningful and those that were not.

Step 3. Identify groups of meanings

When enough examples are collected, they identify recurrent patterns. For example, when clients look back through their diary they may see that they experience moments spent with others as the most meaningful, and time spent alone as the least meaningful. Thus, in this step, scaling-up exercises are used (Section 2.5). For example, in a session they could write out one example per Post-it note, create groups of Post-its with similar meanings, and give every group an overarching name (for instance, 'enjoying coffee' and 'enjoying cheese' will be in the same category as 'physical enjoyment').

Alternatively, practitioners can lead guided exercises based on the **meaning quintet** (Section 3.3). Clients are asked to identify in their past, present or hopes for the future, examples of material-physical, self-oriented, social, higher and existential-philosophical meanings. The treatment manual in Part 3 follows this approach. After several weeks of keeping a diary of his meaningful experiences, John identified patterns among the experiences which had felt the most meaningful. He understood that his most frequently returning meaningful experiences was about helping others.

Step 4. Ranking meanings

Clients are asked to rank their (sub)groups of meaning, ranging from completely not meaningful to completely meaningful. For example, Frankl used a mountain range exercise in which clients draw a mountain on a piece of paper and write their meanings at different heights, in order of importance. Alternatively, clients can put Post-its of each meaning on the mountain, in order of importance. Meaning-centred practitioners use many ranking exercises, such as the Value Awareness Technique (Hutzell, 1990). John identified many different meanings in his diary, such as altruism, being productive at work, socialising and doing adult education. By intuitively exploring his feelings, he realised that being altruistic was the most important.

Step 5. Identify possibility of self-transcendence

Some meaning-centred practitioners explicitly encourage clients to focus on self-transcending meanings. Self-transcendence means that not only we can distance ourselves from our internal and external conditions (e.g. modification of attitudes and de-reflection), but are also able to reach beyond ourselves (Fabry, 1994), by being immersed in social or higher types of meanings. Thus self-distancing is about looking away from one's own problems, de-reflection is about looking away from oneself in the world around us, and self-transcendence is about committing to actions that are more meaningful than oneself. John began to understand that life felt more fulfilling when he was being altruistic and connected with people than when he only focused on his job.

Step 6. Composition of vertical and horizontal axes of meaning

Practitioners can help clients to identify whether they have a pyramidal or a horizontal meaning system. A pyramidal system means that an individual has a small number of meanings that are extremely important and many meanings that are not important. For example, a client mainly organised his life around his academic career and dedicated little energy to his social life and hobbies. This pyramidal system collapsed when he lost his job as an academic and could not find a new position at a university. He developed an existential crisis in which he started to realise that there are other important meanings in life which he should value higher, such as his social life. A horizontal system has many equally important meanings. For example, an adolescent client had difficulties deciding what she wanted to study, as she had a wide range of interests without any topic that had her particular passion.

In meaning-centred practices, clients can be prompted to develop a parallel value system in which there are a few important meanings – for example four or five – which provide a focus and make clients flexible when one value has become lost or unattainable (Lukas, 1996). In the case study described above, John created a hierarchy of meanings, with altruism at the top, socialising and self-education next, and work as the lowest.

Step 7. Identify conflicts, tensions and inconsistencies

In the previous steps, clients may identify conflicts, tensions or inconsistencies between different meanings. Although meaning-centred practitioners often help clients to bear paradoxes and tensions (see next chapter) and develop a **dual attitude**, it could be helpful to identify what these conflicts are about. For example, an individual may experience a tension between family life and work – for example, 'could I work 60 hours per week?' Such a conflict between meanings may lead to passivity or indecisiveness, and a meaning-centred practitioner could help in such a situation, for example by exploring what Clients find the most important in this situation, and using experiential exercises – to distract from the cognitive level of the conflict. John felt frustrated that his job demanded so much time resulting in him being unable to engage in altruistic activities for the charity he worked for; as he had already concluded that altruism is more important than his work, he decided to tell his boss that he wants to work fewer hours (Tables 8.4 and 8.5).

Table 8.4 Examples of self-transcendence

Self-transcendence	Examples
Love, hope, faith and will	Focus on love, hope, faith and will, which cannot be demanded, commanded or ordered like quick happiness or success (Frankl, 1986)
Social and higher meanings	Instead of materialistic-hedonic and self-oriented meanings, focus on social and higher meanings (Vos, 2018b)
Spiritual meanings	Focus on spiritual and religious meanings
Existential-philosophical meaning	Explicitly reflect on existential-philosophical meanings, e.g. freedom, responsibility and uniqueness
Cosmic meaning	Meaning of the universe; how individual life fits into a 'Big Plan'

NB: These are examples from the clinical literature, which are not all evidence-based and which do not necessarily reflect the author's opinion.

Table 8.5 Hierarchy exercises

Hierarchy exercise	Explanation
Mountain range exercise	Draw a mountain range on a piece of paper; write meanings/values at different heights in the mountain, in order of importance. Alternative: put meanings/values on Post-it notes which can be placed on the mountain
Downwards arrow technique	Type of Socratic questioning; successive questions, to uncover underlying intermediate and core meanings. Example, 'why technique': the practitioner starts with a general question about meaningful experiences (e.g. 'Could you describe one moment which you recently experienced as meaningful'), and subsequently asks the client 'Why is this meaningful to you?' (or 'What aspect makes this experience particularly meaningful'), and after each answer, the practitioner asks this same question, until a client cannot further elaborate the answer and seems to finish at an unchangeable core. Cognitive technique (e.g. Beck, 2011)
Card sorting (Q-sort)	Clients write one meaning per card and sorts these in order of importance

Value Awareness Test	Step-by-step application of logotherapeutic principles, emphasising objective activities to stimulate individuals' perceptions of meaning via a series of structured exercises (Hutzell, 1990)
Post-it method	Steps: 1. Individuals collect examples of meaningful moments, and write each on a separate small Post-it note ('micro-meanings'); at least 30 small Post-its need to be created. 2. Small Post-its are organised into coherent groups ('meso-meanings') on the basis of their content – for example, 'drinking coffee' and 'going to restaurants' are about joyful physical experiences. Write a group name on a larger Post-it – for example, 'joyful physical experiences'. Put small Post-its on the corner of the large Post-it. 3. Combine large Post-its/groups into even larger groups ('macro-meanings'). Create approximately five groups. 4. Put large Post-its/groups in order of importance (e.g. on the drawing of a mountain; Post-its could be put on symbolic places and objects in the physical room)
Meaning questionnaires	See Chapter 5

30. *Using a questioning approach*

Meaning-centred practices are strongly based on a questioning approach. The philosopher Socrates compared questioning with being a midwife ('maieutika'). The aim is to help clients give birth to a new understanding, and not to pour the practitioner's ideas into clients, which may block them from experiencing their own meaning. Being a midwife means that the practitioner helps the client to do the work. This also means that the practitioner uses the phenomenological method of temporarily setting aside their own assumptions and biases, helping clients to describe their experiences neutrally and specifically, and not imposing their own hierarchies on clients, but allowing these hierarchies to arise from their experiences. Meaning-centred questions help clients to unpeel their experiences, to differentiate and deepen what is more and what is less meaningful. The question of whether there is a core or not may be regarded an irrelevant question, as it is the process that seems to help clients (Chapter 2). The practitioner may stop asking unpeeling questions when the client seems unable to unpeel the experience any more, as every question leads to the same answer.

A helpful meaning-centred question is phenomenological and focuses on what clients experience as the most meaningful aspect in their experience. More specifically, it has been suggested that naïve questions can be helpful: questions asked from a stance of not-knowing. The questions aim to stretch thinking further, and go from the specific situation to alternative options. Question are open-ended ('How do you feel about ...?') instead of closed ('Do you agree that ...?'). The question words 'why' and 'how' seem to invite more of an open dialogue than 'what' or 'when'. Questions are not merely abstract-philosophical, but also specific with requests for examples. Questions are simple and do not include multiple questions at once ('What do you think about this, and what do you do with this?'). It has also been recommended to use empathic relational skills to tune into the experiences of the clients, and tailor the questions to their experiences. It may be helpful to be sensitive to cues or signals about meaning: 'Are you actually saying that you experience as meaningful ...' It is also recommended that practitioners help clients to recognise nuances in their experiences, seeing different shades and grey areas, rather than generalisations ('Is this so ...?'). Practitioners can tune into symbols and metaphors which clients use in their communication, and ask questions about these.

The philosopher Socrates is well known for his way of asking maieutic questions which helped individuals to develop self-insight by examining the knowledge and experience they already have within themselves, without Socrates pouring his ideas into them. His maieutic method helped individuals to dig beneath the surface of their initial opinions and focus on the most essential aspect in their expertise. The Socratic questioning technique has been used by meaning-centred practitioners for many decades, as this dialogical method may help clients to identify what they experience as the most meaningful in their experiences. Later studies from a cognitive behavioural therapeutic perspective have shown the effectiveness of using Socratic dialogues in treatments. Instructions and training in the Socratic dialogue may be found elsewhere. The unique aim of using the Socratic dialogue in meaning-centred practices is to help clients to identify the most meaningful aspects in their experiences, and to develop self-insight in the way in which they have developed this specific sense of meaning (Table 8.6).

Table 8.6 Possible Socratic questions

Question	Aim of question	Example
Opening	Start a dialogue in which the client feels free to express anything and follow their flow of experiencing	Broad, open, naïve questions. 'How have you been since our last session?'; 'What have you been doing today?'; 'What were some highlights of the recent period?'; 'Could you describe some moments that felt particularly meaningful last week?'

Empathic listening	Create a space in which clients feel free and supported to share anything	No paternalistic, normative or suggestive questions; there are no 'bad answers'; phenomenological bracketing (Chapter 2)
Clarifying	Gain more clarity and understanding about the client's experience	Can you explain this further?'; 'Could you elaborate this?'; 'How do you mean?'; 'Could you put this in another way?'; 'Do I understand you correctly, that …?'
Specifying and concretising	Connect their general vague ideas with specific daily life experiences (Chapter 5)	'Could you give some examples of this?'; 'You have explained some larger examples; could you also tell me how you experience this in your daily life?' If clients stay at an abstract level, the practitioner could ask them to elaborate this: 'How precisely did this happen?'; 'What happened then? What did you feel/think/do?'; 'If I would have had a video camera, what would this camera have recorded?'; 'If we return to my opening question, how does this specific example answer this question?'
Assumptions	Explore the client's implicit and explicit assumptions in the answer	'Is this always the case?'; 'When is this the case, and when not?'; 'How is this possible?'; 'What is needed for this to happen/to be true?'; 'Why do you think this assumption holds here?'
Reason and evidence	Explore the foundations of the arguments	'Why do you say that?'; 'Is this always true?'; 'How do you know this?'; 'Is there reason to doubt this evidence?'; 'Is this logical to say?'; 'So you say, that when X happens, then Y follows: is this logical? What evidence do you have?' Do not pose the questions like an examiner; you are not disputing the client's answers
Multisensory	Help clients explore experiences not only intellectually but also from their embodied lived experience	Different questions elicit different answers: 'What do you think about …?'; 'How do you feel about …'; 'How do you remember …?'; 'How do you interpret …?'; 'What did you do …?'; 'What do others say …?' (Vos, 2011). Individuals could be asked to explore differences and similarities: 'Is there a difference between how you feel and think about this?'
Specifying memory	Memories are often tainted by current emotional state; therefore, ask more specific questions	'Describe a specific example of a precise moment in time. Where were you?; Who were you with?; What did you see, hear, smell, taste, feel?'

(Continued)

Question	Aim of question	Example
Origin	Explore where experiences originate and what they are influenced by	'When was the first time you felt this?'; 'How did this experience/idea start and develop over time?'; 'Where does this experience/idea come from?'; 'Is this your idea or did this come from someone else?'; 'Has anything or anyone influenced the development of this experience/idea, and, if so, which influences did you experience?' 'Is this something you can(not), must (not) and/ or (do not) want?'
Attitudes	Identify helpful and unhelpful attitudes	'How do you feel/think/act regarding this? Does your way of feeling/thinking/ doing change how you experience this? How helpful is this way of feeling/ thinking/doing?'; 'What is the most helpful way to deal with this?'; 'What are unhelpful ways of coping?'
Larger temporal experience	Identify whether or how their experiences are bound to specific periods in time, and to identify the possibility of change	'Is this experience only about the past/ present/future?'; 'How does this also apply to the past/present/future?'; 'Is this the case at all times?'; 'How might this change in future?'; 'Where could this lead to in the long term?'; 'What possibilities are there in the future?'; 'Imagine yourself at the end of your life on your deathbed; how would you answer this question then?'; 'How would you have answered this question as a child?'
Implications	Identify implications and consequences of their answers, experiences and attitudes	'But if ... happened, what else would result?', 'How does ... affect ...?'; 'What effect could this have on how you live your life/the world around you?'; 'What are you implying by that?'
Broadening	Identify similar experiences in other situations; recognise patterns	'Could you give other examples?'; 'Is this your full answer to my question, or are there other answers?'; 'Do you see any pattern?'; 'What is the common thread among these experiences?'; 'What do these experiences have in common?'; 'If you were to put these examples in groups, what would these groups look like and what would you call each one?'; 'If you could look down from a helicopter's perspective on your experiences, what is the most important?'

Top-down	Derive conclusions from a general principle or idea (deduction)	'If you say that, in general, X is the case, what does this look like in daily life?'
Bottom-up	Derive conclusions from specific examples (induction)	'What conclusion/message do you get from these examples?'; 'Where do these examples lead to?'
Hierarchy	Identify hierarchies in their experiences	'What is the most important in these experiences?'; 'What are the highlights?'; 'If you would rank these examples from most important to least important, what would this ranking look like?' The why-question techniques involve repeatedly asking 'Why is this meaningful/important' or 'What makes this meaningful/important?'
Alternative viewpoints	Synthesise the answers, identify conflicts and alternative viewpoints, and explore possible ways to deal with tensions	'What tensions/paradoxes/conflicts do you see in your experiences?'; 'How do you think X relates to Y?'; 'What is a counterargument?', 'Can/did anyone see this another way?'; 'What would X think about this?'; 'If you played devil's advocate, what would you say?'; 'How does this paradox feel? How do you cope with these tensions? How would you like to cope with these tensions?'; 'Between these two conflicting ideas, which is the most meaningful?'; 'Which option is the most meaningful in the long term?'; 'Imagine yourself on your deathbed; which option feels most meaningful?'; 'To what extent are these options really opposites of each other? Could they go hand in hand?'
Summaries	Summarise main findings	'What is the main conclusion from this conversation?'; 'What have we discovered?'; 'Is this everything you would like to say?'; 'Where should we go from these conclusions?'
Meta	Help clients understand the relevance of the dialogue and draw their own conclusions	'Why do you think that I asked that question?'; 'Why was that important?'; 'Which of your questions was most useful?'; 'How did you feel about these questions?'

31. *Using focusing, mindfulness and meditation exercises*

Clinical trials show that meaning-centred practices are significantly more effective when these include focusing, mindfulness and other meditation techniques to help clients focus and explore their inner flow of experiences (Vos & Vitali, 2018). Many exercises include body work, focusing on the body to connect with a fuller and embodied sense of meaning. In general, many empirical studies have shown the beneficial effects of mindfulness and meditation on well-being, particularly in times of stress (Hofmann et al., 2010; Khoury et al., 2013). Several meaning-centred practitioners use these exercises at the beginning of sessions to help clients engage with the topic and other exercises in less hyper-reflective ways.

Focusing

> *Meaning* is not only *about things* and it is not only a certain *logical* structure, but it also involves *felt* experiencing. Any concept, thing, or behavior is mean-ingful only as some noise, thing, or event interacts with felt experiencing. Meanings are formed and had through an interaction between experiencing and symbols or things. ... The task at hand is to examine the relationships between this felt dimension of experience and the logical and objective orders. How can logical symbolizations and operational definitions be related to felt experiencing? Or, to reverse the question: What are the functions of felt expe-riencing in our conceptual operations and in our observable behavior?
>
> (Gendlin, 1962, p. 1)

Focusing helps to pause the ongoing situation and create a space for new experiences. This implies a phenomenological openness to the totality of our experiences, including the unconscious and embodied experi-ences. This focus helps to unpeel our experiences from the mundane and rational to a sensation in the body, called a 'felt sense'. This felt sense lies behind our thoughts and feelings and is full of meaning, like a message from the body to ourselves. Meaning is discovered by focusing on our felt sense. Gendlin summarises this with six steps (Gendlin, 1996, p. 1):

➢ *"First, individuals clear a space, both physically and psychologically: 'be silent, just to yourself, take a moment to relax. Pay attention inwardly, in your body, perhaps in your stomach or chest. Now see what comes there when you ask "How is my life going? What is the main thing for me right now?" Sense within your body. Let the answers come slowly from this sens-ing. When some concern comes, DO NOT GO INSIDE IT. Stand back, say "Yes, that's there. I can feel that, there." Let there be a little space between you and that. Then ask what else you feel. Wait again, and sense. Usually there are several things.'*

➢ *Second, select one personal problem to focus on: 'there are many parts to that one thing you are thinking about – too many to think of each one alone.*

But you can feel *all of these things together. Pay attention there where you usually feel things, and in there you can get a sense of what* all *of the problem feels like.'*

> *Third, let a word, a phrase or an image come up from the felt sense itself, such as* 'tight, sticky, scary, stuck, heavy, jumpy', *a phrase, or an image. Stay with the quality of the felt sense till something fits it just right.*

> *Fourth, 'go back and forth between the felt sense and the word phrase, or image. Check how they resonate with each other. See if there is a little bodily signal that lets you know there is a fit.'*

> *Fifth, ask 'what is it, about this whole problem, that makes this quality (which you have just named or pictured)? Return your attention to your body and freshly find the felt sense again, and ask it again. Be with the felt sense till something comes along with a shift, a slight "give" or release.'*

> *Sixth, 'receive whatever comes with a shift, stay with it a while'."*

Mindfulness

Mindfulness is a mental state, achieved by focusing one's awareness on the present moment, while calmly acknowledging and accepting one's feelings, thoughts and bodily sensations. That is, mindfulness helps individuals to go from a doing-mode to a being-mode. When individuals are in a doing-mode, they are goal-oriented and focused on their rational and superficial wishes. The being-mode emphasises 'accepting and allowing what is', without any immediate pressure to change it. The latter mode helps individuals to concentrate in each moment without judgement; clients may learn that holding on to some of these feelings is ineffective and mentally destructive. This could help individuals to de-reflect and connect with their stream of experiences, so that they can unpeel their daily life experiences and see what is the most meaningful. Mindfulness is a cornerstone of Buddhism, where many mindfulness exercises could be found. Some psychologists have simplified these techniques for use in therapeutic non-religious contexts (Segal, Williams & Teasdale, 2012). However, mindfulness has not been without its critics (Davies, 2015; Van Dam et al, 2018). Populistic forms of mindfulness have been criticised for being **functional** and commercial, suggesting quick solutions to all problems ('McMindfulness'). Furthermore, some hyper-reflective and anxious clients find it difficult not to judge their feelings and thoughts, and shift their focus; consequently, mindfulness creates an even greater focus on themselves, and aggravates their **hyper-reflection**. Therefore, practitioners are recommended to train themselves well in these techniques, and assess which individuals may benefit. Part 3 provides mindfulness examples.

32. *Using non-verbal techniques*

Meaning-centred practices were initially developed as talking therapies, but more and more they also include non-talking exercises to foster de-reflection, as shown in Table 8.7. Research suggests that such non-verbal exercises could be a beneficial addition to talking therapies (Elliott, Greenberg & Lietaer, 2004).

The rationale behind using non-verbal techniques is that meaning is not only a conscious experience, but also (or possibly primarily) part of unconscious or preconscious processes (Damasio, 1999; Kahneman, 2012; Heintzelman & King, 2013). It has been argued that any meaning that comes to consciousness has already been in the unconscious for a long time. Therefore, practitioners have suggested addressing unconscious processes to help clients with meaning-centred concerns connect with their unconscious processes. However, there is little systematic empirical evidence for working with the unconscious meaning.

The psychoanalyst Carl Jung has written extensively on working with unconscious meanings (Jung, 1979). Jung underlined the importance of meaning, and identified materialistic-hedonic and self-oriented meanings as a cause of many psychological problems, such as depression and midlife crises. Through a range of non-verbal techniques, he stimulated clients to focus on perspectives larger than themselves, such as social and higher meanings, particularly connecting with the larger temporality and community. Jung stressed that every client needs to formulate a meaningful life in accord with his/her unique history, personality and destiny. To be able to do so, individuals need to unpeel themselves from conscious rational layers. To reach these unconscious layers, individuals require 'a humbling of the ego mind', 'a sensitivity for what is essential' and 'the attitude of a new-born baby' (Jaffe, 1979). Examples include analysing the client's favourite fairy tale, dreams, fantasies, cultural and personal myths, childhood play, synchronicities ('meaningful coincidences'), physical experiences and so on. According to Jung, these exercises could also help individuals to access their 'shadow', the difficult and most unknown aspect within us.

Empirical research shows that (unconscious) meanings can be found in dreams. Therefore, dream analysis may reveal what is meaningful for us but which we are not consciously aware of (e.g. Hill & Goates, 2004; Hill & Knox, 2010), although there is little evidence for its effectiveness (Domhoff, 2003, 2013). Neuropsychological research suggests that dreams are the result of highly activated parts of the brain which are connected (Antrobus & Bertini, 2013). Some parts are highly activated because they are consciously used during day time, and other parts could be associations or meaningful processes which of individuals may not be conscious. By examining core themes and feelings of a dream, an individual may discover which parts of the brain were highly activated. Thus not every aspect in a dream may be equally meaningful, as certain aspects will be parts of the brain which were activated for example by mundane daytime experience. To explore which conscious and unconscious themes are active and associated with each other, practitioners can use a phenomenological approach. They **bracket** any interpretations ('This symbol must stand for ...'), and instead ask the client to describe the dream via phenomenological questioning, such as: 'What do you feel as the most important/significant/remarkable/meaningful part?; 'What was the overall theme?; 'What was your overall feeling? Subsequently, the client could be asked to relate this to daily life: 'How do you feel that this dream may relate to your life?'; 'What does this dream tell about you and the world around you?' The dream could be used in further imagination: 'If the dream would continue, how would you like the dream to be?'

Table 8.7 Examples of non-intellectualising exercises

Non-intellectual exercise	Description
Act as if	'Act as if what you do makes a difference. It does.' (James, 1902/1985, p. 243) Clients act as if something is meaningful for them: adopt the posture, tone, physical appearance or follow the steps of someone they imagine would be doing this activity
Art	Prescribe art; ask clients about meaningful or symbolic art (Lantz, 2000)
Childhood memories	'What are your earliest childhood memories? What were your favourite stories, fairy tales, movies, radio or television shows? What were your favourite sayings of your mother, father or other important peple? Why do you remember such trivial episodes? What was their importance? Are they still Important? What is their importance today? Do these memories offer an important clue as to what you are today, what your values are? Have your hopes and wishes been fulfilled? What are your hopes now? What was once painful and frightening – is it still so? Did something positive come out of negative experiences? Can you see meaning in those old, painful experiences?' (Fabry, 1988, p. 47)
Collage	Making a collage of meanings, e.g. cutting pictures from magazines or drawing
Drawing	Draw their life; draw their life as a car or a house, draw buried treasure, the end of the rainbow, etc. Drawings are not projective tests, but tools to initiate reflection and conversation (Lantz, 2000)

(Continued)

Non-intellectual exercise	Description
Empty chair	See a dilemma or paradox from multiple perspectives. The practitioner pulls up an empty chair and places it opposite the client. This chair represents a person, situation, meaning or perspective with which the client is in conflict. The clients are asked to speak to the chair, express their feelings. Subsequently, clients sit in the chair, play the represented role and respond to what was just said. The client may move back and forth (Pavio & Greenberg, 1995)
Fast-forwarding techniques	'Various questions are used to help clients see the consequences of their behaviour. (a) What will happen to you 5 years down the road, if you don't make any changes in your life? (b) Deathbed test – imagining yourself on your deathbed, what would be your biggest regrets?' (Wong, 2015, p. 231)
Guided fantasy	Guide clients in a fantasy to discover what is meaningful. Images fit the needs of the client. For example, a client who lacks self-confidence is placed in happy surroundings ('Imagine you are walking in a field full of flowers, on a sunny day'), with a specific direction ('You are walking on a path towards a building in the distance'), etc. Try to be detailed, and use each of the senses. 'Imagine you are at your own memorial service. You hear the music playing. Everyone who loved you is there. How many people are there? Your best friend gives a eulogy about you. What would they say?' (Fabry, 1988, p. 65)
Letter writing	Write a letter to their future self, past self, a lost meaning, unborn child, a lost loved one, etc.
Lifeline exercise	Visualise and reflect highs and lows in life, to identify resources. Draw one horizontal life, running chronologically from birth to where they are now in life, and a vertical axis visualise how meaningful their life is, ranging from not meaningful to totally meaningful. Clients are asked to draw a graph to show the meaningfulness of their line. They could be asked to use different colour pens to represent, for instance, different types of meanings (materialistic-hedonic, self-oriented, social, higher, meta meanings), or to represent a success lifeline (work/education) and personal lifeline. Alternatively, clients could be asked to first draw peaks and valleys in their experience, and then add information (e.g. people, places, occupations, key events, dreams, aspirations, interests, life learnings)
Life mosaic	'Sketch your life with symbols and stick figures to represent situations and people. Start first with early childhood, school years, etc. How many pieces did you draw in dark colours? How many in bright? Do dark lines have silver linings? Give each mosaic piece a name. Do you see a pattern? Are certain parts in your life still dark? You may not be able to change the past, but you can change the colours' (Fabry, 1988, p. 65)

Logo-anchor or logo-hook	Individuals often have specific moments in their past, present or anticipated future which they experience as most meaningful, which could give hope and meaning to the present (Westermann, 1993; Guttman, 1996). Step 1. Find an example of particularly meaningful moment, which answers a lack of meaning in this current life situation. For example, if clients miss love, they could remember a moment of being loved. Step 2. Describe the experience. Imagine you are in that moment again (Close your eyes. What do you see, hear, feel, smell, taste, do, think? Who else is there? What happens before and after?). Step 3. Repeat exercise.
Logodrama	Reflect back on life through dramatisations and find meaning through those experiences. For example, use mindfulness to become aware of present thoughts, feelings and bodily sensations. Stay with uncomfortable experiences. Act out as a drama wherever feels appropriate, for instance by listening to what experiences come up after a body scan, etc. After playing, the client reflects on the acted-out drama from the subsequent perspectives of an unbiased observer, a person/perspective that the client is in conflict with, and the future ideal self. Other psychodrama techniques could also be used, such as exercises for truthful acting, as developed by Meisner and Stanislavski; for example Meisner's 'blue jeans exercise' could help clients to become more aware of their embodied impulses and learn to follow their intuition, beyond learned social behaviour and mannerisms (Krasner, 2012).
Magic wand	Imagine you have a magic wand, and you can wish for whatever you like. What would you wish for in your life? (Bannink, 2010)
Mask making	'Buy or make a mask or do a face painting that suits you. What mask do you usually wear? How do you feel wearing this mask? Would you like to change it? Take it off? For a while, for good?' (Fabry, 1988, p. 87)
Meaning-centred autobiographic writing	Identify what has been meaningful in the past, and how the client could use past meanings in the future. Multiple stages of writing: e.g. write separately about different life periods (childhood, early adulthood, middle adulthood, late adulthood). Focus writing on meaningful, important, defining, life-changing moments or lessons learned in life. Or focus on what they did with the background they came from (the legacy from parents/upbringing), what they have achieved in life up until now (the legacy they live), what they leave to others (the legacy they give) (Breitbart & Poppito, 2014). Give specific instructions to write about specific memories in detail (What happened? Who was there? When? What did you think, feel, see, smell, hear, taste? What happened before and after that?). Clients could present and rewrite their story with feedback. After completion, clients identify common denominators (e.g. types of meaning) and write a science-fiction story about their future. Alternative: clients tell their life story, the practitioner writes the story for them (e.g. Chochinov et al., 2012). Pennebaker and others showed that expressive writing about our life helps to identify meanings in our life, which improves our psychological well-being (Pennebaker & Seagal, 1999; Bohlmeijer, Smit & Cuijpers, 2003; Cho et al., 2008)

(Continued)

Non-intellectual exercise	Description
Movies	Ask clients to develop a film of their life, going from past to present and future. Deepen with questions, e.g. Which genre would this film be? Who would play the lead roles? What would happen at the end? (Schulenberg et al., 2008)
Nudging	Nudging is giving small and easy reminders, positive reinforcements or indirect suggestions to stimulate individuals engaging in meaningful behaviour (Thaler & Sunstein, 2008). Clients remind themselves of the meaningfulness of their life and of possible actions, e.g. putting ideas on a pin board, Post-its on the computer, etc.
Poetry	Read, select or write poems (Lantz, 2000)
Prospective photos exercise	Photographing and subsequently writing about meaningful experiences. Step 1. Over the next week, take photographs of things that make your life feel meaningful or full of purpose. These can be people, places, objects, pets. If you are not able to take photos of these things – for example, if they're not nearby – you can take photos of souvenirs, reminders, websites or even of other photos. Try to take at least nine photographs. These could be of large or small things. Step 2. At the end of the week, if you used a digital camera, upload your photos to a computer. If you used a non-digital camera, have your photos developed. Step 3. Once you have collected all your photos and items, take time to look at and reflect on each one. For each photo, write down a response to the following question: 'What does this photo represent, and why is it meaningful?' (Steger et al., 2013)
Retrospective photos exercise	Look at the pictures that you have taken over the last year. What do you most frequently take pictures of? Where are you? What are you doing? Who are you with? Select the ten most meaningful pictures. What do they tell you about what you may find meaningful? What pictures did you not publish on social media such as Facebook or Instagram but are meaningful to you? Why did you not share these pictures? What does this tell you about what is meaningful for you? Ask others to look at your photos and answer these questions
Rituals	Brainstorm possible small or large rituals to visualise and remember meaningful moments. A ritual can be done alone or with another person; often has multiple types of meaning; connects past, present and future; helps with closure of the past, while looking towards the future. Examples: writing letters to the deceased, burning negative memories, planting a tree, organising a life celebration party, going on holiday to a meaningful place, etc. (Van der Hart, 1983)
Role models	What makes your heroes or role models meaningful? Could you do the same in your life? (Fabry, 1988). Could Frankl's life story be an example for you? (Frankl, 1949/1986)

Running group exercise	A large room is split into three corners, with each having its own meaning. Clients are asked multiple questions with each having three multiple-choice options represented by each of the corners; they have a short time to make a decision and go to the corner that feels the most meaningful. The time for decision-making could become shorter and shorter (30 seconds, 20 seconds, 10 seconds ...), so that clients are forced to start moving intuitively. After the exercise, clients can reflect on questions such as: How did you experience this exercise? How did you make decisions? How did you know what the right decision was? Did you follow others? (Vos, 2009)
Science-fiction exercise	Tell a science-fiction story about the most ideal future, for instance in 10, 20, 100 or 500 years' time. Speak as if you are already there: 'I am living in the year 2150 and I do not work anymore, because robots do all the work for humans.' For example: 'Close your eyes. Tell me what your future would look like. Fantasise. Everything is possible. There are no taboos.' The practitioner asks specific questions to guide the sci-fi fantasy, such as: What is your job? Do you have a partner? Do you earn money? Are you happy? What makes you passionate? Who are your friends? Tell me what you do on an average day? What do you do in your leisure time? This exercise can help clients to distance themselves from their current situation
Self-portrayal	Draw yourself with various colours, not a realistic self-portrait but an abstract picture with lines, colours and symbols. Do not think; just draw. Then talk about the results (Fabry, 1988)
Shoe box	Decorate a shoe box with pictures cut from magazines and drawings. Pictures on the outside represent meanings shown to others, and pictures on the inside meanings that they hide or do not dare to share. Helpful in families (Lantz, 2000)

Key phenomenological, experiential and mindfulness skills

26. Phenomenological unpeeling of experiences.

27. Stimulating an attitude of experiential acceptance.

28. Stimulating clients to immerse themselves in the flow of meaningful experiences.

29. Phenomenologically exploring whether there are any hierarchies in the client's experiences of meaning.

30. Using a questioning approach.

31. Using focusing, mindfulness and meditation exercises.

32. Using non-verbal techniques.

9

Existential Skills

9.1 General existential principles

Meaning-centred treatments are more effective when practitioners explicitly address existential topics (Vos & Vitali, 2018). This is in line with the emergence of so-called second wave psychology and Meaning-Centered Therapies 2.0. Empirical research, clinical experience and philosophical texts have convincingly shown that the experiences of meaning and existential themes are intertwined (Vos, 2014; Ivtzan et al., 2015; Lomas & Ivtzan, 2016; Wong, 2017). The traditional differences between meaning-centred practitioners and other existential practitioners seem to be beginning to fall away, as much theory and practice are starting to intertwine (Correia et al., 2014; Vos, 2018c). The greatest difference seems to about the extent to which existential themes are addressed with a simultaneous focus on meaning. Stereotypically, meaning-centred practitioners aim at 'living a meaningful life in the existential context of life's challenges', while other existential practitioners may be more likely to focus on embracing life as it comes without immediately finding a meaningful answer to it. However, in practice this may only be a relative difference, and not an absolute difference between meaning-centred and existential practitioners. Clinical trials indicate that therapies are the most effective when they address both meaning-centred and existential topics (Vos & Vitali, 2018).

Existential therapy emerged at the beginning of the twentieth century in response to the birth of psychological therapies that reduce individuals to machines of Freudian drives, behaviour or cognition. In contrast, existential therapists take a non-reductionist phenomenological approach to their clients and their experiences, such as not trying to fit their clients into a pregiven theoretical framework (Vos, 2018c). They may help clients not only with their day-to-day challenges, but also with larger questions about life in general. An in-depth explanation of existential therapeutic skills is beyond the scope of this book, but several texts are available on existential skills and case studies (e.g. DuPlock, 1998; Yalom, 2010; Van Deurzen & Adams, 2016; for an overview of existential therapies, see Cooper, 2016).

In this chapter, existential skills are defined as therapeutic activities that focus on helping clients with life's challenges, in particular with life's givens. **Life's givens** are unchangeable facts of life that define all human beings (Vos, 2014, 2018b), such as:

➤ being thrown into existence,

➤ being alive,

➤ being free to make decisions,

➤ being responsible for my own life,

➤ being physically limited and mortal,

➤ being part of the physical and social world,

➤ being in possibilities (having possibilities to change, albeit to change my inner attitude towards the impossibilities),

➤ being an irreducible totality (impossibility to reduce the totality of my being to one specific aspect),

➤ being primarily in daily life (in the first place, we live our daily life, and only in exceptional moments do we experience, for example, peak experiences).

When individuals are faced with life's givens, they often experience **existential moods**, such as:

➤ *Death anxiety*: umbrella term for many different experiences about one's own death and finitude. It is important to explore what the fear of death is specifically about: for instance of physical suffering, not having lived a meaningful life until now, being dependent on others, and so on (cf. Neimeyer, 2015).

➤ *Existential urgency*: the pressure to live life fully in the present, because of the short remaining time in life (Vos, 2014).

➤ *Existential guilt*: feeling guilty about not having made the most of all possibilities in life (Tillich, 2000).

➤ *Existential isolation*: experiencing that we undergo the big events in our life alone (birth, death, suffering); nobody can experience these in our place (Yalom, 1980).

➤ *Existential overwhelming*: being overwhelmed by seeing all of life's possibilities and not knowing how to access them (cf. Heidegger, 1927).

➤ *Fear of taking responsibility and life anxiety*: anxiety about doing what an individual really wants in life, to live life fully, to be in control and so on (cf. 'bad faith' in Sartre, 2012).

➤ *Meaninglessness*: different types exist, which are not necessary the opposite of meaningfulness. It can be helpful to identify the specific type of meaninglessness that the client experiences (Section 3.2).

These existential moods usually do not have a specific object, such as the object of cynophobia is fear about dogs. Existential moods are about life and its givens in general. Some authors have suggested that some existential therapists may be disproportionally obsessed with explicitly asking existential questions and addressing big topics like death (Craig, 2015; Vos, 2018c). They suggest that this obsession with General Givens and Explicit Existential Questions are caused by a misinterpretation of existential philosophers, as the latter wrote that there are many ways to open the gates to full existence, and addressing life's givens and explicit existential moods is only one way of opening these gates (Heidegger, 1927, para. 45). Clinical trials indicate that existential therapies that focus primarily at addressing life's givens and explicating existential moods are less effective than other existential and meaning-centred therapies (Vos, Craig & Cooper, 2014).

Existential moods are first and foremost experienced in day-to-day experiences, according to phenomenologists (see Chapters 2 and 8). For example, existential therapists such as Emmy Van Deurzen (Van Deurzen & Arnold-Baker, 2005) and Ernesto Spinelli (2015) do not explicitly address existential givens or existential moods (Vos, 2018c, d). Instead, Emmy Van Deurzen is interested in the general difficulties, limitations, ambiguities and uncertainties that individuals may experience in everyday life. We do not need confrontations with life's ultimate givens such as the death of our loved ones or our own mortality to understand existence; our daily life gives many examples of the challenges of life. Emmy Van Deurzen phenomenologically stays with the client's descriptions of daily life, and if existential themes or moods arise she explores this, but she would not assume or impose the theme of death on clients. She asks descriptive-phenomenological questions such as 'could you tell me more about your experience' and 'what does this mean for you'?

9.2 Specific existential skills

33. *Empathising, recognising, naming and exploring the existential dimension in client's experiences*

A core skill for meaning-centred practitioners is identifying and, where appropriate, explicating existential themes, moods, behaviours and the unspoken experiences of the client (see Table 9.1).

Table 9.1 Existential themes and moods identification skills

Skill	Description	Example
Naming	Give a name to existential themes or moods	'How would you describe these experiences?'; 'Others have called this death anxiety'
Recognising	Explicit recognition of the existential reality of the client	'This may be difficult for you?'
Normalising & universalising	Explain that the existential experiences are normal and are part of the human condition	'This seems a normal reaction to an abnormal situation'; 'I hear this often'; 'All humans struggle with this'
Empathising	Explicitly show empathy with the client's stories (Chapter 7)	
Questioning	See Chapter 8	
Multisensory exploring	Show sensitivity towards different presentations of existential themes	Existential theoretic themes, moods, behaviours, unspoken processes
Explicating exercises	Exercises to reflect explicitly on existential themes	Looking back from one's death bed what would one need to do now to live a meaningful life; decide what one's epitaph should say; count the number of decisions made this day, and number of activities they did not need to decide on

34. *Stimulating meaning-centred coping with situations of suffering*

Frankl (1989) described how no one can outrun the 'tragic triad' of suffering, death and guilt. Spiritual leaders, for instance in Buddhism, teach that all of us experience moments of pain, death, guilt, turning points and disappointment in ourselves, others or life. Trying to change the unchangeable, and fighting the unfightable, is ineffective and even counterproductive. For example, Karl Jaspers (1919) wrote that individuals' positive intentions are inevitably confronted with injustices, paradoxes and failures in endless numbers of boundary situations. Similarly, Emmy Van Deurzen (2015, p. 181) writes that 'life is an endless struggle where moments of ease and blissful happiness are the exception rather than rule' and reaching heaven-on-earth seems unlikely. Individuals often find it difficult to accept the reality that life is an endless struggle, for instance by fantasising about a life without problems or struggle. Such unrealistic expectations can lead to frustration and suffering, as these expectations will inevitably fail in daily life (Van Deurzen & Adams, 2011).

Therefore, existential philosophers have been arguing for centuries that we should accept what cannot be changed, and change what can be changed. For example, the cancer patient cannot change the disease, the murderer cannot undo the killing, the widow cannot change the loss of the partner and so on. What they can do is change their attitude towards the situation (Chapter 8). This means, in the first place, that they accept the unchangeability of the situation, and in the second place that they commit themselves to a meaningful way to cope with these limitations (Park & Folkman, 1997; Neimeyer, 2010; Park, 2010). For example, in the role of an empathic and non-directive mentor and fellow-human-being, practitioners could help their clients to embrace life as it comes -the totality of being- and wake up from their self-deception. In this process of waking-up, individuals may realise that they are stronger than they think, may overcome a fear of life, discover life's potentiality and experience life as worth living (cf. Van Deurzen, 2015).

For example, after a loss, clients may be inclined to feel that everything has changed. However, clients can be supported in staying connected with what was meaningful in the past. For instance, grieving individuals could continue to experience a bond with a deceased loved one (Klass & Steffen, 2017). Chapter 8 suggested other ways by which individuals could cope in a meaningful way with unchangeable life events, via self-distancing, de-reflecting and self-transcending. In general, individuals may cope with change by reassessing what is meaningful, for example by committing themselves more to specific new or old meanings (Vos, 2016b). Another aspect included in many meaning-centred practices is helping to integrate the experience of loss within the total life story, overarching the past before illness, the present with illness, their own future, and the future after one's death (Section 9.2). This is a limited overview of meaningful coping styles; empirical studies indicate that there is no one best coping style that is the most beneficial for everyone in every situation. Instead, coping flexibility (Cheng, Lau & Chan, 2014), the ability to change coping styles, seems to be a far stronger predictor of long-term well-being; for example, a cancer patient may at some moments pretend as if nothing is going on and at other times express and share emotions with friends and family (e.g. Vos, 2014). Practitioners can help clients to explore what they may experience as a meaningful way to cope with the life changes at this moment in life.

Example

Usually in the first session of meaning-centred treatment for individuals with a chronic physical disease, I start with quite a bold statement when we are discussing our expectations of the treatment: 'This treatment will not change your disease; it will also not get rid of the physical symptoms, or reduce the pain. This treatment will also not

▶

expect you to fight like a hero against your disease, because I do not want you to be like a Don Quixote, fighting the unfightable. However, what this treatment can help you with is living a meaningful and satisfying life despite your disease. I will help you to discover what feels to you as a meaningful way to cope with your disease at this moment. Some clients say that this helps them to better cope with their disease, and they feel better able to distance themselves from their pain and other limitations.'

Many clients find this message a relief as I recognise the reality that their fighting the unchangeable is not helpful, and that instead there is a countless number of ways how they can cope in a meaningful way with their experiences. They often report that friends, family and doctors expect them to fight like an archetypal hero against their disease. I have been told how they feel pressured by health charities which use heroic slogans: 'help us beat cancer'; 'support the fighters against cancer'; 'brave patients'. Journalist and cancer survivor Ehrenreich (2010) called this a 'smile-or-die culture': she felt she not only suffered from cancer but also from not smiling enough.

35. *Exploring paradoxical feelings about meaning, and fostering acceptance of paradoxes and tensions*

> Our greatest challenge today is to couple conviction with doubt. By convic-
> tion, I mean some pragmatically developed faith, trust, or centeredness; and
> by doubt I mean openness to the ongoing changeability, mystery, and fallibil-
> ity of the conviction.
>
> (Schneider, 1990/1999, p. 7)

Multiple paradoxes. Paradoxes are at the heart of living a meaningful life (Schneider, 1999; Vos, 2014; Van Deurzen, 2015). An existential paradox is a combination of experiences that seem logically contradictory or an impossible combination from a rational perspective, but which are under-standable from the subjectively lived experience (i.e. phenomenological perspective). For example, the most important paradoxes described in this book are meaning in life for sceptics (Part 1), meaning in a context of meaninglessness (Section 3.2), meaning as simultaneously at the micro-, meso- and macro-levels (Chapter 2), meaning as authentic but not meta-physical (Chapter 2), meaning as socially connected but independent (Section 3.4), initially bracketing hierarchies but being open to hierarchies (Section 3.5) emerging in the individual's experience (Chapter 2), being in the flow, in the here and now, while distancing and transcending oneself (Chapter 8) and so on.

Denial of paradoxes. Paradoxes can be rationally and emotionally challenging for clients. To deal with the uncertainty and tension of the paradoxes, they may be inclined to give a black-or-white answer: either be sceptical or meaningful; either meaning is metaphysically true or it is not relevant at all; and so on. This denial of paradoxes could limit clients from living life to the full, as they may deny meaningful possibilities that evoke paradoxical feelings (Vos, 2014).

Sensitivity for paradoxes. Practitioners may want to be aware of paradoxes in the experiences of clients. Clients will present their answer to the paradox, thus usually they will not explicitly mention paradoxical feelings. This means that practitioners can be aware of what may be revealed from clients' stories. Key words that may reveal underlying paradoxes when clients speak about meaning are 'absolute', 'true', 'best', 'completely', 'only' and so on, as these may suggest a black-or-white perspective. For example, one client, Elizabeth, felt unfilled in life, although she told me: 'My family is absolutely my true meaning. I do not need anything else.' Her strong focus on family hid underlying tensions.

Specify and de-reflect the paradox. Instead of speaking about the paradox at the abstract level, it can help to specify what the paradox is actually about in daily life, and which ways there are to experience the paradox in a non-intellectualised way. For example, for Elizabeth, 'being a good mother' was the most important ideal in life, which she subsequently generalised to all domains in her life. She said that she could not work as she had to take care of her daughter, but when we looked at her diary she discovered that there were actually many times she could do some work for herself, for example when her husband was at home and could take care of their children.

Unmask false opposites. A seeming contradiction may not be a real contradiction. Critical questioning (Chapter 8) may reveal that there is no real opposite. For example, I helped Elizabeth to examine whether her family life and her career were as contradictory as she thought. I deliberately asked her to give examples of other people and of small moments in her own life when she was both a good mother and successful in her job. As described in Chapter 8, clients may learn to see contradictions not as opposites but as different dimensions which could be combined by developing a **dual attitude** (Vos, 2014).

Learning to tolerate. Paradoxes may evoke tension, uncertainty or lack of control. Such feelings may be so unbearable for some individuals (although not all of them) that they may try to defend themselves existentially against the terror evoked by life's inevitable givens. For example, they deny the facts or shift the focus of their attention away from the frightening experiences. Several existential therapists have argued how such existential defence mechanisms can stop individuals from fully functioning (Yalom, 1980; Becker, 2007), which has been confirmed in several empirical studies (e.g. Pyszczynski, Greenberg & Koole, 2010).

Therefore, several therapists stimulate clients to overcome and 'unpeel' their resistances to life (Bugental, 1987) by suggesting clients stay with their feelings and learn to tolerate them. This is particularly achievable by focusing on what clients experience in the here-and-now and invoking what is 'palpably relevant or charged' (Schneider & Krug, 2010, p. 114). Therapeutic techniques consist of questions about the experiential processes in the here-and-now, staying with feelings, self-expression and free association, identifying and visualising emotions and fostering trust in the ability to bear negative feelings (Cooper, 2017).

Thus, experiential and mindfulness exercises, as described in Chapter 8, can help clients to learn to cope with paradoxical feelings. They could learn to feel paradoxical, and that it is OK to experience this. For instance, start with a mindfulness exercise, such as allowing the client to feel the sensation of sitting on the chair (Where does the body touch the chair? Is there any tension? Focus on breathing. And so on.). Ask the client to bring their awareness to the feeling of the paradox. Ask what precisely the client is feeling and to verbalise this. Ask where in the body the feeling is. Ask the client to stay with the feeling. When the experience becomes too overwhelming, ask the client to shift the focus to their breathing and/or the feeling of the chair, and when the client has calmed down ask the client to bring their attention back to the feeling of the paradox; this shift of attention to and away from the paradox can be repeated several times.

Normalise paradoxes. Some clients seem to have the idea that paradoxes and complex feelings are not normal. Practitioners can explain that such feelings are normal: in life, we do not always have black-or-white answers, and it is possible to live with paradoxes without denying one side of the paradox. For instance: 'I hear you saying that you cannot find any meaning in being ill, but at the same time you want to live a meaningful life in the here and now. That is a paradox. Such paradoxes often occur when individuals are confronted with life's limitations, such as being diagnosed with a disease. I personally think you are right that you cannot find meaning IN the disease: being ill feels tough, negative, sad. Thus, I am not saying that you *should* find meaning *in the experience of being ill*: the illness does not necessarily need to teach you a lesson. However, regardless of being ill, you can live a meaningful and satisfying life.'

36. *Identifying avoidance and denial of meaning-related topics, and flexibly tolerating existential moods*

Existential therapists such as Yalom (1980) have suggested that individuals use existential defence mechanisms to cope with life's givens. This has been confirmed in many empirical laboratory experiments (Pyzscinski,

Greenberg & Koole, 2014; Vos et al., 2015). When individuals become aware of these givens, this may evoke strong **existential moods**, such as death anxiety. To cope with these givens and moods, some individuals may shift their focus away from these experiences and pretend that life is not limited by these givens. Such denial and avoidance may lead to stress-relief in the short term, but predict a lower sense of meaning and fulfilment about life in the long term (Jim et al., 2006; Vos & De Haes, 2007). For example, consider the cancer patient who pretends that she is not ill, by trying to lead life as usual. Or the student who procrastinates in his study as he does not know what to do after graduation. Or the party animal taking drugs and alcohol to sedate himself.

Alternatively, individuals may try to accept life's givens, learn to tolerate existential moods and use this awareness to take responsibility in living an authentic life. Thus, the acceptance of life's givens and existential moods can help individuals to live a more authentically meaningful life. For example, in the face of death, individuals could prioritise their activities in life according to what they experience as the most important. In the face of existential limitations, individuals may reflect on what they want to do with their remaining time, energy and possibilities in life.

Treatments that address life's givens and existential moods without simultaneously addressing meaning have few or no significant effects in clinical trials (Vos, Craig & Cooper, 2014; Vos, 2018c). For example, some existential therapists suggest clients describe how they feel about their death, and subsequently stay with and deepen this experience of their finitude, without connecting this experience with meaning. Focusing only on life's givens can be psychologically unbearable, in the same way as directly staring at the sun can blind individuals, and lead to psychosis or suicide (Yalom, 2008; Vos, 2014). In contrast, when clients reflect in meaning-centred treatments on their finitude, they are simultaneously asked how they can use this experience of their mortality to live a more meaningful life, such as making the best out of life or leaving a positive legacy. Focusing on meaning is not a denial or avoidance of life's givens, but instead an embracing of the fact that all humans have a dual nature: although we know that our death is the end of our possibilities, we are not dead yet and live in the here and now where we have the possibility to live a meaningful life. The existential philosopher Martin Heidegger called our dual nature 'existence', derived from the Latin 'ex-sistere' which can be translated as 'standing out'. We stand in the here and now, where we need to give a meaningful answer to our death that is still outstanding (Vos, 2014). Therefore, meaning-centred practitioners create a **dual attitude**: living a meaningful life despite – or thanks to – our acceptance of life's givens. Meaning-centred treatment is always existential meaning-centred treatment.

Individuals may use avoidance and denial to cope with unbearable feelings. Temporary defences can be useful or even crucial for maintaining one's mental health in crisis situations. However, research shows that avoidance and denial should not be permanent and structural. That is, clients experience the best psychological well-being when they can flexibly switch between different styles of coping, so that they can, for instance, temporarily use denial and avoidance to immediately lower their psychological stress levels, but in the long term they should also be able to use other ways of coping (Cheng, Lau & Chan, 2014; Vos, 2014). For instance, it seems beneficial to have illusions about life – such as feelings of invulnerability, immortality and being in control – while at the same time being (cognitively) aware of their illusory character (Vos, 2016a). Thus, clients may learn to flexibly tolerate existential moods and paradoxes.

Example

Without first accepting the given life situation at this moment, clients may not feel free to be authentically meaningful. I was called to meet a client during the last days of her life. All she did was play computer games on her phone, while she was lying in bed and her daughters wanted her to heal some relationship ruptures and discuss the funeral. When I asked the client, she said playing games was for her the only meaningful activity she could do. When I asked her about her approaching death, her facial expressions remained neutral, and at the same time she killed an enemy in her first-person shooter computer game. The rejection of her imminent death seemed to give her a narrow focus, instead of having the final conversations which were so important for her daughters. Her family told me that she had feared death since the traumatic loss of her parents. After her death, her daughters were very angry at her for not connecting with them, but it helped them to realise that this was caused by her underlying existential anxiety.

Clinical trials indicate that existential-psychotherapies which put a one-sided focus on heroically and/or positively confronting life's givens – regardless of the strength and readiness of the person- are ineffective or even lead to worse mental health such as psychosis (Vos & Vitali, 2018; Vos, Craig & Cooper, 2015).

---

37. *Stimulating clients to take up their own responsibility for living a meaningful life*

Freedom is not the last word. Freedom is only part of the story and half of the truth. The positive aspect of freedom is responsibleness. Therefore I recommend that the Statue of Liberty on the East Coast be supplemented by a Statue of Responsibility on the West Coast.

(Frankl, 1949/1986)

Freedom may seem the last word for some existential therapists, but for some meaning-centred practitioners responsibility seems to be the last word. For them, we not only have the freedom to live a meaningful life despite life's challenges, but we are also responsible for living a meaningful life. For them, life has no meaning except in terms of responsibility (Niebuhr, 1963/1999).

In this context, meaning-centred practitioners often cite Isaiah Berlin's (1958) essay on two different types of freedom. Negative freedom involves an answer to the question, 'What is the area within which the subject – a person or group of persons – is or should be left to do or be what he is able to do or be, without interference by other persons.' Positive freedom is involved in the answer to the question, 'What, or who, is the source of control or interference that can determine someone to do, or be, this rather than that?' The two questions are clearly different, even though the answers to them may overlap. Positive freedom has been interpreted as focusing on the uniqueness of the individual in determining their life and world around them, related to self-regulation and self-worth.

For example, Frankl (1949/1986, p. 135) did not experience much negative freedom in the concentration camp as he was imprisoned, but he described how he had the positive freedom to determine the meaning of his situation: 'Everything can be taken from a man but one thing: the last of the human freedoms – to choose one's attitude in any given set of circumstances, to choose one's own way.' Positive freedom has ultimately been interpreted as responsibility: no one other than us can make the decision for us of how to experience meaning (see Levinas, 1956/1969): when I say 'please, can you make the decision for me to be free' then I am denying my positive freedom. Only I can decide to live life to its fullest, or not. In line with other existential therapies, meaning-centred practitioners stimulate clients to take responsibility for living a meaningful life. The client cannot shift the own unique responsibility of living a meaningful life to others, and the practitioner cannot do this for them. Negative freedom means that others do not determine the direction in our life, and positive freedom means that we have and follow a direction in life.

In line with Frankl, Sartre (2012) spoke about **bad faith** ('mauvaise foi'), individuals' decision to avoid making a commitment, being motivated, acting, having values, experiencing self-worth, understanding and self-regulating; in other words, the decision to avoid meaning (see the definition in Section 3.1). Sartre assumed that individuals are free and responsible to decide their direction in life. We cannot escape this freedom of committing ourselves to motivated action, based on our values, self-worth and understanding of the world and those around us. External circumstances may challenge us, but we should be able to regulate how we live a meaningful life. For instance, an individual in Nazi Germany, such as Adolf Eichmann, might have said, 'I cannot risk my life as I have a family to support' or 'I merely do my job'; this is bad faith. However, an individual could also have resisted the regime, and thus acted in good faith. According to Sartre's friend Hannah Arendt (1963), Eichmann denied his freedom and responsibility, possibly out of anguish, knowing he had to make a choice and this had consequences. He deceived himself and acted out of bad faith. Thus, bad faith is the paradoxical free decision to deny to ourselves our freedom in experiencing meaning.

Following Sartre, some meaning-centred practitioners claim that meaning is inherently about responsibility, and practitioners should stimulate clients to become responsible (Wong, 2016). However, practitioners interpret the call for responsibility in two different ways. In the first place, they could stimulate clients to actively commit to any activity or experience which feels meaningful for the clients. In the second place, practitioners could prompt clients to focus on specific types of meanings, for instance they could impose their idea on clients that they should love and work or completely dedicate their life to other people or larger goals. The first interpretation seems coherent with the existential framework, as clients define responsibility in their own terms. However, clients could experience the second as unethical as this imposes the practitioner's own meanings onto the client.

Example. Strengthening the Will Exercise:

'Many addicts tell themselves "I will not drink again", and certain addiction support programs such as AA suggest addicts say that "I am powerless over the addiction and need a higher Power to rescue me", but this self-talk does not always work as it does not activate their responsibility. Instead, Lukas suggests that they use self-talk such as: "I am not the helpless victim of my drives and emotions. I have a free will. I can feel this inner will, it becomes clearer and clearer, it gives me strength to persist. I shall master my life, master in spite of all the difficulties."' (Lukas, 1984, p. 41)

Key existential skills

33. Empathising, recognising, naming and exploring the existential dimension in clients' experiences.

34. Stimulating meaning-centred coping with situations of suffering.

35. Exploring paradoxical feelings about meaning, and fostering acceptance of paradoxes and tensions.

36. Identifying avoidance and denial of meaning-related topics, and flexibly tolerating existential moods.

37. Stimulating clients to take up their own responsibility for living a meaningful life.

PART 3

A Ten-Session Treatment Manual:
Meaning-Centered Groups for Physically Ill
Individuals

10
Overview of Treatment

Session overview

This treatment manual is called 'Meaning-Centred Groups for Physically Ill Individuals' (MGP). The aim of MGP is to help individuals with a chronic or life-threatening physical disease to live a meaningful and satisfying life despite the limitations of their disease.

Table 10.1 Overview of topics of each session, and typical steps within each session

Overview of topics of each of the ten sessions	Typical steps within each session
1. *Introduction*: what is meaning and why might this be relevant when we are physically ill?	A. *Introduction*: aim and agenda for today; looking back at last week's session
2. *Assessment of meaning*: how do we experience meaning, and how has this changed as a result of the disease?	B. *Emotional check-in*: exploring any important developments since the last session, and reconnecting with each other
3. *Resilience as meaning*: how can we cope in a meaningful way with challenges in life and specifically with the disease?	C. *Didactics and group discussion*: explanation of theory, usually interactive with examples from the group
4. *Materialistic meanings*: how can we experience practical activities, belongings, physical experiences and productivity as meaningful?	D. *Guided experiential exercise*: an experiential or mindfulness exercise is used to help focus on inner experiences instead of merely theoretically speaking about meaning
5. *Self-oriented meanings*: how can we experience self-development, care for ourselves and self-expression as meaningful?	E. *Guided self-reflective exercise*: the experiential exercise flows automatically into an exercise in which the clients are asked to reflect on some questions related to the topic of the session (e.g. 'Find examples of moments that felt particularly meaningful.')
6. *Social meanings*: how can we experience our social relationships, community, children and caring for others as meaningful?	F. *Self-expression*: clients are invited to share their experiences

(Continued)

189

Overview of topics of each of the ten sessions	Typical steps within each session
7. *Higher meanings*: how can we experience larger goals, striving for justice and spirituality as meaningful?	G. *Self-evaluation*: clients are invited to evaluate in an individual exercise followed by a group discussion what was the most meaningful aspect of today, and decide on possible changes in daily life
8. *Being-here as meaning*: how can we experience meaning in the mere fact that we are alive, are free to make decisions and may be grateful?	H. *Session evaluation*: clients are invited to evaluate today's session and write down 'the three most important messages of today'
9. *Applying meaning in daily life*: how can we apply meaning in daily life – how can we set goals, create a plan, make changes, cope with challenges, evaluate and adjust our goals?	I. *Ending*: preview of next session and homework
10. *Ending and starting*: what can we use from these sessions in daily life, and how can we continue living a meaningful life?	

Evidence-based development

This treatment manual offers a guidance for practitioners based on systematic empirical evidence on meaning in life (as described in Part 1 of this book) and effective meaning-centred practices (Part 2). It is based on evidence-based, pluralistic, systematic and pragmatic principles.

First, the manual may be regarded as the common denominator of other effective meaning-centred practices, as it is created by combining their most common evidence-based structures and skills, as explained in Part 2. Components from meaning-centred practices that had little empirical evidence were not included. Although the general structures and skills from other treatments were used, the specific exercises and formulations are unique to this manual.

Second, as every client may have different needs, the manual is as broad and inclusive as possible. The focus lies on the unique needs and capabilities of a unique client at a unique moment in time. Therefore, this treatment manual starts with a systematic assessment session with the individual. It should not be used rigidly (except for clinical trials for its initial validation) but, where needed, tailored to the individual.

Third, a systematic approach to meaning is used to explore all five types of meaning and examine which types are meaningful for individuals and where they may experience problems. Some types of meaning and certain problems may be more relevant to one client than to another. However, from the broad systematic perspective on meaning, individuals may be able to make a more informed decision about how to live their lives.

Fourth, this manual may be regarded pragmatic as it is based on **pragmatic phenomenology,** as explained in Chapter 2. Philosophical discussions are avoided and instead the focus lies on psycho-education, discussion and application based on meaning-oriented empirical research, as summarised in Part 1.

This manual was developed on eight pieces of systematic evidence.

1. A systematic literature review was conducted on the role of meaning in physical diseases (Vos, 2016b).

2. Meta-analyses have revealed how meaning-centred practices are relevant and effective for physically ill individuals (Sections 4.3 and 4.4). As there were no significant differences between different types of meaning-centred practices, it was decided to use the common denominator of all practices. This implies that the most frequently used structure, content and skills are used in this manual, as described in Part 2. Although this treatment may be regarded as the common denominator, the specific formulations of the exercises and didactics are unique.

3. The general style of formulating didactics and exercises is based on the treatment manual from Breitbart and Poppito (2014) for clients with advanced cancer. It has proved that new practitioners can easily be trained in this this treatment method.

4. Both the Breitbart and Poppito manual and most other treatments centred around the **Franklian triad.** It was decided to transform this into the **meaning quintet** (see pages 66–67). The meaning quintet is the most complete evidence-based overview of meanings. There are separate sessions for each type of meaning.

5. To tailor meaning to the specific experience of physical illness Sessions 1–3 introduce how meaning is relevant to coping with physical diseases (following Breitbart & Poppito, 2014).

6. Research shows that clients benefit from translating the insights they gain in treatment sessions to daily life – for example by setting and experimenting with specific goals (Chapter 6). Therefore, clients receive homework, and Sessions 9 and 10 focus on meaning in daily life. For the purpose of providing reminders or 'nudges' (Section 8.2) for themselves about the sessions, clients are given the option to create a pin-up board in their home or workplace where they place relevant text, pictures or anything else. Similar to suggestions by Breitbart and Poppito (2014), clients will give a presentation (a 'life project') in the last session on a newly made or tried meaningful experience.

7. It was decided to offer treatment in groups, as research indicates that physically ill patients may benefit from peer support – for example in order to see that their experiences in their life situation are normal and universal (AGPA, 2007; Yalom & Lezsz, 2005). Groups may also stimulate social meaning-making and de-reflection (Sections 3.3 and 3.6).

8. Several feasibility studies were conducted during the development of this manual (Van der Spek, 2016; Vos & Hutchinson, 2018; Vos, 2016). These suggested significant positive effects on quality of life and reduction in psychological stress in individuals with cancer, cardiovascular disease, chronic pain and other physical problems. Other validation studies are ongoing.

Practical recommendations

Groups consist of six to ten individuals. No new members are admitted after the first session. Weekly sessions last for two hours, with about a ten-minute break halfway through. The location should be accessible and free of distractions. Tables and chairs are arranged in a circle or horseshoe. Before each session, practitioners print tables or texts for each of the clients; Chapters 11–21 provide specific instructions on what should be printed. In Session 1, the clients will be given a file in which they can keep all the texts and exercises; they are asked to bring this file to each session, and are advised to use this file as a source of help for when the sessions end. Practitioners are advised to familiarise themselves with group dynamics and develop group facilitation skills (AGPA, 2007; Yalom & Lezsz, 2005). They should also use manuals in a flexible and client-centred way, and not as a way of imposing their structure and meanings onto the client: they should develop constructive **manual application skills**. Table 10.2 suggests inclusion criteria.

Table 10.2 Recommended inclusion criteria

1. One type of disease in one group (e.g. cancer, stroke, chronic pain)
2. Same stage and prognosis in one group (e.g. palliative care, treatment with curative intent)
3. Expectation to attend at least eight out of ten sessions
4. Psychological capability to contribute to the group process: cognitive and linguistic skills; no acute psychosis or acute mania, issues with aggression, or anti-social behaviour; sufficient social skills
5. Other urgent needs may need to be addressed first (e.g. medical or housing concerns)
6. The client and practitioner can identify at least one way in which the client could benefit from developing meaning-centred skills (Section 4.4; Chapter 5)
7. The client has been informed and agrees with the aim and method (Chapter 5)
8. No inclusion criteria regarding levels of stress or psychopathology such as anxiety or depression

Preparation

Practitioners are advised to prepare themselves in different ways before the first session:

➤ develop group therapy skills

➤ read relevant literature (see reference list)

➤ explore their own meaning-centred experiences – for example, via exercises in this book

➤ participate in personal therapy to develop insights into their own meanings

➤ receive formal training by an expert on evidence-based meaning-centred practices, including tips and techniques for each session (e.g. 'MEANING: an evidence-based training for practitioners' by Dr Vos)

➤ try out giving treatment on other practitioners.

To stimulate self-reflection and self-development, practitioners are advised to evaluate sessions in multiple ways:

➤ At the end of each session, clients summarise the three most important messages from that session, and identify possible wishes for the next session(s).

➤ After each session, practitioners fill in the Meaning Centred Practitioners' Skills Questionnaire.

➤ Co-therapists evaluate the session together.

➤ Provide a verbal evaluation of the treatment with clients in Session 10.

➤ Allow for anonymous feedback after Session 10 via a questionnaire consisting of open questions (e.g. 'Describe helpful aspects of this therapy', 'Describe unhelpful aspects', 'Any recommendations for improvement?') and standardised questionnaires (Chapter 6).

➤ Participate in frequent meaning-centred supervision and/or intervision sessions with senior practitioners. This aims to help with practical questions, improve and practise specific skills, and become aware of the practitioner's own meanings which could influence the treatment. Practitioners could discuss Meaning Centred Practitioners' Skills Questionnaires and session recordings.

11

Individual Assessment Session

11.1 Overview

- *Key session question*: How might the client benefit from participating in a Meaning-Centred Group?

- *Session goals:*
    a. Check to which extent the motivation, needs and preferences of the client match with the aim and format of meaning-centred groups
    b. Check whether the client has sufficient skills to participate in meaning-centred groups
    c. Explain the aims and method of meaning-centred groups
    d. Lay the foundations for a constructive practitioner–client relationship
    e. Create a meaning-centred case formulation
    f. Reach a shared decision on whether the client will join the meaning-centred groups

- *Process:*

  This is an individual session which is usually considered part of the research process and not the treatment process (Vos & Vitali, 2018). However, the assessment stage may already be considered as part of the treatment, for instance because the client starts reflecting on meaning-centred concerns (Lukas, 1986/2014). This session is important for expectation management, laying the foundations for a constructive therapeutic relationship and setting norms, motivating the potential client for participation, helping to connect the individual experiences with the content and format of MCG, and making an informed decision about participation. This session should preferably be given by the practitioner who will lead the group.

- *Recommended reading*: Chapter 10 on assessment skills which includes an example of how to develop a meaning-centred case formulation

– *Clients may be asked to fill in before this session:*
  – Meaning in Life Questionnaire (appendix)
  – Meaning Quintet Questionnaire (appendix)
  – Goal Assessment Form (appendix)

– *Handout provided and explained at end of session:*
  – Handout 11.1. Session overview
  – Handout 11.2 Homework before Session 1 (see below)

11.2 Stages

1. *Introduction* (5 mins)
   The practitioner and client introduce themselves.

2. *Explaining the aim and method of today's session* (5 mins)
   The practitioner explains the aim and method of today's session.

3. *The client's motivation* (10 mins)
   The practitioner asks the client about their motivation for participating in this group, and about their psychological needs at this stage. The practitioner should be aware of the time limitations of today's session, and may need to explain that this is not an in-depth session but intended as an initial assessment. The practitioner may use the following questions in a flexible way tailored to the client, based on strong relational-humanistic practitioner skills.

Example

1. Request for help

   A. What is/are the reason/reasons for your referral and/or for you deciding to participate?
   B. [If not mentioned:] What are the main issues that you are struggling with at this moment in your life?
   C. What would you like to change in your life?
   D. [If not mentioned:] How do these problems impact your daily life? For example, do they influence your emotions, relationships, work, hobbies, physical well-being, etc.

2. History of the problems

   A. What is the reason for you asking for help at this specific moment in your life (any specific triggers)?
   B. [If not mentioned:] Could you describe the first time you experienced these problems? Could you describe that situation?

▶

◄

C. [If not mentioned:] Do you have an idea as to why these problems developed?

D. Are there situations in your life when these problems are worse?

E. Are there situations in your life when you don't experience these problems as much?

[These questions may help to understand the possible underlying causes of the problems.]

3. Attempts for improvement

A. What have you already done to improve your life situation? What was helpful and what was not helpful?

B. *[If not mentioned:]* Have you asked for help from friends or family? What did they say? What was helpful and what was not helpful?

C. *[If not mentioned:]* Have you had any counselling or therapy before, and if so what changes did it make in your life? What was helpful and what was not helpful?

[These questions help identify helpful and unhelpful factors in therapy.]

4. Assess strengths

A. Could you tell me anything about your life situation that may be relevant for me to know? For instance, do you have a partner or children, do you work or study, how is your housing situation, how do you make a living, how is your health, do you have friends and family? Could you describe what you do on an average day?

B. What are some of your strong points?

C. What are the highlights in your life? Could you, for example, describe moments when you felt you were in a flow, forgot the time, things go automatically, etc.?

D. What helps you get through a difficult day? For example, imagine a day when you feel tired or in pain; what helps you to get out of your bed?

E. What do you find particularly important or meaningful in your life? Could you describe some moments that felt particularly meaningful? To what extent are these feelings limited by your problems?

F. To what extent do you feel that you live the life you want to live? To what extent do you feel satisfied about how you live your life? What makes you satisfied and what does not?

[These questions will help to identify a sense of meaning, meaning-related concerns and types of meaning. These questions may also stimulate self-esteem, and help in examining the client's ability to identify meaningful aspects in life. As recommended by Lukas (1986/2014) it is important to prevent hyper-reflection by merely addressing negative aspects in the client's life; the practitioner may want to switch between questions about problems and about positive experiences.]

5. Assess general concerns

A. Are there any problems in your life situation that need to be solved before you could join the therapy group? For example, do you have any social, financial, work, housing or other concerns?

B. *[if not mentioned:]* How is your health at this moment? What is the prognosis and treatment? Are you receiving all the medical care you need? How are you coping with this? How does this feel?

[These questions check whether urgent life issues need to be solved first.]

4. *The aim and method of Meaning Centred Therapy Groups* (15 mins)
The practitioner explains the general aim and method, and checks how relevant this is for the client.

Example formulation

How did you hear about Meaning-Centred Groups and what do you already know about meaning-centred practice? (...) This group is meant for individuals who are questioning how they can live a meaningful and satisfying life despite the limitations of being physically ill. Clients in similar groups have said that this group helped them to find new ways to live a meaningful and satisfying life despite the illness; it also improved their mood and they felt more self-confident and hopeful. You may experience similar benefits but you may possibly also have other experiences, as everyone is different. There are ten weekly sessions. The groups usually consist of six to ten individuals with the same illness as you; many individuals like being in a group with others in the same life situation as they feel supported and get useful advice from each other. Usually, the sessions start with a short explanation of a topic, followed by a group discussion and an individual exercise. For instance, you could be asked to reflect on some moments that felt meaningful for you in the past. The central theme of the sessions is 'living a meaningful life'; we will be searching for examples, ranging from something small – for instance, enjoying a bird in the par – to something large such as raising children, a vocation or helping other people. In each of the sessions, we will discuss another type of meaning: for instance, in one session we will discuss how your family or friends may be meaningful for you – or not – and, in another, how your work or hobby may be meaningful for you – or not. Some types of meaning may be more important for some participants than for others, as everyone is unique. The group members will actively contribute to the group, for instance by doing the exercises and responding to each other's stories. We ask everyone to be open and respectful to each other, and everyone is free to decide for themselves what feels meaningful for them. Usually we will give you a short task to do at home – such as reading or answering some questions – because we believe that to make any changes in your daily life, it is important for clients to not only have two hours of therapy per week but also to do something in their daily life. Do you have any questions? (...) What are your first feelings about this group? (...) What do you think about the topic of meaning? (...) Do you feel that you may benefit from participating, and, if so, how? What would you like to achieve for yourself when you would participate in this group? Could you give some examples of how you might benefit from joining this group?

---

5. *Discussing the match between the therapy and the client* (5 mins)
The practitioner asks specific questions to check inclusion and exclusion criteria; if already clear, these questions do not need to be asked.

Example

I would like to ask some specific questions to see whether you are able to join this group.

1. Do you speak and read English well enough to speak with others in a group and read some texts?

2. How do you feel about being in a group? *[the practitioner may explain that some social anxiety is normal, but that after a while clients usually feel more relaxed and open; this question is intended to check whether the client has some basic social skills and would not feel too overwhelmed; joining a group often helps individuals to learn from each other, and to improve their social interaction skills, thus some anxiety about group participation could even be an indication to join the group]*

3. Do you often forget things, have difficulties keeping your attention on one topic, or have problems with thinking? If so, how limiting are these problems in your life; could you give examples? *[check possible cognitive impairments, particularly in the case of chemotherapy, stroke, brain tumours or neurological disorders; impairments should not be too disturbing for the group process]*

4. Would you be willing to do exercises in the group, speak with other clients and do some exercises at home?

5. Do you expect to be able to attend all the group sessions and do some short exercises at home? *[if a client already knows beforehand that two or more sessions will be missed, the client may miss too much and the group may not be suited for this client]*

6. Have you ever received a diagnosis of a psychiatric disorder? If so, when did you receive this disorder, have you had treatment for this, and are you still experiencing similar problems, and if so which problems? *[a psychiatric diagnosis per se is not an exclusion criterion; the practitioner needs to assess to what extent the symptoms are present and may disrupt the group dynamics, and the benefits for the client]*

7. Finally, are there any specific days or times that you are not able to come to group sessions? Would you be able to come to the location where the sessions will be held, for instance via your own transport, public transport or taxi? Would you need any physical support accessing the location, for instance when you are in a wheelchair?

6. *Discussing questionnaires* (5 mins)

The practitioner discusses the questionnaires filled in by the client, and particularly what the scores could reveal about the relevance of the meaning-centred groups for the client (Chapter 10). This is formulated as hypotheses, to which the client can respond.

7. *Meaning-centred case formulation* (5 mins)
The practitioner shares the case formulation with the client, and discusses how this may relate to the aims and process of the meaning-centred groups (Chapter 10).

8. *Shared decision-making*
Based on the meaning-centred case formulation, the client and practitioner make a shared decision about the client joining meaning-centred groups or not. This decision-making process is phenomenological and relational-humanistic in nature (Chapters 7 and 8), while bearing in mind the inclusion/exclusion criteria.

9. *Ending* (5 mins)
The practitioner provides practical information, and gives homework as preparation for the first session. If the client will not be joining the group, the practitioner refers them to other support options.

Handout 11.1 Session overview

---

1. *Introduction* (5 mins)

2. *Explaining the aim and method of today's session* (5 mins)

3. *The client's motivation* (10 mins)

4. *The aim and method of Meaning Centred Therapy Groups* (10 mins)

5. *Discussing questionnaires* (5 mins)

6. *Meaning-centred case formulation* (5 mins)

7. *Shared decision-making* (5 mins)

8. *Ending* (5 mins)
   a. practical information
   b. homework

Handout 11.2 Homework (to be completed before Session 1):

Prepare what you will share with the group

During this first session, you will get the opportunity to tell the group about yourself, and to share anything you would like others to know about your illness. Everyone will have approximately 5 minutes for this. Some clients have told us in the past that they would like to prepare what they are going to talk about. Therefore, you may wish to use the following questions to prepare, but feel free to do this in your own way: this is your time! Do NOT feel obliged to talk about anything you don't want to.

1. *What is your name?*

2. *What is your age?*

3. *Anything you want to share about your live situation (e.g. single, married, children):*

4. *Anything that feels meaningful or important in your life (e.g. work, children, volunteering, religion, family, study)*

5. *Anything you want to share about your illness (e.g. what it's called, when it was diagnosed, what treatment you have had, whether you are currently undergoing any treatment, any physical limitations you experience in daily life, how you feel about the illness)*

6. *Why did you decide to participate in this group?*

7. *Try to think back over the last two weeks. You could possibly look in your diary. Which moments or activities felt meaningful to you or made you feel 'alive'?*

12

Session 1: Introduction to Meaning in Life

12.1 Overview

– *Key session question*: What is meaning and why might this be relevant for individuals with a chronic or life-threatening physical disease?

– *Session goals:*
   a. introduction to practitioners and clients
   b. general overview of the therapy (treatment goals, weekly topics, logistics)
   c. introduction to meaning and its possible relevance
   d. exploring how meaning can change due to disease

– *Main group process:*
   a. setting group norms
   b. connecting clients

– *Homework completed before this session:*

   Handout 11.1 'Prepare what you will share with the group'

– *Handouts (to be given out in the session):*
   12.1 Session overview
   12.2 Group guidelines
   12.3 Definition of meaning
   12.4 Self-evaluation of today's session
   12.5 Session 2 preview exercise: Identity before and after the illness
   Goal Assessment Form

– *Recommended reading*
   ➤ Chapters 5 and 6

12.2 Stages

1. *Introduction* (15 mins)

   a. *Greeting*

   The practitioner starts with a general introduction to make the clients feel welcome and lower anxiety in the group. The practitioner welcomes the clients, introduce themselves, and asks the group members to say their names. It is useful to ask the clients to make nameplates and put these in front of them, so that everyone can remember each other's names.

   b. *Overview of today*

   The practitioners explain the aims of today's session and give out Handout 12.1.

   c. *Aim of group*

   The practitioner explains the aim of this group therapy in general.

Example formulation

The aim of this group is to help group members live a meaningful and satisfying life despite their illness. That is, individuals with, for example, cancer, cardiovascular illness, chronic pain and so forth, often experience that their illness makes it more difficult to do things that feel meaningful for them; for instance, they may not be able to work, or they may be too tired to go to their daughter's football match. Or they may focus so much on the illness and its treatment that they seem to 'forget' what is really meaningful. Or due to the illness they may now look totally differently at life in general. Many individuals with such illnesses (e.g. cancer, cardiovascular illness, chronic pain, etc.) say that such changes in their meanings make them feel sad, anxious or meaningless. Therefore, in these sessions we will explore how we can live a meaningful and satisfying life despite the illness; we will, for instance, look at what was meaningful for you in the past, and what other new activities could feel meaningful for you.

These sessions are different than traditional psychotherapy or therapy. For instance, we will not tell you, as practitioners, how you should find meaning in life. We will explore together, all group members, how we can live a meaningful life. This is like a 'learning partnership' (*see Breitbart & Poppito, 2014, p. 4*), where we will all be learning from each other. We will do this, by giving you some explanation about meaning, having group discussions and asking you to reflect on some questions about yourself.

We will also not be saying that you MUST find meaning in your illness, like some people say that 'you MUST learn from your illness', 'you must find a positive message in your illness', 'your illness gives you a lesson', or 'you have developed your illness

▶

◀

for a reason'. Friends and magazines often give this message that we must transform our illness into something positive, but we often cannot completely undo or cure the physical disease with mere theorising or positive thinking. It is entirely understandable, that you have moments where you feel that the illness limits you and you feel tired, sad and anxious; you cannot simply get rid of these feelings by trying to make this into something positive. However, we believe that DESPITE being ill, you can live a meaningful and satisfying life. That is, regardless of the illness – or, some would say, thanks to the illness – we can find ways to live a good life. This means that this therapy will NOT cure your illness and will NOT make your illness less painful, but we can help you to live a meaningful and satisfying life despite the illness. This can help you feel less stress and more in control of your life.

d. *Group guidelines*

The practitioner *briefly* discusses the group guidelines handout (Handout 12.2). The practitioner might explain the rationale for this as follows: 'these guidelines help us to create a group atmosphere in which clients feel free and safe to share their experiences, and to learn from each other.' The clients are invited to ask questions and are asked to agree to follow these guidelines; by asking the clients to agree on these rules, the practitioner can refer to these guidelines at a later stage when needed.

e. *Logistics*

Tell the clients about the logistical aspects of the group. For instance, it will meet ten times. Sessions last for two hours, with a short break halfway through. Every session will have a specific topic and follow specific steps. Describe the overview of sessions from Handout 10.1.

2. *Group sharing who you are (prepared in homework before session)* **(45 mins)**

Clients briefly introduce themselves. Mention the time limit of five minutes per person; explain that this may feel insufficient, but it is needed to give everyone the possibility to introduce themselves. It is important to stick to the time limit in this first session, as this sets a group norm about how practitioners deal with time limits. Acknowledge the dissatisfaction of clients when they feel they have not had enough time; explain that they will have more time to get to know each other in the sessions that follow. In the case of extraordinary events (for instance, strong emotions), it may be important to deviate from this time limit, and it should be explained why the time limit is exceeded. The practitioners add that the clients should feel free to tell their story in their way: 'This is your time: do NOT feel obliged to talk about anything you do not want to'.

3. *Explanation and group discussion* (20 mins)

   a. *What does 'meaning' mean for you*

The practitioner asks clients what they think 'meaning' is, and what their associations with this are. Try to create a definition together (for instance on a flip chart). This definition can be connected with the five aspects of meaning in the next step. As a litmus test, the practitioner may ask the clients what the difference is between meaning and 'liking something', 'one-time peak experiences, such as pop concerts', 'happiness', 'things that are popular in the media' and 'drunkenness'.

After the discussion, the practitioner asks whether 'meaning' is the right term for the clients, or whether they have a better term. Previous groups have suggested the terms flow, mojo, importance in life, values, doing your thing, passion, etc. The group is asked whether it is OK to use the term 'meaning', or whether another term needs to be used in group sessions. Usually, the group agrees to use the term 'meaning', and the practitioner could add: 'we will use this term, but you may transpose this with a term that you would prefer.'

   b. *Explaining what 'meaning' is*

Following on from the examples in the previous exercise, the practitioner describes how we use the term 'meaning', via Handout 12.3.

   c. *Five types of meaning*

The practitioner asks the clients for some examples of meaning, and uses these to explain that there are five types of meaning. After having given an overview of these five types of meaning (see the final row in Handout 12.3), the practitioner may then ask whether one or more clients could explain this in their own: 'I realise that I have given you a lot of information. To see whether I have explained this clearly enough, could someone summarise it in your own words? This is not a school examination, but just to see whether I have been clear.'

4. *Guided individual exercise* (10 mins)

   a. *Mindfulness exercise*

The practitioner leads a brief mindfulness exercise, so that the clients have an initial understanding of mindfulness. The next session will go deeper into explaining the mindfulness skills.

Consider the following points:

– Ask whether the clients already have experience with mindfulness or meditation exercises. Ask for examples of experiences, connotations and stereotypes about mindfulness, and provide any additional explanation.

- Explain that the first aim of mindfulness exercises is to become more aware of what we are experiencing, helping us to focus on our inner experiences and on what is important. That is, we often run away from what we are feeling because it may feel too painful or overwhelming but by looking at our experiences, we may better understand where for instance discomfort or happiness come from and how we could solve underlying problems. The second aim is that a mindfulness exercise may help the client to cope better with uncomfortable feelings. Some individuals feel more relaxed and learn to bear pain and discomfort.
- Explain that clients will not and cannot be forced to do anything they do not want to do, and that clients can stop at any time.
- Adjust the exercises to the skills, experiences and preferences of clients.
- Invite clients to close their eyes, drawing their attention to how they sit on the chair; how does the body feel, where does it touch the chair, and so on. This exercise can be creatively extended and adjusted to the personal experiences and preferences of clients.

b. *Reflecting on questions*

While clients have their eyes closed, the practitioner asks them to reflect on the following question:

Try to think of one or more examples when life felt particularly meaningful to you; this could be a big or small experience. For example, when did you feel most alive, or what helped you get through a difficult day?

c. *Writing about the individual exercise*

The clients are invited to open their eyes, and write down key words, whatever they like, about the exercise, as a reminder to themselves. They are requested not to speak with each other just yet.

5. *Group sharing of the individual exercise* (10 mins)

The clients share some of their experiences. This is a good moment for the practitioner to try to connect clients' stories and find common themes. The practitioner could also connect the examples with the theory (for instance with types of meanings).

6. *Self-evaluation in writing* (5 mins)

a. *The three most meaningful aspects of today* &

b. *Wishes for the next session*

The practitioner asks clients to evaluate the session by filling in Handout 12.4.

7. *Group sharing of the self-evaluation* (5 mins)

Clients can briefly share what they experienced as meaningful in today's session, and mention their wishes for the next session. The group should be told that the time for this group sharing is very limited, but if there is anything important that clients want to share, they have the opportunity.

8. *Ending* (5 mins)

a. *Summary*

The practitioner summarises the content and group process of today's session.

b. *Preview of the next session*

The practitioner gives a preview of the next session: 'Next week will be about how physical disease can change how we experience meaning.'

c. *Homework*

The practitioner introduces the homework on Handouts 12.5 and the Goal Assessment Form.

Handout 12.1 Session overview

1. *Introduction* (15 mins)
    a. greeting
    b. overview of today
    c. aim of group
    d. group guidelines
    e. logistics

2. *Group sharing who you are (prepared in homework before session)* (45 mins)

3. *Explanation and group discussion* (20 mins)
    a. what does 'meaning' mean for you
    b. what do we mean by 'meaning'
    c. why could meaning be important when you are ill
    d. four different types of meaning
    e. overview of group sessions

4. *Guided individual exercise* (10 mins)
    a. mindfulness exercise
    b. reflecting on questions
    c. writing about the exercise

5. *Group sharing of the individual exercise* (10 mins)

6. *Self-evaluation in writing* (5 mins)
    a. three most meaningful aspects of today
    b. wishes for next session

7. *Group sharing of the self-evaluation* (5 mins)

8. *Ending* (5 mins)
    a. summary
    b. preview of the next session
    c. homework

Handout 12.2   Group guidelines

1. Protect each other's confidentiality and privacy
   - ➤ It is important that every group member feels safe to share what they would like. Therefore we ask all groups members to respect each other's privacy and not to share any personal stories from other clients outside of this group.

2. Be present in the sessions
   - ➤ Your attendance is important. You will mainly benefit from this group when you are present. The group also needs you, as we learn as a group from each other. Therefore, try to be here every session.
   - ➤ Of course, in life unexpected things happen such as an illness or family matters. If this happens, or there are events you cannot change like a wedding,please inform us about your absence beforehand, and we will give you the handouts and the homework for the next session.
   - ➤ We learn from each other. Therefore, we ask everyone to participate in discussions, exercises and homework. If you find it difficult to participate or speak up, let us know and we will try to help you.

3. Share time with others
   - ➤ Your stories are important. Unfortunately, we only have ten sessions of two hours. This is short. Therefore, we ask you to do some preparation at home before the session (home-work). We want to give all clients equal time to share their stories; therefore, think about others with whom you are sharing the time, and do not demand all the time for your stories. The group leaders will signal when it may be time for someone else to speak.

4. Respect the uniqueness of meaning
   - ➤ Every individual experiences meaning in their own unique way. There is no right or wrong. This group helps you to discover for yourself what is meaningful. Because of this uniqueness, we ask clients to be tolerant of each other, not to judge others, and not to try to persuade others of our own opinion.
   - ➤ We are all equal as human beings, trying to live a meaningful and satisfying life despite our challenges in life: no one is better or more important than another, and everyone deserves equal attention and respect. We ask everyone to treat others as equals, not dominate them, not be racist, sexist, homophobic, etc. Be respectful.

Handout 12.3   Definition of meaning

What meaning is NOT	What meaning is
One Absolute Ultimate Meaning of Life	Multiple meanings
Only for religious or spiritual people	Neutral description of the lives of all people
Only Big Goals in life	Range from small to large meanings
Unchangeable	Changeable, depending on life situation and life events such as becoming ill
One meaning for everyone	Unique to you
Others can tell what your meaning is	You are the only person who can discover what is meaningful for you
You can wait for others to take the initiative in making your life meaningful	You are responsible for discovering meaning in your life; others will not do this for you
Life can be without meaning	It always seems possible to experience meaning in any life situation
You can find meaning randomly: simply pick and choose something	Everyone has a hierarchy of experiences that are less meaningful and experiences that are more meaningful; therefore, you cannot randomly replace one meaning for another meaning
Meaning is an abstract theory	In daily life, we usually do not think about what is meaningful for us; we simply DO things that are meaningful for us
You can find meaning in books and by thinking	Meaning is usually found by intuitively feeling what is meaningful for you, and by engaging in activities in daily life
Meaning is only something in the here and now	Meaning is about the experience of something bigger than daily life; feeling connected with something more important and valuable
We MAKE meaning	What we could experience as meaningful is already implicitly there in our experiences; we only need to discover this by using our intuitive feeling
Meaning can simply be defined as having a goal in life	The definition of meaning has multiple aspects: A. motivation: having a sense of the general direction of where you are going in life or your purpose B. values: living according to your own values C. understanding: generally understanding and feeling connected to the world, to events in your life, to people around you and to yourself D. self-worth: feeling that your life is worthy, significant and relevant E. commitment: committing to specific actions and goals in daily life F. self-efficacy: being able to evaluate, adjust and improve how you live your life
There is only one type of meaning	Generally speaking, there are five types of meaning (and each type has many subtypes): 1. Materialistic and hedonistic meanings; 2. Self-oriented meanings; 3. Social meanings; 4. Larger meanings; 5. Existential-philosophical meanings.

Handout 12.4 Self-evaluation of today's session

List up to three moments in or lessons from today's session that felt particularly meaningful to you

lk - there .

talking work .

How could you use these three meaningful moments or lessons in your daily life?

Do you have any wishes for the next group session?

Handout 12.5 Session 2 preview exercise: Identity before and after the illness

Please take some time to think about these questions. You may want to write some initial answers. We will complete this exercise during Session 2.

Question 1. Think about the period in your life before you became ill. Write down at least five answers to the question about that time: 'who am I?' These answers can be positive or negative, about something small or big, your personality characteristics, things you did or enjoyed, your social roles, or the bigger beliefs, goals or ambitions you had in life. An answer might start with 'I am someone who ...' or 'I am a ...'

Question 2. The previous answers were about your life before you became ill. The illness has (unfortunately) added a new answer that you did not have before: I am also a client with a physical illness who needed/needs medical treatment. Adding 'being a client' as an answer can sometimes change the answers to the previous questions, or cast a different light. Therefore, take a moment to think about how your illness has possibly affected your answers to the question 'who am I?' Are your answers still the same? Have specific answers changed? Do you have any new answers? Do the answers feel different? Has your general view on life changed? Has your illness changed the things that are most meaningful for you?

13

Session 2: Changes in Meaning in Life

13.1 Overview

– *Key session question*: How do we experience meaning in life, and how can disease change this?

– *Session goals:*

1. Supporting **experiential acceptance** in clients
2. Helping clients to start to identify meanings
3. Explaining how illness may have changed the meanings

– *Main group process:*

Stimulating clients to respond to each other; experiencing the universality of the changes in meaning due to illness; stimulating group cohesiveness

– *Homework completed before this session:*

12.5. Homework before Session 2: Preview exercise for Session 2
Goal Assessment Form

– *Handouts:*

13.1. Session overview
13.2. Changes in meaning
13.3. Evaluation of today's session
13.4. Homework (1) for Session 3: Preview exercise for Session 3
13.5. Homework (2) for Session 3: Meaningful moments exercise

– *Recommended reading:*

➤ Chapter 3
➤ Vos, 2016b

13.2 Stages

1. *Group personal/medical check-in* (10 mins)

   The clients are asked to share 'three meaningful aspects of last week'. They can share anything they like, for instance thoughts, feelings and questions about the session or any events that took place in the week. The aim is to become aware of progress and significant life events that may potentially influence the treatment, connect clients with each other and improve group cohesion. The practitioner uses this check-in to connect common themes between clients, to invite clients to respond to each other and to connect stories with the theory of this session. It is recommended that when clients are taking turns to speak their stories should naturally follow on from each other's; for example, the practitioner can elicit connections between clients' stories with the following questions: 'did you recognise this?'; 'did you also experience this this last week?' Before the check-in round starts and during the round, clients need to be gently reminded of the time limit, and the practitioner should acknowledge that 'unfortunately there is not enough catching-up time, because we have a full program today'. Clients are often more succinct when they are asked to describe 'at most three meaningful aspects'.

2. *Introduction* (10 mins)

   a. *Topic and overview of today*

      The practitioner explains that today's session follows on from last week, when the group was introduced to what meaning is in general. Today's session will look specifically at the ways in which individuals experienced meaning before illness and how their illness may have changed this.

   b. *Reflection on previous session*

      The practitioner asks clients to summarise the main message from last week's session. They could invite a client chosen at random to begin: 'Could I ask you to start talking about what was important for you in that session? Other clients can of course help, or add anything.' This is an opportunity for the group to work collaboratively on a task and develop group cohesion. This refresher of last week's session should not last more than a couple of minutes. Based on clients' answers, the practitioner should then provide a summary of the highlights of last week's session.

3. *Individual goals* (20 mins)

   The practitioner asks the clients to share their individual treatment goals, which clients filled in as homework. The practitioner connects the individual goals with the overall aim of the group treatment, connects the themes of the clients with each other, and explores together with clients how realistic these goals are. The clients are then asked to take responsibility for achieving their goals, and asked to pay attention to their goals during the sessions. If needed, clients are encouraged to reformulate their goals, usually by making the goals more specific and achievable within the weeks remaining until the final session.

4. *Explanation and group discussion* (15 mins)

a. *Explanation about 'Experiencing meaning, and changes in meaning'*

Step 1. What you wanted to become when you were a child, as an example

The practitioner asks whether the clients can still remember from their childhood what they wanted 'to become when they grew up'. The practitioner asks for some examples, and asks whether the clients have become what they had wanted to become, whether they would still like to become this, why they have not become this or why their interests have changed. The practitioner uses this as an example to explain that what feels meaningful at a certain moment in life can change over time – for example, due to a change in interests, growing up or life circumstances. Becoming ill is an example of a life event that can change what we feel is meaningful.

Step 2. Overview of possible changes in meaning after illness

The practitioner refers to Handout 13.2. to explain how developing a chronic or potentially life-threatening illness can influence how individuals experience meaning.

Example formulation

Developing illness (cancer, cardiovascular illness, chronic pain, etc.) often places many practical and physical limits on how you live your life: for instance, you need to undergo medical treatment, you need to take sickness leave from work, or you are often exhausted. Thus, an illness can make you aware of your physical, emotional or personal limitations. This can change what you experience as meaningful in life, according to other clients with a similar illness – that is, specific meanings in your life could change, or your perspective on life in general can change. You may recognise some of the following examples, but not everything.

You can of course still experience the same things as meaningful as before the illness. A specific previous meaning could suddenly become more valuable; for instance, many clients report that they suddenly experience their family connections

▶

◀

as being much more important to them. A previous meaning could feel less valuable; for instance, your work may feel less important. Something that felt meaningful for you before may have become unattainable; you may, for instance, be too tired to go your daughter's football match, or you may not be able to do the sports you did before. A new meaning may have come into your life; for instance, you develop new friends with fellow clients, or you feel proud about the fact that you managed to get out of bed, or you find meaning in your perseverance, in the fact that you do not give up but continue fighting your illness. Your general priorities in life may have changed; for instance, your family becomes more important to you and your work less so. You could start to experience life more intensely; everything is still the same, but it feels deeper and you feel more alive and connected to the world and others. Some clients say that they have become more aware of who they really are; they report that they are more authentic and more truly themselves; they see more clearly what is authentic for them and what is not. Some clients report that they focus all their attention on the illness and the treatment; due to this, their focus becomes really narrow and they seem to forget other things in life that are meaningful for them; for instance, a client told me that she felt that she was only a client and she had forgotten that she was also a mother, a wife, a music lover, and so on. Some individuals start to think so much about life that they become entirely absorbed in thinking and worrying, and they feel that they cannot simply immerse themselves in their ordinary meaningful daily life; they are completely absorbed in thinking that they cannot live their normal daily life anymore. Some individuals say that they have become aware of how meanings are created in general, and they start to relativise all meanings in life, and feel everything is meaningless.

b. *Group discussion*

The practitioner asks the group to give some examples of changes in meaning, how they think and feel about this overview of possible changes and whether they have any questions.

5. *Guided individual exercise* (20 mins)

a. *Mindfulness exercise*

The practitioner repeats the rationale of doing a mindfulness exercise (previous session), and guides the clients.

We are going to do a mindfulness exercise. Like always, do not feel obliged to participate; please take care of your needs; for instance, if it feels too overwhelming you can stop at any time. To start, I would like to invite you to sit up straight in your chair, have your feet on the floor and your hands alongside your body or in your lap. I also invite you to close your eyes, but if this does not feel comfortable, you can simply gaze gently at a point just in front of you. Please bring your awareness to your body. How does your body feel today? Relaxed? Tense? Warm? Cold? Are there any parts of the body that feel painful? If you are ready, bring your attention to your breathing. Do not change your breathing, but simply be aware of it. Do you breathe quickly or slowly? Do you breathe from your chest or your belly? Feel the air come in and go out of the body. It may be that you become distracted and your attention drifts away from your breathing; that is normal; just kindly bring your attention back to your breathing.

b. *Reflecting on questions*

The practitioner directly follows the mindfulness exercise with the self-reflective exercise. While the clients are in a relaxed mindful state with their eyes closed, the practitioner asks them to reflect on some meaning-related questions.

Now that you are focusing on your breathing, I would like to ask you to reflect on some questions.

First, reflect on the period before your illness. What felt meaningful for you during that period in your life? This can be anything: something small or big, things you did or enjoyed, your social roles, or the bigger beliefs, goals or ambitions you had in life. [give the clients some time to think about this]

Second, reflect on how your illness has changed what feels meaningful for you in your life. Something may feel less important since your illness, or something else may have become more important. Some meanings may have become unattainable. Your general priorities in life may have changed, you may experience life more intensively, or feel more authentic. It could also be that you focus so much on your illness that you have forgotten what was meaningful for you. Or you may be thinking too much about your illness, or relativise everything and feel that everything is meaningless. Any answer is good. How have the meanings in your life changed since your illness? [allow some time]

Third, how do these changes in your life feel? Are you sad about the changes? Happy? Or do you have any other feelings about these changes? [allow some time]

c. *Writing about the exercise*

The practitioner invites the client to write down some key words, without analysing and without sharing with the other clients (yet) – for example: 'When you are ready, I invite you to open your eyes, and write down some key words from your exercise so that you will not forget it.'

d. *Drawings of the exercise (optional)*

If there is enough time, the practitioner could ask the clients to do five quick drawings (allow about 2–3 minutes per drawing; the short time may help preventing over-thinking the exercise):

1. *Draw your life before your illness, with some of the most meaningful experiences. For instance, if going to college was important, draw the* *college building; or draw your marriage, the birth of your child, etc. You do not need to be a perfect artist. Don't think long about what you are drawing; do this intuitively! You have two minutes.*

2. *Draw what is meaningful now in your life. This could be meanings that are still there from the past, or it could be new meanings. For instance, if you are still married you could draw your partner, or if you are still enjoying nature draw the park you walk in, etc. If you have discovered which friends are your true friends, you could draw them.*

3. *Draw those meanings you have lost or you can no longer achieve in your life. For instance, if you do not have enough energy to play sports, draw your football field.*

4. *Draw how you would like your future to be if you were able to do anything you wanted and were not ill. What meaningful aspects would be there?*

5. *Draw a realistic but meaningful future. Look at the other drawings, and look at which meanings you can still achieve. Also try to find alternatives for meanings that have been lost – for instance, if you can no longer play football due to your physical limitations, you could consider coaching, supporting or watching soccer.*

6. *Group sharing of individual exercise* (20 mins)

Step 1. Process evaluation

First, the practitioner asks the group how they felt about doing this exercise, and in particular how it felt to close their eyes and focus on what they were experiencing. For some clients, this may be one of the first times that they have really focused on their inner stream of experiences, and this may feel overwhelming or strange to them. Usually in the first sessions clients report that they could not do the exercise perfectly, for instance because their thoughts were continually drifting to other topics; the practitioner uses this feedback to explain that this is totally normal: the attention of every human being drifts off and it's only after a lot of practice that it may be possible to stay focused; the clients are encouraged to be kind and gentle in their self-judgement, to simply be aware that their attention has changed, and then return to the exercise until their attention drifts off again (*'it is like clouds in the sky: we cannot prevent the fact there are clouds, but we can decide whether we put all our attention on the clouds or on the blue sky behind the clouds; suggest that they allow their thoughts/distractions to be like clouds in the sky'*).

Step 2. Group sharing of experiences

The practitioner invites the clients to share any experiences. The practitioner uses this to elicit common themes, connect the clients' stories and identify types of change (e.g. 'Thus, when we look at the figure in Handout 12.3, you would say that ...').

Step 3. Mourning over lost meanings and meaning potential

The practitioner identifies the common theme that will likely arise about 'lost meanings' and 'lost meaning potential', and the sadness or bereavement over this loss. The practitioner asks how this loss felt for the clients, and acknowledges the pain (e.g. 'that must be painful'). The practitioner helps clients to stay with the feelings of loss, and avoids immediately searching for solutions or false hope, to facilitate experiential acceptance (Chapter 8). The practitioner might explain that this loss is painful, although new meanings can and will come ('You cannot simply change your life to how it was before the disease'). Existential skills may be needed (Chapter 9).

7. **Self-evaluation in writing** (10 mins)

   The practitioner invites the clients to evaluate today's session by answering the questions in Handout 13.3.

8. **Group sharing of self-evaluation** (10 mins)

   The practitioner asks clients to share their evaluation. The clients need to be reminded of the limited time. The focus should be on any wish for change, any plans and any wishes for the next session. This discussion could be used to establish common themes between clients, set concrete goals and make plans for changes in daily life (Chapter 6).

9. **Ending** (5 mins)

   a. **Summary**

   The practitioner summarises the content and group process of today's session.

   b. **Preview of the next session**

   The practitioner explains that the next session's topic is resilience: 'how can we cope in a meaningful way with the challenges of the disease?'

   c. **Homework**

   The clients are asked to do a preview exercise for Session 3.

Handout 13.1 Session overview

1. *Group personal/medical check-in* (10 mins)

2. *Introduction* (10 mins)
   a. topic and overview of today
   b. reflection on previous session

3. *Individual goals* (20 mins)

4. *Explanation and group discussion* (15 mins)
   a. explanation about 'Experiencing meaning, and changes in meaning'
   b. group discussion

5. *Guided individual exercise* (20 mins)
   a. mindfulness exercise
   b. reflecting on questions
   c. writing about the exercise
   d. drawings of the exercise (optional)

6. *Group sharing of individual exercise* (20 mins)

7. *Self-evaluation in writing* (10 mins)

8. *Group sharing of self-evaluation* (10 mins)

9. *Ending* (5 mins)
   a. summary
   b. preview of the next session
   c. homework

Handout 13.2 Changes in meaning

Changes in specific meanings

 ➤ All specific pre-event meanings stay the same
 ➤ A specific pre-event meaning becomes more valuable
 ➤ A specific pre-event meaning feels less valuable
 ➤ A specific pre-event goal is adjusted
 ➤ A specific pre-event meaning become unattainable
 ➤ A specific new meaning develops

Changes in general perspectives

 ➤ General priorities in life change
 ➤ Experiencing life more intensively
 ➤ Focusing more on authentic meanings
 ➤ Such a narrow focus on life's limitations that other meanings are forgotten or denied
 ➤ Hyper-reflection or hyper-intention
 ➤ Experiencing meaninglessness
 ➤ More realistic about life's limitations
 ➤ Existential moods, e.g. existential anxiety

Handout 13.3 Evaluation of today's session

Question 1. In today's session, you have reflected on different examples of meanings in your life. What were the three most important or valuable meanings to you?

Question 2. Think about three new meanings that today's session has made you aware of? These can be examples of new meanings that other clients talked about, old meanings in your life that you had forgotten about or a new perspective on your life.

Question 3. Looking at your two previous answers, is there anything you would like to change in your life? Would you, for instance, like to try something new, or focus more on one particular meaning?

Question 4. If there is anything you would like to change in your life, how realistic is it that you can change this, and what do you concretely need to do to make it happen?

Question 5. Do you have any wishes for the next group session?

Handout 13.4   Homework (1) for Session 3: Preview exercise for Session 3

Question 1. When you look back at your life, what were significant moments of change? This can be anything: starting your first job, becoming a parent, moving, losing a loved one, etc.

Question 2. What helped you to make these changes? This can be anything: support from others, active planning, educating yourself, distracting yourself, talking to others, etc. Try to be as specific and concrete as possible; give examples. Generate as many helpful resources as possible.

Question 3. When you look back at your life, what were difficult moments? This can be anything: losing a job, losing a loved one, struggling during your education, a difficult job, marital problems, etc.

Question 4. How were you able to get through these difficult moments in your life? This can be anything: support from others, active planning, educating yourself, distracting yourself, talking others, etc. Try to be as specific and concrete as possible; give examples. Generate as many helpful resources as possible.

Question 5. Overall, what have you learned from these moments of change and these difficult moments in life?

Question 6. How could you use these lessons or ways of coping with previous life events to cope with your current life situation?

Handout 13.5   Homework (2) for Session 3: Meaningful moments exercise

---

This exercise is intended to make you become more aware of moments that feel meaningful in your life. At the end of **every day**, take five to ten minutes to write down **at least three moments** that felt relatively important, significant or valuable to you. This does not need to be something big: it is often something small, such as deeply enjoying the birds in the park, feeling connected to a friend during a conversation, being able to get out of bed despite feeling miserable, etc. If you forget to write these down, no problem: simply write down the meaningful moments later on when you're thinking about the exercise.

14

Session 3: Resilience as a Source of Meaning

14.1 Overview

– *Key session question*: How can we cope in a meaningful way with challenges in life, and specifically with physical diseases?

– *Session goals:*
   1. Raising awareness of multiple ways of coping with difficult life changes
   2. Reminding clients of sources of resilience, and fostering a sense of self-efficacy by exploring how previous times of hardship were overcome
   3. Creating a historical sense of continuity between past, present and future

– *Main group process:*

   Stimulating clients to actively contribute to the group, and reveal more of themselves to each other.

– *Homework completed before this session:*
   13.3. Homework for Session 3 (1): Preview exercise for Session 3
   13.4. Homework for Session 3 (2): Meaningful moments exercise

– *Handouts*
   14.1. Session overview
   14.2. Overview of theory on resilience
   14.3. Homework for Session 4 (1): Preview exercise for Session 4
   14.4. The meaningful objects exercise
   14.5. Homework for Session 4 (3): Breathing exercise
   13.3. Evaluation of today's session (can be found on p. 220)

– *Recommended reading*
   ➢ Vos, 2014; Ehrenreich, 2010; Frankl, 1949/1986

14.2 Stages

1. *Group personal/medical check-in* (**10 mins**)

   See Stage 1 in Session 2

2. *Introduction* (**10 mins**)

   a. *Topic and overview of today*

   The practitioner introduces the topic of today – resilience as meaning: how can we cope in a meaningful way with challenges in life and specifically with disease?

   b. *Reflection on previous session*

   See Stage 2(b) in Session 2

   c. *Reflection on homework*

   See Stage 2(c) in Session 2

3. *Explanation and group discussion* (**15 mins**)

   a. *Explanation of today's topic*

   The practitioner explains what resilience is, and gives the life story of Viktor Frankl as an example (Handout 14.2).

Example formulation

All humans are confronted with limitations and challenges in life; that is an unavoidable part of life. We cannot prevent being confronted with such challenges, but we can change the way in which we cope with challenges; the way in which you cope with challenges can also be a source of meaning. There is a Chinese saying about this: 'You cannot prevent the birds of sorrow from flying over your head, but you can prevent them from building nests in your hair.'

As I mentioned, resilience is about our ability to get through difficult situations in life. There are many different ways to cope with such situations. For instance, how do you manage to get out of bed in the morning, and how do you keep yourself going despite all your problems? Many psychologists have carried out scientific research on the best way to deal with challenges in life. Are you overwhelmed and passive? Or are you courageous? Do you ask for help and express your feelings to others? Do you accept your situation or fight it? Do you help others? Do you focus on your emotions or do you stay rational?

What is effective differs for each situation. There is no one typical best way of coping; overall, there is no good or bad. The only thing that scientific research shows to be important is coping flexibility, that is, our ability to use to different strategies at different moments in time. When we always use the same coping style, we may get stuck. For instance, denying the situation and pretending as if nothing serious has happened can be beneficial in the short term – playing cool keeps you cool in the short term – but it can be problematic long term – playing cool can leave you frozen.

▶

◄

In this session, we focus on how we dealt with difficult moments in our past. The reason for this is that difficult moments in life may be painful but they can also be a learning curve and an opportunity to develop yourself *(see Karl Jaspers, 1925)*; that is, in moments of suffering, we often learn much about ourselves and about what life is really about. There are three other reasons why we focus on past moments of resilience. First, it is good to remind ourselves that we can actually cope effectively with difficult moments in general; when we are in a difficult moment in our life it may seem impossible to overcome the problems but when we look back we see that we have already dealt with difficult moments: 'Yes, we can do this!' Second, by looking back we may find concrete examples of how we can potentially cope with the current situation. Third, we may also check whether the general coping styles that we have developed in the past are still useful or whether we want to change them.

In this group, we will focus on one specific way of coping with challenging life situations, namely by focusing on what is meaningful for you. I will explain this with the life story of the Austrian psychiatrist Viktor Frankl as an example. This group therapy is indirectly based on his work, and more specifically on his book *Man's Search for Meaning*. In this book, he describes his experiences as an inmate at a concentration camp. He describes how he saw many fellow inmates lose hope and meaning, and consequently fall into despair. Individuals who were not able to experience any meaning in life seemed more prone to becoming ill and weak, and dying sooner. However, there were inmates who were able to grasp and hold on to anything meaningful, albeit a smile to another inmate, looking at a bird, having hope for rescue or believing in a God; their meaning helped them to survive. Frankl wrote about this experience: 'He who has a why to live for can bear almost any how.' In the meantime, many researchers have shown that this is indeed true: individuals who can experience meaning in life cope better with difficult times, and they feel emotionally and physically better.

Based on his experiences in the concentration camp, Frankl developed three fundamental beliefs. First, every human being searches for meaning in life, and meaning in life is important for our general well-being. Second, life always holds the possibility of being meaningful; even in a concentration camp, you can find meaning in small things. Third, we are free to find meaning in our life, and to choose our attitude towards difficult life situations, that is, although we cannot possibly change the situation itself, we can change how we perceive the situation and what our inner attitude to the situation is. For instance, you may not be able to get rid of your illness, but you can decide whether to give up hope and behave like a victim of your situation, or you could try to make the best it, within the limitations of the situation.

This last point is important. It is important to be able to differentiate between the things you can change and the things you can't. You may not be able to cure your illness, but you can take medication to reduce the pain and other symptoms. This is what some religious individuals call the Serenity Prayer: 'God, grant me the serenity to accept the things I cannot change, the courage to change the things I can, And the wisdom to know the difference.' Our resilience seems to depend on knowing this difference.

Finally, when Frankl said that it is important to focus on meaning, he was not saying that you would no longer experience any difficulties or pain. In the concentration camp, the inmates still felt pain and they were not happy, but they were able to get through that difficult moment. Experiencing meaning and experiencing difficulties and pain often go hand in hand with each other.

b. *Group discussion*

Step 1. The practitioner asks how clients feel about this explanation, and whether they have any questions.

Step 2. The practitioner asks what friends, family, colleagues, the media or society tell us about how we should cope with our illness. Often clients will mention this themselves in the group discussion, without the practitioner needing to ask the question. It may be important to identify the social pressure that individuals may feel as a result of their social context, particularly to cope in an optimistic, active and heroic way with the illness. The practitioner can ask questions such as: 'Are their expectations realistic?'; 'How do their expectations make you feel?'

4. *Guided individual exercise* (30 mins)

a. *Mindfulness exercise*

The practitioner guides the group in a mindfulness exercise which leads to self-reflective questions.

Exercise

1. We are going to do a mindfulness exercise. As always, do not feel obliged to participate please take care of your needs; for instance, if it feels too overwhelming you can stop at any time. To start, I would like to invite you to sit up straight in your chair, have your feet on the floor and your hands alongside your body or in your lap. I also invite you to close your eyes, but if this does not feel good, you can simply gaze gently at a point just in front of you.

2. If you are ready, bring your awareness to you breathing, like we did last week. Do not change your breathing, but simply be aware of it. Do you breathe quickly or slowly? Do you breathe from your chest or your belly? Feel the air come in and go out of the body. It may be that you become distracted and your attention drifts away from your breathing; that is normal; just kindly bring your attention back to your breathing.

---

b. *Reflecting on questions*

The practitioner asks the clients to examine how they were able to stay resilient in previous difficult moments in their lives.

Example

1. *Think about* 'difficult moments in your life in the past; this can be anything: losing a job, losing a loved one, struggling during your education, a difficult job, marital problems, etc. When you remember one difficult memory, try to remember another one.'

▶

◄

2. Select one of the most difficult moments in your life. How were you able to get through it? This can be anything: support from others, active planning, educating yourself, distracting yourself, talking to others, etc. [give the clients some time to think about this]

3. Select another difficult moment in your life. How were you able to get through this? [allow some time and repeat the question]

4. Overall, what have you learned from these moments of change and these difficult moments in your life? [allow some time]

5. How could you use these lessons or ways of coping in previous life events to cope with your current life situation?

c. *Writing about exercise*

See Stage 4(c) in Session 2

5. *Group sharing of individual exercise* (20 mins)

Step 1. Process evaluation

Step 2. Group sharing of individual experiences

See Step 6 in Session 2

6. *Self-evaluation in writing* (10 mins)

See Handout 13.3. stage in Session 2

7. *Group sharing of self-evaluation* (10 mins)

See in Session 2

8. *Ending (5 mins)*

a. *Summary*

b. *Preview of the next session*

The practitioner explains that the next session's topic is 'material meanings in life: how can we experience having nice material things and doing pleasurable physical activities as meaningful?'

c. *Homework*

Handout 14.1   Session overview

1. *Group personal/medical check-in* (10 mins)

2. *Introduction* (10 mins)
   a. topic and overview of today
   b. reflection on previous session
   c. reflection on homework

3. *Explanation and group discussion* (15 mins)
   a. explanation of today's topic: 'how can we cope with challenges in life and with illness in particular?'
   b. group discussion

4. *Guided individual exercise* (30 mins)
   a. mindfulness exercise
   b. reflecting on questions
   c. writing about the exercise

5. *Group sharing of individual exercise* (20 mins)

6. *Self-evaluation in writing* (10 mins)

7. *Group sharing of self-evaluation* (10 mins)

8. *Ending* (5 mins)
   a. summary
   b. preview of the next session
   c. homework

Handout 14.2 Overview of theory on resilience

1. Everyone experiences difficult moments in life.

2. Chinese saying: '*You cannot prevent the birds of sorrow from flying over your head, but you can prevent them from building nests in your hair.*'

3. Resilience = our ability to get through difficult situations in life, like the branches of a tree that bend in the wind but do not break.

4. There is no one best way of coping with a difficult situation. There is no right or wrong! Psychologists recommend 'coping flexibility', which means that you can use different ways of coping in different situations.

5. Difficult moments in life are not only painful but can also offer an opportunity to learn 'what life is about' and to develop oneself.

6. We look back at previous moments of resilience, for three reasons:
   1. to remind ourselves that 'yes, we can!'
   2. to find concrete examples of how we may be able to cope with the current situation
   3. to check whether the general coping styles that we developed in the past are still useful and whether we may want to use other styles now

7. An important source of resilience is focusing on meaning.

8. Viktor Frankl (1905–1997), an Austrian psychiatrist, was an inmate at a World War II concentration camp.

9. Our general well-being depends on our ability to experience meaning despite a difficult life situation.

10. Frankl's three beliefs:
    i. Everyone needs meaning, and meaning is important for well-being
    ii. We can find meaning in every life situation
    iii. If we cannot change the situation, we can change our inner attitude towards the situation (e.g. how we think and feel about it)

11. Recognise the difference between the things we can change and those we cannot. For example, think of the Serenity Prayer: '*God, grant me the serenity to accept the things I cannot change, the courage to change the things I can, and the wisdom to know the difference.*'

12. Experiencing meaning does not deny the difficulties or the pain: both often go hand in hand with each other.

Handout 14.3   Homework for Session 4 (1): Preview exercise for Session 4

Please take some time to think about these questions. You may already have written down some answers, but we will complete this exercise during Session 4.

The next session will be about materialistic meanings. These meanings are about having nice material things and taking part in pleasurable physical activities; these are typically things you can literally see and/or things you can feel in your body. The following questions ask for examples of materialistic meanings you may have experienced in the past or that you are experiencing now. Of course, it is possible that you may not experience every question as relevant; thus, it is also fine to answer: 'I do not experience this as meaningful.' Try to find as many answers as possible, but do not worry if only one or two are forthcoming.

Question 1. Give some examples of material things that are meaningful for you now, or that have been meaningful for you in the past. Examples are enjoying your possessions, such as your house, clothes, DVD collection, enjoying the process of trying to get possessions, or enjoying having an income, savings or financial security.

Question 2. Give some examples of visible success that is currently meaningful for you or that has been meaningful for you in the past. For example, this could be success in your education, work, voluntary work or hobbies (e.g. sporting success).

Question 3. Give some examples of nice physical experiences that are currently meaningful or that were meaningful for you in the past. For instance, this could be that you enjoy your health, feel connected with your body, feel good about your body, take care of your body, wear nice clothes or make-up, engage in sports, are physically intimate with another person, or enjoy good food and drink.

Question 4. Give some examples of leisure time activities that are currently meaningful for you or that were meaningful for you in the past. This could be for instance about your hobbies, enjoying humour, having an appreciation of beauty, art or nature, going on holiday, watching television, or reading for pleasure.

Question 5. Look again at the previous questions and use your imagination. Are there any examples of materialistic meanings that you are currently not experiencing but that you would like to try? These examples could be realistically attainable or entirely fantasy.

Question 6. Would you like to experience more material meanings in your life? If so, what could you do to experience this?

Handout 14.4   The meaningful objects exercise

Description:

– Sit in your living room and notice the meanings of the objects in the room. Often, these are memories of important moments in your life.

> *Examples: the clock reminds me of my strong connection with my father who gave me this clock; the picture reminds me of the warm relationship with my friends and our great holidays; my sports shoes remind me of how important sports are for me; my books remind me of my education and self-development; the concert ticket reminds me how important music is for me; the political leaflet reminds me how meaningful my political activism is; my nail polish reminds me of my self-care; the crucifix reminds me of my religion; etc. Try to find at least five objects that feel very meaningful to you.*

– Do this exercise every time you go into another room in your house.

> *Examples: Observe the meaningful objects when you go into your bedroom, kitchen, bathroom, other rooms, your office at work, etc. Try to make it a habit that every time you change rooms, you briefly notice the meaning of the things around you. You will start to feel that you are surrounded by meaningful experiences. Even frustrating housing conditions can start to feel meaningful, and you may feel more at home.*

– If you feel that you do not have many meaningful objects around you, consider putting more meaningful things around you.

> *Examples*: Put pictures of your friends and holidays on the wall; have books around you; things you inherited from people important to you; buy flowers and plants reminding you of nature's beauty; deliberately leave nice CDs and DVDs lying around instead of returning them to a shelf; pieces of art you love such as prints and paintings, etc. Put a pin-up board on your wall, on which you pin reminders of meaningful moments, e.g. pictures and concert tickets. Consider having cupboards with open shelves instead of putting meaningful things behind closed doors; paint the room in your favourite colour, etc. Bring souvenirs back from holidays to put in your room as a reminder of great times. Often, the fuller and more chaotic a room looks like, the more personal and meaningful it feels to live in. If you are going to be in bed for a while in a hospital or another type of care unit, consider bringing objects with you that feel meaningful and put these at your bedside: pictures often work very well, flowers, etc.; you will feel less estranged and disoriented.

– If you are travelling a lot, feel that the place where you travel to is impersonal or even threatening, or you feel homesick, consider bringing meaningful objects.

> *Examples: Many people have pictures of their family and friends in their wallet; others put hangers on their key rings that remind them for instance about their holiday; others wear bracelets from music festivals, or necklaces with a specific meaning, for instance which they bought at a special place or were given by an important person; bring a book you like; use meaningful pictures as a screensaver and background photo on your phone and laptop; put stickers or buttons on your jacket or bag; wear clothes with meaningful memories; etc.*

Why we do this exercise:

In our daily life, we often forget how meaningful our life already is, because things around us feel familiar and we are often too busy. However, when we were a child we were much more aware of the meaning of our surroundings. For instance, we were fascinated by the birds in the trees, and we could play for hours with some paper; but now we do not even see this anymore. This exercise reminds us how meaningful our life already is. This can also help us to feel more at home in places where we live and work. We will literally feel surrounded by meaning.

Handout 14.5   Homework for Session 4 (3): Breathing exercise

In Session 3, we did a 'breathing exercise'. The aim of this exercise is to learn to focus on our breathing, and to use shifting our focus to cope with stressful moments in life. Try this exercise at home at least once. It is important to try this exercise in the first instance when you feel relaxed, so that you know how to do the exercise even when you feel overwhelmed by your emotions and, for example, feel anxious. If you want to do this at home, you could follow these steps. As always, do not feel obliged to do this; take care of yourself; for instance, if it feels too overwhelming you can stop at any time.

1. *To start, you could sit in a chair or lie on a bed. Make sure that you are in a quiet room, and that no one will disturb you during the exercise. If you sit in a chair, sit up straight, have your feet on the floor and your hands alongside your body or in your lap. Close your eyes, but if this does not feel comfortable, you can simply gaze gently at a point just in front of you.*

2. *Feel how you sit on the chair or lie on the bed. Notice how your body feels, where it touches the chair or the bed, etc. Notice how your body is feeling today: is it relaxed, or is there tension or pain? Do not try to change how it feels; just be aware of it. It is normal for your attention to drift away during the exercise. This may be, for example, because you hear something around you or you think about other things; simply notice that your attention has drifted elsewhere and come back to the exercise.*

3. *Do not change your breathing, but simply be aware of it. Do you breathe quickly or slowly? Do you breathe from your chest or your belly? Feel the air come in and go out of the body. Take some time to stay with your breathing.*

Open your eyes and allow yourself some time to 'come back to reality again'. Stay in your chair or bed for a while, and evaluate for yourself how this exercise felt today. Be gentle on yourself; for instance, the first few times you do this exercise may be difficult, and there are simply some days when it is more difficult to focus your attention on the exercise; it is also normal to feel sleepy or even fall asleep, especially when you are doing the exercise in bed.

(See also Handout 13.3 'Evaluation of today's session' on p. 220)

15

Session 4: Materialistic-Hedonic Sources of Meaning

15.1 Overview

– *Key session question*: How can we experience having material things and doing pleasurable activities as meaningful?

– *Session goals*:

1. Explaining materialistic and pleasurable meanings as possible sources of meaning
2. Helping clients to find and evaluate examples of materialistic-hedonic meanings
3. Helping clients to evaluate and commit to concrete actions

– *Main group process*:

Clients should have become more open and self-expressive, and interact spontaneously with each other. If not, the group practitioner may mention this (meta-communication) and invite specific individual clients to contribute more to the group. Due to this increased openness and interaction, some anxieties and differences in opinion may appear, which has been called 'the storming phase of group development' (AGPA, 2007). The practitioner needs to be aware of possible storming and stimulate an atmosphere of collaboration where differences in opinion are accepted, and where individuals start to feel responsible for the group process. In the storming stage, there is a likelihood that individuals may drop out; therefore, practitioners need to be aware of how each individual is behaving, as from this session onwards, there will be less didactics and more opportunity for the group process.

– *Homework completed before this session*:

14.3. Homework (1) for Session 4: Preview exercise for Session 4
14.4. Homework (2) for Session 4: The meaningful objects exercise
14.5. Homework (3) for Session 4: Breathing exercise

– *Handouts*:

15.1. Session overview

15.2. Overview of theory

15.3. Homework for Session 5 (1): Preview exercise for Session 5

15.4. Homework for Session 5 (2): The meaningful pin-up board (optional)

15.5. Homework for Session 5 (3): The safe place exercise

13.3. Evaluation of today's session (can be found on p. 220)

– *Recommended reading*:

➤ Sheldon & Kasser, 1998. This article describes why materialistic/extrinsic goals do not bring greater well-being.

15.2 Stages

1. *Group personal/medical check-in* (10 mins)

2. *Introduction* (10 mins)

   a. *Topic and overview of today*

   b. *Reflection on previous session*

   c. *Reflection on homework*

   See Stages 1 and 2 in Session 2

3. *Explanation and group discussion* (15 mins)

   a. *Explanation of today's topic*

   The practitioner explains that when psychologists asked individuals in the past for examples of meaning in their life, these individuals often mentioned materialistic-hedonic meanings. The name of this group 'material' may seem a bit odd: for instance, success in your job is an example of materialistic meanings but this success is not necessarily something material (e.g. when you are a teacher, how do you show success you have had with an individual pupil?); if the clients have a better name, they can mention this. However, this term is used to differentiate between this type of meanings and others which are less concrete and visible; for instance, self-oriented meaning is about developing yourself and coping with difficult life situations, social meaning is about feeling socially connected and helping others, and larger meaning is often quite abstract. Thus, materialistic meanings are the most concrete and visible types of meaning. Describe the four different types of material meanings in Handout 15.2. Stress that it is possible that individuals may not experience every material meaning as relevant to them; for them, these examples may not be meaning-ful and that is fine. Research indicates that materialistic meanings are less beneficial for someone's well-being than other types of meaning, to the extent that these are external to the client (Vos, 2016a).

b. *Group discussion*

    Step 1. The practitioner asks how the clients feel about this explana-tion, and whether they have any questions.

    Step 2. The practitioner asks for some personal examples.

4. *Guided individual exercise* **(20 mins)**

    a. *Mindfulness exercise*

Example

1. We are going to do an exercise that we call 'the safe place'. The aim of this exer-cise is to learn to use pleasant memories to cope with stressful moments in life. You could do this exercise at home when you feel overwhelmed by your emotions and, for example, feel very anxious.

2. As always, do not feel obliged to participate; take care of yourself; for instance, when it feels too overwhelming you can stop at any time. To start, I would like to invite you to sit up straight in your chair, have your feet on the floor and your hands alongside your body or in your lap. I also invite you to close your eyes, but if this does not feel comfortable, you can simply gaze gently at a point just in front of you.

3. If you are ready, I invite you to feel how you are sitting on the chair: how does your body feel, where does it touch the chair, etc. Notice how your body is feeling today: is it relaxed, or is there tension or pain?

4. I invite you to recall a positive memory of when you felt safe and happy. For exam-ple, this could be the memory of a holiday, a concert, a great evening with a part-ner, the birth of a child, etc. It needs to be a memory of a specific moment at a specific place, thus not a general feeling. We will call this memory 'the safe place'. When you have found a safe and happy memory, raise your hand and stay with that memory. If you cannot find a safe place, just focus on any place where you felt OK. [wait until everyone has raised their hand; repeat the instruction to raise the hand if needed]

5. You may lower your hand again. Go back to the memory. What do you see: any specific people or objects? How the general colours look: bright or soft? What do you hear: other people or animals, cars, the heating in the house? How does your skin feel: warm or cold, do you feel air or wind, anything hard or soft, etc.? What do you smell? What do you taste: sweetness, salt, bitterness? [allow some time between each question]

b. *Reflecting on questions*

While the clients have their eyes closed, the practitioner asks them to reflect on the following questions (not all examples need to be mentioned):

1. *Find some examples of material things that are meaningful for you now, or that have been meaningful for you in the past. Examples are enjoying your possessions, such as your house, clothes, DVD collection, enjoying the process of trying to get possessions, or enjoying having an income, savings or financial security.*

2. *Find some examples of visible success that is currently meaningful for you or that has been meaningful for you in the past. For example, this could be success in your education, work, voluntary work, or hobbies (e.g. sports success).*

3. *Find some examples of nice physical experiences that are currently meaningful or that were meaningful for you in the past. For instance, this could be that you enjoy your health, feel connected with your body, feel good about your body, take care of your body, wear nice clothes or make-up, engage in sports, are physically intimate with another person, or enjoy good food and drink.*

4. *Find some examples of leisure time activities that are currently meaningful for you or that were meaningful for you in the past. For instance, this could be about your hobbies, enjoying humour, appreciating beauty, art or nature, going on holiday, watching television, or reading for pleasure.*

c. *Writing about the exercise*

See Stage 4(c) in Session 2

5. *Group sharing of individual exercise* (30 mins)

Step 1. Process evaluation

Step 2. Group sharing of experiences

See Stage 5 in Session 2

6. *Self-evaluation in writing* (10 mins)

See Handout 13.3. in Session 2

7. *Group sharing of self-evaluation* (20 mins)

See Step 7 in Session 2

8. *Ending* (5 mins)

a. *Summary*

b. *Preview of the next session*

The practitioner explains that the topic of the next session is 'Self-oriented meanings: how can we experience developing ourselves, taking care of ourselves and expressing ourselves as meaningful?'

c. *Homework*

Handout 15.1 Session overview

1. *Group personal/medical check-in* (10 mins)

2. *Introduction* (10 mins)
   a. topic and overview of today
   b. reflection on previous session

3. *Explanation and group discussion* (15 mins)
   a. explanation of today's topic: materialistic meanings
   b. group discussion

4. *Guided individual exercise* (20 mins)
   a. mindfulness exercise
   b. reflecting on questions
   c. writing about the exercise

5. *Group sharing of individual exercise* (30 mins)

6. *Self-evaluation in writing* (10 mins)

7. *Group sharing of self-evaluation* (20 mins)

8. *Ending* (5 mins)
   a. summary
   b. preview of the next session
   c. homework

Handout 15.2 Overview of theory

I. MATERIALISTIC-HEDONIC INSTEAD OF MEANINGS

Underlying value: the value of having material goods, objective success, nice physical experiences

A. Material conditions

   Finances, housing, possessions, practical activities, physical survival

B. Professional-educational success

   General success, professional success, educational success, social status, power

C. Hedonistic-experiential activities

   Hedonism, fun, leisure and joyful activities, aesthetic enjoyments (music, art, food and drink, etc.), sex, nature and animals, peak experiences, pain avoidance

D. Health

   Being healthy, healthy lifestyle, sports

Handout 15.3   Homework for Session 5 (1): Preview exercise for Session 5

Please take some time to think about these questions. You may already have written down some answers, but we will complete this exercise during Session 5.

The next session will be about self-oriented meanings. These meanings are about YOU, such as developing yourself, showing yourself to others and expressing yourself in creative ways, knowing yourself, accepting who you are and taking care of yourself. The following questions ask for examples of self-oriented meanings you may have experienced in the past or that you are experiencing now. Of course, it is possible that you do not experience every question as relevant for you; thus, it is also fine to answer 'I do not experience this as meaningful'. Try to find as many answers as possible, but do not worry if you can only think of one or two examples.

Question 1. Give some examples of how you have developed yourself in the past, or how you are developing yourself now. This self-development could be about education, therapy, psychotherapy or psychological counselling. One example could be that you are participating in this meaning-centred group therapy.

Question 2. Give some examples of how you let yourself be seen to others, how you express yourself and how you are creative. This could be expression and creativity in your work or hobbies, such as making music, writing, being artistic, making jokes and telling stories, or having a creative lifestyle in general.

Question 3. Give some examples of aspects of yourself as a person that you are proud of. For instance, being proud of being a good friend, always being on time, carrying on even in times of hardship, etc.

Question 4. Give examples of aspects of yourself that you do not like but still accept of yourself. To find these examples, you may want to first look at some aspects of yourself that you do not like, and subsequently evaluate for yourself how bad you think that aspect of yourself is. For instance, you know that you are often late for appointments, but this may be something you accept about yourself: 'this is simply who I am.' Or you may know that you are bad with computers, and therefore you usually ask others to help you to do things at the computer. Or you know that you are bad at learning, but find it OK that you do not get the highest scores at school. Or you know you are bad at fixing things in the home, but you still try to fix things yourself as far as you can, and you laugh at yourself when something fails.

(Continued)

Question 5. Give some examples of moments in your life when you took care of yourself. This could mean that you gave yourself what you needed at that time. This could be something like making some time for yourself, taking a bath, making a phone call to a friend when you wanted to talk, giving yourself a break from your work, etc.

Question 6. Look again at the previous questions and use your imagination. Are there any examples of self-oriented meanings that you are currently not experiencing but that you would like to try? These examples could be realistically attainable or entirely fantasy.

Question 7. Would you like to experience more self-oriented meanings in your life? If so, what could you do to experience this?

Handout 15.4   Homework for Session 5 (2): The meaningful pin-up board (optional)

Reason for the exercise: It is easy to forget the lessons we learn in life or via training and therapy groups. This exercise may help by placing reminders for ourselves in our house where we can see them daily.

Exercise:

- Decide how you could remind yourself of what you have learned in therapy. For instance, put a pin-up board in your kitchen, put Post-its on your wall next to the computer, etc.
- Look at the last session. Put reminders of the last session on the wall, particularly reminders of what you experience as meaningful in life and the decisions you have made. For instance, if you have concluded after the last session that you want to subscribe to an education course put a reminder on the board saying, 'subscribe to course'. Some people like to put a to-do list with deadlines on this board: 'subscribe before the end of next week.'
- You could also use it to remind yourself of meaningful moments in your life – for example, by putting pictures of friends and family on it, or a ticket of a great concert, etc.

Handout 15.5   Homework for Session 5 (3): The safe place exercise

---

In the session we did the 'safe place exercise'. The aim of this exercise is to learn to use pleasant memories to cope with stressful moments in life. Try this exercise at home at least once. It is important to try this exercise in the first instance when you feel relaxed, so that you know how you to do the exercise even when you feel overwhelmed by your emotions and, for example, feel anxious. If you want to do this at home, you could follow these steps. As always, do not feel obliged to do this; take care of yourself; for instance, if it feels too overwhelming you can stop at any time.

1. Sit in a chair or lie on a bed. Make sure that you are in a quiet room and that no one will disturb you. If you sit in a chair, sit up straight, have your feet on the floor and your hands alongside your body or in your lap. Close your eyes, but if this does not feel *comfortable, gaze gently at a point* in front of you.

2. Feel how you sit on the chair or lie on the bed. Notice how your body feels, where it touches the chair or the bed, etc. Notice how your body is feeling today: is it relaxed, or is there tension or pain? Do not try to change how it feels; just be aware how it. It is normal for your attention to drift away during the exercise. This may be, for instance, because you hear something around you or you think about other things; that is no normal; simply notice that your attention has drifted elsewhere, and come back to the exercise.

3. Recall a positive memory of when you felt safe and happy. For example, this could be the memory of a holiday, a concert, a great evening with a partner, the birth of a child, etc. It needs to be a memory of a specific moment at a specific place, and thus not a general feeling. We will call this memory 'the safe place'. Take some time to find your safe and happy memory, and stay with it.

4. Try to focus on the memory, to feel as though you are really there again. For instance, you could focus on what you see: any specific people or objects? How the general colours look: bright or soft? What do you hear: other people or animals, cars, the heating in the house? How does your skin feel: warm or cold, do you feel air or wind, anything hard or soft, etc.? What do you smell? What do you taste: sweetness, salt, bitterness?

5. Stay for a while with the memory. Be aware of the emotions that the memory can evoke, such as happiness, but sometimes also some sadness.

6. Open your eyes and give yourself some time to 'come back to reality again'. Stay in your chair or bed for a while and evaluate for yourself how doing this exercise felt today. Be gentle on yourself; for example, the first few times you do this exercise may be difficult, and there are simply some days when it is more difficult to focus your attention; it is also normal to feel sleepy or even fall asleep, especially when you are doing the exercise in bed.

(See also Handout 13.3 'Evaluation of today's session' on p. 220)

16

Session 5: Self-oriented Sources of Meaning

16.1 Overview

– *Key session question*: How can we find meaning in developing ourselves, taking care of ourselves and expressing ourselves?

– *Session goals:*

   1. Explaining self-oriented meanings as possible sources of meaning
   2. Helping clients to find and evaluate examples of self-oriented meanings
   3. Fostering self-acceptance and self-care
   4. Helping clients to evaluate and commit to concrete actions

– *Main group process:*

   Managing differences, stimulating interaction, transforming feelings of anxiety or conflict to cohesion

– *Homework completed before this session:*

   15.3. Homework (1) for Session 5: Preview exercise for Session 5

   15.4. Homework (2) for Session 5: The meaningful pin-up board (optional)

   15.5. Homework (3) for Session 5: The safe place exercise

– *Handouts*

   16.1. Session overview

   16.2. Overview of theory (1): Self-oriented meanings

   16.3. Overview of theory (2): Self-acceptance

   16.4. Homework (1) for Session 6: Preview exercise for Session 6

   16.5. Homework (2) for Session 6: Body scan exercise

   13.3. Evaluation of today's session (can be found on p. 220)

   15.4. Repeated homework: the meaningful pin-up board (optional; can be found on p. 238)

List of self-care activities. Downloaded from:
www.calswec.berkeley.edu/files/uploads/activity_6c-f_self-care_activities.doc

– *Recommended reading*

➢ On acceptance and meaning: Steger et al. (2008)

➢ On self-compassion therapy: Gilbert (2009)

➢ On acceptance and commitment therapy: Hayes (2012)

16.2 Stages

1. *Group personal/medical check-in* (**10 mins**)

2. *Introduction* (**10 mins**)

   a. *Topic and overview of today*

   b. *Reflection on previous session*

   c. *Reflection on homework*

      See Stages 1 and 2(b) in Session 2

3. *Explanation and group discussion* (**10 mins**)

   a. *Explanation of today's topic*

      Step 1. The practitioner explains that when psychologists asked indi-
      viduals to reflect on past examples of meaning in their life, they often
      mentioned these self-oriented meanings. Describe the different types
      of self-oriented meanings in Handout 16.2. Stress that it is possible
      that individuals do not experience every self-oriented meaning as rel-
      evant to them.

      Step 2. Explain that self-acceptance is an important self-oriented
      source of meaning. Give an overview of theory with Handout 16.3.
      This theory is based on other meaning-centred treatments, com-
      bined with insights from Acceptance and Commitment Therapies,
      and clinical experience.

Example formulation

One example of self-oriented meanings is about self-acceptance. Many individuals
experience this as a difficult type of meaning, especially when they are confronted
with a physical illness. Your body often does not feel and look how you would like it

▶

◀

to, and you may not be able to do everything that you did in the past. Developing a physical illness is often a strong challenge for someone's self-acceptance. Therefore, I will explain what some psychologists believe about self-acceptance.

In summary, these psychologists say that self-acceptance is about not judging yourself, understanding who you really are, understanding the things you are good at and knowing your limitations – saying to yourself, 'I am OK, regardless of anything in my life such as my illness', and feeling worthy and significant. That is a lot! Let us look at this in more detail.

Self-acceptance does not mean that you are perfect – you can always improve – but self-acceptance says that fundamentally you are OK, regardless of the situation and of the aspects of yourself that you could improve. This means, for instance, that you not only accept the good aspects of yourself but also accept your failures and that you sometimes feel bad. It is about knowing what you can do, and knowing what you cannot; you are not perfect, and it is OK not to be perfect. You are a human being – you are not Superman – and failures and sometimes feeling bad are part and parcel of this. Self-acceptance is also about understanding the reason and context behind why you feel or acted this way; for instance, you may say 'I feel bad now, because of my physical illness'; 'Although I would like to go to my daughter's football match I can't because I'm ill'; or 'I would like to be able to repair some problems in my house but I am simply bad at fixing things, and therefore it is OK to ask someone to help me with this'. Knowing WHY you failed can help you accept THAT you failed.

Our body is always changing as we age: there are things that we can no longer do. Our illness has made these changes occur more quickly or severely than we expected. Self-acceptance is also about saying, 'My body does not feel or look perfect, but it is as it is'. That means, that you could look in the mirror and see how beautiful you are, while also seeing your imperfections. This is often difficult in our society with its 'Photoshopped' models: we want to look perfect. But when you look at real human beings around you, you see that no one is perfect. Did you know that Tom Cruise is actually a very short man? Do you know that the queen actually has many wrinkles? And so on. You are a human being, and your body is how it is. It can take time to learn to accept your body as it is after an illness. Allow yourself that time; it is normal to not be able to accept your body immediately.

From our past experiences and from society, we may have been given the message that 'I am only OK when I do this or that'. For instance, our parents gave us love and praise when we achieved good marks in school. Or magazines tell us that we must wear certain clothes or have a lot of friends 'to be cool'. We may try to live up to these expectations and criteria from other people. Self-acceptance does not say 'I am only OK if I do…' but 'I am OK, whatever I do'. Instead of accepting ourselves, we may create a 'fake self' – pretending to be someone other than who we really are.

Some psychologists say that self-acceptance is about being your own best friend and taking care of yourself. Give yourself the care that you need and deserve, regardless of your situation and your success. Taking care of yourself can be meaningful, and self-acceptance is the basis of true meaning in life (understanding what is meaningful for YOU). You are worthy of taking care of yourself. You are worthy of living a meaningful and satisfying life, despite your imperfections and illness. You are worthy of investing in your self-development, like coming to this therapy group.

▶

◀

My explanation could give the false impression that you MUST accept yourself. No, self-acceptance is also about accepting the fact that there are periods in our lives when we find self-acceptance and self-care difficult. Especially when you are physically ill, self-acceptance can be difficult and can take time to grow. It seems to be a life-long process, and at every stage of your life you may struggle with accepting another part of yourself.

Finally, we will talk about self-acceptance today because some individuals say that they find meaning in the fact that they accept themselves, take care of themselves and educate themselves – that is, in itself, important to them. Furthermore, accepting yourself also means that you accept what you experience as meaningful: you are worthy of living a meaningful life – you are worth it!

b. *Group discussion*

Step 1. The practitioner asks how the clients feel about this explanation, and whether they have any questions.

Step 2. The practitioner asks for some personal examples, specifically about self-acceptance.

4. *Exercise 1: Self-care exercise* (15 mins)

The practitioner presents the list of possible self-care activities, and asks the clients to 'Put a cross before the self-care activities that you are already doing' and 'Put a circle around new self-care activities you may want to do'. The reason for using this list is that individuals often have difficulties finding examples of self-care, and this is an evidence-based list of possible types of self-care (downloaded from: www.calswec. berkeley.edu/files/uploads/activity_6c-f_self-care_activities.doc) Have a discussion about the following statement:

> *The best self-care is engaging in truly meaningful activities. We often forget this in our daily life. When you feel you are struggling too much in your daily life, this may be due to not doing enough self-care or the right type of self-care.*

5. *Guided individual exercise* (20 mins)

a. *Self-compassion exercise*

Step 1. I invite you to close your eyes; if you do not want to close your eyes gently gaze at a point in front of you. Assess how your body is feeling today. Is it relaxed or tense? (...) Is there any discomfort or pains? Do not try to change your body's position, just notice what you are experiencing. (...) How would you like your body to feel: for instance, more relaxed, more energised, without pain? (...) Reflect for a moment on the statement:

'I cannot force my body to feel how I want to feel.' (...) Reflect on the statement: 'I sometimes feel I am struggling in life.' (...) Reflect on the question: 'It's OK to say that I am sometimes struggling in life.'

Step 2. I would like to invite you to hold each other's hand, and then close your eyes again. Feel the hand of your neighbour. How does the hand feel: warm, cold, sweaty, soft, hard? (...) How does it feel to touch another person? Relaxed, supportive or a bit frightening? (...) How does it feel to connect with someone who is in a similar life situation as yourself? (...) Reflect for a moment on the statement: 'I am not alone; others are also struggling.' (...) Reflect for a moment on the statement: 'I can ask for help from others when I need it.'

Step 3. You can let go of your neighbours' hand. Take three deep and satisfying breaths. Put your hand on your heart, and feel your chest going up and down – feel the pressure and possibly the warmth of your hand on your heart. You may even feel the beating of your heart. (...) How does this feel, to feel your heart, and take care of your heart? (...) Reflect on the statement about taking care of your heart as a metaphor: 'I allow myself to listen to my heart.' (...) Reflect on the statement: 'I am OK.' (...) 'I am worthy of love.' (...) 'I try to love myself.'

Step 4. With your right hand, gently stroke your left hand. Be as kind to yourself as you can. How does this feel? How does your skin feel when it gets stroked? (...) Does anything change in how your skin feels? (...) Now stop stroking your hand. How does your skin feel now? For instance, does it feel soft and relaxed? (...) Now stroke your right hand with your left hand. How does this feel? How does your skin feel when it gets stroked? (...) Does anything change in how your skin feels? Now stop stroking your hand. How does your skin feel now? For instance, does it feel soft and relaxed? (...) Reflect on the statement: 'I allow myself to take care of myself.' (...) Reflect on the statement: 'I am worthy of taking care of myself.'

  b. *Writing about the exercise*

  c. *Reflecting on questions*
    See Stage 5 in Session 2

6. *Group sharing of individual exercise* (10 mins)
   Step 1. Process evaluation
   Step 2. Group sharing of experiences
   See Stage 5 in Session 2

7. *Self-evaluation in writing* (5 mins)
   See Stage 6 and Handout 13.3. in Session 2

8. *Group sharing of self-evaluation* (5 mins)

   See Stage 7 in Session 2

9. *Ending* (5 mins)

   a. *Summary*

   b. *Preview of the next session*

   The practitioner explains that the next session's topic is 'materialistic meanings in life: how can we experience having nice material things and doing pleasurable physical activities as meaningful?'

   c. *Homework*

   The clients are invited to do the preview exercises in the handouts for the next session. Also make the clients aware of the fact that they will be asked in Session 10 to present any meaningful change they have made or tried to make: this could be anything, such as enrolling on a course you have always wanted to do, booking a holiday, speaking with your children about meaningful things in life, writing your last will, writing up recipes that you have learned from your parents for your children and grandchildren, writing your life story, etc.

Handout 16.1 Session overview

1. *Group personal/medical check-in (10 mins)*

2. *Introduction* (10 mins)
   a. topic and overview of today
   b. reflection on previous session
   c. reflection on homework

3. *Explanation and group discussion* (10 mins)
   a. explanation of today's topic: self-oriented meanings
   b. group discussion

4. *Self-care exercise* (15 mins)

5. *Guided individual exercise* (20 mins)
   a. self-compassion exercise
   b. reflecting on questions
   c. writing about the exercise

6. *Group sharing of individual exercise* (10 mins)

7. *Self-evaluation in writing* (5 mins)

8. *Group sharing of self-evaluation* (5 mins)

9. *Ending* (5 mins)
   a. summary
   b. preview of the next session
   c. homework

Handout 16.2   Overview of theory (1): Self-oriented meanings

II. SELF-ORIENTED SOURCES OF MEANING

Underlying value: the value of the self

A. Resilience (coping successfully with difficult life situations)

   Flexibility, perseverance and hardiness, accepting challenges, effective coping skills

B. Self-efficacy

   Effective actions in daily life (setting specific activities or goals, planning, organising, discipline, evaluating and adjusting daily life activities or goals), being in control

C. Self-acceptance

   Self-insight, self-acceptance, self-worth, self-esteem

E. Autonomy

   Self-reliance, non-selfish balance within social context

F. Creative self-expression

G. Self-care

Handout 16.3   Overview of theory (2): Self-acceptance

1. Self-acceptance is about:

   a. Not judging yourself

   b. Understanding who you really are

   c. Understanding your strengths and limitations

   d. Saying to yourself 'I am OK, regardless of my situation and what I do'

   e. Feeling worthy and significant

2. Self-acceptance does not mean you are perfect: you can always improve, but self-acceptance says that fundamentally you are OK, regardless of the situation and of the aspects of yourself that you could improve.

3. Accepting not only good aspects but also failures and feeling bad. Know what you can do, and know what cannot do: you are not perfect, and it is OK to be not perfect. Self-acceptance is also about understanding the reason and context why you feel or did this way.

4. 'My body does not feel or look perfect, but it is as it is.' Often difficult in our society with Photoshopped models.

5. In our past and society, we could have received the message that 'I am only OK when I do this or that'. We may try to live up to other people's expectations and criteria. Self-acceptance does not say, 'I'm OK if I do ...' but 'I am OK, whatever I do.'

6. 'Fake self': pretending to be someone other than who we really are.

7. 'Being your own best friend.'

8. Self-acceptance is the basis of self-care. Self-care can be meaningful.

9. You are worthy of living a meaningful and satisfying life, despite your imperfections and the illness.

10. Self-acceptance is also about accepting the fact that there are periods in our life that we find self-acceptance and self-care difficult. Self-acceptance needs time to grow.

Handout 16.4   Homework (1) for Session 6: Preview exercise for Session 6

Please take some time to think about these questions. You may already have written some of the answers, but we will complete this exercise during Session 6.

The next session will be about social meanings. These meanings are about being connected with others and improving the well-being of others. The following questions ask for examples of self-oriented meanings you may have experienced in the past or that you are experiencing now. Of course, it is possible that you do not experience every question as relevant for you; thus, it is also fine to answer 'I do not experience this as meaningful'. Try to find as many answers as possible, but do not worry if can you only think of one or two examples.

Question 1. Give some examples of social connections now or in the past. For instance, you may feel connected to friends, relatives, intimate relationships and parents, or feel that you are part of a larger community, tradition or culture.

Question 2. Give some examples where you feel or felt socially accepted by others. For instance, communities you feel part of, and feeling accepted for who you are.

Question 3. Give some examples that you are or have been altruistic, that is moments where you have selflessly invested in and helped others, or moments where you have contributed to the wider society or world.

Question 4. Give some examples that you take or have taken care of children and young people, such as being a parent, being a foster or adoptive parent, or working in education.

Question 5. When did you feel deeply connected to other people?

Question 6. Look again at the previous questions, and use your imagination. Are there any examples of materialistic meanings that you are currently not experiencing but that you would like to try? These examples could be realistically attainable or entirely fantasy.

Question 7. Would you like to experience more materialistic meanings in your life? If so, what could you do to experience more material meanings in your life?

Handout 16.5   Homework (2) for Session 6: Body scan exercise

In the session we have done the 'body scan exercise'. This exercise can help us to pay attention to our bodily experiences, but not be overwhelmed by them. You are invited to scan your body with your attention, sweeping your awareness through differ-ent parts of your body – starting from the top of your head, to your toes – without judg-ing what you are aware of but as best as you can, bringing attention to your experience moment to moment. It is important to try this exercise in the first instance when you feel relaxed, so that you know how you to do the exercise even when you feel over-whelmed by your emotions and, for example, feel anxious. If you want to do this at home, you could follow these steps. As always, do not feel obliged to do this; take care of yourself; for instance, if it feels too overwhelming you can stop at any time.

1. *To start, I would like to invite you to lie on the floor or on a bed. Close your eyes, if that feels comfortable to you, and notice how your body feels, where it makes contact with the floor, etc.*

2. *Bring your attention to the crown of your head; notice any sensations here – tingling, numbness, tightness or relaxation. Feel the weight of your head (as it rests on your shoulder/the cushion). Be aware of your forehead; notice whether or not you can feel the pulse in the forehead, whether there is tightness or ease. Then include the eyes, the nose, cheeks, mouth and chin and finally the ears, noticing any sounds you can hear. Being aware moment by moment of the changing pattern of sensations, feelings of warmth, coolness, ease. If you notice your mind wandering this is perfectly natural and what minds do. Noticing your mind has wandered is a moment of awareness; just gently guide your awareness back to the part of the body you are focusing on.*

3. *Now let go of the head and face, and move your awareness into the neck and shoulders. Notice the strong muscles in this part of the body, be aware of any tension in the neck and throat, perhaps be aware of the sensation of air in the throat.*

4. *Move your awareness now to the shoulders, the places where there is contact between the shoulders and the floor; extend your awareness into the arms, elbows, wrists, hands and fingers, aware of what is here in each moment.*

5. *Shift the focus to the chest area; notice the subtle rise and fall of the chest with the in and out breath; turn your awareness now to the ribcage, front and back of the ribs, sides of the ribs, the upper back resting on the floor. Notice any aches and pains here and see if you can bring a sense of gentleness and kindness to these areas.*

6. *Turn your awareness now to the abdomen and stomach, the place where we feel our 'gut feelings', notice your attitude to this part of your body, see if you can allow it to be as it is, taking a relaxed and accepting approach to this part of the body. Then extend your awareness to the lower back, the lumber spine; feel the gentle pressure as the back meets the floor/chair. Move your awareness to the pelvis area, the hip bones, and sitting bones, genitals and groin; notice any sensations or lack of sensations that are here, perhaps being aware of the breath in this part of the body. Bring a kindly attention here.*

7. *Now let go of the torso as the centre of your awareness and move your attention into the thighs of both legs, feel the weight of the legs; gently notice what other sensations there are here; tune into the skin, bone and muscle of the legs here.*

(Continued)

8. *Next turn your attention gently towards the knees, bringing a friendly attention; notice if there is any discomfort here, and if there is none then notice what is present already here.*

9. *Take your attention into the calves of both legs; notice how your muscles feel here; feel this part of the legs from the inside out – the flesh and bone of the lower legs. And, again, check in with where your attention is from time to time and notice the quality of your attention, seeing if it is possible to bring a gentleness and kindliness into your awareness, not forcing yourself, but bringing a lightness of touch to your attention in this part of the body.*

10. *Finally, move your attention into both feet, the heels of the feet, the instep, the balls of the feet, the tops of the feet, skin and bone and finally the toes, seeing if it is possible to distinguish one toe from another. Notice whether there is tension here, sensations, numbness, tingling and allowing any tension to soften as you bring a gentle awareness to it.*

11. *Now, take one or two deeper breaths and widen your focus, filling the whole body with awareness; noticing whatever is present; sweeping the body with your awareness from top to bottom; experiencing the body from the inside out. Notice whether there is any non-acceptance towards any parts of the body as you fill the body with a gentle aware-ness and see if you can have compassion for any judgements or for any tension or pain that might be present as and when you notice it. Be aware of this amazing body that you have; be compassionate towards its pains and appreciate its capacities and the wonder of it.*

(See also Handout 13.3 'Evaluation of today's session' on p. 220 and Handout 15.4 'The meaningful pin-up board on p. 238)

17

Session 6: Social Sources of Meaning

17.1 Overview

- *Key session question*: How can we experience meaning in our social relationships, belonging to a community and taking care of others and children?

- *Session goals:*
  1. Explaining social meanings as possible sources of meaning
  2. Helping clients to find and evaluate examples of social meanings
  3. Fostering social interactions between clients
  4. Helping clients to evaluate and commit to concrete actions in their life

- *Main group process:*

  Explicit reflection and meta-discussion about the group dynamics and about the meaning of the group for the members.

- *Homework completed before this session:*

  16.4. Homework (1) for Session 6: Preview exercise for Session 6
  16.5. Homework (2) for Session 6: Body scan exercise
  15.4. Repeated homework: The meaningful pin-up board (optional)
  Preparation for presentation in Session 10

- *Handouts*

  17.1. Session overview
  17.2. Overview of theory
  17.3. Exercise: Whose meaning is it?
  17.4. Homework for Session 7 (1): Preview exercise for Session 7
  13.3. Evaluation of today's session (can be found on p. 220)
  15.4. Repeated homework: The meaningful pin-up board (optional; can be found on p. 238)

– *Recommended reading*
Group dynamics: e.g. American Group Psychotherapy Association (2007), Yalom & Lezcs (2005).

17.2 Stages

1. *Group personal/medical check-in* (10 mins)

2. *Introduction* (10 mins)

    a. *Topic and overview of today*

    b. *Reflection on previous session*

    c. *Reflection on homework*

    See Stages 1 and 2 in Session 2

3. *Explanation and group discussion* (15 mins)

    a. *Explanation of today's topic*

    The practitioner explains that when in the past psychologists asked individuals for examples of meaning in their life, these individuals often mentioned social meanings. Describe the different types of social meanings in Handout 17.2. Stress that it is possible that individuals do not experience every social meaning as relevant for them.

    b. *Group discussion*

    Step 1. The practitioner asks how the clients feel about this explanation, and whether they have any questions.

    Step 2. The practitioner asks for some personal examples.

    Step 3. If clients do not mention it themselves, the practitioner could ask how it feels to belong and to contribute to each other in this group ('Does this feel meaningful?'; 'How do the social meanings in this group relate to social meanings outside of this room?'). The practitioner asks clients to tell each other what they have contributed to the group process up until now (it is important that the clients communicate this to each other, to stimulate group cohesion). This discussion also offers an opportunity for meta-communication about the group process, and, for instance, asks whether the clients have any wishes for the group dynamics in the next sessions. The group may, for example, reflect on the meaning of different roles in the group dynamics: What social meaning could it have to be relatively silent in the group? What social meaning could it have to be speaking too much, etc.? The practitioner could also ask the quieter and shy members in the group whether they would like to use this group as an opportunity to try out new ways of social interaction.

4. *Guided individual exercise* (20 mins)

   a. *Compliment exercise*

   Step 1. The practitioners give all clients an equal number of Post-it notes based on group size (ten Post-its for a group of ten).

   Step 2. The practitioners ask: 'Write the name of every group member on top of the Post-it. Write at least one compliment for every group member on one Post-it, including for yourself. Try to be specific – for instance, try to not write 'you are a nice person' but write why you think this person is nice.

   Step 3. Give the Post-its to each other. Read the Post-its for yourself. (Alternatively ask every client to read aloud the Post-its they have received.) *Do not say to yourself: 'this person is wrong', but simply accept the compliment: this is simply how others see you.*

   Step 4. I invite you to close your eyes. Be aware of the impact of these compliments by others. What are you feeling? Do you, for instance, feel happy, connected, possibly a bit shy? (...) How does it feel to be a member of this group and be accepted for who you are? (...) How does it feel to give compliments to others? (...) How does it feel to listen to the others in the group and help them with your responses, support and presence in the group?

   Step 5. Try to visualise yourself as being a spider sitting in the middle of a web. See how you have a silky spider thread going from you to your neighbours, and other threads to the other people in this room. See how longer threads run from you to your close friends and family. And still more threads run to your colleagues, friends from the past and acquaintances. See how threads extend to your parents, and your grandparents and their parents ... back many generations. See how threads run from you to the next generation: your children and/or to other young people you are taking care of and/or anyone else whose lives you have influenced; see how these threads to the next generation are followed by threads to their children and their friends, and all the following generations. Finally, feel how big your web is: you are connected with an infinite number of people in the past, present and future. How does it feel to be at the centre of this big social web?

   b. *Reflecting on questions*

   While the clients have their eyes closed, the practitioner asks them to reflect on the following questions:

   1. *Give some examples of social connections now or in the past. For instance, you might feel connected to friends, relatives, intimate relationships and parents, or feel that you are part of a larger community, tradition or culture.*
   2. *Give some examples that you feel or felt socially accepted by others. For instance, communities you feel part of, and feeling accepted for who you are.*

3. *Find some examples that you are or have been altruistic, that is, moments where you have selflessly invested in and helped others, or moments where you have contributed to the wider society or world.*
4. *Find some examples that you take or have taken care of children and young people, such as being a parent, being a foster or adoptive parent, or working in education.*
5. *When did you feel deeply connected to other people?*

c. **Writing about the exercise**

See Session 2.

d. **Social context exercise**

This second exercise can be skipped if there is not enough time left. It is particularly recommended for groups with individuals experiencing **separation-individuation** issues and having difficulties in independent decision-making, such as young people and students.

Explanation

The practitioner explains that what we experience as meaningful is often influenced by our social context: our parents, friends, social group such as neighbourhood church or political community, education and media. For instance our parents give us an example ('role model') of what they experience as meaningful, and often they let us know how they expect us to live our lives ('socialisation'): for instance, the child of a political activist is more likely to also be politically active (larger type of meaning), or a child in an academic family often hears from their parents how important education is and subsequently the child can start to feel for themselves how meaningful education is (self-oriented meaning) (this describes the process of internalisation and socialisation of meanings). Thus, the people around us influence what we feel is meaningful.

However, we can also change and select some of the people who influence us: for instance, you can decide to find other friends who believe more in the same meanings and values as yourself. For example, we could find friends with similar hobbies via online forums, or join a political party in line with our world view.

Therefore, this is a cycle of being influenced and selecting the influence based on what you experience as meaningful (the figure below is intended only for the practitioners). In daily life, we are often unaware of this cycle: we simply follow what others expect us to do, and we find meaning in the same place as our context finds meaning.

This can be OK, but sometimes it can be useful to re-evaluate for ourselves: Is this something I really find meaningful for myself or am I just doing this because others say this is meaningful?; Is this really the group of people that I want to be in? Thus, the main question is: Is this something I experience as truly meaningful for myself (**authentic self**) or is it something I find meaningful because I am only adjusting myself to the expectations of others and want their approval/recognition (**inauthentic self**)? Such questions often arise when an individual is confronted with a chronic or life-threatening disease: individuals start to ask themselves who they are and what is truly meaningful to themselves.

About everything we experience as meaningful we can ask ourselves: am I only conformist or authentic? The answers to this question could be: (1) I experience this as meaningful because my context has taught me to experience this as meaningful, and that feels authentic to me; (2) My context taught me to experience this as meaningful, and this does not feel authentic to me; (3) I have selected the people around me to support my authentic meaning, and they are confirming what I experience as meaningful; (4) I experience something as truly meaningful that the people around me do not experience as meaningful.

The following exercise is meant to allow you to become aware of this circular pattern, and analyse how authentic we feel in our meanings.

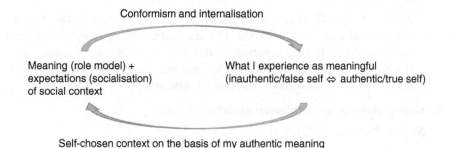

Conformism and internalisation

Meaning (role model) + expectations (socialisation) of social context

What I experience as meaningful (inauthentic/false self ⇔ authentic/true self)

Self-chosen context on the basis of my authentic meaning

Step 1. Fill in Table 17.3.

Step 2. Now that you have done this exercise, reflect on the following questions:

- *How much do you follow the people around you in what you experience as meaningful?*
- *How would the people around you react if you were to do the opposite of what they expected, e.g. if your parents expect you to have a successful career and you deliberately chose not to be successful? How would their response make you feel?*
- *How authentic does it feel to primarily follow these people around you?*
- *Look again at Table 17.3: which three meanings and expectations of the people around you feel the most authentic to you (the meanings you deeply agree with)? Which three meanings feel the least authentic to you (meanings that you do not entirely agree with)?*

  – *To what extent have you deliberately selected the people around you, based on what you experience as meaningful in relationships (e.g. find friends with similar hobbies via online forums; join political party in line with your world view)?*

Step 3. Reflect on the following questions: *(step can be skipped)*

  – *Imagine that you are to be born again, but this time you can select the people around you, and you can decide completely how you will live your own life. What would your life look like? Who would be your friends and family?*
  – *How much does this fantasy differ from your current life?*

Step 4. Reflect on the following questions: *(step can be skipped)*

  – *What dreams did you have for your own future when you were a small child? How different are these dreams now?*
  – *Have you ever changed direction in life, or decided to follow other dreams? To what extent did the people around you influence this change?*

Step 5. Reflect on the following questions:

  – *To what extent is what you think as meaningful originally what others think is meaningful?*
  – *Which of the following options would you like to aim for in life: be conformist and experience your life as inauthentic; OR be independent, find your own friends and experience your life as authentic? Explain why. Would you prefer other options – for instance, sometimes be conformist-inauthentic and sometimes independent-authentic?*

5. **Group sharing of individual exercise** (30 mins)

   Step 1. Process evaluation

   Step 2. Group sharing of experiences

   See in Session 2

6. **Self-evaluation in writing** (10 mins)

   See Stage 5 and Handout 2.4. in Session 2

7. **Group sharing of self-evaluation** (20 mins)

   See Step 7 in Session 2

8. Ending (5 mins)

   a. *Summary*

   b. *Preview of the next session*

   c. *Homework*

   The clients are invited to do the preview exercises in the handout for the next session. Remind clients that they will be asked in Session 10 to present any meaningful change.

Handout 17.1   Session overview

1. *Group personal/medical check-in* (10 mins)

2. *Introduction* (10 mins)
   a. topic and overview of today
   b. reflection on previous session
   c. reflection on homework

3. *Explanation and group discussion* (15 mins)
   a. explanation of today's topic: social meanings
   b. group discussion

4. *Guided individual exercise* (20 mins)
   a. compliment exercise
   b. mindfulness exercise
   c. reflecting on questions
   d. writing about the exercise
   e. social context exercise (optional)

5. *Group sharing of individual exercise* (30 mins)

6. *Self-evaluation in writing* (10 mins)

7. *Group sharing of self-evaluation* (20 mins)

8. *Ending* (5 mins)
   a. summary
   b. preview of the next session
   c. homework

Handout 17.2　Overview of theory

III. SOCIAL SOURCES OF MEANING

Underlying value: the value of being connected with others, belonging to a specific community and improving the well-being of others and children in particular

A. Feeling socially connected
Sociability, friends, family, intimate relationships/partner

B. Belonging to a specific community
Family, community, history and society

C. Following social expectations
Doing what is socially expected, following social virtues, conformism

D. Altruism

E. Giving birth to and taking care of children

Handout 17.3 Exercise: Whose meaning is it?

Social group	Names of at most three important individuals	What do they experience as meaningful for themselves? (Give most important examples)	What are their expectations of you? (Give most important examples)	How important is their opinion for you? 1 = totally unimportant; 10 = extremely important	How much do you experience the same things as meaningful as they do, and follow their expectations? 1 = totally not; 10 = completely
Parents and/or others raising you					
Friends until your twenties					
Social group until your twenties, e.g. neighbourhood, church, political group					
Education, e.g. teachers					
Current friends and partner					
Current social group					
Current colleagues					
Media, e.g. books, blogs, news, newspapers, Facebook pages					
Other important individuals, e.g. therapist					

Handout 17.4   Homework for Session 7 (1): Preview exercise for Session 7

Please take some time to think about these questions. You may already have written down some answers, but we will complete this exercise during Session 7

The next session will be about larger meanings in life. These meanings are about setting large goals in life and trying to achieve them. The following questions ask for examples of larger meanings you may have experienced in the past or that you are experiencing now. Of course, it is possible that you do not experience every question as relevant for you; thus, it is also fine to answer 'I do not experience this as meaningful'. Try to find as many answers as possible, but do not worry if you can only think of one or two examples.

Question 1. Give some examples from the past or present of when you tried to achieve the best you are capable of in life. For instance, you may have tried to achieve your largest potential as a person, or follow deeper values and norms in life (e.g. being a courageous, modest or honourable person), or tried to become who you really are in life (some call this 'being authentic' and 'listening to your true self').

Question 2. Give some examples of the legacy you may leave when you die. This could be about contributing or having contributed something positive to other people, based on what you have done in the past, are doing now or are going to do in the future. This could also be about how you want to be remembered by others when you are have died.

Question 3. Give some examples of moments when you feel or may have felt connected to the generations before you (your parents, grandparents and the people before them), and the generations that come after you (your children, grandchildren, etc.). This could, for instance, be an experience where someone in your family was born or died, a marriage or funeral, a family gathering, a meeting with children at a school, etcetera.

Question 4. Give examples of intense spiritual moments in the past or present, such as feeling connected to your religious community, feeling the presence of God or a higher power or energy, feeling connected with nature or the world as such, or experiencing a cosmic and Ultimate Meaning of Life. Like all other questions in this group therapy, it may be possible that you have not had such experiences.

Question 5. Look again at the previous questions and use your imagination. Are there any examples of larger meanings that you are currently not experiencing but that you would like to try? These examples could be realistically attainable or entirely fantasy.

Question 6. Would you like to experience more self-oriented meanings in your life? If so, what could you do to experience more materialistic meanings in your life?

_____

(See also Handout 13.3 'Evaluation of today's session' on p. 220 and Handout 15.4 'The meaningful pin-up board on p. 238)

18

Session 7: Larger Sources of Meaning

18.1 Overview

– *Key session question*: How can we experience meaning in larger goals, striving for justice and spirituality?

– *Session goals*:

1. Explaining larger meanings as a possible source of meaning
2. Helping clients to find and evaluate examples of larger meanings
3. Fostering a sense of 'belonging to something that is bigger than my individual situation in the here and now'
4. Helping clients to evaluate and commit to concrete actions

– *Main group process:*

Clients may feel anxious in this session owing to the fact that their death anxiety is addressed; therefore it is important to create an atmosphere of safety and of universality of mortality.

– *Homework completed before this session:*

17.4. Homework for Session 7: Preview exercise for Session 7
15.4. Repeated homework: The meaningful pin-up board (optional)

– *Handouts*

18.1. Session overview
18.2. Overview of theory
13.3. Evaluation of today's session (can be found on p. 220)
15.4. Repeated homework: The meaningful pin-up board (optional; can be found on p. 238)

– *Recommended reading*

Existential skills: Chapter 9; Yalom, 1980; Schneider, 2004; Becker, 2007; Pyszczynski et al, 2010; Vos, 2014.

18.2 Stages

1. *Group personal/medical check-in* (10 mins)

2. *Introduction* (10 mins)

   a. *Topic and overview of today*

   b. *Reflection on previous session*

   c. *Reflection on homework*

   See Stages 1 and 2 in Session 2

3. *Explanation and group discussion* (15 mins)

   a. *Explanation of today's topic: larger meanings*

   The practitioner explains that when in the past psychologists asked individuals for examples of meaning in their life, these individuals often mentioned larger meanings. It is good to clarify from the start that this term 'larger meanings' is not necessary spiritual, but is about specific goals that individuals may strive for in life, other than materialistic, self-oriented and social meanings. Describe the different types of larger meanings in Handout 18.2. Stress that it is possible that individuals do not experience every larger meaning as relevant for them. As this can be an abstract topic, explicitly ask the group for examples and prepare some examples in advance.

Example formulation

- Being-alive as meaning: e.g. the mere fact that I am breathing, the fact I was born, the fact I am not dead yet.

- The four groups of meanings from the previous sessions are about specific objects or identifiable goals in life (e.g. enjoying material things, self-development, social connections, larger goals in life). The meaning of being-alive is not about objects, it is about the general feeling that 'it is significant to be here'. We do not need to possess things, be successful or achieve goals to live a meaningful life. Some individuals compare experiencing meaning in the mere fact of being-alive with a toddler who looks into the world without all big expectations, and who just enjoys the here-and-now. A child plays, and the playing in this moment is enough to feel alive and to feel meaningful. A child seldom asks questions about the meaning in

▶

◀

life, because for a child every moment is by definition meaningful: 'just being-there' (based on Nietzsche, 1891/2017).

– In line with Albert Schweitzer (1969) we may say: 'every life matters, because it is alive/a life'. It has been said that it is a fundamental life instinct to appreciate the mere fact that we exist. In most situations individuals will clamp onto life, despite their life circumstances.

– Finding meaning in being-alive can be particularly helpful when all other meanings are not attainable, particularly in difficult life situations. 'I cannot experience many meanings in life at this moment, but fortunately I am alive and that is enough!'

– Example 1: Viktor Frankl, the founder of meaning-centred therapy, survived a concentration camp. He said that the inmates survived not because of the things they possessed or extraordinary things they did – that was all impossible – but rather because people found meaning in the mere fact that they were still alive, that they had got through another day and had not died.

– Example 2: After a car accident, Emma lost all control and feelings of her limbs, and had difficulties speaking. She said she felt like a plant, 'but I am grateful for being a plant and not an impersonal stone: I breathe, my heart beats, my skin protects my numb limbs. Just being-there is a miracle that I am grateful for every day.' When Emma was dying, she said that there was not much she looked back on positively, 'but it was meaningful to have been here; thanks, life!' Thus, in the worst of situations, it seems possible to find meaning in the mere fact that you are alive. This gratitude could replace any bitterness you may feel about all the lost meanings and the unlived life that could have been but never was.

– Example 3: John had lung cancer, and he felt dissatisfied about the fact that he cannot do much more than lie in bed, eat, speak with his wife and sometimes go to the living room. Until he started to see what a big achievement this is: to be able to get through a day; to add another day to his calendar. He felt proud and grateful for still being here.

– What does this mean, to find meaning in the mere fact of being alive? Existential philosophers have written extensively on this; they say, for instance, that being alive means being the unique individual that I am, being free to make decisions and being able to connect with the world and the people around me (based on: Heidegger, 1927/2001). Finally, the mere fact that I am alive means that I am connected with people around me and influence the world. The world would not have been the same without me. People take care of me, I take care of people, I have friends, I am a consumer, etc. – there are an endless number of ways in which I influence the world. Although my influences may seem small, the indirect effects may be huge, like a small snowball rolling down a snowy hill. This fact that my being-there influences the world makes my life significant *(note: the practitioner may want to cover this only very briefly due to its abstract nature).*

– Some practitioners and philosophers add that 'life is a gift', that is, they find meaning in the fact that life is given to us: we did not ask for it, and we may sometimes not like it and sometimes we do, but in the end it is a gift to us – because of

▶

◀

our parents or some may say a higher power or God. Such philosophers say we can decide to accept life as a gift, by living it responsibly *(based on: Breitbart & Poppito, 2015)*.

– Some individuals do not experience life as a gift, are not grateful and do not experience meaning in the mere fact that they are alive; their life feels more like an unwanted or absurd burden. These experiences are not denied by acknowledging the fact that I am alive, and that my life feels – at least in the past or in moments – significant and important, to me at least. Some philosophers say that there is no ultimate meaning in life and everything is random and absurd; this does not equate with the fact that my life can feel meaningful to me. As Aristotle wrote: the form of the stone that is brought into the workshop of a sculptor may look meaningless – as the stone has no shape yet but it offers many options to the sculptor. But we can experience meaning in the fact that there is a stone that is being shaped. The current form of my life may not feel meaningful, but the fact that I am alive can feel meaningful.

b. *Group discussion*

Step 1. The practitioner asks how the clients feel about this explanation, and whether they have any questions.

Step 2. The practitioner explicitly asks for some personal examples of this type of meanings.

4. *Guided individual exercise* (20 mins)

a. *Mindfulness exercise*

Today's mindfulness is a repetition of the 'the safe place exercise'. Explain that today this will be followed by an exercise in which the clients imagine the last moments in their life; explain the rationale for this exercise: we often become aware of the larger meanings in our life, when we look at our life as a whole, for instance when we are dying. See the 'safe place exercise' in Session 4.

b. *Reflecting on questions*

While the clients have their eyes closed, the practitioner asks them to reflect on the following:

'I invite you to imagine the last moments of your life. If imagining this becomes too much for you, you can always go back to the safe place; take care of yourself.

    Imagine you are on your deathbed. Your loved ones are around you. You have your eyes closed; it is too much effort to keep them open. You feel tired; your body is totally exhausted from fighting. You are breathing slowly, and your heart rate is slowing down. You feel that your body will stop functioning soon. [allow some time]

1. *It is in these last moments of your life, that you look back on how you have lived your life. Imagine how you feel about your life. Are you satisfied or unsatisfied about how you have lived, and has your life been meaningful? [allow some time]*
2. *What feels the most meaningful in your life? This can be anything, something small or something large. [allow some time]*
3. *What do you need to do in your life to be able to feel on your deathbed that you have lived a meaningful and satisfying life? This can be something you have already done in your life, or something you may still need to do.*
4. *Which larger meanings do you need to achieve in your life to be able to die with a sense of meaning and satisfaction about your life? This could be about setting important goals in life, the person you have been, your values, the legacy you leave, your contribution to justice, your position among the generations, or your sense of religion and spirituality?*
5. *Are you now living your life in such a way that you will be able to look back with a sense of meaning and satisfaction when you die? Why, or why not?*
6. *What could you change in your life to be able to die with a stronger sense of meaning and satisfaction about your life?*

c. **Writing about the exercise**

See Session 2

5. *Group sharing of individual exercise* (30 mins)

   Step 1. Process evaluation

   Step 2. Group sharing of experiences

   See Step 5 in Session 2.

6. *Self-evaluation in writing* (10 mins)

   See Stage 6 and Handout 2.4. in Session 2

7. *Group sharing of self-evaluation* (20 mins)

   See Stage 7 in Session 2

8. *Ending* (5 mins)

   a. *Summary*

   b. *Preview of the next session*

   c. *Homework*

   There is no preview exercise. Clients can catch up with some homework that they have not done in previous weeks. Remind the clients that in Session 10, they will present any meaningful change they have made or tried.

Handout 18.1   Session overview

1. *Group personal/medical check-in* (10 mins)

2. *Introduction* (10 mins)
   a. topic and overview of today
   b. reflection on previous session
   c. reflection on homework

3. *Explanation and group discussion* (15 mins)
   a. explanation of today's topic: larger meanings
   b. group discussion

4. *Guided individual exercise* (20 mins)
   a. mindfulness exercise
   b. reflecting on questions
   c. writing about the exercise

5. *Group sharing of individual exercise* (30 mins)

6. *Self-evaluation in writing* (10 mins)

7. *Group sharing of self-evaluation* (20 mins)

8. *Ending* (5 mins)
   a. summary
   b. preview of the next session
   c. homework

Handout 18.2 Overview of theory

IV. LARGER SOURCES OF MEANING

Underlying value: values of something bigger than their materialistic-hedonic experiences, themselves and other human beings, merely for the sake of that larger value.

A. Purposes
     Specific larger goals, purposes, aims or dreams in life

B. Personal growth
     Self-development, self-transcendence, self-realisation, fulfilling one's potential, authenticity, wisdom

C. Temporality
     Sense of coherence, future-oriented, reflection on the past, legacy and after-life

D. Justice and ethics
     Following ethical standards, being treated in a just way, contributing to a just world

E. Spirituality and religion
     Spirituality and religion, beliefs, worship and religious practices, insight into cosmic meaning, spiritual union, peace harmony and balance, Platonic Idea or Largest Good

---

(See also Handout 13.3 'Evaluation of today's session' on p. 220 and Handout 15.4 'The meaningful pin-up board on p. 238)

19

Session 8: Being Here as Source of Meaning

19.1 Overview

- *Key session question:* How can we experience meaning in the fact that we are alive?

- *Session goals:*

  1. Explaining existential-philosophical meanings
  2. Helping clients to find and evaluate examples of existential-philosophical meanings
  3. Exploring opportunities of meaning in case other meanings are not experienced
  4. Exploring relationship to death and life

- *Main group process:*

  The clients may start becoming aware of the finiteness of this therapy group, which could evoke feelings of bereavement and loneliness. Individuals who have not really progressed up until now may start to feel negative about the possibility of experiencing meaning. This could create a negative group atmosphere; therefore, it is important to focus on possibilities of change and hope.

- *Homework completed before this session:*

  15.4. Repeated homework: The meaningful pin-up board (optional)

  Preparation for presentation in Session 10

- *Handouts*

  19.1. Session overview
  19.2. Overview of theory
  19.3. Lifeline exercise
  19.4. Letter to a friend exercise
  19.5. Homework for Session 9: Preview exercise for Session 9

13.3. Evaluation of today's session (can be found on p. 220)

15.4. Repeated homework: The meaningful pin-up board (optional; can be found on p. 238)

MQQ Meaning Quintet Questionnaire

– *Recommended reading*
  ➤ Chapter 9

19.2 Stages

1. *Group personal/medical check-in* (10 mins)

2. *Introduction* (10 mins)

　a. *Topic and overview of today*

　b. *Reflection on previous session*

　c. *Reflection on homework*
　　See in Session 2

3. *Explanation and group discussion* (15 mins)

　a. *Explanation of today's topic*
　　The practitioner explains that when psychologists asked individuals for examples of meaning, they sometimes mentioned the mere fact of being alive as a source of meaning. That is, individuals have said that simply the fact that they are breathing is meaningful to them. The practitioner gives the following theory, bearing in mind that this theory may be quite difficult for some members to follow, and some examples may be too confrontational so the practitioner may decide for clinical reasons to offer other examples.

　b. *Group discussion*
　　Step 1. The practitioner asks how the clients feel about this explanation, and whether they have any questions.

　　Step 2. The practitioner explicitly asks for personal examples. The practitioner is particularly sensitive about feelings of existential anxiety and suicidal ideation.

4. *Guided individual exercise* (20 mins)

　a. *Lifeline exercise*
　　Step 1. The practitioner gives out Handout 19.3 and asks the clients to put a cross next to the place where they are now in life, on the line ranging

from birth to death. The clients are asked to look at the position of this cross, and be aware of any feelings that arise in them (approx. 2 minutes).

Step 2. The practitioner asks the clients to lift up the paper, place it in front of their eyes with the long right-hand side of the paper in front of their eyes, so that they can look back on their lives from the perspective of their death. The clients are asked to look at the line, and be aware of any feelings that arise in them (approx. 2 minutes).

Step 3. The practitioner asks the clients to turn over the paper again, so that they can see their lifeline from the perspective of their birth. The clients are asked to look at the line, and be aware of any feelings that arise in them (approx. 2 minutes).

Step 4. The practitioner asks the clients to compare the position of the cross on their lifeline with the three shorter lines below this line, which represent the lives of people who have not lived as long. The clients are asked to look at the lines, and be aware of any feelings that arise in them (approx. 2 minutes).

Step 5. The practitioner asks the clients to put a cross on the lifeline with many ups and downs in life, and compare this to the original straight lifeline. The clients are asked to look at the lines, and be aware of any feelings that arise in them (approx. 2 minutes).

Step 6. The practitioner asks the clients to look at the next lifeline which gives many options for the future: there is not one predetermined direction in which life will develop. The clients are asked to look at the line, and be aware of any feelings that arise in them (approx. 2 minutes).

Step 7. The practitioner asks the clients to look at the last line, which extends before the start of life and continues after the end of life. This means that someone is born on a lifeline that was already there: every individual is born to parents, into a family, into a neighbourhood, into a pre-existing country, etc. After one's death, the lifeline will continue: someone's legacy will still be there, the impact on their family and friends, the indirect influence on other people by being part of this society having a job, paying taxes and buying things.

b. *Writing about the exercise*

See Session 2.

c. *Letter writing exercise*

Today's session is about experiencing meaning in the fact that we are alive, and that feeling-alive can be a motivational and uplifting experience. This meaning can be particularly helpful when searching for any other meanings temporarily fail. Therefore, the clients are invited to write a letter to themselves for a moment in their lives that they may feel negative and may not experience any meaning. The clients are recommended to write this letter as if they are writing this letter to a good friend: What would you tell a good friend who feels very down? Clients can write the letter in any way they would like, although the handout gives some suggestions. It is likely that clients will not finish this letter during the session; they can complete it at home. The clients could reread the letter for moments they feel down in future.

5. *Group sharing of individual exercise* (30 mins)

   Step 1. Process evaluation

   Step 2. Group sharing of experiences

   See Stage 5 in Session 2

6. *Self-evaluation in writing* (10 mins)
   See Stage 5 and Handout 13.3 in Chapter 13

7. *Group sharing of self-evaluation* (20 mins)
   See Stage 7 in session 2

8. *Ending* (5 mins)

   a. *Summary*

   b. *Preview of the next session*

   c. *Homework*

The clients are invited to do the preview exercises in the handout for the next session. Remind the clients that they will present any meaningful change they made or tried in Session 10. If they have not finished the letter, they could finish this at home.

Handout 19.1   Session overview

1. *Group personal/medical check-in* (10 mins)

2. *Introduction* (10 mins)
    a. topic and overview of today
    b. reflection on previous session
    c. reflection on homework

3. *Explanation and group discussion* (15 mins)
    a. explanation of today's topic: being alive as meaning
    b. group discussion

4. *Guided individual exercise* (20 mins)
    a. lifeline exercise
    b. writing a letter to one's self

5. *Group sharing of individual exercise* (30 mins)

6. *Self-evaluation in writing* (10 mins)

7. *Group sharing of self-evaluation* (20 mins)

8. *Ending* (5 mins)
    a. summary
    b. preview of the next session
    c. homework

Handout 19.2 Overview of theory

- Being alive as meaning: e.g. the mere fact that I am breathing, the fact I was born, the fact I am not dead yet

- The four groups of meanings: specific objects or identifiable goals
- Meaning of being alive: general feeling that 'it is significant to be here', 'just being there'

- 'Every life matters, because it is alive/a life' (Albert Schweitzer, 1969)

- Helpful to focus on being alive when other meanings are temporarily not attainable, particularly in difficult life situations

- Example 1: Viktor Frankl's concentration camp experience

- Example 2: Emma: terminally ill, but finds meaning in the mere fact that she is alive. This gratitude could replace the bitterness about all the lost meanings and the unlived life that could have been but never was.

- Example 3: John: physically limited. Depressed until he started to see what a big achievement it is to be able to get through a day and add another day to his calendar

- Existential philosophers: being the unique individual I am, being free in making decisions and being able to connect with the world and the people around me. I am connected with people around me and influence the world. The world would not have been the same without me. People take care of me, I take care of people, I have friends, I am a consumer, etc. The fact that my being there influences the world makes my life significant.

- Spirituality: 'life is a gift'

- The current form of my life may not feel meaningful, but the fact that I am alive can feel meaningful

---

Handout 19.3   Lifeline exercise

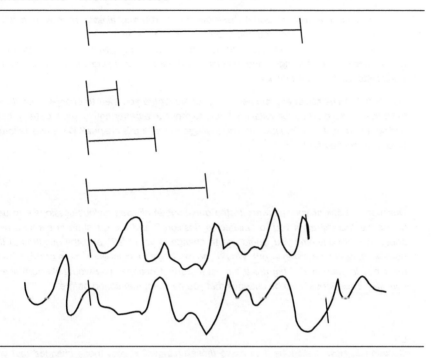

Handout 19.4   Letter to a friend exercise

What would you tell a good friend who feels very down? Write a letter to yourself, as if you were that friend giving yourself advice. You can write this in any way you would like. Some suggestions:

– Start with 'Dear Me,'

– Acknowledge how hard life can feel and that feeling bad is an inevitable part of life, like there are downs in the lifeline with ups and downs.

– Underline the meaning of being alive.

– Remind of meanings in the past.

– Give some hope and belief in yourself: you can do this!

– Give examples of meanings from previous sessions.

– Suggest specific steps to be reminded of what is meaningful in life, e.g. 'call aunt Agatha', 'eat better', etc.

– Remind to re-read the texts and exercises from this training/therapy.

Handout 19.5   Homework for Session 9: Preview exercise for Session 9

Please take some time to think about these questions. You may already have written down some answers, but we will complete this exercise during Session 9.

The next session will be about 'just doing it: how can we set goals, create a plan, make a change, cope with challenges and evaluate, and experience trying this as meaningful?' Psychologists call this 'self-efficacy'.

> *Question 1. Think about any moments in your life where you tried to change your life for the better. This could be for instance, trying to move to a better house, get a better job, or ending a bad relationship. How did you manage to make this change? What was helpful? What was not helpful?*

> *Question 2. Look at your answers to the questions in all the previous sessions – in particular the therapy aims you formulated in Session 2 and the question in each session about 'is there anything you would like to change in your life?', and the question in the homework of each session about 'Would you like to try to experience more of this type of meanings in your life?' What are the most important changes you would like to make in your life? These could also be changes that you have not mentioned before.*

> *Question 3. How realistic is it to make these changes? Select those changes that you think are the most realistic. Remember that we spoke about this in Session 3, when we mentioned the Serenity Prayer: 'God, grant me the serenity to accept the things I cannot change, the courage to change the things I can, and the wisdom to know the difference.'*

> *Question 4. Look at the most important change you want to make. Have you already tried to make this change before; if so, what worked and what did not work? What do you need to be able to make this change (e.g. help from someone, more self-confidence, etc.)? Which concrete steps do you need to take to make this change really happen?*

> *Previous try-outs: what worked and what did not?*

> *What do you need to make this happen?*

> *Which specific steps do you need to take?*

Question 4. Do the same for the second most important change you want to make. If you have more changes you want to make, you can add some additional pieces of papers to describe this.

Previous try-outs: what worked and what did not?

What do you need to make this happen?

Which specific steps do you need to take?

Question 5. If you know what you want to change in your life, and you know how to change it, give it a try! Describe below your experiences of trying to make this change in your life. It could be that you are not immediately successful; that is OK, as this is only about TRYING to make changes in your life (experimenting!). Why are the things you did successful or unsuccessful?

Be aware that for the homework in Session 9, you will be asked to talk about changes you have tried to make in your life: this could be anything, such as enrolling on a course you have always wanted to do, booking a holiday, speaking with your children about meaningful things in life, writing your last will, writing up recipes that you have learned from your parents for your children and grandchildren, writing your life story, etc.

(See also Handout 13.3 'Evaluation of today's session' on p. 220 and Handout 15.4 'The meaningful pin-up board on p. 238)

20

Session 9: Doing Meaning in Daily Life

20.1 Overview

– *Key session question*: How can we find meaning by setting goals, making a plan, evaluating, adjusting and improving our goals?

– *Session goals:*
  1. Helping clients to identify priorities in life
  2. Explaining how clients can set goals, create a plan, make an actual change in their life, cope with challenges and evaluate this
  3. Explaining how this process of meaning in daily life can create a sense of meaning
  4. Fostering a sense of pride and self-efficacy

– *Main group process:*

  Feelings about termination may emerge as this is the penultimate session, and these feelings may be reflected in the group process. As this session is about making practical changes in life, clients will be encouraged to brainstorm together how these changes can be made.

– *Homework completed before this session:*

  19.5. Homework for Session 9(1): Preview exercise for Session 9
  13.3. Evaluation of today's session (can be found on p. 220)
  15.4. Repeated homework: The meaningful pin-up board (optional)

  MQQ Meaning Quintet Questionnaire (online supplementary material)

– *Handouts*

  20.1. Session overview
  20.2. Homework for Session 10
  Copy of the individual Goal Assessment Form completed in Session 2
  13.3. Evaluation of today's session (can be found on p. 220)
  15.4. Repeated homework: The meaningful pin-up board (optional; can be found on p. 238)

– *Recommended reading*
  ➤ Chapter 6, specifically on goal-setting.
  ➤ To help clients find solutions to practical problems: O'Connell, 2005.

20.2 Stages

1. *Group personal/medical check-in* (10 mins)

2. *Introduction* (15 mins)

   a. *Topic and overview of today*

   b. *Reflection on previous session*

   c. *Reflection on homework*
      See Stages 1 and 2 in Session 2

3. *Explanation and group discussion* (10 mins)

   a. *Explanation of today's topic*
      The practitioner explains that today's topic is about evaluating all previous sessions, and examining which concrete steps they want to make in daily life. The clients are stimulated to develop a sense of self-efficacy. There are no theoretical didactics in this session.

   b. *Group discussion*

      Step 1. The practitioner asks how the clients feel about this brief explanation, and whether they have any questions.

      Step 2. The practitioner explicitly asks for some personal examples of this type of self-efficacy in life.

4. *Guided individual exercise* (20 mins)

   a. *Mindfulness exercise*
      Today's mindfulness exercise is called 'the prioritising exercise', which will help the individuals to become aware of their priorities and facilitate intuitive decision-making.

      Step 1. Invite the client to bring their attention to how he/she sits in the chair; how does the body feel; where does it made contact with the chair, etc. This exercise can be creatively extended and adjusted to the personal experiences and preferences of the individual client.

      Step 2. Explain that the client will be asked to make quick decisions between multiple options that the practitioner will ask. There is no right or wrong. This is only an exercise in learning how to make quick decisions. The clients should focus on what they feel is appropriate in the here and now.

Step 3. The practitioner will ask the following questions, each followed by a silence of five seconds (in the beginning more time can be given, and after several questions the time can be shortened).

a. *Would you prefer a cup of coffee or tea now, or something else?*
b. *Would you prefer to be doing some physical exercise like walking or sports, or to be lying on bed now?*
c. *Would you prefer to be dancing or singing now?*
d. *Would you prefer to be listening to dance music, R&B, jazz, classical or another type of music now?*
e. *Would you prefer to be rich without friends, or poor with lots of friends?*
f. *Would you prefer to be healthy and feel you are living a meaningless life, or be ill and living a meaningful life?*
g. *Imagine you are walking outside now. Would you prefer an easy but boring route to your destination, or the longer but exciting way?*
h. *Would you prefer to read a good book or be with friends?*
i. *Would you prefer to have a successful career or make the world a better place to live in?*
j. *Would you prefer to be an intelligent or a social individual?*
k. *Would you prefer to make the effort to try new activities that could give you a new sense of meaning in daily life, or to continue your life as it is and not expend energy on new activities?*

b. **Mountain range exercise**

The clients are requested to stay silent. The practitioner gives a stack of Post-its to each client and a piece of A3 paper. The practitioner gives the following explanation:

Example

1. *Write the most important meanings on 5–15 Post-its*
Look at all your answers from the last few weeks – or think back over these sessions – and identify which are the most important meanings in your life. Write one meaning on each Post-it. Try to have between 5 and 15 Post-its; if you have more, decide to throw way the least meaningful ones.

▶

◀

2. *Make large and abstract meanings more specific*
Try to make these selected meanings on the Post-its more specific, and to break big meanings into specific meanings. For instance, do not write 'being social', but instead 'helping my neighbours', 'emotionally supporting my friend John who is going through a divorce', etc. Write these specific meanings on new Post-its, and only use these Post-its.

3. *Draw a mountain on a large piece of paper.*

4. *Put the Post-its on the mountain in order of importance*
Put the Post-its on the mountain in the order of priority, with less important meanings low on the mountain and the important meanings high up.

5. *Find what the meanings have in common*
   A. Reflect on what the Post-its that are all relatively high on the mountain have in common; how are these meanings in your life related, and could you possibly combine these changes?
   B. If you want, you can compile Post-its or use new ones to write common themes.

6. *Make the meanings on the mountains neither too 'peaky' nor too 'flat'*
   A. Look at the shape of the mountain of meanings. Does your mountain have one sharp peak; that is, are there only one or two extremely important meanings in your life, and are there very few other meanings that are relatively important? Or is your mountain very flat, because you have many meanings which are equally important?
   B. Try to rearrange your meanings so that there are four or five relatively important meanings high up in the mountain and several meanings which are somewhat less important lower down.

   NB: The reason to rearrange the meanings, is that when you have only one meaning at the peak of your life, and you fail to achieve this peak then you will feel very unsatisfied; to ensure that you can deal with problems in life, make sure that you have multiple meanings. If you have too many equally important meanings, you may have difficulties in spreading your time and energy, and in the end you may be too exhausted to even fulfil one meaning.

c. *Goal-setting exercise*

1. *Evaluate existing meaning experiences (this step can be skipped)*

I invite you to evaluate the current goals in your life. To do so, I ask you to look at the highest meaning or group of meanings on your mountain. Write on the back of the Post-it to what extent you already experience this meaning in your daily life, and what steps you usually take to realise this meaning? What can you learn from how you set and achieve these goals?

  2. *Select realistic meaning*

      a. Which highest meaning or group of meanings on your mountain would you like to experience but are you not yet experiencing? Select one.

      b. How realistic is it to realise this in your life?

      c. Which problems could arise when you would try to realise it?

      d. How can you overcome each of these problems?

  3. *Formulate a goal*

  Formulate a goal for yourself: 'I want to do ... to achieve ... and to be able to achieve this I need to do/overcome ...'

  Try to make the goal: important, specific and simple, not too far in the future or, challenging but attainable, and provide other supporting goals as well ('two birds with one stone'). Try to formulate this in a positive way ('I want to have more friends') instead of a negative way ('I want to feel less lonely'). By the way, one meaning can be formulated as many different goals.

  4. *Make a stepwise plan to realise this goal*

  For example: Step 1... Step 2...
  Ask yourself: Who? What? When? Where? How long?
  Try to be as precise as possible, and prepare an emergency plan in case you fail.

  5. *Make a timeline and set a deadline for evaluation of the stepwise plan*

  Add a timeline to the steps: When are you going to do this? When do you want to have finished this? When are you going to evaluate your plan? When are you going to decide to adjust the plan (e.g. change the steps)?

  6. *Action*

  What can you already do here and now to realise this plan? For instance, can you put the deadlines in your diary?

  7. *Repeat Steps 2–6 for other meanings high on the top of your mountain which you have not realised yet* (Handout 20.2)

5. *Group sharing of individual exercise* (**20 mins**)

    Step 1. Process evaluation

    Step 2. Group sharing of experiences

    See Stage 5 in Session 2

6. *Self-evaluation in writing* (**10 mins**)

    See Stage 6 in Session 2

7. *Group sharing of self-evaluation* **(20 mins)**

See Stage 7 in Session 2

8. *Ending* **(5 mins)**

a. *Summary*

b. *Preview of the next session*

c. *Homework*

Handout 20.1 Session overview

1. *Group personal/medical check-in* (10 mins)

2. *Introduction* (10 mins)
   a. topic and overview of today
   b. reflection on previous session

3. *Explanation and group discussion* (15 mins)
   a. explanation of today's topic
   b. group discussion

4. *Guided individual exercise* (30 mins)
   a. mindfulness exercise
   b. mountain range exercise
   c. goal-setting exercise

5. *Group sharing of individual exercise* (20 mins)

6. *Self-evaluation in writing* (10 mins)

7. *Group sharing of self-evaluation* (20 mins)

8. *Ending* (5 mins)
   a. summary
   b. preview of the next session
   c. homework

Handout 20.2   Homework for Session 10

1. Finalise the exercises from Session 9. This exercise could help in preparing your presentation.

2. Prepare a presentation on any meaningful change that you have tried to make during these sessions. This could be anything, such as enrolling on a course that you have always wanted to do, booking a holiday, speaking with children about meaningful things in life, writing your last will, writing up recipes that you have learned from your parents for your children, writing your life story, etc. You could also bring something creative, such as a painting or a homemade cake, if these are hobbies that you have started again. Or you could bring your pin-up board or a photo of this pin-up board. Share this with other group members in the way you want to share.

3. Reflect on the questions:

   a. Is there anything you would like to say to the other group members?
   b. Is there any ritual you would like to do to mark the end of the last session?

4. Add scores in the Goal Assessment Form based on to what extent you have achieved the goals that you set in Session 2.

(See also Handout 13.3 'Evaluation of today's session' on p. 220 and Handout 15.4 'The meaningful pin-up board on p. 238)

21

Session 10: Ending and a New Beginning

21.1 Overview

– *Key session question*: What can we use from these ten group sessions in our daily life, and how can we continue to live a meaningful life?

– *Session goals*:

1. Presenting meaningful changes in life, and coping with successes and failures
2. Evaluating the group sessions
3. Identifying how the clients could continue their changes
4. Saying goodbye and coping with feelings of termination

– *Main group process:*

Termination and feelings of bereavement; taking stock of the group process: what was meaningful and what was learned in the group process?

– *Homework completed before this session:*

20.2. Homework before Session 10

Goal Assessment Form (see Appendix; filled in again and compared with scores filled in in Session 2)

– *Handouts*

21.1. Session overview

Table 21.1 Session overview

1. *Group personal/medical check-in* and discussion about the closing ritual (10 mins)
2. *Introduction (5 Mins)*
a. topic and overview of today
b. reflection on previous session
c. reflection on homework

(Continued)

3. *Individual presentations (60 mins)*
4. *Group evaluation: three aspects: (10 mins)*
 a. individual achievements; individual continuation of changes (what will you continue + which concrete steps + what do you need for this continuation)
 c. development of the group, and contributions to each other
 d. general evaluation
5. *Closing ritual (5 mins)*

21.2 Stages

1. *Group personal/medical check-in* (10 mins)

See Stage 1 in Session 2

2. *Introduction* (5 mins)

a. *Topic and overview of today*

See Stage 1 in Session 2

Specific attention: The individuals are asked to reveal how they feel about the fact that this is the last session. They are also asked whether there is anything they would like to say to other clients, and whether there is any closing ritual they would like to do at the end. The group decides together how they would like to finish this session. Depending on the group process, the practitioners could mention their own feelings about finishing this group and their own proposal how to finish this group. For example, as finishing ritual, the group could stand in a circle, hold each other's hands, look each other in the eyes, and say 'thank you' to each other, and subsequently give each other a hand, kiss, hug or whatever feels appropriate. The practitioner could mention the possibility of sharing contact details if they would like to stay in touch with each other, although this is something that the clients need to initiate themselves.

b. *Reflection on previous session*

See Stage 2 in Session 2

c. *Reflection on homework*

Ask whether there were any questions about the homework. For instance, has everyone tried one change in their life? The practitioner can mention that it is not important how big or how successful the change was, but that it was trying something that was important. If individuals say they cannot present anything, the practitioners ask them to talk about which life project they would have tried, or share what they have learned during these sessions; this individual could be the last person to present the changes, so that they have time to generate ideas. If a group member does not want to share anything this should of course be respected.

3. *Individual presentations* (60 mins)

Each of the clients present their life project. The practitioner encourages other clients to respond to and recognise the effort. The practitioner could ask the group to identify the type of meaning and the concrete plan of action that this individual has tried. Both in cases of success and failure, it may be useful to assess how the individual has achieved this, for instance by analysing how realistic the goals set were and the plan of actions. In case of (partial) failure, the practitioner could mention that trying and adjusting aims and strategies are part of the process of achieving aims in the long term. The main group atmosphere should be positive and stimulate a sense of self-efficacy. It may be helpful to ask not only about the final product, but also about the process of working on these life lessons projects.

4. *Group evaluation* (10 mins)

The clients are asked to reflect on:

a. individual achievements and lessons learned
b. individual continuation of changes (what will you continue doing + via which concrete steps + what do you need for this continuation)
c. development of the group, and contributions to each other (clients are encouraged to tell each other what they have meant to each other, and to thank one other)
d. general evaluation

It may be beneficial to encourage clients to respond to each other, acknowledge the effort, be concrete in the steps that are required to continue change, and to create a positive atmosphere.

5. *Closing ritual* (5 mins)

The practitioners summarise today's session and acknowledge the individual contributions. The group closes with the ritual that the group has agreed upon at the beginning of this session.

Questionnaires

Meaning Quintet Questionnaire (MQQ)

© Dr Joel Vos, 2016

Aim

This questionnaire aims to help you understand better what you experience as meaningful in life. It also aims to help you discover which meaningful activities you are already doing and which you would like to do more in life.

Instruction

Below is a list of possible meaningful experiences in life. Give three scores to each experience.

1. In the first column, score how important this experience has been in your life (in any period in your life):

   1 = totally unimportant
   2 = somewhat unimportant
   3 = neither unimportant, nor important
   4 = somewhat important
   5 = totally important

2. In the second column, score how much you are experiencing, trying or doing this in this specific period in your life (since approximately six months ago):

   1 = seldom
   2 = not often
   3 = sometimes
   4 = often
   5 = very often

3. In the second column, score how much you would like to be experiencing, trying or doing this in future:

1 = seldom
2 = not often
3 = sometimes
4 = often
5 = very often

Some suggestions for scoring

All three questions are <u>not</u> about how successful you are; for example, if trying to become a billionaire is 'somewhat important' to you, although you are not a billionaire yet, you fill in 'somewhat important'.

When multiple examples are given, only one of these examples need to apply to you; for example, if you experience only one example 'often' and the other examples 'seldom', then you score 'often'. Ignore examples you do not understand.

Try not to think too long about the items, and try to give the scores intuitively. If you do not know which score to give, do what feels relatively the best.

Meaningful experience	How important has this been in your life until now?	How much are you doing, trying or experiencing this now?	How much would you like to be doing, trying or experiencing this in future?
	1 = totally unimportant 2 = somewhat unimportant 3 = neither unimportant, nor important 4 = somewhat important 5 = totally important	1 = seldom 2 = not often 3 = sometimes 4 = often 5 = very often	1 = seldom 2 = not often 3 = sometimes 4 = often 5 = very often
1 Being in a good, safe or enjoyable material situation E.g. good finances, good house, nice possessions, not needing to fight for physical survival	1 2 3 (4) 5	1 2 3 (4) 5	1 2 3 (4) 5
2 Having success E.g. being generally successful in life, having a successful career, being successful in school/education, having high social status or power	1 2 3 (4) 5	1 2 (3) 4 5 ←	1 2 3 (4) 5 ←
3 Enjoying nice physical experiences E.g. hedonism, fun, leisure, joyful activities, enjoying beauty (music, art, eating, drinking, etc.), sex, nature, animals, peak experiences	1 2 (3) 4 5	1 2 (3) 4 5	1 2 (3) 4 5
4 Enjoying good health E.g. being healthy, healthy lifestyle, sports	1 2 3 (4) 5	1 (2) 3 4 5 ←	1 2 3 4 (5) ←

	Meaningful experience	How important has this been in your life until now?					How much are you doing, trying or experiencing this now?					How much would you like to be doing, trying or experiencing this in future?				
		1	2	3	4	5	1	2	3	4	5	1	2	3	4	5
5	Coping successfully with difficult life situations E.g. being flexible, resilient, perseverance, hardiness, accepting challenges, effective coping skills, knowing what to do in stressful situations				④			②							④	
6	Being effective in achieving daily life activities or goals E.g. being effective in setting specific activities or goals, planning, organising, discipline, evaluating and adjusting, being in control			③					③					③		
7	Knowing myself E.g. self-insight					⑤			③						④	
8	Knowing myself and/or accepting myself for who I am E.g. self-acceptance, self-worth, self-esteem					⑤			③						④	
9	Being autonomous or self-reliant					⑤			③						④	
10	Expressing myself in creative ways E.g. speaking, writing, art		②					②					②			

Meaningful experience	How important has this been in your life until now?					How much are you doing, trying or experiencing this now?					How much would you like to be doing, trying or experiencing this in future?				
11 Taking good care of myself E.g. self-care	1	2	③	4	5	1	②	3	4	5	1	2	3	4	⑤
12 Feeling socially connected E.g. having good social skills, good connections with friends, family, intimate relationships or partner	1	2	③	4	5	1	2	③	4	5	1	2	3	④	5
13 Belonging to a specific community E.g. feeling that I am part of my family, community, history, society	1	2	③	4	5	1	②	3	4	5	1	2	3	④	5
14 Following social expectations E.g. doing what is socially expected, following social virtues, being conformist	1	2	③	4	5	1	2	③	④	5	1	2	3	④	5
15 Being altruistic E.g. helping other people, improving the well-being of others, being selfless or generous	1	2	3	4	5	1	2	3	4	5	1	2	3	4	5
16 Giving birth and/or taking care of children	1	2	3	4	5	1	2	3	4	5	1	2	3	4	5
17 Following higher purposes E.g. trying to achieve specific larger goals, purposes, aims or dreams in my life	1	2	3	4	5	1	2	3	4	5	1	2	3	4	5

Meaningful experience	How important has this been in your life until now?					How much are you doing, trying or experiencing this now?					How much would you like to be doing, trying or experiencing this in future?				
18 Trying to get the best out of myself E.g. personal growth, self-development, fulfilling my potential, self-transcendence, self-realisation, trying to become authentic or wise	1	2	3	4	5	1	2	3	4	5	1	2	3	4	5
19 Focusing on the future E.g. future-oriented, leaving a positive legacy to people who will live after my death, focusing on an afterlife, heaven or hell	1	2	3	4	5	1	2	3	4	5	1	2	3	4	5
20 Trying to overcome the past E.g. reflecting on the past, making something better of the background that I grew up in, solving mistakes in my past	1	2	3	4	5	1	2	3	4	5	1	2	3	4	5
21 Living in the here and now E.g. mindfulness	1	2	3	4	5	1	2	3	4	5	1	2	3	4	5
22 Being ethical and just E.g. following high ethical standards, being treated in a just way, contributing to a more just world	1	2	3	4	5	1	2	3	4	5	1	2	3	4	5

Meaningful experience	How important has this been in your life until now?					How much are you doing, trying or experiencing this now?					How much would you like to be doing, trying or experiencing this in future?				
23 Being spiritual or religious E.g. spirituality, religion, beliefs, worship or religious practices, insight in cosmic meaning, spiritual union, peace harmony and balance, belief in Absolute Beauty, Platonic Idea or Highest Good	1	2	3	4	5	1	2	3	4	5	1	2	3	4	5
24 Feeling alive	1	2	3	4	5	1	2	3	4	5	1	2	3	4	5
25 Being aware that I will die one day E.g. mortality, finitude, knowing that everything in life is temporal and can change	1	2	3	4	5	1	2	3	4	5	1	2	3	4	5
26 Being a unique individual: E.g. being unique as a person, having my own unique experiences, my own life and world around me	1	2	3	4	5	1	2	3	4	5	1	2	3	4	5
27 Being fundamentally connected with the world and people around me E.g. I am always in the world, in social relationships; I am always influenced by the larger context and I always influence a larger context	1	2	3	4	5	1	2	3	4	5	1	2	3	4	5

Meaningful experience	How important has this been in your life until now?					How much are you doing, trying or experiencing this now?					How much would you like to be doing, trying or experiencing this in future?				
28 Being individually free: E.g. I am free to make decisions, free to decide my attitude towards problems in life; I am able to leave a legacy to people who will live after my death	1	2	3	4	5	1	2	3	4	5	1	2	3	4	5
29 Being grateful for being alive: E.g. experiencing the mere fact that I am born and that I am still alive as a gift or a miracle; although I did not ask to be born, I see being-born as highly precious and special, for which I need to be grateful	1	2	3	4	5	1	2	3	4	5	1	2	3	4	5
30 Being individually responsible E.g. I and only I am responsible to make something from my life, no one else can do this instead of me; I am responsible to live up to my highest values	1	2	3	4	5	1	2	3	4	5	1	2	3	4	5
31 Other meaningful experiences (write down your own examples)	1	2	3	4	5	1	2	3	4	5	1	2	3	4	5

Coding instructions

Types of meanings (create a sum for each type of meaning in each column =
5 scales × 3 columns = 15 sums)

– Materialistic-hedonic meanings: sum of items 1–4; range = 4–20

– Self-oriented meanings: sum of items 5–11; range = 7–35

– Social meanings: sum of items 12–16; range = 5–25

– Higher meanings: sum of items 17–23; range = 7–35

– Meaning of being alive: sum of items 24–30; range = 8–40

Validity

– This scale has not been validated in scientific trials and there are no norm groups.

Alternative instruction

– Let individuals write examples from their own life for each item in the questionnaire.

Suggestions for interpretation

– What are extreme low or extreme high scores on individual items or on sum-scores for the types of meanings?

– Which type of meaning is more important than the other meanings? Is there one specific type of meaning specifically important ('pyramidal meaning system')? Or are all meanings equally important ('broad meaning system')? Or are there 4–5 parallel important meanings ('parallel meaning system')?

– Is there a discrepancy for types of meanings and/or for specific items between what is regarded important on the one hand and what individuals are experiencing, doing or trying at this moment in their life on the other hand?

– Is there a discrepancy for types of meanings and/or for specific items between what is regarded important on the one hand and what individuals would like to be experiencing, doing or trying in future on the other hand?

– Is there a discrepancy for types of meanings and/or for specific items between what individuals are experiencing, doing or trying at this moment in their life and what individuals would like to be experiencing, doing or trying in future on the other hand?

Meaning-Centred Practitioner Skills Questionnaire (MCPQ)

© Dr Joel Vos, 2016

Your level of confidence/competence in practising meaning-centred practice

For each of the principles of meaning-centred therapies below, please rate how well you feel you applied them. Use the following rating scale:

1	Much improvement in application needed: I felt like a *beginner*, as if I didn't have the concept.
2	Moderate improvement needed: I felt like an *advanced beginner*, who is beginning to do this, but needs to work on the concept more.
3	Slight improvement in application needed: I need to make a focused effort to do more of this.
4	Adequate application of principle: I did enough of this, but need to keep working on improving how well I do it.
5	Good application of principle: I did enough of this and did it skilfully.
6	Excellent application of principle: I did this consistently and even applied it in a creative way.

1. Exploring the client's request for support in a non-reductionist and multi-dimensional way	1	2	3	4	5	6
2. Assessing the immediate needs and life situation of the client	1	2	3	4	5	6
3. Developing a meaning-oriented case formulation	1	2	3	4	5	6
4. Using assessment as start of the meaning-centred change process	1	2	3	4	5	6
5. Using meaning-centred assessment tools and developing a meaning-centred profile	1	2	3	4	5	6
6. Providing meaning-centred didactics	1	2	3	4	5	6
7. Focusing on long-term meaning in life instead of on short-term gratification and pleasures, and showing the potential benefits of this focus	1	2	3	4	5	6
8. Identifying and explicating meaning-centered topics in the experiences of the clients	1	2	3	4	5	6
9. Offering clients a guided discovery of their meaning potential via specific exercises	1	2	3	4	5	6
10. Showing an unconditional positive regard about the possibility of finding meaning	1	2	3	4	5	6

(Continued)

	1	2	3	4	5	6
11. Addressing the totality of possible meanings in the client's life	1	2	3	4	5	6
12. Concretising and specifying meaning in daily life	1	2	3	4	5	6
13. Stimulating effective goal-management	1	2	3	4	5	6
14. Stimulating the client to connect with the larger temporal experience of past-present-future-legacy	1	2	3	4	5	6
15. Exploring meanings in the client's past, as a potential source for improving self-esteem, hope and inspiration for future meaning	1	2	3	4	5	6
16. Stimulating the client to give an independent-but-connected answer to the social context	1	2	3	4	5	6
17. Focusing on meanings that are based on and that stimulate self-worth and self-compassion	1	2	3	4	5	6
18. Tailoring the practice to the needs, skills and wishes of the client	1	2	3	4	5	6
19. Shared decision-making (macro-level)	1	2	3	4	5	6
20. Exploring and macro-communication about which meanings the client expresses in the relationship with the practitioner	1	2	3	4	5	6
21. Improving and deepening the practitioner-client relationship	1	2	3	4	5	6
22. Following the tempo of progress of the client	1	2	3	4	5	6
23. Empathizing with the client's struggles in life, and stressing that existential struggles are common to all human-beings	1	2	3	4	5	6
24. Recognising the importance of existing meanings, religious and cultural context	1	2	3	4	5	6
25. Helping the client to develop ethical and authentic relationships, and having an ethical stance towards the client and their situation	1	2	3	4	5	6
26. Phenomenological explorations of the experiences of the client	1	2	3	4	5	6
27. Stimulating an attitude of experiential acceptance	1	2	3	4	5	6
28. Stimulating clients to immerse themselves in the flow of meaningful experiences	1	2	3	4	5	6
29. Phenomenologically exploring whether there are any hierarchies in the client's experiences of meaning	1	2	3	4	5	6
30. Using a questioning approach	1	2	3	4	5	6
31. Using experiential exercises focusing on inner awareness and intuition	1	2	3	4	5	6
32. Using non-intellectual therapeutic techniques	1	2	3	4	5	6
33. Empathising, recognizing, naming and exploring the existential dimension in the clients' experiences	1	2	3	4	5	6
34. Stimulating meaning-centred coping with situations of suffering	1	2	3	4	5	6

35. Exploring paradoxical feelings about meaning in life, and fostering acceptance of paradoxes and tensions	1	2	3	4	5	6
36. Identifying avoidance and denial of meaning-related topics, exploring the reasons of avoidance and denial, and trying to overcome this	1	2	3	4	5	6
37. Stimulating clients to take up their own responsibility for living a meaningful life	1	2	3	4	5	6
Total score for assessment, meaning-centred, relational, phenomenological and existential skills	**SUM SCORE**					
38. Setting up the parameters of the group, establishing rules and limits (e.g. safety), managing time, and interceding when the group goes off course in some way ('executive function')	1	2	3	4	5	6
39. Establishing group norms	1	2	3	4	5	6
40. Stimulating group interaction and feedback between group members, and fostering constructive interpersonal skills	1	2	3	4	5	6
41. Identifying the different roles that individual group members have in the group	1	2	3	4	5	6
42. Identifying the stage of the group development, and leading the development towards the next stage and towards group cohesion	1	2	3	4	5	6
43. Stimulating meta-communication about roles and exploration of alternative roles of group members with disruptive roles in the group	1	2	3	4	5	6
44. Maintaining the cohesion of the group in case of any specific group-specific events	1	2	3	4	5	6
45. Balancing a focus on the task of the session and the group process	1	2	3	4	5	6
Total score for group skills	**SUM SCORE**					
46. Following the structure of the practice manual	1	2	3	4	5	6
47. Having meta-communication and fostering shared decision-making about the decision to use the therapy manual	1	2	3	4	5	6
48. Using the manual in a flexible client-oriented way	1	2	3	4	5	6
49. Continuously assessing and evaluating outcomes and processes in practice, to tailor the practice optimally to the client.	1	2	3	4	5	6
Total score for flexible treatment manual skills	**SUM SCORE**					

Meaning in Life Questionnaire (MLQ)

© Dr Michael Steger, 2002

The Meaning in Life Questionnaire

MLQ Please take a moment to think about what makes your life feel important to you. Please respond to the following statements as truthfully and accurately as you can, and also please remenber that these are very subjective questions and that there are no right or wrong answers. Please answer according to the scale below:

Absolutely Untrue	Mostly Untrue	Somewhat Untrue	Can't Say True or False	Somewhat True	Mostly True	Absolutely True
1	2	3	4	5	6	7

1. ____ I understand my life's meaning.

2. ____ I am looking for something that makes life feel meaningful.

3. ____ I am always looking to find my life's purpose.

4. ____ My life has a clear sense of purpose.

5. ____ I have a good sense of what makes my life meaningful.

6. ____ I have discovered a satisfying life purpose.

7. ____ I am always searching for something that makes my life feel significant.

8. ____ I am seeking a purpose or mission for my life.

9. ____ My life has no clear purpose.

10. ____ I am searching for meaning in my life.

MLQ syntax to create Presence and Search subscales:
Presence = 1, 4, 5, 6, & 9-reversed-coded
Search = 2, 3, 7, 8, & 10

Goal Attainment Form

© Dr Mick Cooper, 2015

Instruction:

As we have discussed in the first group session, the overall aim of this group is to 'help individuals live a meaningful and satisfying life despite any problems they may be experiencing in life'. This overall aim is deliberately formulated in a general way, so that every group member can formulate their own specific goals within this overall aim, and to try to achieve this aim during the nine group sessions. Therefore we would like to ask you to write any specific goals you would like to achieve by participating in this group. During the last session, we will ask you to fill in to which extent you have achieved each goal (these are the numbers in grey in the Goal Assessment form below). During the next sessions, you can share your goals with the group if you'd like. You do not need to fill in each goal.

Goal 1:						
Not at all achieved						Completely achieved
1	2	3	4	5	6	7

Goal 2:						
Not at all achieved						Completely achieved
1	2	3	4	5	6	7

Goal 3:						
Not at all achieved						Completely achieved
1	2	3	4	5	6	7

Goal 4:

Not at all achieved   Completely achieved

| 1 | 2 | 3 | 4 | 5 | 6 | 7 |

Goal 5:

Not at all achieved   Completely achieved

| 1 | 2 | 3 | 4 | 5 | 6 | 7 |

Reading Suggestions

1. American Group Psychotherapy Association (AGPA). (2007). *Practice guidelines for group psychotherapy.* New York: American Group Psychotherapy Association.
2. Andresen, R., Oades, L. G., & Caputi, P. (2011). *Psychological recovery: Beyond mental illness.* Hoboken, NJ: John Wiley & Sons (Overview of the recovery model of mental health).
3. Batthyany, A., & Russo-Netzer, P. (2014). *Meaning in positive and existential psychology.* New York: Springer (Overview of empirical studies).
4. Cooper, M. (2008). *Essential research findings in counselling and psychotherapy: The facts are friendly.* London: SAGE (Introduction to therapy research).
5. Cooper, M. (2016). *Existential therapies.* London: SAGE (Overview of existential therapies).
6. Cox, G. (2014). *How to be an existentialist or how to get real, get a grip and stop making excuses.* London: Bloomsbury (Introduction to Sartre's existential philosophy).
7. Frankl, V.E.(1948/1985). Man's search for meaning. Simon and Schuster.
8. Frankl, V. E. (1985). *Man's search for meaning.* New York: Simon and Schuster (Cornerstone of most meaning-centred treatments).
9. Gilbert, P. (2010). *Compassion-focused therapy: Distinctive features.* New York: Taylor & Francis.
10. Hayes, S. C., Strosahl, K. D., & Wilson, K. G. (2012). *Acceptance and commitment therapy. The process and practice of mindful change.* The Guildford Press.
11. Mearns, D., & Cooper, M. (2005). *Working at relational depth in counselling and psychotherapy.* London: SAGE (Introduction to relational-therapeutic skills).
12. Neimeyer, R. A. (2001). *Meaning reconstruction and the experience of loss.* Washington, DC: American Psychological Association (Introduction to meaning reconstruction).
13. O'Connell, B. (2005). *Solution-focused therapy.* London; Sage.
14. Russo-Netzer, P., Schulenberg, S. E., & Batthyany, A. (eds.). (2016). *Clinical perspectives on meaning: Meaning in positive and existential psychotherapy.* New York: Springer (Overview of meaning-centred practitioner skills).
15. Segal, Z. V., Williams, J. M. G., & Teasdale, J. D. (2012). *Mindfulness-based cognitive therapy for depression.* New York: Guilford Press (Examples of mindfulness exercises).
16. Spinelli, E. (2005). *The interpreted world. An introduction to phenomenological psychology.* London: SAGE (An introduction to phenomenology and phenomenological skills).

17. Steger, M. F., Kashdan, T. B., Sullivan, B. A., & Lorentz, D. (2008). Understanding the search for meaning in life: Personality, cognitive style, and the dynamic between seeking and experiencing meaning. *Journal of Personality, 76*(2), 199–228.

18. Vos, J. (2014). Meaning and existential givens in the lives of cancer clients: A philosophical perspective on psycho-oncology. *Palliative & Supportive Care, 12*(9), 1–16.

19. Vos, J. (2014). Meaning and existential givens in the lives of cancer clients: A philosophical perspective on psycho-oncology. *Palliative & Supportive Care, 12*(9), 1–16 (Relationship between existential and meaning-centred skills).

20. Vos, J. (2016a). Working with meaning in life in mental health care: A systematic literature review and meta-analyses of practices and effectiveness. In: Russo-Netzer, P., Schulenberg, S. E., & Batthyany, A. (eds.). *Clinical perspective on meaning: Meaning in positive and existential psychotherapy.* New York: Springer (Overview of meaning-centred coping with physical disease and other life changes).

21. Vos, J. (2016b). Working with meaning in life in chronic or life-threatening disease: A review of its relevance and effectiveness of meaning-centred therapies. In: P. Russo-Netzer, S. E. Schulenberg & A. Batthyany (eds.). *Clinical perspectives on meaning: Meaning in positive and existential psychotherapy.* New York: Springer (Overview of evidence-based meaning-centred treatments).

22. Vos, J. (2018a). Death in existential psychotherapies: A critical review. In: Menzies, R. G., Menzies, R. E. Iverach, L. *Curing the dread of death: Theory, research and practice.* Sydney: Australian Academic Press (On coping with death in existential therapies).

23. Vos, J. (2018b). A review of research on phenomenological-existential therapies. In: Van Deurzen et al. (eds.) *World handbook on phenomenological-existential therapies.* London: SAGE (Review of evidence-based phenomenological competences in therapy).

24. Vos, J. & Vitali, D. (2018). Psychological meaning-centered therapies: A systematic literature review and meta-analyses. *Journal of Supportive and Palliative Care* (in print) (Evidence for effectiveness of meaning-centred practices in clinical trials worldwide).

25. Wong, P. T. (ed.). (2013). *The human quest for meaning: Theories, research, and applications.* London: Routledge (Overview of research on meaning).

Index

This index shows subjects and authors mentioned in the main text. A full reference list with the names of all authors can be found on the companion website. Authors are printed in *italics*. Terms in **bold** are defined on the companion website of this book:

absurdity   16, 61, 86, 265
acceptance
  experiential acceptance   148–50, 154, 217
  of life's givens and paradoxes 179–83
  self-acceptance, example of self-oriented meaning   65–7, 240–50
Acceptance and Action Questionnaire   112, 149
  see also Flexibility Scale
Acceptance and Commitment Therapy   91, 149, 156, 241
act as if   84, 154, 169
addiction   12, 24, 79, 185
Adler, Alfred   88, 127
aesthetic enjoyment
  materialistic-hedonic meaning   66–7
aetiology   90, 97, 100, 105–9
Africa   28–30, 52
aims
  in life   19, 21, 68–9, 84, 123–7, 152, 256, 268
  of meaning-centered practices xv–xvii, 81–2, 91–3, 109–10, 137–40, 147, 174, 189, 197, 202, 276
  see also goals, Goal Assessment Form
alternative list making exercise   156
altruism   17, 65–6, 248, 251–21
Altruism Scale   112

Animals
  example of materialistic-hedonic meaning   5, 10, 32, 65
  see also nature
animal rationale   7, 9, 36
anxiety   118–9,125, 127, 153–6, 167, 192, 198, 202–3, 232–4, 239
  see also death anxiety, life anxiety
appealing technique   249
Arendt, Hannah   185
Aristotle, see also teleology   7, 11, 28, 34, 80, 265
art
  example of materialistic-hedonic meaning   66–7
  using in sessions   168–73
attitude
  change of, *or* modulation of   89, 95, 175–7, 228
  modulation interventions   154, 157–8, 164, 224, 226, 228, 276
  collectivistic   152
  dual attitude   59, 64, 111, 151–154, 159, 180
  fanatical   152
  fatalistic   152
  letting-be, *see also* bracketing, Gelassenheit   27
  obsessive   153
  passive   153
  phenomenological, *see also* bracketing, phenomenology   13, 168
  provisionary   152

attitude (*continued*)
  route to meaning, *see* Franklian triad   66
  sceptical   17, 26, 35
  towards life situation   xxiv, 66, 68, 89, 95, 120, 122, 146, 175, 178, 184, 224, 228
  unhelpful attitudes, overview of   40, 148–52, 164
  See also acceptance, experiential acceptance, hyper-intention, hyper-reflection, pyramidal or horizontal meaning system
authenticity
  example of hot inside flow of experiencing   80–2
  relevance   XV, 15, 38, 40, 42–7, 51, 59, 67, 74, 84, 89, 98, 132, 136, 142–4, 147, 179, 182, 219, 255–6
Authenticity Scale   112
authobiographic writing exercise   95, 171
automatic pilot
  example of cold outside reflections   74, 77
autonomy   65–8, 72, 96, 130–2, 247
avoidance   41, 67, 131, 153, 181–5
  see also existential defence mechanism, experiential avoidance
Aztecs   28

Bad faith   175, 184–5
  see also responsibility
balance in life   xiv, 47, 65–8, 113, 121, 130–1, 247, 268
Basic Psychological Needs Assessment Scale   112
Baumeister, Roy   55, 79–80
Becker, Ernest   59, 180, 263
Becker, Gary   20
behaviour   80, 113, 118, 122, 125, 132, 142, 145–6, 156, 170–2, 174, 176–7
  see also passive attitude, obsessive attitude
behaviourism, behavioural therapy, cognitive behaviour therapy   xvi, 9, 27, 63, 90–3, 97, 99, 100, 105, 119, 135, 151, 162

being-alive
  example of existential-philosophical meaning   66, 68, 175, 263–4, 269–78
being-here, *see* being-alive
being until death   66, 68
beliefs, religious
  example of larger meaning   66–8, 268
belonging to a community, sense of
  example of social meaning   65–8
benevolence, example of fundamental assumption   82–3
bereavement   62, 101, 217, 269, 285
Berman, Marshall   15, 18
birth, giving
  example of social meaning   65–68, 216, 234, 239, 258, 260
body scan exercise   249–250
Bohlmeijer, Ernst   129, 130, 171
Bonaventura, Giovanni   11
Borderline Personality Disorder   63
Born, being
  existential-philosophical meaning   65–68, 70, 175, 256, 263, 271, 274
  see also lifeline exercise
Boszormenyi-Nagy, Ivan   131
Breitbart, William   146, 171, 191, 202, 265
bottom-up meanings   48–51, 165
  see also scales of meaning
boundary situation   88, 141, 177
breathing exercise   148, 181, 214–5, 225, 231
Buddhism   26–27, 37, 40, 77, 79, 167, 177

Cancer, *see under* physical disease
Can (not), *see also* meaning development triangle
Capitalist life syndrome   18, 22–5
Card Sorting Test (Q sort)   160
challenges
  coping with, as self-oriented meaning   62–8
  existential   174–15
  addressing in sessions   222–33, 278–84
  see also copingstyle, resilience

change in life, *or* changeability 179,
202, 208–21, 242, 254, 256
see also attitude change, boundary
situation
changes in therapy 125–126
childhood, experiences of 48, 62,
69–72, 129–31, 164, 168–70,
213, 230
children, giving birth and caring
example of social meaning 65–9,
74, 79, 126–9, 248, 251–8, 260
choice overload 16, 25
Chochinov, Harvey 129, 171
clergy, priest, vicar, theologian xiii,
10, 12–13, 88
see also pastoral care
Climacus, John 10
Clinical trial, outcomes of 72, 90,
93–102, 130, 139, 147, 149,
165, 174, 176, 182–3, 190–2
cognitive behaviour therapy
see behaviourism
cognitive dissonance reduction 11
coherence, sense of 19, 57, 68, 94,
102, 126–9
cold outside reflections on meaning in
life 27, 73–6, 87, 145
see examples theorising,
intellectualising, hyper-
reflection, hyper-intention,
automatic pilot, following
others, crisis
collectivism 15, 36, 152
see also attitude, collectivist
common denominator of practices
xv, xx, xxv, 100, 102, 171, 190
common factor in practices xvi,
92, 101
commitment xix, 25, 58, 60, 61, 73,
79, 83, 96–7, 108, 117, 123–7,
152, 156–7, 178, 184–5
cognitive behaviour therapy
see behaviourism
cognitive defusion 156
cognitive subliminal experiments 59,
112–113
Conceptual Well-Being Scale 112
**Concretising and specifying
meaning in daily life** 123,
147,150, 154, 163, 180

conformism 17, 65, 68–72, 255–6
Confucius 26
confrontation
exercises 142, 153, 154, 270
in life xxiv, 16, 41, 59, 61, 63, 83,
96, 117, 141–2, 176–7, 181, 183,
223, 241
see also boundary situation, life's
givens
connectedness
example of social meaning 65–8,
130–2, 159, 179, 248, 251–7,
260, 274
construction of meaning 46, 51,
53, 61, 91, 130, 148
constructivism, *see* construction of
meaning
**continuum of meaning-centered
practices** 91, 101
control, sense of 152–3, 175, 180,
183–5
example of fundamental
assumption 82–3
example of self-oriented meaning
65–8
Cooper, Mick 16, 56, 106, 109,
111, 126, 135, 136–7, 139,
141–2, 147, 174, 176, 181–3,
301–302
coping, or coping style 16, 50,
56–9, 65, 76–7, 96, 98, 106–7,
121, 127, 139, 164–5, 177–83,
222–8, 247, 276, 278–84
see also challenges, resilience
Coping Schema Inventory 112
cosmic meaning 57, 66–8, 160,
268
creative self-expression xxiv, 65–7,
78, 125, 237, 247
creativity in exercises 151, 154,
169–73, 284
see also art, creative self-expression
crisis 98, 108, 183
example of cold outside reflections
on meaning in life 73–6
existential xxiv, 59, 75, 83, 85,
111, 159
identity 75, 85
meaning 75, 83, 85, 111, 152
midlife 12, 168

crisis (*continued*)
  psychological   23, 75, 153
  religious *or* spiritual   75, 85
  societal   23, 88, 90
Csikszentmihalyi, Mihaly   xvi, 37, 77,
  124

Daoism   27, 30
death   63, 66, 68, 88–9, 141, 175–7,
  182–3, 262–8
  anxiety, Angst   16, 63, 127–8,
    175–7, 182–3, 262–8
  Death Attitude Profile   112
  deathbed exercise   164–5, 170, 177,
    265–6
Dennett, Daniel   14, 49
Descartes, Rene   14
decision-making   xix–xx, xxv, 13, 18,
  25, 46, 52, 57, 61, 66–71, 74,
  81, 83–4, 96, 109, 130–3, 150,
  175, 184–5, 264, 274, 279–80
  exercises   46, 71 3, 109, 132–3,
    173, 177, 238
degrees of authenticity   81
denial   8–10, 16, 34, 59, 83, 148, 152,
  179–85, 223, 228
  see also existential defence
    mechanism
depression   12, 32, 44, 75–6, 79,
  90, 94, 99, 125, 130, 152, 168,
  274
de-reflection   xxii–xxiii, 89, 99, 155,
  158, 167, 180
  exercises   xxiv, 154, 156
Deurzen, Emmy Van   141, 147, 174,
  176–9
diagnosis, psychological   105, 107–9,
  198
  see also **meaning-centered
    assessment**
Dialectical Behaviour Therapy   63
didactics   xviii, xix, 52, 76, 96, 106,
  116–7, 119, 122, 137, 154, 164,
  189, 191
  see also psycho-education
Diener, Ed   23, 79, 82, 125
directivity, *see also* **non-directive**
  137
discontent   75, 150, 154, 205

discovery of meaning   22, 26, 39,
  43, 45, 51, 119, 141, 147, 149,
  166–8, 170, 208–9, 297
double hermeneutics   46–7
Downwards Arrow Technique   160
Drama, *or* logodrama   171
Drawing exercise   169, 173, 215–6,
  284
dual attitude
  see under attitude
Duintjer, Otto   39

effectiveness, *see under* empirical
  research
Eckhart, Meister   4–8, 13, 27, 30, 36–7,
  43
education
  in sessions, *see* didactics,
    psycho-education
  Meaning in Life Education   100
  of practitioners   96
  example of self-oriented
    meaning   65–8, 235–8
eudaimonia   7–8
effective goal-management   123–6
Egypt, Ancient   28
embodiment of meaning   xviii, 9,
  20, 27–9, 35, 38, 40, 44–5, 54–7,
  96, 147, 163, 166–8, 171
Emmons, Robert A.   56–58, 125
empathy, of practitioner   105, 110,
  119, 121, 136, 141–2, 147, 149,
  162–3, 176–8
empirical research
  on meaning   66–87
  on effectiveness of meaning-
    centered practices   93–6
  on effectiveness of practitioner
    skills   103–86
  see also evidence-based, trial
empiricism   14
empty chair technique   170
Enlightenment   14–1, 22
equifinality   64
Erikson, Erik   72–3
eschatology   10–11
ethics, ethical stance   8, 17, 51, 53,
  65, 142–144, 185, 268
evidence-based, *see* empirical research

existential
existential analysis   89, 91, 149
Existential Anxiety
    Questionnaire   112
existential avoidance *or* denial
    see avoidance, denial, existential
    defence mechanisms
existential defence mechanisms   16,
    59, 88, 179–85
    see also avoidance, denial
existential moods   xvii, 16, 45, 84,
    113, 175–7, 181–3
    existential anxiety   94, 183, 219,
        270
        see also death anxiety
    existential isolation *or*
        loneliness   118–9, 175, 269
    existential vacuum   11, 62, 75, 98
    guilt   12, 18, 24, 35, 61, 72, 86, 89,
        121, 175, 177
    overwhelmed   16, 63, 84, 119,
        149–150, 175, 181, 198, 205,
        214, 216, 223–5, 231, 234, 239
    urgency   175
existential limitation   68–69, 74,
    83–6, 92–6, 102, 106, 120–1,
    129, 131, 150, 154, 175–82,
    197, 213, 219, 223, 224, 247
    see fundamental assumption
existential paradoxes   39, 96, 141,
    151, 154, 165, 170, 179–85
existential-philosophical meanings
    definition   65–8
    relevance   80, 98, 106, 158, 160, 209
    session on   269–77
    see examples being alive, being born,
        feeling alive, being until death,
        uniqueness, being in the world,
        connectedness, freedom of
        decision, gratitude to life as a
        gift, responsibility
existential practitioner skills   96,
    174–86
experiences, *see* Franklian triad
experiential acceptance   148–54,
    157, 217
    see also acceptance
experiential avoidance   146, 149
    see also experiential acceptance

experiential exercise   xviii, 145–73, 189
external perspective on meaning,
    see cold outside reflection on
    meaning
extremism   25, 34

Fabry, Joseph   47, 60, 91, 143,
    155–156, 158, 169–73
faith   89, 154, 160, 179
    see also religion
family, example of social meaning
    65–73, 107, 114, 119, 130–132,
    157, 159, 178–183, 196–197,
    213–4, 225, 230, 238, 253, 256,
    258, 260, 271
fast forwarding technique   170
fat ego   24
feeling culture   18
finances, example of materialistic-
    hedonic meaning   65–68
Financial Worries and Illness
    Perception Questionnaire   112
Finding Positive Meaning Scale   112
finitude, *see* death, mortality
flexibility, *see also* coping style   58–59,
    65–68, 98, 106, 111, 138, 159,
    178, 181–3, 192, 228, 247
Flexibility Scale, *also called* Acceptance
    and Action Questionnaire   112
flow
    example of hot inside flow of
        experiencing   29, 43, 44, 51–4,
        73, 76–87, 98, 102, 108, 124–5,
        145–73, 196
Flourishing Scale   112
focusing exercise   165–7
following others
    example of cold outside
        reflections   73–6
FOMO, Fear Of Missing Out   21, 61
Fonagy, Peter   97, 122–3, 142
Foucault, Michel   22
Frankl, Viktor   xxii, 18, 20, 30, 34,
    56, 60, 62, 66, 75, 89–91, 106,
    115, 120–21, 127, 129, 143,
    151, 154–5, 158, 160, 172, 177,
    183–4, 222–5, 228, 264, 274
Franklian triad   66, 89, 98, 191
    compare meaning quintet

friends, *see* social meaning

Fromm, Erich 20

freedom xiv, xxiv, 21, 37, 46–8, 52–5, 59, 66, 68, 70–3, 78, 85–6, 127, 129–32, 143, 160, 175, 181, 183–5, 264, 274

freedom of will 89

see also freedom, frustrated will to meaning

Freedom Questionnaire 112

frustrated will to meaning 75, 98

functional meanings or **functionalism** xx, 17–33

future orientation 43, 56, 65, 68, 77, 82, 122, 124–32, 148, 158, 164, 170–3, 216, 253, 256, 260, 271

Gelassenheit *or* let-it-be 27, 43

Gendlin, Eugene 166–7

gift, life as a gift
  example of larger meaning 66–6, 264–5, 274

goal
  Goal Assessment Form xx, 112, 301
  in daily life
  of clients, *see* shared informed decision-making
  of each session 189–190
  of meaning-centered practices
  limitations of
  management, *see* effective goal-management
  setting exercise xxv, 94, 97, 122–6, 140, 191, 212–3, 217, 219

Goethe, Johan Wolfgang von 16

Good, The Highest, *see* larger meaning

gratitude, *see also* gift 66–8, 154, 264–5

Gratitude Scale 112

Greenberg, Jeff 59, 113, 180, 263

grief, *see* bereavement

Grief and Meaning Reconstruction Scale 112

group skills 192, 299

guided exercises 95–96, 116, 119, 123, 158

Guided fantasy 170

guilt, *see* existential guilt

happiness
  difference from meaning 9, 33, 85, 204–5
  example of hot inside flow of experiencing
  happiness paradox 23–5, 32, 69, 80, 85
  quick happiness 18, 24, 35, 54, 79–80, 90, 108
  slow happiness 19, 79–80, 108

hardines 65–8, 247

Hardiness Scale 112

harmony 65–8, 79, 268

Hayes, Steven C. 140, 149, 156, 241

hedonism
  example of materialistic-hedonic meaning 9, 23, 27, 28, 32, 44, 65–68, 79, 143, 152, 209, 237

Hedonic Experiences Scale 112

Hedonism Scale 112

Heidegger, Martin 10, 16, 27, 28, 30, 37, 39, 40, 43–9, 56, 61, 74, 128, 150, 175–6, 182, 264

hierarchy exercises, *see also* mountain range exercise 156–61

hinduism 26–8, 37, 128

history, social-cultural, *see* social meaning

holism 106–07, 111

hot inside flow of experiencing 27, 73–82, 85, 87, 98
  compare cold outside reflection

Hilton, Walter 11

Hoffman, Louis 26

horizontal axis of meaning 159

housing *or* living conditions
  example of materialistic-hedonic meaning 65–68

Hume, David 14

humor 153, 156, 229, 235, 237

Husserl, Edmund 17, 38, 42, 147

horizontal axis of meaning 153, 159, 170

hyper-intention 84, 99–100, 153, 155–156, 219
  example of cold outside reflections 73–6

hyper-reflection 84, 92, 99–100, 110, 113, 123, 153, 155–156, 167, 196, 219
example of cold outside reflections 73–7

identifying and explicating topics in the experiences of the clients 117–9, 154, 156, 176–83
ikigai 28–9, 31
inclusion criteria 107, 109, 192
individualism 70, 130
informed decision, *see* shared decision
immortality, example of fundamental assumption 82–3
inner conflict 142, 159–60, 165, 170, 171, 240–6
integration in life story 48, 177–8
intellectualising, *see also* rationalising, theorising 62, 110, 138, 169, 180
example of cold outside reflections on meaning in life 73–6
internal perspective on meaning, *see* hot inside flow of experiencing
Intimate relationships
example of social meaning 65–8
intuitive hierarchy xxii, xxiv, 38–9, 43, 46–8, 62, 95, 101, 147, 156–61, 165, 179, 209
see also hierarchy exercises
intuition, *see* phenomenological intuition
Invulnerability, example of fundamental assumption 82–3
Islam 29

Jainism 26
James, William 41, 88, 169
Jaspers, Karl 26, 88–89, 141, 177, 224
joy, or enjoyment xvii, xxiii, 21, 50, 65–8, 120, 125, 133, 139, 141, 148, 158, 161, 197, 210, 215, 221, 229, 235, 237, 263
see also happiness, hedonism
Judaism 29, 128
Jung, Carl Gustav 46, 61, 137, 168
justice 65–8, 141, 177, 262–8

Kant, Immanuel 14, 52
Kierkegaard, Soren 37, 128

ladder of nature 3–12, 14, 21, 29, 32–3, 37–8, 43
Langle, Alfried 64, 81, 91, 146, 149
Lantz, Jim 131, 169, 172–173
larger meaning
definition 65–8
relevance 14, 23–4, 43, 48, 118, 209
session on 233, 254, 260–268
see examples purposes, aims, personal growth, self-transcendance, self-realisation, authenticity, temporality, sense of coherence, future-oriented, past reflection on, legacy, lifeline, justice, ethics, spirituality, religion, beliefs, cosmic meaning, union, peace, harmony and balance; Platonic Idea, Highest Good
legacy
example of larger meaning 66–8, 126–30, 171, 182, 260, 265–71
leisure
example of materialistic-hedonic meaning 52, 65–8
Lerner, Michael 17
letter to a friend exercise 271–72, 275
letter writing exercises 132, 170, 172, 271–2, 275
Levinas, Emmanuel 39, 128, 184
life anxiety
example of existential mood 175–7, 262–8
life Fulfilment Scale 112
life lessons exercise 112
lifeline exercise 170, 270–1, 275
life mosaic exercise 170
Life Orientation Scale 112
life review exercise 95, 129
life satisfaction
example of hot inside flow of experiencing xvii, 23, 76, 82, 98, 108, 113–4, 129, 132

Life Satisfaction Test 112
life's limits, life's givens, *see*
  existential limitation
life span, *see* existential-philosophical
  meaning
living a meaningful and satisfying
  life despite life's limitations
  aim of meaning-centered
    practices 73, 76–82, 92, 99,
    151, 174, 179, 182, 242–3, 280
logo-anchor, *or* logo-hook 171
  see also safe place exercise
logo-test 112
logotherapy 89–91
loss, *see* bereavement
love
  example of social meaning xiii, 4,
    6, 11, 13, 16, 20, 26, 28–9, 36–7,
    131, 146, 154, 156, 160, 170,
    185, 242–4
Lukas, Elizabeth 56, 76, 89–91, 96–7,
    105–7, 110, 137, 151, 159, 185,
    194, 196
Luther, Marten 5, 13, 37

macro level of the therapeutic
    relationship 136–8
magic wand exercise 171
Major Life Goals Measure 112
manual application skills, *or*
  flexible treatment manual
  skills 192, 299
map/landscape-fallacy 16, 38, 74
Marshall, Maria & Marshall,
    Edward 106, 151, 154–6
mask making exercise 171
materialistic-hedonic meanings
  definition 65–8
  relevance 43, 49, 65–8, 80, 98, 106,
    143, 147, 153, 160, 168
  session on 232–9
  see examples finances, housing,
    possessions, success, hedonism,
    fun, leisure, aesthetic
    enjoyments, art, sex, nature
    and animals, peak experiences,
    pain avoidance, physical health,
    sports
McIntyre, Alisdair 21

McMeanings, *see* functional meanings
meaning-centered assessment
  skills 105–115, 194–200
meaning-centered case formulation
    107–110, 194–200
meaning-centered coping, *see*
  coping
Meaning-Centered Practices (MCP),
  explanation of terminology
  xv, xviii, xix
meaning-centered profile 113–114
meaning-centered unconditional
  positive regard xxiv, 120–121
meaning development triangle
    69–73
meaningful life projects 125–6,
    142, 146, 151, 191, 286, 287
meaningful objects exercise 230
meaning in life, explanation of
  term xv–xviii, 55–60, 201–10
meaninglessness 61–64, 84–85, 108,
    118, 130, 176, 179–181
meaning-making 18–20, 208
meaning of being-alive, *see*
  existential-philosophical
  meaning
Meinung 29–30, 36–7, 149
Meaning-centered Practitioner Skills
  Questionnaire 112, 297–9
Meaningful Life Measure 112
meaningful moments exercise 221
meaningful pin-up board exercise 238
Meaning in Life Questionnaire
    111–2, 300
Meaning Quintet Questionnaire
    288–96
Meaning Reconstruction Scale 112
Mearns, David 135–7, 139
meso-level of the therapeutic
    relationship 136–8
meta-communication, *see also*
  macro-level of the therapeutic
  relationship 51, 299
metaphysics 38, 51, 81, 147, 148,
    178
method of meaning-centered practices,
    summary of xviii–xix
micro level of the therapeutic
    relationship 136–8

micro-, meso-, macro- meanings, *see* scales of meaning

micro-, meso-, macro- perspectives on the client-practitioner relationship 136–8

middle ages 3–11, 88

mindfulness
example of cold outside reflections 77–78
relevance xv, xviii, 44–5, 77–8, 94–8, 108, 122–3, 132, 139
practitioner skills 145–173

mindfulness exercises 189, 204–5, 214–5, 225, 234, 265, 279–80

modelling, being a role model 47, 136, 143, 172, 254–5

modulation of attitudes, *see* attitude change

Montaigne, Michel de 14

Morita therapy 27

mourning over lost meanings 95, 170, 217, 264, 274

motivation 50, 55–60, 73, 108–109, 124–126, 142

motivational interviewing 91

mountain range exercise 95, 124, 158, 160, 280–283

mortality, *see also* death, existential limits, finitude 59, 175–176, 182–183

multifinality 64

multi-sensory, *see also* embodiment, Sinn 13, 27, 29, 35, 37, 39, 41, 43, 44, 77, 122, 163, 166–167

music, example of materialistic-hedonic meaning 65–8

must (not), *see* meaning development triangle

mysticism 26, 27, 29, 42, 128

narcissism 62, 229

nature, connection with as *type of meaning* 65–68, 229–230, 235, 260

Neimeyer, Robert 61, 62, 81, 91, 175, 178

Nietzsche, Friedrich xiii, 14, 27, 37, 43, 48, 69, 76, 80, 125, 128, 264

nine-Eleven, 9/11 59, 83

non-intellectualising exercises 169–173

No Meaning Scale 112

non-directivity, *see also* directivity 137–138, 141, 178

normalising xvii, 141, 177, 181

nudging 172, 191

observation, as assessment skill 112

obsession, *see* obsessive attitude

optimism, example of self-oriented meaning 65–8

organising, *see* goal management, self-oriented meaning

pain, physical, *see under* physical health

paradoxes 39, 96, 141, 151, 154, 159, 165, 170, 177–185

paradoxical intention 89, 156, 159

past, reflection on 65–73, 95, 109, 117–118, 126–130, 141, 158, 164, 170–171, 178, 197, 211–218, 237, 268

pastoral care, *see also* clergy xv, xvi, 88, 91

pathoplastics 106

peace, *see* social meaning 65–68

peak experiences
example of hot inside experiencing 78
relevance 43, 50, 65–68, 98, 108, 117, 175, 204

Pennebaker 171

perseverance 65–68, 214, 247

personal growth, *see* larger meaning 65–68, 144, 268

Personal Meaning Profile 112

phenomenology, method xix, 3, 9, 16–17, 22, 25–32, 36–54, 62–64, 76–82, 101, 108, 111, 113, 128, 137–138, 143, 145–173, 199

phenomenological assessment, *see* meaning-centered assessment

phenomenological intuition 117, 120

intuition

phenomenological meanings 56–57, 60

phenomenological, experiential and mindfulness skills 145–173

phenomenological steps 43–43, 146

phenomenological unpeeling 27, 35, 39–44, 77, 146–148, 161

physical
 cancer xx, 83–4, 118, 130, 177–9, 182, 191–2
 disease, health, well-being xvi–xviii, 5, 83, 95, 98, 100–1, 107, 177–81, 191–2, 201–31
 effects of meaning-centered practices 93–96
 pain 177, 192, 196, 202–5, 213, 217, 224, 231, 234, 237, 239, 241, 243, 249

photo exercise 172

planning, see goal management, self-oriented meaning

Plato 7, 11, 66–8

pluralism 137, 140

possessions
 example of materialistic meaning 65–8, 232–9

post-it method 129, 158, 160–1, 280–1

Post-Traumatic Growth Inventory 112

preparation, of session 193

pragmatic phenomenology 40, 47, 51–2, 81, 101, 121, 147–8, 191

predictability of life, example of fundamental assumption 82–3

productivity-creativity, see Franklian triad

projective tests 113, 169

process evaluation, in sessions 216

psychoanalysis, or psychodynamic xvi, 56, 62–13, 127, 139–140

psycho-education, see didactics

psychological Resilience Scale 112

psychological stress xvi–xvii, 32, 40, 52, 75, 83, 94, 98–102, 122, 153, 166, 182–3, 192

psychopathology 88, 99, 101, 192

purpose in life questionnaire 112

pyramidal or horizontal value-system 98, 153, 159, 296

Pyrrho from Ellis 14

Pyszcinski, Tom 59, 113, 180, 263

qi 29

quality of life xvi–xviii, 40, 92–9, 99, 129

Quest for Meaning Scale 112

questioning approach 119, 147, 151, 154, 161–165, 177, 188
 examples 162–165

ranking meanings 158, 165
 see also hierarchy exercises, mountain range exercise

rationalising, see also intellectualising, theorising 37, 146
 example of cold outside reflections on meaning in life 73–6

recognising of difficulties 132, 137, 148, 176–19

recovery, or recovery model xvi, xxii, 91

reductionism xvi, 16–7, 20, 29, 36, 62, 74, 88, 128

reflection and reflexivity xxiii, 3, 31, 35, 47, 51, 96, 109, 115, 140, 143, 193

relational depth 47, 135–136

Relational Depth Inventory 112

relational skills 135–144

relationship between practitioner and client, see also relational skills

relevance of meaning 97–9

religion, see also clergy, crisis, spirituality 4, 28, 46, 48, 66–8, 266–8

request for help 106, 195

resilience 25, 65–8, 86, 98, 117, 132–3, 222–30, 247

responsibility 19, 36, 55, 59, 60, 66–8, 96, 130–3, 138–9, 152, 160, 175, 182, 183–5, 209, 213, 265

responsibility Scale 112

rituals 6, 26–9, 37, 92, 172, 284–7

Rogers, Carl 81, 136, 144

role model, see modelling

Rorschach Test   113
running group exercise   173
Russell, Bertrand   9
Ryff, Carol   99

safe place exercise   239
Sartre, Jean-Paul   41
scala naturae, *see* ladder of nature
**scale of phenomenological
    experiences,** *or* scale of
    meaning   48–51
scaling-up exercise   50–51
scepticism, sceptics   xiii, xiv, 3,
    12–8, 26, 29, 34–43, 51–53,
    61–2, 74, 77, 88, 93, 108, 127,
    152, 179
Schneider, Kirk J.   179, 181, 263
Seeking of Noetic Goals
    Questionnaire   112
self   39–42, 80–81
    authentic self, *see* authenticity,
        degrees of authenticity, true self
    future self in exercises   170–1
    inauthentic self, *see* authenticity,
        degrees of authenticity, true self
    letter to the self exercise, *see* letter to
        a friend exercise
self-acceptance   65–8, 241–3, 247
self-care   xxiii, 65–8, 126, 132–3,
    238, 241–4, 247
self-care exercise   243
self-compassion   65–8, 132–133, 241
self-compassion exercise   243–4
self-congruence scale   112
self-deception   62, 141, 178, 185
self-denial   8–10
self-determination   22
self-discipline, *see also* goal
    management, self-oriented
    meaning   8–10
self-disclosure   141
self-distance   xvii, 47, 150–1, 154–5,
    157–9, 178
self-efficacy   xxiii, 65–8, 94, 97, 108,
    117, 125, 129, 209, 222–31,
    247, 276, 278–83, 287
    see also flexibility, goal
        management, self-regulation
self-esteem   71–5, 129–30, 196, 247

self-evaluation of session   190,
    205–6, 210
self-expression, *see* creative self-
    expression
Self Esteem Scale, Rosenberg   112
self-obsession, *see* fat ego
self-portrayal exercise   173
self-realisation   26, 56, 65–8, 113,
    262–8
self Realisation Scale   112
self-regulation   55, 58–60, 65–8, 108,
    157, 184
self-reflection, *see* reflection and
    reflexivity
self-reliance, *see* autonomy, self-
    oriented meaning
self-talk   185
self-transcendence   xxii, 56, 65–8,
    89, 99, 122, 128, 131, 143,
    153, 155–6, 158–60, 178–9,
    262–8
self-worth   12, 55, 58, 60, 65–8, 79,
    81, 94, 97, 102, 108, 113–4,
    125, 132–3, 157, 184, 209, 247
true self, *see also* authenticity, degrees
    of authenticity   80
self-oriented meaning
    definition   65–8
    relevance   80, 98, 110, 117, 127,
        139, 153, 158, 160, 168, 209
    session on   237–238, 240–249, 254
    see examples resilience, flexibility,
        perseverance, hardiness,
        accepting challenges, coping,
        hope, optimism, self-efficacy,
        goal management, planning,
        self-discipline, control, self-
        acceptance, self-worth, self-
        esteem, autonomy, creative
        self-expression, self-care,
        authenticity, true self
Seligman, Martin   xvi, 76, 91
Sennett, Richard   19, 21, 25
Sense of Coherence Scale   112
Sentence Completion Test   112
serenity prayer   130, 224
session overview   189
sex, example of materialistic-hedonic
    meaning   65–8

shame 72
shared informed decision-making
105–115, 136–139, 194, 199
shoebox exercise 173
should (not), *see* meaning
development triangle
Sinn 13, 29–31, 36–37, 39, 149
Sloterdijk, Peter 21, 39, 56, 88, 98
sociability, *see* social meaning
Social Connection Scale 112
social context exercise 254–9
social meanings
definition 65–8
relevance 98, 130–2, 248
session on 251–61
see examples sociability, friends,
family, intimate relationships,
belonging, tradition, social-
cultural history, conformism,
altruism, giving birth and
taking care of children
social status, *see* materialistic-hedonic
meaning
societal-cosmic-divine order 4–13,
18, 26–9, 36, 56, 69, 88
Socratic dialogue, *see also*
questioning approach 147,
154, 162
Smith, Jonathan 147
source of meaning, *see* type of
meaning
Sources of Meaning Profile 112
Spinelli, Ernesto 41–2, 146, 147,
176
spiral structure of sessions 122–3
spirituality xxiii, xxiv, 10, 11, 15,
26, 43, 47–8, 56–7, 66–8, 75, 88,
93–4, 101–2, 128, 160, 177, 190,
208, 260–8
Spirituality Questionnaire 112
Sports 65–8
STAR, Situation, Task, Action,
Results 123
Stoicism 9, 27, 79
Steger, Michael 56–7, 97–9, 111, 113,
128, 172, 241, 300
Stress Appraisal Measure 112
structure, of sessions xviii, 93–96
121–2, 135–9, 190–2

success 18–19, 22, 33, 56, 65–8, 82,
84, 151, 170, 180, 229, 233–6,
255, 263, 277, 280, 287, 290
suffering 88–9, 95, 120, 132, 141,
143, 154, 175, 177–9
suicidal ideation 99, 106, 182, 270
systematic literature review and
meta-analysis 107, 191

tailoring xx, 90, 101, 105, 110–1,
116, 119, 136–8, 141, 162,
190–1
Taylor, Charles 5, 21
telos, *see also* teleology, purpose
teleology, *see also* ladder 9, 11–25,
36–40, 42, 1–53, 55, 69, 77–8,
82, 93, 128, 149
temporality 63–8, 126–9, 164, 168,
268
terrorism, *see* extremism 142–3
thematic analyses 49, 69,
94–5
Thematic Apperception Test 112
theorising, *see also* intellectualising,
rationalising 45, 73–5, 122, 146
example of cold outside reflections
on meaning in life 73–6
Tolle, Eckhart 127
toleration of feelings, *see also*
experiential acceptance xvii,
96, 152, 154, 180–3
top-down meanings 48–51
totality of possible meanings 20, 90,
106, 121–3, 166, 175, 178
trauma, *see also* nine-eleven 62, 83,
101, 150
tradition, *see also* social meaning
65–8, 248, 253
traditional approaches to
meaning 1–35
see also teleologic meaning, sceptic
meaning, functionalistic meaning
Tragic Optimism Scale 112
tragic triad 89, 177
trapeze, metaphor of therapeutic
change 125–126
treatment, explanation of term xvi
Trent Attribution Profile 112
types of meaning 65–68

unconditional positive regard,
    see also meaning-centered
    unconditional positive regard
understanding   39
    union, spiritual, *see also* social
        meaning   66–8
uniqueness   16, 66–8, 90, 152, 160,
        184, 208
unpeeling, *see* phenomenological
    unpeeling

values   19–20, 24, 31, 43, 46, 47,
        57–60, 64–8, 80–1, 95, 97–8,
        130, 143, 153, 159, 209
Value Awareness Technique   158, 161
value conflict   160–1
vedic texts   26, 28
vertical axis of meaning   159
Verhaeghe, Paul   9, 21–2, 24, 98
vicious cycle   123
virtue   7, 9, 65–8, 72–3, 258
Visser, Gerard   19, 22, 27, 28, 45, 128
Vos, Joel   xiv, xvi–xviii, 16, 18, 23, 31,
        39, 43, 45, 49, 55, 59, 61–2, 64,
        66–7, 72, 74–6, 80, 82, 83–4, 88,
        89–95, 98–101, 107, 111, 117,
        121–2, 126, 128, 135–6, 141, 145,
        147–9, 151, 160, 163, 166, 173–
        83, 191–4, 211–2, 263, 288, 297

want (not), *see also* meaning
    development triangle
Weber, Max   10, 21
whose meaning is it? Exercise
    259
will to meaning   xxiii, 56, 75, 113
wisdom, *see* larger meaning
    65–8
Wong, Paul   55–6, 98, 113, 117, 170,
    174, 185
work   4–8, 19–20, 22, 46, 57, 59,
    72–7, 77, 98, 125–12, 151, 157,
    159–10, 200, 213–21, 229, 235,
    237
working alliance   95, 137, 140
Working Alliance Scale   112
World Assumptions Scale   112
worship, *see* religion, broader
    meaning
writing exercise, *see* autobiographic
    writing, letter writing
wu wei   27
worlds (Eigenwelt, Mitwelt,
    Uberwelt, Umwelt)   47–8, 54,
    57, 64, 147

Yalom, Irvin   59, 141, 174–5, 180–2,
    192, 252, 263
YOLO, You Only Live Once   21